THE POWER AND AUTHORITY OF THE BELIEVER

Godsword Godswill Onu

Second Edition: 2014
ISBN: 978-1508515111
Copyright © 2014 by Godsword Godswill Onu

Many Scriptural quotations or citations were paraphrased, abridged, edited, or summarized, and a combination of the New King James Version and the King James Version of the Holy Bible were used, except where indicated otherwise.

Published by:
Godsword Christian Publications,
Okigwe, Nigeria.

All Rights Reserved
Never duplicate this book/ebook for any commercial purpose, by any means (paper, electronic, digital, internet, etc), without an express permission from either Apostle Godsword or the publisher. Excerpts can be used for those doing research, preaching, teaching, writing, etc.
For the ebooks, if you want to share to another person's computer/electronic system or to the public on any platform, do not share the whole/complete ebook (except to your husband or wife); but you may share/post/use or reshare/repost/reuse an excerpt or part of the ebook.

For order, enquiry, seminar, prayer, sponsorship, comments, programmes, etc, contact:
APOSTLE GODSWORD GODSWILL ONU
WHOLE LIFE SPIRIT-WORD MINISTRIES
A.k.a. HOLY GHOST AND GODSWORD CHRISTIAN NETWORK,
OKIGWE, IMO STATE, NIGERIA.
Call or text: +234 8030917546, 8052563967, 8020648283, 8092582282.
E-mail: godswordgodswill@yahoo.com

Never Say That God Said What He Did Not Say!

TABLE OF CONTENTS

Dedications..4
Appreciation/Acknowledgments...5
Preface..7
Introduction...9
The Believer and the Supernatural..13
The Signs of the Believers..17
The Weapons and Armour of Our Warfare...21
The Old Testament Believers' Exploits..25
The Nothingness of All Contrary Things..29
The Believer and Love..33
When You Pass Through the Fire...37
The Hope of the Believer..41
God's Original Intention for Man..45
How Is Your Foundation?...53
Divine Protection..57
Angels Surround Us!...61
No Weapon Formed Against You Shall Prosper.......................................63
The Power-filled Life..67
Great Power Given to Men...71
You Are Gods..75
Taking It by Force...87
The Weapons and Armour of Our Warfare...89
I Give You Dominion..91
The Light and Salt of the World..93
They that Know Their God..95
The Name of Jesus Christ..99
Decree a Thing to Be Established..101
Kings and Priests...105
Full of the Word and the Spirit of God..109
We Are More Than Conquerors..121
The Strong and Untouchable Christian...129
Secrets to God's Miracle-working Power...143
The Place of Faith..147
Be a Prayer-warrior...151
You Must Be Led by the Holy Spirit...157
The Place of Obedience, Holiness, and Righteousness...........................165
Having a Strong Relationship with God..183
Becoming an Example to the Believers..187
Go from Glory to Glory...191
Psalms Concerning God's Provisions..199
Demonic and Satanic Activities Today...203
Divine Revelations and Near Death Experiences (NDE's).....................207
Dressing and Outward Appearance (Special Edition).............................227
Books by Apostle Godsword...260

DEDICATIONS

I dedicate this work to the Almighty God the Father, Who loves us so dearly; to His Son, the Lord Jesus Christ, Who is my Lord and Saviour; to the Holy Spirit of the Living God, Who is my Great Helper and Comforter; and to all those, who love the Lord Jesus Christ sincerely, and want to know and practice the Truth.

ACKNOWLEDGMENTS/APPRECIATION

I appreciate my Heavenly Father, Who gave me Jesus Christ – my Lord and Saviour. I thank my Lord Jesus Christ, Who gave me the Holy Spirit – the Spirit of Wisdom and of Power. Thank You, Holy Spirit, for making the writing of this book possible; when I consider the strength of the teaching anointing, and when I feel it, I marvel how awesome the Anointing of the Holy Spirit is!

I acknowledge the efforts, prayers, contributions, and encouragements, in one way or the other, of my Christian brothers and sisters, who equip and are being equipped, for the work of the ministry, for the edifying of the Body of Christ, till we all come to the unity of the faith and of the Knowledge of the Son of God, to a perfect man, to the measure of the stature of the Fulness of Christ; that we should no longer be children, tossed to and fro and carried about with every wind of doctrine, by the trickery of men, in the cunning craftiness of deceitful plotting, but, speaking the Truth in love, grow up in all things into Him Who is the Head: Christ.

I appreciate all those who contributed positively, in one way or the other, to my Christian life, my ministry, and the writing and publication of this book. As we look forward to the Rapture of the Saints and Second Coming of our Saviour, Lord, and Master: Jesus Christ the Son of the Living God, don't lose your focus. Look unto Jesus Christ, the Author and Finisher of our faith, Who for the Joy that was set before Him, endured the Cross, despising the Shame, and has sat down at the Right Hand of the Throne of God.

God did not call us to serve Him in vain, but He will reward us abundantly for the labour we have laboured in His Name. He shall also give us the Crown of Life. Remember that there is a Heaven to gain, and there is a Hell Fire to avoid. Live in total obedience to the Word of God; live in righteousness and holiness, without which no eye shall see the Lord. God bless you!

Never Say That God Said What He Did Not Say!
Jesus Christ Is Coming Very Soon: Heaven And Hell Are Real!
Let No One Deceive You: Without Holiness, No One Will See The Lord
This hymn will help keep us focused:

IT PAYS TO SERVE JESUS

1. It pays to serve Jesus; I speak from my heart,
   He'll always be with us, if we do our part,
   There is nothing in this wide-world can pleasure afford,
   There is peace and contentment in serving the Lord.

Chorus:
   I'll love Him far better than in days gone by,
   I'll serve Him more truly than ever before,
   I'll do as He bids me whatever the cost,
   I'll be a true soldier; I'll die at my post.

2. And often when I am tempted to turn from the track,
   I think of my Saviour, my mind wanders back,
   To the place where they nailed Him on Calvary's Tree,
   I hear a Voice saying, "I suffered for thee."

3. There is no one like Jesus can share me today,
   His Love and Kindness can never fade away,

In winter, in summer, in sunshine and rain,
His Love and Affection is always the same.
                              APOSTLE GODSWORD

PREFACE

When the Lord Jesus Christ arose from the dead, He said, "All authority (power) in Heaven and on earth has been given to Me. Go therefore...." He was speaking to the Church (His Body), and handing the authority and power He got for them to them.

The Lord Jesus Christ has given us the authority and power to tread and trample on serpents and scorpions and over all the power (ability) of the enemy, and nothing shall by any means hurt or harm us.

We have been given authority and power over satan, his fallen angels and demons, and the agents of the kingdom of darkness (witches and wizards). Never fear them, because greater is the Holy Ghost in you than the devil in the world.

We are god-men and supernatural beings. We represent God on this earth, and we must never disappoint God. We must carry out the assignments God has given us faithfully, so that in the end, the Lord will tell us: "Well done, good and faithful Servants; enter into the Joy of your Lord!"

GODSWORD GODSWILL ONU,
2012.

INTRODUCTION

Do we have any authority or power as Believers? If so, are we using it? We shall give account of our lives to God. How will you feel, if, when you get to Heaven, you realize you didn't use the things God provided for you?

When Jesus Christ rose up from the dead, He said that all authority in Heaven and on earth has been given to Him. "Go therefore…" He said to His apostles and to His Church (Matt. 28:18). He transferred the authority over to us, because that is what He came to collect for us. That was the authority and dominion which God gave to Adam, but Adam lost it to the devil because of sin and disobedience.

The Lord Jesus Christ says He has given us authority and power over serpents and scorpions, and over all the power of the enemy, and nothing shall by any means hurt us (Lk. 10:19). He has given us authority and power over satan, his demons and cohorts, and their works. We have the power and authority to destroy the works of the enemy, and nothing will harm us.

God has given us authority and power to uproot and to build (Jer. 1:10). We uproot anything that is contrary to God, and we build that which God wants to be. We have not used the ability, authority, right, and privilege that God has given us. We have used just a small portion or percentage of them. We can put rulers of our nations in place, and we can remove bad rulers over our nations from their positions.

The weapons of our warfare are not carnal, natural, or man-made. They are spiritual and mighty through God to the pulling down of strongholds (2 Cor. 10:4). The weapons of our warfare can destroy and break any mountain, barrier, or obstacle. We can even speak to mountains and obstructions, and they will disappear (Mk 11:23). We have power and authority with God, because we are sons of God.

The Lord said that, because we believe in Him, we shall cast out devils, we shall speak with new tongues, serpents or poisons shall not hurt us, and we shall heal the sick by laying hands on them (Mk 16:17-18). Do you know what that means? It means that you share in the Divine Nature, and you are a super-human.

We have the ability to change the course of nature. There is nothing impossible with God (Mk 10:27). And because we believe in God and His Word, because we carry God's Presence and Power, nothing shall be impossible to us (Lk. 1:37). Have you been putting them into practice?

God does not take delight in disappointments, and we must not disappoint Him. If we don't use what He has given us to use, then we disappoint Him. When we disobey God, the devil is happy, and we must never make the devil happy. The devil is our arch-enemy, and we have the mandate to pull down and scatter his works.

However, we must not war or exercise our authority and power recklessly. Do you know that power can be abused? Jesus Christ, our Captain and Lord, says that we should be as wise as serpents (Matt. 10:16). We should know when to say, 'Yes,' and when to say, 'No.' Let the Word of God, which is the Wisdom of God, dwell in you richly in all wisdom (Col. 3:16).

The Lord says that, because we are Believers, the works that He did when He was on earth, the same works we will do. We will even do greater works than them, because He went to the Father (Jn 14:12). This is fantastic!

We are god-men, and not ordinary men. We are supernatural beings. No wonder the Word declares that we are gods, and all of us are the children of the Most High.

But the pitiable thing concerning it, is that many of us die and will die like men, and fall like one of the princes (Psa. 82:6-7). Did you notice that princes are nothing compared to our status? But many trust in princes instead of in the Living God.

The early apostles and Disciples stunned their opponents by operating in the supernatural and extra-ordinary realm. Concerning their Master (Who also is our Master), their opponents had said, "What shall we do? For this Man works many signs…" (Jn 11:47-48).

As they planned against their Master, they found out that He waxed stronger, and they couldn't help it but said, "You see that you are accomplishing nothing. Look, the world has gone after Him!" That is a remarkable statement. Can people say this about us?

God does not change, and He has never changed. The Old Testament Servants of His who believed in Him performed mighty exploits, signs, and wonders. If the Believers and Christians who lived in the early New Testament time did the same (and greater), we must also do the same.

As we dedicate ourselves to prayer, the study of God's Word, fasting, obedience, and faith, we will see results that will blow our minds. God is able to do exceedingly abundantly above all that we ask or think, according to the power that works in us (Eph. 3:20).

The Kingdom of God is not in word, but in the Power of the Spirit of God. If all we do is preach and teach, how shall we prove to the world that our God is alive and all-powerful?

If you have not been filled with the Holy Spirit, don't wait again, but be filled now. Receive Him in faith, for you receive power when the Holy Spirit comes upon you. That empowerment by the Holy Spirit is to make you a witness (a proof-provider) to the Lord Jesus Christ (Acts 1:8).

Being conscious of the fact that we wrestle not against flesh and blood, but against a host of fallen angels and demons, you must be alert and watchful always. You must recognize the weapons that the Lord has provided for your use in spiritual warfare.

Also, put on the whole Armour of God so that no plan of the enemy will succeed on you. The armour is for your protection. The Armour of God include: the belt of truth, the breastplate of righteousness, the preparation of the Gospel of Peace, the shield of faith, the helmet of salvation, the Sword of the Spirit, and prayer.

In this fight of faith we are involved in, you must be conscious of the fact that life and death are in the power of the tongue. Therefore, speak positive words and words that correspond to the Word of God always. Don't give in to the enemy when he tells you to speak negative words.

No plan of the devil will harm or hurt you. The gate of Hades shall not prevail over the Church of Jesus Christ. Don't be afraid of anything, because the Holy Spirit in you is greater than the devil in the world. Also, God has given His angels Charge over you, to keep you in all your ways.

His Divine Power has given to us all things that pertain to life and Godliness, through the Knowledge of Him Who called us by glory and virtue, by which have been given to us exceedingly great and precious promises, that through these we may be partakers of the Divine Nature (2 Pet. 1:3-4).

But just as Jesus Christ and the early apostles and Disciples passed through persecutions, you will have to expect the same. Don't think that you can never be met by persecutions. On the contrary, they will come, since you call on the Name of the Lord.

Remember that the Word does not tell us to kill demons, but to cast them out (Mk 16:17). If you cast them out from this place, they will go to another place, but they are still in this world, because their time has not reached. But at the fulness of time, God will expel satan and his fallen angels and demons, and banish them forever.

Also, remember that, after the Lord had defeated and overcome satan (when the devil tempted Him), the Word says, "Now when the devil had ended every temptation, he departed from Him until an opportune time." He didn't leave forever.

Though the Lord has promised that whatever you may leave for His Sake, you will receive them a hundred fold in this life, and in the life to come Eternal Life, notice that He said that you will have all those things with persecutions (Mk 10:29-30).

Therefore, don't be discouraged if persecutions, trials, and temptations come. And know that they are the trials of your faith, and not the trials of your sin (Jas 1:3). God may test you as he tested Abraham. Pass your test as did Abraham.

For to this you were called, because Christ also suffered for us, leaving us an Example, that we should follow His Steps. (1 Pet. 2:21). Therefore, since Christ suffered for us in the flesh, arm yourselves also with the same mind, for he who has suffered in the flesh has ceased from sin (1 Pet. 4:1).

Let us lay aside every weight, and the sin, which so easily ensnares us; and let us run with endurance the race that is set before us, looking unto Jesus Christ, the Author and Finisher of our faith, Who for the joy that was set before Him endured the Cross, despising the shame, and has sat down at the Right Hand of the Throne of God (Heb. 12:1-2).

But no matter what the devil may bring across your way, you will pass through it without being hurt, though it may pain you. Cast your faith on the Lord, Who cannot fail. All will be well.

Your journey and hope will not finish here. There is hope for you, for our hope in Christ Jesus is not only in this world. God has promised us the Resurrection from the dead and Eternal Life. Yes, we will dwell with Him forever in His Kingdom.

Not only that we will live with Him forever, we will also be abundantly rewarded for the work we have done for Him. This is why you must strive to labour for the Lord with all that you have.

He who loses his life for the Sake of Jesus Christ will find it. God owns everything, and He has power over all things. Don't be afraid of anyone. Be faithful until death, and the Lord will give you the Crown of Life.

Deal with any faulty foundation in your life. Let your foundation be strongly grounded in Jesus Christ and in the Word of God. It is not the Will of God for you to live in wretchedness and abject poverty. Though trials, tests, or hardship may come, yet God will make all things well with us at His Appointed Time. Yes, we have to pray fervently in faith; but learn to wait for God's Time.

Never Say That God Said What He Did Not Say!

THE BELIEVER AND THE SUPERNATURAL

Who is the Believer? The Believer is the one who believes that Jesus Christ came in the flesh, suffered, died (shedding His Blood), and resurrected on the third day for the redemption, salvation, and justification of the human race. The Believer is the one that believes in the Sacrifice of which, Jesus Christ gave His Life for the salvation of mankind. He believes that Jesus Christ did it for him personally, and accepts that Sacrifice on his behalf.

When you receive and accept Jesus Christ as your Lord and personal Saviour, you receive the right and power to be a child of God (Jn 1:12). That power gives you the ability to overcome the world (1 Jn 5:5). It gives you the ability to say, 'No' to sin. This is why, if you commit sin, you are responsible for it. *our power comes from Jesus*

Jesus Christ declares that except a man is born again, he cannot see the Kingdom of God (Jn 3:3). When you receive Jesus Christ, the Holy Spirit quickens, regenerates, or makes alive your spirit. Your spirit is your real you, your inner man.

When Adam sinned by disobeying God, his spirit died, and he was separated from God and His Life. Man therefore became an enemy of God, even though God still loved him. It was for the salvation and restoration of man that God sent His Son to die for mankind.

Since all men came from Adam, all men inherited that separation from God through Adam. This is why the Word of God declares that all men have sinned and come short of the Glory of God (Rom. 3:23).

But when you accept Jesus Christ, He cleanses you with His Precious Blood, and you are justified and made righteous before God, so that you appear before God as if you have never sinned. However, God expects you to live the life of obedience, righteousness, and holiness.

This is why the Word says that he who does righteousness is righteous, just as Jesus Christ is righteous (1 Jn 3:7). If you live in sin and disobedience, you don't know God, but you are of the devil (1 Jn 3:8,10). *God's word is true*

However, if you fall into sin, repent and confess the sin to God, and He will forgive you. But don't say, "I will obey God in this area, but as for this other area, not now." That attitude is the attitude of a backslider and a sinner. God deserves our total and complete obedience.

The Believer has the authority that the unbeliever does not have. When Jesus Christ rose up from the dead, He declared that all power, all authority, has been given to Him. All authority in Heaven and on earth has been given to Jesus Christ!

The Lord handed the authority to us, Believers, who are the members of His Church (Body), and said, "Go therefore…." He gave us the promise that He is with us till the end of the age (Matt. 28:18-20).

The authority Jesus Christ got, He got it for us, His Church. And this is why the Word says that whatever we bind on earth will be bound in Heaven, and whatever we loose on earth will be loosed in Heaven (Matt. 18:18). This authority is great and beyond science and technology. We are super-humans!

We are supernatural beings, who live and operate with the Divine Power. The power we operate with, is greater than any natural force. This power is greater than any satanic, demonic, or witchcraft power. Before the Holy Ghost that lives in us, satan and his host are powerless.

But this power is beyond your reach if you are not born again. Even if you go to church, even if you have been baptized and made a full-member of your church, if you are not born again, you don't have this power and authority of the Believer. *I have been born again and crucified with Christ*

Jesus Christ Is Coming Very Soon: Heaven And Hell Are Real!

When a Believer in the Lord Jesus Christ is baptized and filled with the Holy Ghost, he receives the In-filling of the Holy Ghost, the Spirit of Power, by Whom the Almighty created the whole universe. The Father created all things through Jesus Christ by the Holy Spirit (Col. 1:16).

The Word declares that Believers receive power after/when they are filled with the Holy Ghost, and they are thereby empowered to be witnesses (or proof-providers) to the Lord Jesus Christ to the ends of the world (Acts 1:8).

When the apostles and the early Believers and Disciples were filled with the Holy Spirit, they were empowered to do exploits for the Lord Jesus Christ. Few of their deeds and exploits are recorded in the Book of the Acts of the Apostles. The acts of the Believers are still being written today.

The Lord had told them never to leave Jerusalem until they were empowered from Heaven. In His Words, "Behold, I send the Promise of My Father upon you, but tarry in the city of Jerusalem until you are endued with power from on High" (Lk. 24:49).

When the power came on the Day of Pentecost, the first preaching, given by Apostle Peter, brought about three thousand souls to the Lord (Acts 2). They kept on increasing in number, because the Gospel was preached in the Power of the Holy Spirit.

Souls were drawn to the Lord when the people saw the mighty signs and wonders that the apostles and the Believers performed. Peter healed the lame man at the gate called Beautiful (Acts 3). Peter's shadow brought healing to many.

One of the deacons, who turned out to become Evangelist Philip, stunned the people of Samaria with miracles and healings. The signs and wonders performed by his hands were so spectacular that even a sorcerer, Simon, could not deny the superiority of what he saw, and submitted to the Lord (Acts 8).

When Prophet Paul, who later became Apostle Paul, came to the scene, he amazed the Gentiles, as he preached and taught the Word of God, in the demonstration of the Power of the Holy Ghost (1 Cor. 2:4; 1 Thes. 1:5). The former persecutor of Christians – Saul – accepted Jesus Christ and became a changed man (Acts 9).

When Ananias laid hands on Saul, he received his sight and was filled with the Holy Spirit. Saul, later known as Paul, grew and matured in the Lord that by the thirteenth chapter of the Book of Acts, he had become a prophet and a teacher.

After the Lord sent them forth as apostles to the Gentiles, Apostle Paul (in company of Apostle Barnabas) did mighty signs and wonders among the people. Handkerchiefs and aprons from his body were taken to the sick, and the diseases left them, and evil spirits went out of them (Acts 19:11-12).

The Lord tells us in His Word that the Believers are to do the same works that He did, and even greater works (Jn 14:12). If you are a Believer in the Lord Jesus Christ, those mighty signs, wonders, and miracles that you read about in your Bible, that Jesus Christ and the Disciples did, you will do also.

Move in faith, and do not give in to doubt, and you will see the Manifestations of the Holy Spirit through you that will blow your mind! If you have not been baptized and filled with the Holy Spirit, ask God to fill you, and receive the Holy Ghost in faith.

If your child is still crawling at the age of five, you will not like it. If he still asks for pocket-money at the age of forty, you will be greatly displeased. This is the same with God. God expects us to grow and mature in Him, so that we can live for Him, and do exploits for Him.

This is why you must take enough time to read and study the Bible, and allow the Holy Spirit minister and reveal Divine Secrets to you. Studying your Bible will expose your rights and privileges to you. It will also make you know your authority and power over the devil, so that you can destroy his works in the Name of the Lord Jesus Christ.

Prayer is one thing you must never joke with, as a Believer. Pray always, without ceasing. Pray with all kinds of prayer. 'All kinds of prayer,' because there are the prayer of faith, of worship, of supplication and petition, of intercession, of confession, of binding and loosing, of agreement, of commitment, etc.

It was as the apostles and Disciples went out and preached everywhere, that the Lord worked with them, and confirmed the Word through the accompanying signs (Mk 16:20). Don't wait for your church's pulpit before you preach. Preach in schools, in streets, in markets, in buses, etc. He that wins souls is wise.

If you are ashamed of Jesus Christ in this sinful and adulterous generation, He also will be ashamed of you before His Father and before the holy angles (Mk 8:38). Jesus Christ gave up His Life for the salvation of mankind. Your evangelizing and winning souls will make His Blood cleanse and save more souls.

Learn to be thankful to God. In everything, give thanks. When the Israelites blew the trumpet, after Jericho had been encircled seven times, the walls of Jericho fell down, and the people of Israel overcame their enemies because they praised God.

When the people of Ammon, Moab, and Mount Seir came up against King Jehoshaphat and the people of Judah, the Lord told them not to worry, because the battle is the Lord's. When they began to sing and to praise the Lord, the Lord set ambushes against their enemies, and they were defeated (2 Chron. 20).

The Lord is a Man of War, the Lord is His Name. In the greatness of His Excellence He overthrows those who rise against Him. Who is like our God among the gods? He is glorious in holiness, fearful in praises, doing wonders!

Instead of complaining and murmuring, worship the Lord, and you will see what the Lord will do. As Paul and Silas prayed and sang hymns to God, suddenly there was a great earthquake, so that the foundations of the prison were shaken, and immediately all the doors were opened, and everyone's chains were loosed (Acts 16:25-26).

Brother, there are no two ways about it. If you want to move consistently in a concentrated red-hot anointing, you must do some fasting often. You may have to fast for one, two, three, or even seven days. Some have fasted longer than seven days.

This is not to say that you can't perform or receive miracles, signs, and wonders without fasting. However, why will it take someone days to destroy a demonic stronghold, while another can do it in seconds or minutes? The difference is the anointing and faith.

You may start by fasting till 12:00 p.m., 3:00 p.m., or 6:00 p.m., for the day. If you do three days straight fasting, you will not die. In the Book of Esther, fasting averted an impending national disaster.

In the words of Esther: "Go, gather all the Jews who are present in Shushan, and fast for me; neither eat nor drink for three days, night or day. My maids and I will fast likewise. And so I will go to the king, which is against the law, and if I perish, I perish!" (Esth. 4:16).

That was a straight non-stop three days fasting. Instead of dying from the fasting, the fasting wrought wonders for them. And the king, when Esther met him, said, "What do you wish, Queen Esther? What is your request? It shall be given to you – up to half of the kingdom!" (Esth. 5:3).

Some demons will not go out, except by prayer and fasting (Matt. 17:21). Some say that it was before Jesus Christ defeated the devil. But why do you think that Jesus Christ Himself fasted?

Apart from the fact that fasting helps you bring your flesh under subjection, and gets you more sensitive to the Holy Spirit, fasting activates your faith and brings the anointing you wouldn't get by avoiding fasting.

Never Say That God Said What He Did Not Say!

THE SIGNS OF THE BELIEVERS

Apostle Paul told us that the Kingdom of God is not in words but in power (1 Cor. 4:20). It is not in too much talk or speech; rather, it is in power. It is in the Demonstration of the Holy Spirit and power, that the faith of your hearers should not be in the wisdom of men, but in the Power of God (1 Cor. 2:4-5).

The Lord gives Believers power to trample on serpents and scorpions, and over all the power of the devil, and nothing shall by any means hurt them (Lk. 10:19). As a Believer, you have the authority, you have the power to tread on serpents and scorpions, and they will not harm you.

As a Believer, you are supposed to be a terror to demons and their human agents. You are empowered to destroy their works and activities, and render them ineffective.

Jesus Christ came to destroy the works of the devil (1 Jn 3:8). We are His Body, and members of His Body (the Church) in particular. Therefore, we are to carry on with what He started. Let God be proud of us!

The Word tells us of the signs that are to accompany/follow us (Mk 16:17-18). Each and every one of these signs is for every Believer. If any Believer is not experiencing any of them, let the fellow check himself, and let him work on himself; he will see them in his life.

The Believer casts out demons in the Name of Jesus Christ. The Name of Jesus Christ is above other names, and in His Name, every knee should bow, of things or beings in heaven, on earth, and under the earth. In His Name, every tongue should confess that Jesus Christ is Lord, to the Glory of God the Father (Phil. 2:9-11).

It is the Finger of God, the Spirit of God, that expels demons when you give a word of command in the Name of Jesus Christ (Lk. 11:20; Matt. 12:28). Even, when you are endued with a strong anointing, your presence alone can drive out demons.

This is why handkerchiefs and aprons taken from Apostle Paul's body could heal the sick and drive out demons. It is not you that they fear, but the Fire and Power of the Holy Spirit. Therefore, do not fear, because the Holy Spirit in you is greater than them.

Believers take up serpents. If you encounter a snake, it will not harm you. This is the Word of God that is forever settled in Heaven. God cannot lie, and He is able to perform His Word.

This is why Apostle Paul did not suffer any harm when he was attacked by a viper. The heathen expected that he would swell, but when he was not harmed, they changed their mind and said that he was a god (Acts 28).

Well, they were right because he was a god. The Bible declares that we are gods and the children of the Most High (Psa. 82:6). But do you know that even though you are a god, you can die like men, and fall like one of the princes? (verse 7).

No wonder the Word of God says that God's people are destroyed, because of lack of knowledge (Hos. 4:6). Ignorance of God and His Ways, ignorance of the devices and tricks of the enemy, can make you suffer loss and fall into the trap of the enemy.

As a Believer you are supposed to speak (to be speaking) in new tongues. When the Holy Spirit came upon the Believes on the Day of Pentecost, they spoke in tongues, as the Spirit of God gave them utterance (Acts 2:4). Speaking in tongues is the evidence of being baptized and filled with the Holy Spirit.

Some argue whether every Believer must speak in tongues when he is filled with the Holy Spirit. In the Bible, under the New Testament, when people were filled with the Holy Spirit, they spoke in tongues; we are in the same dispensation, and we have the promise also.

THE POWER AND AUTHORITY OF THE BELIEVER

Apostle Paul was filled with the Holy Spirit when Ananias laid hands on him. He spoke in tongues, because he told the Corinthians that he spoke in tongues more than them all (1 Cor. 14:18). While Apostle Peter was still speaking, the Holy Spirit fell on Cornelius and his household, and they spoke in tongues (Acts 10:44-46).

When Paul found some Ephesian Disciples, he asked them whether they have received the Holy Spirit. They told him that they have not heard that there is a Holy Spirit. When he laid hands on them, they were filled with the Holy Spirit, and they spoke in tongues and prophesied (Acts 19:6).

As you speak in tongues, you speak mysteries (Divine Secrets) to God (1 Cor. 14:2), you edify yourself (1 Cor. 14:4), and the Holy Spirit helps you pray for the things you don't know of, the right way (Rom. 8:26-27). Don't stop speaking in tongues after you have been baptized in the Holy Ghost; continue to speak everyday.

If a Believer takes poison or harmful drink, it will not harm him. Whether it is chemical or witchcraft poison, you will not be poisoned. The life you live flows from the Holy Spirit. The Holy Spirit that raised Jesus Christ from the dead, will give an extra-ordinary life to your body.

But the Word instructs you to bless your food. Your food and drink are blessed by the Word of God and by prayer (1 Tim. 4:5). Don't be afraid, the Holy Ghost in you is greater than any other force or power. But why do poison kill Christians? Because they don't live in obedience to the Word of God and the Spirit of God. Many mix doubt with their confession.

And when you lay hands on the sick, they shall recover. Notice that here speaks of recovery, instead of instant healing. Yes, healings can be instant, especially when the gifts of healings are in operation. But when you pray the prayer of faith for the sick, they shall be healed, instantly or progressively.

Even when you may feel symptoms of sickness as a Believer, don't welcome that sickness by confessing that you are sick. Confess health in the Name of Jesus Christ, and every bit of those symptoms will leave you.

By the Stripes of Jesus Christ, we were healed (1 Pet. 2:24). Jesus Christ Himself took our infirmities and bore our sicknesses (Matt. 8:17). If our Lord has borne our sicknesses and diseases, let us not bear them again. Though the situation may look hopeless, let us believe the Lord instead of our feelings.

Is any among you sick? Let him call for the elders of the church, and let them pray over him, anointing him with oil in the Name of the Lord. And the prayer of faith will save the sick, and the Lord will raise him up. And if he has committed sins, he will be forgiven.

Confess your trespasses to one another and pray for one another, that you may be healed. The effective fervent prayer of a righteous man avails much.

Elijah was a man with a nature like ours, and he prayed earnestly that it would not rain, and it did not rain on the land for three years and six months. And he prayed again, and the heavens gave rain, and the earth produced its fruits (Jas 5:14-18).

One thing that makes a Believer (a true Believer) different is that he doesn't live in sin. He recognizes that without holiness, no one can see the Lord. He knows that God doesn't like sin, disobedience, hypocrisy, and compromise.

The true Believer knows that it is only those that do the Will of the Father that will enter the Kingdom of Heaven. The Word says that we must be holy, for the Lord is holy. The Father, without partiality, judges according to each one's work (1 Pet. 1:17).

Conduct yourselves throughout the time of your stay in this world in fear. Work out your salvation with fear and trembling. Strive to be a child of God, who is blameless and harmless,

Let No One Deceive You: Without Holiness, No One Will See The Lord

without fault in the midst of a crooked and perverse generation, among whom you shine as lights in the world.

Not everyone who says to the Lord, "Lord, Lord," shall enter the Kingdom of Heaven, but he who does the Will of His Father in Heaven. Is there any ambiguity in this Statement by the Lord?

Many will say to Him on that Day, "Lord, Lord, have we not prophesied in Your Name, cast out demons in Your Name, and done many wonders in Your Name?" Then He will declare to them, "I never knew you, depart from Me, you who practice lawlessness!" (Matt. 7:21-23).

Friendship with the world is enmity with God. Whoever therefore wants to be a friend of the world makes himself an enemy of God. Walk in the Spirit, and you shall not fulfill the lust of the flesh. If we live in the Spirit, let us also walk in the Spirit.

But fornication and all uncleanness or covetousness, let it not even be named among you, as is fitting for Saints; neither filthiness, nor foolish talking, nor coarse jesting, which are not fitting, but rather giving of thanks.

For this you know, that no fornicator, unclean person, nor covetous man, who is an idolater, has any inheritance in the Kingdom of Christ and God. Let no one deceive you with empty words, for because of these things the Wrath of God comes upon the sons of disobedience.

Therefore do not be partakers with them. For you were once darkness, but now you are light in the Lord. Walk as children of light (for the Fruit of the Spirit is all goodness, righteousness, and truth), finding out what is acceptable to the Lord.

And have no fellowship with the unfruitful works of darkness, but rather expose them. For it is shameful even to speak of those things, which are done by them in secret (Eph. 5:3-12).

Whoever commits sin also commits lawlessness, and sin is lawlessness. And you know that He was manifested to take away our sins, and in Him there is no sin. Whoever abides in Him does not sin. Whoever sins has neither seen Him nor known Him.

Let no one deceive you. He who practices righteousness is righteous, just as He is righteous. He who sins is of the devil, for the devil has sinned from the beginning. For this purpose the Son of God was manifested, that He might destroy the works of the devil.

Whoever has been Born of God does not sin, for His Seed remains in him, and he cannot sin, because he has been Born of God. In this the children of God and the children of the devil are manifest. Whoever does not practice righteousness is not of God, nor is he who does not love his brother.

Love God with all your heart, mind, and strength. Love your neighbour and brother as yourself. Whatever you will want others to do to you, do the same to them. Love thinks no evil; therefore love is the fulfilment of the Law.

The Fruit of the Spirit is love, joy, peace, longsuffering, kindness, goodness, faithfulness, gentleness, self-control. Love suffers long, does not parade itself, is not puffed up.

Love does not behave rudely, does not seek its own, is not provoked, thinks no evil, does not rejoice in iniquity, but rejoices in the truth. Love bears all things, believes all things, hopes all things, endures all things (1 Cor. 13:4-7).

If you are a Believer, seek those things which are Above, where Christ is. Set your mind on things Above, not on things on the earth. For you died, and your life is hidden with Christ in God.

When Christ Who is our Life appears, then you also will appear with Him in glory. When you live the Life of Christ, then are you truly a Christian and a Believer in Christ Jesus.

Never Say That God Said What He Did Not Say!

THE WEAPONS AND ARMOUR OF OUR WARFARE

As a Believer, you must know that we do not wrestle against flesh and blood, but against principalities, against powers, against the rulers of the darkness of this age, against spiritual hosts of wickedness in the heavenly places.

Therefore, be strong in the Lord and in the power of His Might. Put on the whole Armour of God, that you may be able to stand against the wiles of the devil. Take up the whole Armour of God, that you may be able to withstand in the evil day, and having done all, to stand (Eph. 6:10-13).

For though we walk in the flesh, we do not war according to the flesh. For the weapons of our warfare are not carnal but mighty in God for pulling down of strongholds.

We cast down arguments and every high thing that exalts itself against the Knowledge of God, bringing every thought into captivity to the Obedience of Christ, and being ready to punish all disobedience when your obedience is fulfilled (2 Cor. 10:3-6).

Did you notice that you will punish all disobedience when your obedience is complete? In our wrestling with the devil, it is not a matter of who has power, because the devil's power is nothing before the Holy Ghost. It is a matter of who has the legal ground to use his power.

Therefore, if you live in disobedience, demons may refuse to go when you tell them to go. This is why the Word says that in the Name of Jesus Christ, every knee should bow (not 'shall bow'). 'Should bow' because sin, doubt, and life of compromise may make them refuse to bow, even in the Name of Jesus Christ.

Therefore, if the Spirit tells you to pray, pray. If He tells you to fast, fast. If He tells you to study the Bible, study the Bible. If the Holy Ghost tells you to evangelize, evangelize and win souls.

Your life of obedience will lead to urgent response, by the Holy Spirit and the angels of God, to your declarations and commands. He will not, necessarily, speak to you by an audible voice; but even if He gives you a witness or prompting in your spirit, respond to it.

Concerning the Armour of God, the Word tells us to gird our waist with truth, and to put on the breastplate of righteousness. We are to shoe our feet with the preparation of the Gospel of Peace.

Above all, we are to take the shield of faith with which we will be able to quench all the fiery darts of the wicked one. And take the helmet of salvation, and the Sword of the Spirit, which is the Word of God.

We are to pray always with all prayer and supplication in the Spirit, being watchful to this end with all perseverance and supplication for all the Saints (Eph. 6:14-18). It is prayer that holds all the armour together. Therefore, if you don't pray, there is a big problem with you.

To this end, the Word tells us to watch and pray, that we do not fall into temptation. The spirit is willing to pray, but the body (the flesh) says, "I am weak; therefore I need rest, sleep, and food" (Matt. 26:41).

If you pray without watching, you may still fall into the trap and device of the devil. If you watch without praying, even if you see the trap, you may still be overpowered, because prayerlessness leads to weakness.

You must gird your waist with the belt of truth. You must be honest and transparent. Never allow lie or exaggeration into your life. Speak truth with your neighbour, and do not lie to one another.

The Bible tells us that the Word of God is truth. Jesus Christ prayed that the Father will sanctify us by His Truth, and He states that the Word of God is truth (Jn 17:17). Let the Word of Christ dwell in you richly in all wisdom (Col. 3:16), and divide the Word aright (2 Tim. 2:15).

Put the Word where it belongs, and don't misinterpret or distort the Word of God to suit your desires. Interpret the Word of God in the right context, and compare Scripture with Scripture, staying open to the Holy Spirit.

You must put on the breastplate of righteousness. When you receive the Lord Jesus Christ as your Saviour, you receive the righteousness He gives to the Believers in Him. This righteousness justifies you before God, and gives you a right-standing with God.

Many have erred a lot from the truth and the faith, because they have depended on this definition of righteousness, and they live however they want. They live in sin, and say that they have a right-standing with God. But God asks, "Shall you continue in sin that grace may abound?" (Rom. 6:1).

As a child of God, you have received the power and ability to live above sin and overcome the world. If you don't use that power, God will hold you responsible. Don't let the Lord tell you that He never knew you. Don't allow the devil ask you, "So you later came here?"

Whoever commits sin also commits lawlessness, and sin is lawlessness. And you know that He was manifested to take away our sins, and in Him there is no sin. Whoever abides in Him does not sin. Whoever sins has neither seen Him nor known Him.

Child of God, let no one deceive you. He who practices righteousness is righteous, just as He is righteous. He who sins is of the devil, for the devil has sinned from the beginning. For this purpose the Son of God was manifested, that He might destroy the works of the devil.

Whoever has been Born of God does not sin, for His Seed remains in him, and he cannot sin, because he has been Born of God. In this the children of God and the children of the devil are manifest: whoever does not practice righteousness is not of God, nor is he who does not love his brother (1 Jn 3:4-10).

You have to shoe your feet with the preparation of the Gospel of Peace. Preach the Word! Be ready in season and out of season. Convince, rebuke, exhort, with all longsuffering and teaching (2 Tim. 4:2). Preach the Gospel of the Kingdom of God. The Gospel brings peace to men.

Peacemakers shall be called sons of God (Matt. 5:9). Don't encourage strife, envy, division, and quarrels. Where there is no talebearer, strife ceases. Pursue peace with all men (Heb. 12:14). If it is possible, as much as it concerns you, live peaceably with all men (Rom. 12:18).

Take the shield of faith with which you will be able to quench all the fiery darts of the wicked one. Faith comes by hearing, and hearing by the Word of God (Rom. 10:17). If you think you don't have faith, take enough time to feed your spirit with the Word of God, and you will get amazed by what you will experience.

However, even if your faith is as small as the mustard seed, if you don't doubt, you can say to a mountain to be removed and to be planted in the sea, and the mountain will obey you (Matt. 17:20; Mk 11:23). Activate your faith by action, and remove fear from you.

However the devil may come against you, stand your ground, believing the Word of God, and do not shake. The devil will bow and withdraw, if you don't give up. Resist the devil, and he will flee from you (Jas 4:7).

Be sober, be vigilant, because your adversary the devil walks about like a roaring lion, seeking whom he may devour. Resist him, steadfast in the faith (1 Pet. 5:8-9).

Take the helmet of salvation in order to protect your head. In warfare, it is the helmet that protects your head. Your head has your eyes and your brain. Brother, if your head is gone, you are also gone!

Don't joke with your salvation. Your salvation cost God His Only Begotten Son. Your salvation did not come cheap, even though you got it by grace through faith. If you are careless, the devil will tell you that this or that does not matter. He will repeat what he did to Eve to you.

The Word tells us that because iniquity shall abound, the love of many shall wax cold, but he that endures to the end will be saved (Matt. 24:12-13). The Word tells us to hope for the salvation ready to be revealed in the Last Day (1 Pet. 1:13).

The Word says that Jesus Christ, for the Joy that was set before Him, endured the Cross, despising the shame, and has sat down at the Right Hand of the Throne of God (Heb. 12:2). Take your Lord as your Example, and look to Jesus Christ, the Author and Finisher of our faith.

We are looking for a reward, which cannot be compared to anything in this world. Don't fall down to worship the devil in order to have the things of this world. The devil does not love anyone. He is no good entity.

Take the Sword of the Spirit, which is the Word of God. The Sword is an offensive weapon used for attacking an enemy. It is the confession and declaration of the Word of God that pierces the devil. No wonder God, through Apostle Paul, tells us that the Word of God pierces (Heb. 4:12).

The Word of God is fire, and it is hammer (Jer. 23:29). The fire of the Word burns up the works of the devil. The hammer of the Word breaks to pieces the things that are opposed to God and His people.

Apostle John saw the Lord with the double-edged sword coming out of His Mouth. That is the sword of the Word of God. It is by the Word of God that the heavens and the earth were created, and it is the Word that will judge people on the Last Day.

Don't joke with the Word, for it is forever settled in Heaven (Psa. 119:89). Don't remove from His Word, so that He will not remove your blessing and reward. Don't add to His Word, so that He will not add punishments to you (Prov. 30:6; Rev. 22:18-19).

As you speak the Word of God, and declare what the Lord has said, to the devil and his demons, the Word comes out of your mouth as sword, fire, and hammer, and no devil can withstand that Word you speak. They will flee and be rendered powerless.

Then, you must pray always with all prayer and supplication in the Spirit. Pray in the Holy Ghost. As you pray in the Spirit, your spirit prays, but your understanding is unfruitful. Pray with the spirit, and pray with the understanding also. Sing with the spirit and sing with the understanding also (1 Cor. 14:15).

Also, you must learn to plead the Blood of Jesus Christ: the Blood of Jesus Christ! The Blood of Jesus Christ speaks mercy, peace, forgiveness, protection, deliverance, etc. No devil can cross the Blood-line.

You must also use the Name of Jesus Christ always. The Name of Jesus Christ is the Name above all other names. At His Name, every knee should bow, of things (those) in heaven, of things (those) on earth, and of things (those) under the earth.

Speaking in tongues should become part and parcel of you. Speaking in tongues is a way of praying in the Holy Ghost. As you speak in tongues, you speak to God, speaking mysteries to Him. You pray for things you don't know of, the right way, by praying in the Holy Ghost.

For we do not know what we should pray for as we ought, but the Spirit Himself makes intercession for us with groanings which cannot be uttered. Now, He Who searches the hearts knows what the Mind of the Spirit is, because He makes intercession for the Saints according to the Will of God.

The Fire of the Holy Ghost works wonders in spiritual warfare. God showed me, by revelation, the effectiveness of it, in destroying the works and plans of the devil.

Prophet John the Baptist said that Jesus Christ will baptize with Holy Ghost and fire (Matt. 3:11). The Word that comes out of your mouth as fire (Jer. 23:29) is actually a form of the Fire of the Holy Ghost. Even those who may say they don't believe in the Fire of the Holy Ghost still use it, because, many times, when you say, "Jesus!" it is actually fire that comes out of your mouth.

THE OLD TESTAMENT BELIEVERS' EXPLOITS

In the Old Testament, we see people who believed in God, and the exploits they did. God empowered them, because they were His spokesmen and prophets. In the Old Testament, the anointing was upon the prophets, the priests, the kings, and any other people God selected for special works.

The ordinary people didn't have the Spirit of God upon them. However, in the New Testament, the Holy Spirit dwells inside the Believers, and comes upon them at the baptism in the Holy Spirit and the Infilling of the Holy Spirit.

All Believers that have been filled with the Holy Spirit have the anointing upon them. This is why the Word says that the Believers receive power after the Holy Spirit comes upon them, and they are thereby anointed and empowered to be witnesses for the Lord Jesus Christ.

No wonder the Believers are called Christians. The word 'Christian' means being like Christ, the Anointed. Christ is the Greek for Messiah. Messiah is the Hebrew word for the Anointed. Of course, to be Christian or to be a Christian is to be like Jesus Christ, both in anointing and in character.

Therefore, if you call yourself a Christian without the Anointing of the Holy Spirit, you still have some distance to cover. But all Believers have the Holy Spirit, at least to a level. You can have Him at the well-level (Jn 4:14) or at the river-level (Jn 7:38-39).

This is why the Word of God says that if any person does not have the Spirit of Christ, he is not of Christ. Therefore, if you have the Indwelling Presence of the Holy Spirit, because you are born again, go for the in-filling presence of baptism in the Holy Spirit.

Another thing you should know is that under the New Testament, all Believers are kings and priests. Jesus Christ loved us and washed us from our sins in His Own Blood, and has made us kings and priests to His God and Father (Rev. 1:5-6).

The Lord redeemed us to God by His Blood out of every tribe and tongue and people and nation, and has made us kings and priests to our God, and we shall reign on earth (Rev. 5:9-10).

As kings, we are supposed to reign; and just as there is power wherever the word of the king is, our word should carry power and dynamic ability to cause change, and bring to pass what we declare.

God created the heaven and the earth by the power of His Word. When He declared that anything should be, the Holy Spirit brought it to pass. The visible world was created from the invisible world.

No wonder the Word says that God calls those things that are non-existent by name as though they existed. The good news is that when He calls them, they come to be. We should speak and act like God.

This is one reason why you should be careful how you speak, because life and death are in the power of the tongue. Don't curse yourself with your own mouth; rather, learn to bless yourself. Speak positive things about yourself according to the Word of God.

If anyone does not stumble in word, he is a perfect man, able also to bridle the whole body. Indeed we put bits in horses' mouths that they may obey us, and we turn their whole body.

Look also at ships: although they are so large and are driven by fierce winds, they are turned by a very small rudder wherever the pilot desires. Even so the tongue is a little member and boasts great things.

See how great a forest a little fire kindles! And the tongue is a fire, a world of iniquity. The tongue is so set among our members that it defiles the whole body, and sets on fire the course of nature, and is set on fire by Hell.

No man can tame the tongue. It is an unruly evil, full of deadly poison. With it we bless our God and Father, and with it we curse men, who have been made in the Similitude of God. Out of the same mouth proceed blessing and cursing. My brethren, these things ought not to be so (Jas 3:2-10).

Don't curse your children in the name of correcting them. Yes, you must discipline your children to train them aright. Flog them when it is necessary, but don't curse them with your own mouth.

As priests, we ought to offer the sacrifice of praise to our God and King. We also have to stand in the gap between God and people, and make intercession on behalf of others.

You are a chosen generation, a royal priesthood, a holy nation, His Own special people, that you may proclaim the Praises of Him Who called you out of darkness into His Marvelous Light (1 Pet. 2:9).

The Old Testament has great examples of men and women who did mighty things for God, and glorified His Name, both among the people of God (Israelites and Jews) and the Gentile nations. They did those exploits through the power and authority God gave them.

Think of Prophet Moses. When God sent Moses to Pharaoh, Moses went with great power and boldness. When Moses asked Pharaoh to let the Israelites go, Pharaoh asked, "Who is the Lord, that I should obey His Voice to let Israel go?"

The devil (satan) got lifted up in pride, thinking within himself that he could acquire a position that God didn't give him by himself. Why did he do that? It was because he thought he knew God, while he didn't. If Lucifer had known what would befall him, he wouldn't have tried what he did.

Concerning satan, God said, "You were the seal of perfection, full of wisdom and perfect in beauty. You were the anointed cherub who covers; I established you; you were on the holy mountain of God. You were perfect in your ways from the day you were created, till iniquity was found in you (Ezek. 28:11-15).

"How you are fallen from Heaven, O Lucifer, son of the morning! How you are cut down to the ground, you who weakened the nations! For you have said in your heart: 'I will ascend into Heaven, I will exalt my throne above the stars of God;

'I will also sit on the mount of the congregation on the farthest sides of the north; I will ascend above the heights of the clouds, I will be like the Most High.' Yet you shall be brought down to Sheol" (Isa. 14:12-15).

Pharaoh was lifted up in pride, just as the devil was also lifted up in pride. But whereas Pharaoh was a kind of a stranger to God, satan was not. Rather, Lucifer actually related closely with God.

We are talking about the power and authority of the Believer. Many people that God uses to demonstrate His Power, in signs and wonders, have become lifted up in pride and taken the glory due to God to themselves.

God resists the proud, but He gives grace to the humble (Jas 4:6). God is a Jealous God, Who will not share His Glory with another (Isa. 48:11). If God did not give you life, health, and understanding, you couldn't do or become anything.

Pharaoh said, "Who is the Lord that I should obey Him?" Why do the nations rage, and the people plot a vain thing? The kings of the earth set themselves, and the rulers take counsel together, against the Lord and against His Anointed.

They say, "Let us break Their Bonds in pieces and cast away Their Cords from us." He Who sits in the Heavens shall laugh, the Lord shall hold them in derision. Then He shall speak to them in His Wrath, and distress them in His Deep Displeasure (Psa. 2:1-5).

Pharaoh did not know that the Lord is too much for him. God, by the hands of His Servant Moses, brought many plagues upon and against the Egyptians. The Egyptians suffered so much; yet Pharaoh refused to let the Israelites go.

But Moses, a type of a Believer who has been anointed by the Spirit of God, glorified the Lord in demonstrating signs and wonders that shook Pharaoh and his people.

The Lord said to Moses, "See I have made you as God to Pharaoh, and Aaron your brother shall be your prophet. You shall speak all that I command you. And I will harden Pharaoh's heart, and multiply My Signs and My Wonders in the land of Egypt.

"But Pharaoh will not heed you, so that I may lay My Hand on Egypt and bring My armies and My people, the children of Israel, out of the land of Egypt by great judgments.

"And the Egyptians shall know that I am the Lord, when I stretch out My Hand on Egypt and bring out the children of Israel from among them." Then Moses and Aaron did so; just as the Lord commanded them, so they did.

When Aaron's rod became a serpent, the Egyptian magicians and sorcerers threw down their rods also, so that their rods also became serpents. However, Aaron's rod swallowed up their own rods.

Rivers, streams, ponds, and pools of Egypt became blood, so that the people couldn't drink it. God smote their territory with frogs. Dust of the earth became lice in man when Aaron stretched his rod and struck the dust.

Thick swamps of flies came upon Egypt. God brought pestilence on their cattle. They were attacked by boils. Hail fell on the land of Egypt when Moses stretched out his rod toward Heaven. God brought locusts into their territory.

Pharaoh kept on hardening his heart until the last plague in which all the firstborn of Egypt died. Whoever hardens his heart against God's Purpose for your life, and refuses to repent is committing himself to God's Judgment. God of Vengeance will fight for you!

Even after the people of Israel had left, Pharaoh still pursued them. God divided the Red Sea, and the Israelites passed on dry ground. But when the Egyptians wanted to pass, they were drowned. God sent quails and manna to them to feed them.

God, by the hand of Moses, did mighty signs and wonders in the sight of Israel as they wandered in the desert. When Moses struck the rock, water came out for them to drink. The Gentile nations were afraid of them, because they heard what happened to Pharaoh.

Joshua commanded, and the sun stood still. The walls of Jericho fell down after it had been encircled seven days and the trumpets were blown. The Book of Judges has many accounts of mighty deeds done by men of God.

Ehud saved Israel from Moab. At that time they killed about ten thousand men of Moab, all stout men of valour, not a man escaped. So Moab was subdued under the hand of Israel. And the land had rest for eighty years.

Barak, working with Prophetess Deborah, subdued Sisera and his armies. Gideon defeated the Midianites with only three hundred men. Jephthah, a son of a harlot was used by God to subdue the Ammonites.

When Sampson came on the scene, the Philistines saw and felt pepper; the man gave them sleepless nights. Sampson, a one-man army, was so much anointed and empowered that he killed a lion with bare hands. He used a fresh jawbone of a donkey to kill one thousand Philistines.

Sampson pulled the doors of the gate to a city and the two gate posts; he carried them, bar and all, up a hill. Cords used to tie him became as flax that is burned with fire, and his bonds broke loose from his hands. Even at his death, he killed more people than in his lifetime.

David was empowered and emboldened by the Spirit of God, so that he killed the giant, Goliath, with a stone and a sling; and there was no sword in David's hand. David defeated the enemies of Israel in many battles, because God was with him.

Think of Elijah that called down fire from Heaven. Prophet Elijah stopped rainfall for three and half years, and brought back rain afterwards. Prophet Elisha cured Naaman of leprosy, healed the water of a land, and brought back the dead to life.

When the Syrian army came to fetch him, he prayed and the entire army became blinded, so that he arrested them, even though he released them to go. Even at death, his bones brought somebody back to life when the dead person came in contact with his bone.

Prophet Daniel and his friends: Shadrach, Meshach, and Abed-Nego, made up their minds to stay faithful and true to God; God blessed them so much that when they were tested, after their training, in all matters of wisdom and understanding about which the king examined them, they were excellent.

The king found them ten times better than all the magicians and astrologers who were in all his realm. And they served before the king. God gave them knowledge and skill in all literature and wisdom, and Daniel had understanding in all visions and dreams (Dan. 1).

When Shadrach, Meshach, and Abed-Nego were threatened with death by fire, they believed that God could save them. They decided that it was better to die than to bow down to King Nebuchadnezzar's gold image. God delivered them from the fiery furnace (Dan. 3).

When Daniel was thrown into the den of lions through an evil plot, God delivered him so that the lions couldn't touch him. So Daniel was taken up out of the den, and no injury whatever was found on him, because he believed in his God (Dan. 6).

The things the Old Testament prophets and Servants of God did were spectacular. Yet we are to do them, and we will do greater things than the things they did, because we are in the New Testament, which is established upon better promises (Heb. 8:6).

And if the ministry of death…was glorious…how will the Ministry of the Spirit not be more glorious? For if the ministry of condemnation had glory, the ministry of righteousness exceeds much more in glory.

For even what was made glorious had no glory in this respect, because of the glory that excels. For if what is passing away was glorious, what remains is much more glorious (2 Cor. 3:7-11).

The Old Testament Believers in God, through faith, subdued kingdoms, worked righteousness, obtained promises, stopped the mouths of lions, quenched the violence of fire, escaped the edge of the sword, out of weakness were made strong.

They became valiant in battle, and turned to flight the armies of the aliens. Women received their dead raised to life again. Others were tortured, not accepting deliverance, that they might obtain a Better Resurrection (Heb. 11:33-35).

If you know that they did mighty exploits, in signs and wonders, for the Lord, by which they stunned the people and brought glory to God, then you have to know that God is expecting greater results from us!

THE NOTHINGNESS OF ALL CONTRARY THINGS

As a Believer, you are God's Property. Not one hair of your head can fall to the ground without God's Permission. No matter how the devil and his demons come against you, you will prevail over them and overcome them.

The Church of Jesus Christ is marching on, and the gates of Hades shall not prevail against it (Matt. 16:18). Why? Because the Church is the Body of Christ, and her Head – Jesus Christ – is above all. He is the Commander-in-chief of the Heavenly host.

Therefore, do not fear him, who after killing the body has no power over the soul. Rather fear Him Who can destroy both the body and the soul in Hell (Matt. 10:28). God cares for you, and He has you in His Heart.

The Believer who dwells in the Secret Place of the Most High shall abide under the Shadow of the Almighty. To dwell in the Secret Place of the Most High is to stay long in the Presence of God, in prayer, praise, Bible study, and waiting on Him.

The Lord is your Refuge and your Fortress; your God, in Him you will trust. Surely He shall deliver you from the snare of the fowler and from the perilous pestilence.

He shall cover you with His Feathers, and under His Wings you shall take refuge; His Truth shall be your shield and buckler. You shall not be afraid of the terror by the night, nor of the arrow that flies by day.

You shall not be afraid of the pestilence that walks in darkness, nor of the destruction that lays waste at noonday. A thousand may fall at your side, and ten thousand at your right hand; but it shall not come near you.

Only with your eyes shall you look, and see the reward of the wicked. Because you have made the Lord, Who is my Refuge, even the Most High, your Dwelling Place, no evil shall befall you, nor shall any plague come near your dwelling.

God shall give His angels Charge over you, to keep you in all your ways. In their hands they shall bear you up, lest you dash your foot against a stone.

You shall tread upon the lion and the cobra, the young lion and the serpent you shall trample underfoot. With long life God will satisfy you, and show you His Salvation.

Because you have set your love upon God, therefore He will deliver you; He will set you on High, because you have known His Name. You shall call upon Him, and He will answer you; He will be with you in trouble; He will deliver you and honour you (Psa. 91).

In righteousness you shall be established; you shall be far from oppression, for you shall not fear; and from terror, for it shall not come near you.

Indeed evil men and workers shall surely assemble, but not because of God. Whoever assembles against you shall fall for your sake. This is the Word of God, Who can neither lie nor disappoint.

God created the blacksmith who blows the coals in the fire, who brings forth an instrument for his work; He created the spoiler to destroy.

No weapon formed against you shall prosper, and every tongue, which rises against you in judgment, you shall condemn. This is the heritage of the Servants of the Lord, and their righteousness is from Him (Isa. 54:14-17).

This tells you that you shall not be afraid of guns and other destructive weapons. Do you know that a gun can refuse to shoot, because it is pointed at you? Even if it shoots, God can give you a supernatural bullet-proof.

This is not to say that you should go for guns and other destructive weapons to prove that they will not harm you. Also, learn to listen to your spirit, and be sensitive to the Prompting and Leading of the Holy Spirit, so that you will not fall into danger.

You remember that an angel of God told Joseph to take Jesus Christ and Mary to Egypt, because Herod wanted to kill Jesus Christ. Why didn't God save Jesus Christ and the rest of them the trouble of going to Egypt by killing Herod? God has a purpose in everything.

Also, when the Egyptians were destroying the male-children of the Israelites, when Moses was born (when he could no more be hidden by his mother), God led the mother to form a basket for him.

With Moses inside the basket, the basket floated on the river, and Pharaoh's daughter picked him up. Moses, who was the deliverer, was brought up right inside Pharaoh's home, with all the privileges and opportunities he enjoyed. They were doing all they could to stop the freedom of Israel, while they were feeding and clothing the deliverer without their knowledge. God is too much for the devil. But you've got to be sensitive to His Holy Spirit.

No wonder the Word of God says that if the kingdom of darkness had known the Wisdom of God, they wouldn't have killed Jesus Christ, because it was in killing Jesus Christ that they destroyed themselves (1 Cor. 2:8).

The devil and his demons are confused people. Who told or tells them that they can overcome God? Brother, it is not possible. All things will be perfected by God in due course. At the appointed time, the devil will be banished!

The Everlasting God, the Lord and the Creator of the ends of the earth, neither faints nor is weary. His Understanding is unsearchable. He gives power to the weak, and to those who have no might He increases strength.

Even the youths shall faint and be weary, and the young men shall utterly fall, but those who wait on the Lord shall renew their strength; they shall mount up with wings as eagles, they shall run and not be weary, they shall walk and not faint (Isa. 40:28-31).

Fear not, for God is with you; be not dismayed, for He is your God. He will strengthen you, yes, He will help you, He will uphold you with His Righteous Right Hand.

Behold, all those who were incensed against you shall be ashamed and disgraced; they shall be as nothing, and those who strive with you shall perish. You shall seek them and not find them – those who contended with you.

Those who war against you shall be as nothing, as a nonexistent thing. Fear not, for God will help you. Fear not, you worm Believer, you Christian! The Lord God will help you (Isa. 41:10-14).

The Lord is your Shepherd; you shall not want. He makes His people lie down in green pastures; He leads them beside the still waters. He restores their souls; He leads them in the paths of righteousness for His Name's sake.

Yea, though they walk through the valley of the shadow of death, they will fear no evil; for God is with them; His Rod and His Staff, they comfort them.

God prepares a table before them in the presence of their enemies; He anoints them with the Holy Spirit; their cups run over. Surely goodness and mercy shall follow them all the days of their lives; and they shall dwell in the House of the Lord forever (Psa. 23).

Even in the presence of your enemies, God prepares a table before you. Isn't it wonderful? They shall watch you prosper and succeed, in spite of all their charms, incantations, and invocations against you.

This is what happened to Isaac. He was in the land of the Philistines and prospered so much that the Philistines envied him. Yet, because God was with him, they couldn't touch him. God told Isaac that He would bless him, because of his father Abraham who obeyed Him.

What God told Joshua is applicable to us Believers, and it is very nice. God said, "Every place that the sole of your foot will tread upon, I have given you.... No man shall be able to stand before you all the days of your life.... I will be with you.

"I will not leave you nor forsake you. Be strong and of good courage.... Only be strong and very courageous, that you may observe to do according to all the Law which Moses My Servant commanded you; do not turn from it to the right hand or to the left, that you may prosper wherever you go.

"This Book of the Law shall not depart from your mouth, but you shall meditate in it day and night, that you may observe to do according to all that is written in it. For then you will make your way prosperous, and then you will have good success. Have I not commanded you? Be strong and of good courage; do not be afraid, nor be dismayed, for the Lord your God is with you wherever you go" (Josh. 1:3-9).

Now it shall come to pass, if you diligently obey the Voice of the Lord your God, to observe carefully all His Commandments...that the Lord your God will set you high above all nations of the earth.

And all these blessings shall come upon you and overtake you, because you obey the Voice of the Lord your God. Blessed shall you be in the city, and blessed shall you be in the country.

Blessed shall be the fruit of your body, the produce of your ground and the increase of your herds.... Blessed shall be your kneading bowl.

Blessed shall you be when you come in, and blessed shall you be when you go out. The Lord will cause your enemies who rise against you to be defeated before your face; they shall come out against you one way and flee before you seven ways.

The Lord will command the blessing on you in your storehouses and in all to which you set your hand, and He will bless you in the land which the Lord your God is giving you.

The Lord will establish you a holy people to Himself...if you keep the Commandants of the Lord your God and walk in His Ways. Then all the peoples of the earth shall see that you are called by the Name of the Lord, and they shall be afraid of you.

And the Lord will grant you plenty of goods, in the fruit of your body, in the increase of your livestock, and in the produce of your ground, in the land....

The Lord will open to you His Good Treasure, the heavens, to give the rain to your land in its seasons, and to bless all the work of your hand. You shall lend to many nations, but you shall not borrow.

And the Lord will make you the head and not the tail; you shall be above only, and not be beneath, if you heed the Commandments of the Lord your God...and are careful to observe them.

So you shall not turn aside from any of the Words...to the right or the left, to go after other gods to serve them (Deut. 28:1-14).

The mountains and obstacles you may meet along the way in your Heavenly race are as nothing. All that is opposed to God and His Word is nothing!

THE BELIEVER AND LOVE

Love is the fulfilment of the Law (Rom. 13:10). Loving God with all and more than all, and loving your neighbour as yourself are the whole duty of man. Yes, the whole duty of man is to fear God and keep His Commandments; and love is the beginning and the end of His Commandments.

Why? This is because Jesus Christ Himself states in the Bible that if you love Him, you will keep His Commandments (Jn 14:15). And we know that His Commandments are neither burdensome nor grievous (1 Jn 5:3). Yes, your flesh will hate to obey Him; but you must bring your flesh into obeying your spirit, who is always willing.

The Commandments of the Lord are not meant to punish or destroy us. No, they are for our well-being. God knows better than any of us; in fact, God loves you more than you love yourself. You may not believe it, but it is true.

Do you know that God felt Job's pains more than he felt them? Yes, it was God that permitted satan to touch him, to prove to the devil that Job's love for Him, and his commitment to obeying Him were not because of conditional things. I tell you, God felt what Job felt.

This is why the Word says that even when the Lord chastens us, He does so, that we may become partakers of His Holiness (Heb. 12:10). This is why the Word says that even when we are judged by the Lord, the Lord chastens us so that we will not be condemned with the world (1 Cor. 11:32). God loves you; He cares for you.

When Jesus Christ was asked to state the great Commandment in the Law, He answered, saying, "You shall love the Lord your God with all your heart, with all your soul, and with all your mind. This is the first and great Commandment. And the second is like it: You shall love your neighbour as yourself.

"On these two Commandments hang all the Law and the Prophets" (Matt. 12:36-40). This is wonderful and amazing; isn't it? Mark added something when he reported (quoting Jesus Christ): "And you shall love the Lord your God with all your heart, with all your soul, with all your mind, and with all your strength" (Mk 12:30).

Brother, if you love God, you will not disobey Him, and you will not want Him to be disappointed in you. Even when your flesh wants to have its way, your spirit will always side with God. Can you see that the real issue in obeying God is a matter of the heart? Of our course, discipline and self-control are involved.

If you love your neighbour as yourself, you will not steal his property, you will not bear false witness against him, and you will not kill him. No wonder the Word says, "Do to others as you would have them do to you" (Matt. 7:12). It will require making up your mind (once and for all) in order to obey that Statement.

The Word of God says that love covers multitude of sins (I Pet. 4:8). This does not mean that love hides and covers sins, because the Bible tells us to rebuke those that sin publicly, so that others may fear (I Tim. 5:20). Rather, love overlooks wrongdoings done against it.

So, if you are always finding faults with somebody, check your love for that person. When you want somebody to commit faults so that you may accuse him, it is because you hate the person. There is much hatred among Believers today. He who hates his brother is a murderer (I Jn 3:15). And no murderer will enter the Kingdom of God.

There is no fear in love, but perfect love drives out fear (I Jn 4:18). Think of the love that will make a man accept a woman into his life and home, thereby committing his life in the hands of the woman! But the love we are talking about is greater than husband-wife love.

It was love that made the good Samaritan to go to the man that was brutalized by robbers on his way to Jericho. That love removed the fear that it may be assumed that the good Samaritan knows what happened to the man, if he was caught with him.

These days are fearful sometimes, because someone who wants to help put things in order, may be accused of being responsible for that very thing. Satan tries to get us away from doing the right things, because of fear of the unknown. But we must obey God instead of our reasoning.

However, in connection to what I just said, is that you should be sensitive to the Leading of the Holy Spirit. To escape evil and a possible set-up, you must be led by the Holy Spirit. Don't try to correct or help a matter when you have been directed by the Holy Spirit (even if it is by the inward witness, sign, or check in your spirit or heart) to leave and depart.

Love is listed as a Fruit of the Spirit. The Fruit of the Spirit is love, joy, peace, longsuffering, kindness, goodness, faithfulness, gentleness, self-control (Gal. 5:22-23). Actually, this is talking about the fruit of the recreated human spirit. It is like to say: "The human spirit, by the Holy Spirit, brings out or produces...."

The Fruit of the Spirit is in all goodness, righteousness, and truth (Eph. 5:9). If the Holy Spirit lives in you, love, joy, peace, longsuffering, kindness, goodness, faithfulness, gentleness, self-control, etc will be seen in you. Yes, all those attributes and all that have to do with goodness, righteousness, and truth will be in your life.

Of course, there are different levels of fruitfulness and productivity. Therefore, strive to bear much fruit in each of those areas of the Fruit of the Spirit. If any of them is not showing as supposed, work on yourself to excel in it. Amen.

Yes, we are speaking about the power and authority of the Believer. The power and authority that God gave us is astonishing, amazing, surprising, and wonderful. But there is a higher life, and that is the life of love. God took time to describe the life of love to us in the thirteenth chapter of the Book of First Corinthians.

Brother, if you speak with the tongues of men and of angels, but have not love, you have become a sounding brass or a clanging cymbal. And though you have the gift of prophecy, and understand all mysteries and all knowledge, and though you have all faith, so that you can remove mountains, but have not love, you are nothing.

And though you bestow all your goods to feed the poor, and though you give your body to be burned, but have not love, it profits you nothing. How can somebody bestow all his goods to feed the poor, and even give his body to be burned without love? Is it possible? Yes. Then what is love?

Love suffers long. Did you notice that longsuffering is one of the Fruit of the Spirit? And love is longsuffering! Love can bear pains and wrongs for a very long time. This Heavenly race we are running requires patience and endurance. If you don't endure to the end, you will not be saved (Matt. 24:13).

Love is kind. What does it mean to be kind? According to the Longman Dictionary of Contemporary English, to be kind is: "Saying or doing things that show that you care about other people and want to help them or make them happy."

Kindness has to do with tenderness of the heart. You are not strong-willed to having your own things to the detriment of others. You consider others, and put yourself in their positions. Kindness has to do with having compassionate feeling toward others.

Love does not envy. Don't be envious of your neighbour. God holds the key to your life; He will supply all your needs according to His Riches in glory in Christ Jesus. Be patient and wait for God; and even if your promotion or prosperity is delayed, it will surely come.

Love does not parade itself, is not puffed up. God resists the proud but gives grace to the humble (Jas 4:6). Herod was smitten by an angel and eaten by worms, because he took the glory due to God to himself. You could become nothing without God. God gave you life, health, gifts, talents, and even help.

Love does not behave rudely. To be rude is to speak or behave in a way that is not polite and is likely to offend or annoy people. To be polite is to behave or speak in a way that is correct, and showing that you are careful to consider other people's needs and feelings.

Love does not seek its own. It is not selfish. To be selfish is be caring only about yourself and not about other people. When Jesus Christ gave up the comfort of Heaven, and came to this earth, He was saying 'No' to selfishness. When He gave His Life for us, He was showing that He cared for us.

Love is not provoked. This is wonderful. To not be provoked is to be tempted with provocative situations and factors, and yet not being provoked. To not be provoked at all is more than not being quick-tempered. Someone who is not quick-tempered can be provoked after some time; but love is not provoked. Beware of destructive anger!

Love thinks no evil. It didn't say that love acts no evil, but that it thinks no evil. That is to say that when the Almighty God, Who searches the heart, screens your inner thoughts, He will say: "I see no evil hidden in this man's thoughts." Don't plan evil against your fellow human being.

Love does not rejoice in iniquity. It does not take delight in living in sin. If you live in sin, if you take delight in committing sin (and the sin(s) may be hidden from men), then you lack love. And you know that he who does not love is heading towards Hell and not Heaven.

Love rejoices in the truth. Love is honest and transparent. It does not hide sin (and you can't hide any sin from God). The Word of God is truth; therefore, love rejoices in the Word of God. But he who lives in sin, he who has no repentance, does not like hearing the true unadulterated Word of God.

Love bears all things. Forgiveness and forbearance are necessary for you as a Believer. Don't be given to grumbling and bearing of grudges. If you don't forgive others, God also will not forgive you. Don't be like the unmerciful servant.

Love believes all things. Blessed are those who have not seen and yet have believed (Jn 20:29). Love believes that the Word of God is true. Love believes that the Promises of God are 'Yes' and 'Amen.' And it hopes for and looks forward to having what God has promised.

Love endures all things. The burden may be heavy, the pain may be great, but love endures all things. Love does not blame God when it is passing through harsh and difficult situations. Rather, love will praise God in the midst of tests, trials, and persecutions.

Love never fails: it has no ending. But whether there are prophecies, they will fail, whether there are tongues, they will cease; whether there is knowledge, it will vanish away. We wouldn't need the Gifts of the Spirit when Jesus Christ comes, but love will last forever. Of course, we will always need the Holy Spirit, even in Heaven, because He is the One that will make us the super-beings we will become in Heaven!

And now abide faith, hope, love, these three; but the greatest of these is love. If the greatest is love, what shall we do? We will do everything to get matured in love. No matter the level of love you may be in, you can improve and mature in it. Remember that love is a more excellent way (I Cor. 12:31).

WHEN YOU PASS THROUGH THE FIRE

As a Believer, you must realize that many are the afflictions of the righteous, but the Lord delivers him from all of them (Psa. 34:19). Inasmuch as you are still in this world, you shall have tribulations; but be of good cheer, because the Lord has overcome the world (Jn 16:33).

This is why the Word says: "When you walk through the fire…" instead of, "If you walk through the fire…" (Isa. 43:2). Many times, afflictions and tribulations will not require your permission before they come. Of course, you will not permit them.

Before you know it, you see afflictions. If you ask, "Affliction, why are you here?" it will say, "I am already here, take care of me." However, remember that all things work together for good for those who love God, to those who are the called according to His Purpose (Rom. 8:28).

Think about it! If Joseph was not hated by his brothers, they wouldn't have sold him. If he hadn't been tempted by Portiphar's wife, he wouldn't have been imprisoned. If he was not imprisoned, he wouldn't have interpreted the dreams of the Pharaoh's servants that were imprisoned.

It was that interpretation of their dreams that introduced him to Pharaoh, and he became the prime minister of Egypt. The dream that Joseph dreamt was a big dream, and his father's house was too small for the fulfilment of that dream. He had to be hated to go out from there.

Joseph was sold into slavery, not because of what he did, but because God, in His Divine Plan, had already told Abraham that his children will be slaves in a foreign country for four hundred years. So, when demons incited Joseph's brothers against him, they were helping to fulfil a prophecy.

The same thing was applicable to Jesus Christ. When the devil incited the Pharisees and the priests against Him, they were helping to fulfil the prophecy that the chastisement of our peace was upon Him, and by His Stripes we are healed (Isa. 53:5).

God can allow you enter into a trouble that will stagger your mentality, and even make you despair life. But you may find out that before you come out of it, you have become a prayer-warrior (a consistent prayerful Christian).

This is why people (even ministers) may pray for you, and yet you will not have your answer, because you have not learned your lesson. God can use afflictions and troubles to make you wiser and get you matured spiritually.

Notice that Jesus Christ passed through extreme sufferings and persecutions. And the Word of God says that Jesus Christ, for the Joy that was set before Him, endured the Cross, and despised the shame, and has sat down at the Right Hand of the Throne of God (Heb. 12:2).

Consider Him Who endured such hostility from sinners against Himself, lest you become weary and discouraged in your souls. You have not resisted to bloodshed, striving against sin.

Christ Jesus, being in the Form of God, did not consider it robbery to be equal with God, but made Himself of no reputation, taking the form of a bondservant, and coming in the likeness of men.

And being found in appearance as a Man, He humbled Himself and became obedient to the point of death, even the death of the Cross. Therefore God also has highly exalted Him and given Him the Name which is above every name.

That at the Name of Jesus Christ every knee should bow, of those (things/beings) in heaven, and of those on earth, and of those under the earth, and that every tongue should confess that Jesus Christ is Lord, to the Glory of God the Father (Phil. 2:6-11).

Had you known it that the Word says that Jesus Christ learnt obedience through the things He suffered? (Heb. 5:8). There are some things you can never learn, except by experience, no matter how you read and study about them. 'Experience is the best teacher' is applicable to spiritual things also.

The Saints of both the Old Testament and the early New Testament suffered afflictions and persecutions, and the case can't be different with you. As a matter of fact, even the Lord Jesus Christ told us about it (or rather promised us persecutions) (Jn 15:20).

They had trials of mockings and scourgings, yes, and of chains and imprisonment. They were stoned, they were sawn in two, were tempted, were slain with the sword. They wandered about in sheepskins and goatskins, being destitute, afflicted, tormented – of whom the world was not worthy. They wandered in deserts and mountains, in dens and caves of earth.

However, you must know that the Lord will not allow any temptation, test, or trial that is greater than you to come your way. Therefore, don't disappoint God by yielding to temptations.

No temptations has overtaken you except such as is common to man; but God is faithful, Who will not allow you to be tempted beyond what you are able, but with the temptation will also make the way of escape, that you may be able to bear it (1 Cor. 10:13).

Fear not, for God has redeemed you; He has called you by your name; you are His. When you pass through the waters, He will be with you; and through the rivers, they shall not overflow you.

When you walk through the fire, you shall not be burned, nor shall the flame scorch you. For He is the Lord your God…. He will give men for your ransom…since you are precious in His Sight (Isa. 43:1-4).

The tests and trials you will pass through, the wilderness experiences you will experience, may be different from the ones I will pass through. But in all, they will work out for our good and promotion.

God loves us more than we love ourselves. When we are in hard times, some of us tend to think that God has forgotten us; but God cares for us, and He is aware of whatever you may be passing through.

Do not despise the Chastening of the Lord, nor be discouraged when you are rebuked by Him; for whom the Lord loves He chastens, and scourges every son whom He receives. If you endure chastening, God deals with you as with sons; for what son is there whom a father does not chasten?

But if you are without chastening, of which all have become partakers, then you are illegitimate and not sons. Furthermore, we have had human fathers who corrected us, and we paid them respect.

Shall we not much more readily be in subjection to the Father of spirits and live? For they indeed for a few days chastened us as seemed best to them, but He for our profit, that we may be partakers of His Holiness.

Now no chastening seems to be joyful for the present, but painful; nevertheless, afterward it yields the peaceable fruit of righteousness to those who have been trained by it (Heb. 12:5-11).

Though you walk through the valley of the shadow of death, you need not fear any evil; for God is with you; His Rod and His Staff, they will comfort you. He will be with you in trouble; He will deliver you and honour you.

God may tell you something, which you may have to wait for long, before you see it physically. In your mind, you may assume that it will come to pass next week, but the vision is yet for an appointed time.

At the end, the vision will speak, and it will not lie. Though it tarries, wait for it; because it will surely come, it will not tarry. Write the vision or grab it in your heart and mind, waiting on God patiently. It will come to pass (Habk. 2:2).

Think of what Apostle Paul passed through, even though he desired and worked passionately to fulfil his ministry! Apostle Paul wrote: "We are hard pressed on every side, but not in despair;

"Persecuted, but not forsaken; struck down, but not destroyed – always carrying about in the body the Dying of the Lord Jesus, that the Life of Jesus also may be manifested in our body. For we who live are always delivered to death for Jesus' Sake, that the Life of Jesus also may be manifested in our mortal body. So then death is working in us, but life in you" (2 Cor. 4: 8-12).

He also wrote, "But in all things we commend ourselves as ministers of God: in much patience, in tribulations, in needs, in distresses, in stripes, in imprisonments, in tumults, in labours, in sleeplessness, in fastings;

"By purity, by knowledge, by longsuffering, by kindness, by the Holy Spirit, by sincere love, by the Word of Truth, by the Power of God, by the armour of righteousness on the right hand and on the left, by honour and dishonour, by evil report and good report;

"As deceivers, and yet true; as unknown, and yet well-known; as dying, and behold we live; as chastened, and yet not killed; as sorrowful, yet always rejoicing; as poor, yet making many rich; as having nothing, and yet possessing all things" (2 Cor. 6:4-10).

Apostle Paul also wrote, "Are they ministers of Christ? – I speak as a fool – I am more: in labours more abundant, in stripes above measure, in prisons more frequently, in deaths often. From the Jews five times I received forty stripes minus one.

"Three times I was beaten with rods; once I was stoned; three times I was shipwrecked; a night and a day I have been in the deep; in journeys often, in perils of waters, in perils of robbers, in perils of my own countrymen, in perils of the Gentiles,

"In perils in the city, in perils in the wilderness, in perils in the sea, in perils among false brethren; in weariness and toil, in sleeplessness often, in hunger and thirst, in fastings often, in cold and nakedness.

"Besides the other things, what comes upon me daily: my deep concern for all the churches. Who is weak, and I am not weak? Who is made to stumble, and I do not burn with indignation? In Damascus, the governor desired to arrest me; but I was let down in a basket through a window in the wall, and escaped from his hands (2 Cor. 11:23-33).

Apostle Paul lived his life that he may know Christ and the power of His Resurrection; and the fellowship of His Sufferings, being conformed to His Death, if by any means he might attain to the Resurrection from the dead (Phil. 3:10-11).

The suffering of this present time is not worthy to be compared with the glory which shall be revealed in us. Paul called all those things he suffered light afflictions (Rom. 8:18; 2 Cor. 4:17).

Who shall separate us from the Love of Christ? Shall tribulation, or distress, or persecution, or famine, or nakedness, or peril, or sword? Yet in all these things we are more than conquerors through Him Who loved us.

I am persuaded that neither death nor life, nor angles nor principalities nor powers, nor things present nor things to come, nor height nor depth, nor any other created thing, shall be able to separate us from the Love of God, which is in Christ Jesus, our Lord (Rom. 8:35-39).

As a Believer, you must have patience. If you don't have patience, you will fall by the way. Many don't like to hear of patience, but this is to get into trouble. Count it all joy when you fall into various trials, knowing that the testing of your faith produces patience.

But let patience have its perfect work, that you may be perfect and complete, lacking nothing (Jas 1:2-4). Remember that after Job persevered and endured, God blessed his later end so that it was, by far, better than his earlier life.

Remember that if your wilderness experience was caused by sin and disobedience (as in the case of Prophet Jonah), it is only repentance and yieldedness that will get you out of it. No man of God can pray you out, except if by Divine Mercy, God has compassion on you.

THE HOPE OF THE BELIEVER

The Word says that if it is only in this world that we have hope in Christ Jesus, we are of all men the most miserable (1 Cor. 15:19). The Believer in Christ Jesus has the hope of being with the Lord forever.

No wonder the Lord, speaking to His apostles, said, "Let not your heart be troubled; you believe in God, believe also in Me. In My Father's House are many mansions; if it were not so, I would have told you.

"I go to prepare a Place for you. And if I go and prepare a Place for you, I will come again and receive you to Myself; that where I am, there you may be also" (Jn 14:1-3).

This is the hope of the Believer: the Believer looks forward to being with the Lord in His Kingdom forever. He looks forward to receiving a worthy reward from the Lord, as He says, "Well done, good and faithful Servant."

Why do we labour and work for the Lord? It is because we love the Lord, our God. We love Him because He first loved us (1 Jn 4:19). The Father sent His Son Jesus Christ to die for us, even while we were yet sinners.

When the Lord Jesus Christ came, He suffered many things for us. He was obedient to the Father in all things, even to the point of dying on the Cross of Calvary, so that, by shedding His Blood, we might be redeemed from bondage.

He qualified us to be partakers of the inheritance of the Saints in the light. He delivered us from the power of darkness and conveyed us into the Kingdom of the Son of His Love, in Whom we have redemption through His Blood, the forgiveness of sins (Col. 1:12-14).

The Word gives us a parable (as given by the Lord) of a man who called his own servants and delivered his goods to them. And to one he gave five talents, to another two, and to another one, to each according to his own ability; and immediately he went on a journey.

Then he who had received the five talents went and traded with them, and made another five talents. And likewise he who had received two gained two more also. But he who had received one went and dug in the ground, and hid his lord's money.

This is speaking of Believers or Christians. Some have got more than five talents. Some have gained more than five talents. And some have buried more than two talents. The talents are in your talents and abilities; they are also in the Gifts and Enablements of the Holy Spirit, and the Callings of God.

But what happened? After a long time, the lord of those servants came and settled accounts with them. So he who had received five talents came and brought five other talents, saying, "Lord, you delivered to me five talents; look, I have gained five more talents besides them."

His lord said to him, "Well done, good and faithful servant; you were faithful over a few things, I will make you ruler over many things. Enter into the joy of your lord." The same was the case with the one who received two talents.

Then he who had received one talent came and said, "Lord, I knew you to be a hard man, reaping where you have not sown, and gathering where you have not scattered seed. And I was afraid, and went and hid your talent in the ground. Look, there you have what is yours."

But his lord answered and said to him, "You wicked and lazy servant, you knew that I reap where I have not sown, and gather where I have not scattered seed. So you ought to have deposited my money with the bankers, and at my coming I would have received back my own with interest.

"Therefore take the talent from him, and give it to him who has ten talents. For to everyone who has, more will be given, and he will have abundance; but from him who does not have, even what he has will be taken away.

"And cast the unprofitable servant into the outer darkness. There will be weeping and gnashing of teeth" (Matt. 25:14-30). I want to hear: "Well done, good and faithful Servant" from the Lord, instead of, "You wicked and lazy Servant."

The hope of the Believers is that the Lord Jesus Christ will reward their faithfulness and diligence in the service of His Kingdom. But whether or not they expect it, unfaithful Believers will be punished in the Outer Darkness, out of the Presence of the Lord.

Strive to be commended by the Lord at the end. It is not he who commends himself that is commended, but he who the Lord commends (2 Cor. 10:18). If your pastor and church-members speak well of you while the Lord is angry with you, you will be punished (contrary to your expectation).

You may have a different reason for not putting your talent or gift to profitable labour/work for the Lord; however, know that God will surely punish unfaithfulness. Therefore, be faithful to the assignment the Lord has for you.

Apostle Paul's passion, desire, and commitment should challenge all of us. Apostle Paul said, "Do you not know that those who run in a race all run, but one receives the prize? Run in such a way that you may obtain it.

"And everyone who competes for the prize is temperate in all things. Now they do it to obtain a perishable crown, but we for an imperishable crown. Therefore I run thus: not with uncertainty. Thus I fight: not as one who beats the air.

"But I discipline my body, and bring it into subjection, lest, when I have preached to others, I myself should become disqualified" (1 Cor. 9:24-27). All of us should have the same thought, passion, and commitment in our lives.

This is a faithful saying: For if we died with Him, we shall also live with Him. If we endure, we shall also reign with Him. If we deny Him, He also will deny us. If we are faithless, He remains faithful; He cannot deny Himself (2 Tim. 2:11-13).

You therefore must endure hardship as a good soldier of Jesus Christ. No one engaged in warfare entangles himself with the affairs of this life, that he may please him who enlisted him as a soldier.

And also if anyone competes in athletics, he is not crowned unless he competes according to the rules. The hardworking farmer must be first to partake of the crops (2 Tim. 2:3-6). The Lord has told us to be of good cheer. Our tears shall be turned to laughter!

Writing to the Philippians, Paul said, "...that I may know Him and the power of His Resurrection, and the fellowship of His Sufferings, being conformed to His Death, if by any means, I may attain to the Resurrection from the dead.

"Not that I have already attained, or am already perfect; but I press on, that I may lay hold of that for which Christ Jesus has also laid hold of me. Brethren; I do not count myself to have apprehended;

"But one thing I do, forgetting those things which are behind, and reaching forward to those things which are ahead, I press toward the goal, for the prize of the Upward Call of God in Christ Jesus" (Phil. 3:10-14).

What is the prize of the Upward Call of God in Christ Jesus? It is the reward we are hoping for, if we endure to the end. God did not call us to serve Him in vain. He will reward us exceedingly abundantly, above our imagination.

Jesus Christ, writing to the seven churches in Asia Minor, tells us of our hope in Him. God cannot lie; God cannot disappoint us. The things He says He has provided for us are true, and they are waiting for us.

In the second and third chapters of the Book of Revelation, the Lord tells us that He will give him who overcomes to eat from the Tree of Life, which is in the midst of the Paradise of God. He who overcomes shall not be hurt by the Second Death.

To the overcomer, the Lord will give some of the hidden manna to eat. He will give him a white stone, and on the stone a new name written which no one knows except him who receives it.

He who overcomes, and keeps His Works until the end, to him the Lord will give power over the nations. He will give him the morning star. He who overcomes shall be clothed in white garments.

He who overcomes will have his name not blotted out from the Book of Life; but the Lord Jesus Christ will confess his name before His Father and before His angels. He who overcomes will be made a pillar in the Temple of His God.

Jesus Christ will write on the overcomer the Name of His God and the name of the City of His God, the New Jerusalem, which comes down out of Heaven from His God. And He will write on him His Own New Name.

To him who overcomes the Lord will grant to sit with Him on His Throne, as He also overcame and sat down with His Father on His Throne. He who has an ear, let him hear what the Spirit says to the Believers and the Church of Jesus Christ.

Our hope is to attain to the Resurrection from the dead. The Word says that many of those who sleep in the dust of the earth shall awake, some to Everlasting Life, some to shame and everlasting contempt. Those who are wise shall shine like the brightness of the firmament, and those who turn many to righteousness like the stars forever and ever (Dan. 12:2-3).

The Lord Himself will descend from Heaven with a shout, with the voice of an archangel, and with the Trumpet of God. And the dead in Christ will rise first. Then the Believers who are alive and remain shall be caught up together with them in the clouds to meet the Lord in the air. And thus we shall always be with the Lord.

We, according to His Promise, look for New Heavens and a New Earth in which righteousness dwells. Therefore, beloved, looking forward to these things, be diligent to be found by Him in peace, without spot and blameless (2 Pet. 3:13-14).

He who overcomes shall inherit all things, and the Lord will be His God and he shall be His son. The Lord is coming quickly, and His Reward is with Him, to give to everyone according to his work.

Blessed are those who do His Commandments, that they may have the right to the Tree of Life, and may enter through the gates into the City. But outside are dogs and sorcerers and sexually immoral and murderers and idolaters, and whoever loves and practices a lie.

As a Believer, you are not foolish. As a Christian, you are not mentally deranged. Though you may appear like one to the people of the world, yet the foolishness of God is wiser than men. They may say many things against us, because they are blinded; they will come to terms with the reality in the end.

My brother, be faithful until death. Be faithful until the end. All you may lose for the Cause of Christ cannot be compared to what you will gain from Him in the end. If your eye causes you to sin, pluck it out and cast it from you. It is better for you to enter life with one eye than, having two eyes, to be cast into Hell Fire. Jesus Christ is coming soon, and without holiness, no one can see the Lord!

GOD'S ORIGINAL INTENTION FOR MAN

It is God that created the heavens and the earth (Gen. 1:1). Even after the creation of the earth, it was still without form and void; and darkness was over the surface of the deep. The Spirit of God, the Spirit of Power, was hovering over the face of the waters, and yet nothing happened until God spoke, and said, "Let there be light"; and there was light.

Even though you have been born again and the Spirit of God is for you, and in you, there are things that will not happen in your life, or in the life of your beloved ones, until you pray or give a word of command. The Spirit of God will do what you say, because you are a god (Psa. 82:6), and a representative of God.

After God had finished creating other things, He said, "Let Us make man in Our Image, according to Our Likeness; let them have dominion over the fish of the sea, over the birds of the air, and over the cattle, over all the earth and over every creeping thing that creeps on the earth."

So God created man in His Own Image; in the Image of God He created him; male and female He created them. You were created in the very Image and Likeness of God, and you have to function as God does; for example, by calling those things which do not exist by names as though they did exist. When you call them, they will exist (Rom. 4:17; Heb. 11:3).

Then God blessed them, and God said to them, "Be fruitful and multiply; fill the earth and subdue it; have dominion over the fish of the sea, over the birds of the air, and over every living thing that moves on the earth." This explains why God created man, and the ability that He gave man.

Man has to be fruitful in every area of his life. God did not create any barren woman. And if for any reason, one seems to be barren, there is hope for fruitfulness to her. Let her pray; God will answer her. Then, if God wants to use another Christian or preacher to minister to her, He will bring him her way. But let her depend on God.

And man was made to multiply. He didn't only have to be fruitful, he had to multiply. In any area you are, that is good and acceptable to God, increase and multiply! Your God is all-powerful; therefore you don't have to have the begging and let-me-survive mentally. Man, by procreation and multiplication, was to fill the earth.

Not only did he have to fill the earth, he had to subdue the earth, wherever he may be. Man was (and is) to take control of the earth, and if the devil wanted to intrude, he had to stop him by force. Even now, we have been authorized and empowered to stop the works of the devil.

Then, man was given dominion over the things in the earth. This is just wonderful! Man is to lord it over the created things in the earth. But how many of us will see a snake or a lion, and not run away? You were given dominion over them. Joshua gave a command, and the sun stood still. This is worthy of sober reflection.

And God said, "See, I have given you every herb that yields seed which is on the face of all the earth, and every tree whose fruit yields seed; to you it shall be for food." He gave man and animals the power or freedom to eat plants and crops – their leaves, fruit, seed, etc (Gen. 1).

Of course, this does not mean that you can't eat meat; you can if you want, and you know that meat is sweet to your taste! After the Flood, when Noah offered a burnt offering to God, God smelled a sweet aroma and was glad. He then gave Noah and men the freedom to eat meat.

Concerning the Israelites, God permitted them to eat certain kinds of meat, and never to eat the unclean ones (as they were called). But in the New Testament, the Lord told us that it is not what enters your mouth that defiles you, but what comes out of your mouth, because it comes from your heart (Matt. 15:11,17-20).

He reaffirmed this when He told Peter to kill and it, even the so-called unclean animals, because He has called them clean now. Sin is the transgression of the Law (1 Jn 3:4), and where there is no Law or Command, there is no sin (Rom. 5:13). Do you think God counted Abraham and Isaac as sinners because two of them lied concerning their wives? (Gen. 20; Gen. 26).

At that time, God had not said, "You shall not lie." But now, He has said: "You shall not lie," "You shall not commit sexual immorality," "You shall not love the world or the things in the world." He says that whoever loves the world is an enemy of God (Jas 4:4). Those who dress and appear like the people of the world, take note.

Apostle Paul, speaking by the Holy Spirit, said that false teachers and preachers will forbid people from marrying, and command people to abstain from foods (meats, according to KJV) which God created to be received with thanksgiving by those who believe and know the truth. For every creature of God is good, and nothing is to be refused if it is received with thanksgiving; for it is sanctified by the Word of God and prayer" (1 Tim. 4:3-5).

However, you must be able to interpret the Word well. God did not say that you must eat all things, but that you may eat all things. Is there really any person that eats all things, without anything that is offensive to him? I, for instance, like well-fried fish of a kind, but if that kind of fish is not fried and I put it into my mouth, I feel like to vomit. Of course, there are kinds of fishes I will like in cooked form.

But another person will like it, and that is good for him. I think I used to like fish that is not fried when I was younger. Also, I like chicken, fried or not fried; but if you bring cattle meat (beef) that is not fried to me, I will have a repulsive feeling to eating it. Even if it is fried, and it is in big cuts or pieces, I will still feel that way. That is I for you, brother; but if you choose to eat all of them and more, you have not sinned; go on!

Let me explain further: Paul told us not to eat meat that is sacrificed to idols, although we are not to ask questions when we want to buy (1 Cor. 8). Jesus Christ condemned eating things sacrificed to idols (Rev. 2:20). Why then did He say that nothing that enters your mouth can defile you? Brother, you can't eat everything, though you may eat if you want. But you must exercise self-control over your appetite.

Also, when Jesus Christ spoke on the issue of divorce, the Disciples said, "If this is so with a man (if a man cannot divorce his wife, except because of fornication), it is better not to marry." That teaching was hard, even to His Own Disciples. Those that want to divorce, have you seen it? Even if he or she commits fornication (and, it must never happen), you can still forgive him or her!

But see what the Lord said, "All cannot accept this Saying, but only those to whom it has been given: For there are eunuchs (impotent men) who were born thus from their mother's womb, and there are eunuchs (castrated men) who were made eunuchs by men, and there are eunuchs who have themselves eunuchs for the Kingdom of Heaven's sake. He who is able to accept it, let him accept" (Matt. 19:10-12).

The Lord said that some made themselves eunuchs for the sake of the Kingdom of Heaven, and if you are able, do it. But this is not for married people, because, if you say that you can separate and stay alone, you are putting the other person into temptation, and God will require it from you in judgment.

Jesus Christ did not marry. Paul, also, did not marry. And Paul said that he wishes that all men were as he is. Why? So that they can serve God as they want, unhindered by wives and children. But he said that instead of you to burn with lust and passion, it is better for you to marry. Lust is equal to fornication.

Also, remember that Paul's time was full of violent persecutions against the Christians. So, if you say that you will not marry with the temptations of these days, be careful, lest you fall. But if you can do it, it is better (study 1 Cor. 7). So, brother, get married to a lovely, spiritual, and sincere lady!

Let me conclude with this portion of the Scripture: "Receive one who is weak in faith, but not with disputes over doubtful things. For one believes he may eat all things, but he who is weak eats only vegetables. Let not him who eats despise him who does not eat, and let not him who does not eat judge him who eats; for God has received him.

"Who are you to judge Another's Servant? To his own Master he stands or falls. Indeed, he will be made to stand, for God is able to make him stand. One person esteems one day above another; another esteems every day alike. Let each be fully convinced in his own mind.

"He who observes the day, observes it to Lord; and he who does not observe the day, to the Lord he does not observe it. He who eats, eats to the Lord, for he gives God thanks; and he who does not eat, to the Lord he does not eat, and gives God thanks. For none of us lives to himself, and no one dies to himself.

"For if we live, we live to the Lord; and if we die, we die to the Lord. Therefore, whether we live or die, we are the Lord's. So then each of us shall give account of himself to God. The Kingdom of God is not eating and drinking, but righteousness and peace and joy in the Holy Spirit. For he who serves Christ in these things is acceptable to God and approved by men" (Rom. 14).

And on the seventh day, God ended His Work, which he had done, and He rested on the seventh day from all His Work, which He had done. Then God blessed the seventh day and sanctified it, because in it He rested from all His Work, which God had created and made.

Those that want to work throughout the week, with no day or days to rest, can you see that the Almighty God Himself rested? Unless the Lord builds the house, they labour in vain who build it; unless the Lord guards the city, the watchman stays awake in vain.

It is vain for you to rise up early, to sit up late, to eat the bread of sorrows; for so He gives His beloved sleep (Psa. 127:1-2). It is not because you work always that you get rich. Of course, hardwork is good, but by the arms of the flesh shall no man prevail. It is not by might nor by power, but by the Holy Spirit of the Lord God Almighty (Zech. 4:6).

The Lord God formed man out of the dust of the ground, and breathed into his nostrils the breath of life; and man became a living being. The Lord God planted a garden eastward in Eden, and there He put the man whom He had formed.

And out of the ground the Lord God made every tree grow that is pleasant to the sight and good for food. The Tree of Life was also in the midst of the garden, and the Tree of Knowledge of God and Evil. Now a river went out of Eden to water the garden. Then the Lord God took the man and put him in the Garden of Eden to tend and keep it.

God has taste! See the good things He made for man! The garden that was well watered, served as his home. Also, notice that man was to tend and keep the garden. Man was to carry out a level of work, even before the fall, but not to suffer; for the Glory of the Lord God covered and empowered him. Even angels work. If you love laziness, beware! God created man to have fellowship and communion with Him.

And the Lord commanded the man, saying, "Of every tree of the garden you may freely eat; but of the Tree of the Knowledge of Good and Evil you shall not eat, for in the day that you eat it you shall surely die." Even though God gave man all good things, yet He gave him a Command to keep. Those Believers who delight in unrestricted freedom, can you see?

And the Lord God said, "It is not good that man should be alone; I will make him a helper comparable to him." Among the beasts, which Adam named, none was found a helper comparable to him. And the Lord God caused a deep sleep to fall on Adam, and he slept; and He took one of his ribs, and closed up the flesh in its place.

Then the rib, which the Lord God had taken from man, He made into a woman, and He brought her to the man. And Adam said: "This is now bone of my bones and flesh of my flesh; she shall be called Woman, because she was taken out of man."

Therefore a man shall leave his father and mother and be joined to his wife, and they shall become one flesh. And they were both naked, the man and his wife, and were not ashamed (Gen. 2). Who told Adam that Eve was his bone, since he was in a deep sleep and God had closed up his flesh? The man was still very spiritually sensitive. And if you have an intimate relationship with God, you will be sensitive too.

You can also notice from here that sometimes, sleep may not be natural. Demons and their human agents manipulate people to oversleep, so that they will neither pray nor read their Bible in the night period. They spread sleep-waves in the early morning hours to many Believers, so that they will not pray well, thereby getting ready for the day.

When King Saul pursued David to kill him, Saul went with three thousand chosen warriors of Israel; a time came when they encamped and slept. David and Abishai came into their camp in the night and took Saul's spear and jug of water, which were by Saul's head without any of them awaking, even though Saul was surrounded by soldiers.

The Bible says: "For they were all asleep, because a deep sleep from the Lord had fallen on them" (1 Sam. 26:12). How can none of three thousand soldiers not awake, when two men came into their camp and collected things, except that they were supernaturally remote-controlled? Both the Kingdom of Light and the kingdom of darkness can do this.

Now, the serpent was more cunning than any beast of the field, which the Lord God had made. Was it a serpent or a snake that deceived Eve? It was a serpent possessed by the devil. Satan saw all the good things that God had provided for man, and noticed the position that God had placed man, and it staggered his mentally.

Many times, we read about how disobedient and stubborn the Israelites were, both in the wilderness and in their promised land. When we read about their worldliness, we criticize them a lot. By worldliness, I mean being like and following the Gentile (unbelieving) nations. Yet many of us do terrible things like they did, without paying attention to the Spirit of God.

We read and believe the Word, because they were written in the Bible. I will tell you that many of the Israelites never believed that some of the things that they were told, actually came from God at the time they were instructed. If the ways many Believers live, is written down for the next generation, they will cry for us, as we cry and weep for the Israelites now. And they will believe that it is God that told us many of the things we don't believe God is telling us now.

To be very sincere with you, how many Believers dress and appear like the people of the world, pains me a lot and staggers my mentality. Many preachers had spoken against it; but now they are weak and unwilling to speak any more on it, because they feel that it seems that the Believers are not paying attention to their message.

But does God change because His Word is not heeded? However, the most regrettable part of it, is that by the time many will realize the truth, there will not be a second chance, because they would have died or Jesus Christ would have come, and they would be facing judgment at that time.

And the devil said, "I must destroy this man." The devil has no good plan for man. Those that go to the devil, in the names of cults, secret societies, witch-doctors, fortune-tellers, sorcerers, palm-readers, astrologers, necromancers, etc, for power, money, protection, guidance, children, healing, breakthrough, etc are deceiving themselves.

The devil has no free gift for anyone. His ultimate goal is to enslave you, and to get you into Hell Fire at last, so that you will suffer eternal damnation like him. Why? Because he rebelled against God, and God condemned him to Hell Fire. He is looking for companions!

Concerning the devil, the Word says: "How you are fallen from Heaven, O Lucifer, son of the morning! How you are cut down to the ground, you who weakened the nations! For you have said in your heart: 'I will ascend into Heaven, I will exalt my throne above the stars of God;

'I will also sit on the mount of the congregation on the farthest sides of the north; I will ascend above the heights of the clouds, I will be like the Most High.' Yet you shall be brought down to Sheol, to the lowest depths of the Pit" (Isa. 14:12-15).

It goes on to say, "You were the seal of perfection, full of wisdom and perfect in beauty. You were in Eden, the Garden of God; every precious stone was your covering: the sardius, topaz, and diamond, beryl, onyx, and jasper, sapphire, turquoise, and emerald with gold.

"The workmanship of your timbrels and pipes was prepared for you on the day you were created. You were the anointed cherub who covers; I established you; you were on the Holy Mountain of God; you walked back and forth in the midst of fiery stones.

"You were perfect in your ways from the day you were created, till iniquity was found in you. By the abundance of your trading you became filled with violence within, and you sinned; therefore I cast you as a profane thing out of the Mountain of God.

"And I destroyed you, O covering cherub, from the midst of the fiery stones. Your heart was lifted up because of your beauty; you corrupted your wisdom for the sake of your splendor; I cast you to the ground, I laid you before the kings that they might gaze at you.

"You defiled your sanctuaries by the multitude of your iniquities, by the iniquity of your trading; therefore I brought fire from your midst; it devoured you, and I turned you to ashes upon the earth in the sight of all who saw you. All who knew you among the peoples, are astonished at you; you have become a horror, and shall be no more forever" (Ezek. 28:11-19).

Having been thrown down, the devil was not happy concerning what man was, and he entered the serpent. And he said to woman, "Has God indeed said ("Did God really say..." according to the New International Version), 'You shall not eat of every tree of the garden?'"

Look at this wicked being! He tells Believers, "Did God really say that you must not do this or that?" How does it concern him? Was the Commandment given to him? But he does not come but to steal, and to kill, and to destroy (Jn 10:10). And the woman did not know this, because he came cunningly.

And the woman said to the serpent, "We may eat the fruit of the trees of the garden; but of the fruit of the tree which is in the midst of the garden, God has said, 'You shall not eat it, nor shall you touch it, lest you die,'" Did God tell them not to touch it? No, He told them not eat it; but the woman misquoted God by adding something.

No wonder Apostle Paul said, "Let a woman learn in silence with all submission. And I do not permit a woman to teach or to have authority over a man, but to be in silence. For Adam was formed first, then Eve. And Adam was not deceived, but the woman being deceived, fell into transgression. Nevertheless she will be saved in childbearing if they continue in faith, love, and holiness, with self-control" (1 Tim. 2:11-15).

Why didn't he permit them to teach? It may be because most of them don't hear well. Did Eve hear well? At least, she did not quote well. No wonder the writer of Ecclesiastes said, "Here is what I have found, adding one thing to the other to find out the reason, which my soul still seeks but I cannot find: one man among a thousand I have found.

"But a woman among all these I have not found. Truly, this only I have found: that God made man upright, but they have sought out many schemes" (Eccl. 7:27-29). Even though God made man upright, yet many men have sought out many evil schemes. But, could Solomon say that, even among the billions of women, ladies, and girls in the world today, he can't find one?

And Apostle Paul, speaking to the Corinthians said, "Let your women keep silent in the churches, for they are not permitted to speak; but they are to be submissive, as the Law also says. And if they want to learn something, let them ask their own husbands at home;

"For it is shameful for women to speak in church. Or did the Word of God come originally from you? Or was it you only that it reached? If anyone thinks himself to be a prophet or spiritual, let him acknowledge that the things, which I write to you, are the Commandments of the Lord. But if anyone is ignorant, let him be ignorant" (1 Cor. 14:34-38).

Why did Paul have to tell Pastor Timothy this, and also the church at Corinth? Is it not written that in the mouth of two or three witness, a case is established (not invisible witnesses, you understand?). I guess many people don't see these portions of the Scripture.

Why? Maybe because they want to be presidents and their wives vice-presidents of their churches or ministries, so that if peradventure they die before the woman, she will become the general-overseer, and his children bishops!

Let me explain something here, so that you will not misunderstand me. I am not saying that a woman shouldn't do anything in a church or the ministry; after all, Apostle Paul spoke of women praying and prophesying with covered or long hairs (1 Cor. 11:1-16). So, they can pray and prophesy.

But some women will come into church with low-cut hair, and wouldn't even use any covering to cover their head. I wonder what some women think of themselves to be. I think some, if they had the opportunity, will rewrite the Bible to read, "The woman and the man are equal."

The worldliness of women liberation movements is creeping into churches (or, should I say, "...has crept into churches"?). This is why in some advanced countries, people divorce anyhow they want. I wonder whether the gate of Heaven will be opened to such people. However, I am not the judge; but the Word of God is the judge!

So that you will not misquote me, let me state my own belief, according to the Word of God, "Women can do very many things in the church; but they must do whatever they do with the permission of men, being in submission. Apostle Paul said he didn't permit a woman to teach.

I myself can permit a woman to teach, if I am satisfied with her knowledge and spirituality; but I can never permit a woman to usurp authority over a man, whether in the church or at home. If you choose to be ignorant, be ignorant.

Maybe, you have never seen it in the Bible that women are weaker vessels, according to Apostle Peter, speaking by the Holy Ghost (1 Pet. 3:7). Maybe, you have not noticed that it was the carelessness of Eve that led humanity into enmity with God. By the way, why didn't she just eat it alone?

I wonder whether Adam even knew it was the forbidden fruit, or whether she came with a fruit to Adam, and said, "If you really love me, eat this fruit." And Adam said, "Let me show you how much I love you," and took the fruit and ate.

Man, you are the head of your wife; if you take decisions suggested by your wife, and you don't examine them well to see whether they are alright, God will hold you responsible for whatever comes out of it. Was Adam free when he told God that it was the woman whom God gave him that caused him to sin against Him?

We have talked so much of Islam, Muslims, and the Arabs. Who brought them? A woman, my brethren! God told Abraham in the fifteenth chapter of Genesis that He will give him a son. And in the sixteenth chapter, maybe because of unbelief or impatience, Sarah confused the man.

And the Word says, "Now Sarai, Abram's wife, had borne him no children. And she had an Egyptian maidservant whose name was Hagar. So Sarai said to Abram, 'See now, the Lord has restrained me from bearing children. Please, go in to my maid; perhaps I shall obtain children by her.' And Abram heeded the voice of Sarai" (Gen. 16:1-2). She wanted a child by any means, so that she can boast of being a mother.

"If I am really your sweetheart, and you have no other woman in your life, do this or that!" Many women have threatened their husbands with those kinds of words. But Abraham got Ishmael; and all these Arabs came from Ishmael, brother, and they will tell you that they are Abraham's offsprings also (even of the first son of Abraham).

And God said to Abraham, after the birth of Isaac, "Take now your son, your only son Isaac, whom you love, and..." (Gen. 22:2). Brother, can you see that Sarah's mathematics and family management didn't work out? Why? Because, to God, Isaac was Abraham's only son.

I will not go to the story of Samson and Delilah, because that would mean what an unbeliever can do to a Believer. But I have shown you what a believing wife can do to a believing husband.

Please, don't misquote me; all women will not lead their husbands into grave-mistakes. There are very good Christian women, but if you are not careful, even the very good ones can lead you into serious mistakes, even sincerely. Remember that Sarah, Abraham's wife, is not noted for wickedness; yet she led Abraham into a grave mistake.

What many people have failed to realize, is that women are easily manipulated by the devil. And this is not to say that all women are manipulated by the devil always. Many of them have grown well in character and spirituality, and they can notice the devil's devices. Also, some men are so weak, that it is even their wives that keep them up spiritually.

I will tell you that many of the women that led some ministers into different kinds of sins never consciously had the intention of leading them into those sins; but they were manipulated by the devil, and they yielded themselves to the devil unknowingly. Yes, many of them do it knowingly, but some do it unknowingly.

This is why, in the family, many women are manipulated by the devil to cause quarrels and disagreements in the home, so that the man will either overreact or be weakened spiritually. And when you are weak spiritually, the devil will rejoice, and many of his plans will succeed in the home.

Many women will even cry and weep, when they realize themselves; but then, the devil will have accomplished his purpose. His evil deeds and intents might have come to pass, before the woman realizes herself.

Yes, a man can also be manipulated by the devil, but the devil's usage of women in this connection, is more than his usage of men. There is a difference when evil men yield themselves to the devil knowingly, and when women yield themselves to the devil unknowingly, even sincerely.

Then the serpent said to the woman, "You will not surely die. For God knows that in the day you eat of it your eyes will be opened, and you will be like God, knowing good and evil." Who knows whether the serpent had given that destructive hope to Adam before? But Adam didn't want to be like God.

But the woman wanted to be like God; this is the same thing that destroyed Lucifer. He wanted to be like God. Many women have put their husbands into situations that have killed and destroyed them, because they wanted to be like other women in town: wearing the costliest dresses, driving the latest cars, and living in the best mansions.

So when the woman saw that the tree was good for food, that it was pleasant to the eyes, and a tree desirable to make one wise, she took of its fruit and ate. She also gave to her husband with her, and he ate. Then the eyes of both of them were opened, and they knew that they were naked; and they sewed fig leaves together and made themselves covering (Gen. 3:1-7). Man had fallen!

HOW IS YOUR FOUNDATION?

In building construction, the foundation of the building is more important than the appearance of the building. In the construction of a building, different factors are considered, such as: safety, economy, and comfort. Of those three factors, safety is of paramount importance.

This is because, no matter how the economy may be, and no matter how comfortable you may think that you are, if the safety is compromised, the building may collapse on you and you may be found a dead man. And when the building collapses, even all the money you had economized will be lost, and you would have also lost every comfort.

The foundation of the building is where the safety of the building starts. If the foundation is weak, how will it carry the building safely? Another thing you should be aware of, is that the size of the building (its height, width, and length) is very crucial in the laying on of the foundation of the building.

The higher the building, the deeper the foundation should be. Of course, the foundation is dependent on other factors, like the nature of the soil. A rocky basement or land will require a shallower foundation than a clayey or sandy basement. But the fact is that, if you want the building to stand safely, the foundation should be strong and durable.

The Bible has something to say about building science and technology. In the Words of Master Jesus Christ, "Therefore whoever hears these Sayings of Mine, and does them, I will liken him to a wise man who built his house on the rock; and the rain descended, the floods came, and the winds blew and beat on that house; and it did not fall, for it was founded on the rock.

"But everyone who hears these Sayings of Mine, and does not do them, will be like a foolish man who built his house on the sand; and the rain descended, the floods came, and the winds blew and beat on that house; and it fell. And great was its fall" (Matt. 7:24-27).

Brother, if the foundation of a building is weak to carry the building, how will the building stand? The Bible asks the question this way: If the foundations are destroyed, what can the righteous do? (Psa. 11: 3). My brother, how is your foundation? There are many things to foundations in the life of a Believer.

First, the Bible says, "Nevertheless the Solid Foundation of God stands, having this seal: 'The Lord knows those who are His,' and, 'Let everyone who names the Name of Christ depart from iniquity' (2 Tim. 2:19). The Solid Foundation of God is the basis on which God relates with men, and does His Things.

That foundation stands forever settled in Heaven. The first thing to the seal it has, is that the Lord knows those who are His. The second thing to its seal, is that everyone who names the Name of Christ must depart from evil. How does the Lord know those who are His? Because they depart from evil.

You can't deceive God, because God cannot be deceived. To this end, the Word of God says, "Do not be deceived, God is not mocked; for whatever a man sows, that he will also reap. For he who sows to his flesh will of the flesh reap corruption, but he who sows to the Spirit will of the Spirit reap Everlasting Life" (Gal. 6:7-8).

He who names the Name of Christ must depart from iniquity! This is consistent with what Jesus Christ told the multitude that followed Him. In His Words, "Not everyone who says to Me, 'Lord, Lord,' shall enter the Kingdom of Heaven, but he who does the Will of My Father in Heaven.

"Many will say to Me in that Day, 'Lord, Lord, have we not prophesied in Your Name, cast out demons in Your Name, and done many wonders in Your Name?' And then I will declare to them, 'I never knew you; depart from Me, you who practice lawlessness!'" (Matt. 7:21-23).

The Lord knows those who are His, because they depart from evil/iniquity. The Lord never knew many people, because instead of departing from evil, they practiced lawlessness or iniquity. The more pitiable thing to it, is that they named the Name of Christ, and they called Jesus Christ their Lord.

This is worthy of sober reflection. They were not just speaking to people, telling them that Jesus Christ is their Lord; no, they were talking to the Master directly, and saying, "Lord, Lord." And Jesus Christ asks, "Why do you call Me, 'Lord, Lord,' and do not do what I say?" (Lk. 6:46).

Many call themselves Believers and Christians, and they don't care how they live their lives. They live in immorality and dress however they want, while they speak in tongues, prophesy, and do miracles. Do you want to work in the Lord's Vineyard and be rejected by Him on the Last Day?

How I wish people read the Bible and mediate on it! I am not talking about studying it; I am speaking of just reading it, and mediating on what they read. If they will do these two things, many will change by themselves. Many pastors and preachers don't tell people the truth. They are after their money, and not their souls.

The worst is that many don't even know that many of those people who call themselves pastors and ministers are actually agents of the kingdom of darkness, who have been sent to deceive people with the Bible and the Name of Jesus, by telling them that this and that don't matter.

But what will you do when you stand before God on the Judgment Day, and He tells you that they matter to Him? Then there will be no second chance. You will spend eternity in Hell Fire in anguish, wailing, and shouts of pains and torment. The Book of James says: "You believe that there is One God. You do well. Even the demons believe – and tremble! (Jas 2:19). Faith without work is dead (Jas 2:17).

In conclusion, the Word says, "Whoever abides in Him does not sin. Whoever sins has neither seen Him nor known Him. Little children, let no one deceive you. He who practices righteousness is righteous, just as He is righteous. He who sins is of the devil, for the devil has sinned from the beginning" (1 Jn 3:6-8).

Speaking of foundations, the second thing you must know is that your foundation must have a solid base on the Word of God. You must be rooted and grounded in the Word of God. And the Lord God speaks to us the same things He spoke to Joshua.

And He says, "This Word of God shall not depart from your mouth, but you shall mediate in it day and night, that you may observe to do according to all the things that God has said. For then you will make your way prosperous, and then you will have good success" (Josh. 1:8).

And the Book of James says, "Therefore lay aside all filthiness and overflow of wickedness, and receive with meekness the implanted Word, which is able to save your souls. But be doers of the Word, and not hearers only, deceiving yourselves" (Jas 1:21-22)

The Book of Proverbs puts it this way: "My son, give attention to My Words; incline your ear to My Sayings. Do not let them depart from your eyes; keep them in the midst of your heart; for they are life to those who find them, and health to all their flesh" (Prov. 4:20-22).

Don't decide how you will live your life, but let God and His Word decide it. There are so many benefits to this decision. The Word of God is a sure foundation. If your life is built on any other thing outside the Word of God, it will crumble. Confess it, mediate on it, look at it, and do it.

Another thing to the foundation of a Believer – having a solid foundation – is that your life should be powered by prayer. A consistent prayerful life will give you a firm stand. Watch and pray, so that you will not fall into the traps and devices of the enemy. The human spirit indeed is willing, but the flesh is weak, and says, "Nowhere!" (Matt. 26:41).

Through prayer, you will receive what you need and want from God. This is why the Bible says, "Ask, and it will be given to you; seek, and you will find; knock and it will be opened to you. For everyone who asks receives, and he who seeks finds, and to him who knocks it will be opened" (Matt. 7:7-8).

Also, through prayer, you will stop the plans of the devil from coming to pass in your life and in the lives of others. It is through prayer that the works of the devil are destroyed. And the Word tells us to give no place to the devil, but to resist him, so that he will flee (Eph. 4:27; Jas 4:7).

Prayer is power, and prayerlessness is powerlessness. A prayerful Christian is a powerful Christian. Please, learn to discipline yourself in order to pray well consistently.

And your life must be powered by the Anointing and Power of the Holy Spirit. Be filled and be being filled with the Holy Spirit! It is not by might nor by power, but by the Holy Spirit of the Living God, Who is the Spirit of Power and Might (Zech. 4:6).

Your life must never be built on falsehood. As a minister, don't build your ministry on false testimonies. If you supplanted your friend to marry her fiancé, go and ask for her forgiveness. Do all necessary restitutions that the Spirit of God leads you to do. Repentance and restitution go together many times. Of course, it is not everything that needs restitution, but you will restitute whatever is necessary.

Deal with all faulty, bad, and evil foundations. If you are working with fake or impersonated certificate, you need restitution. If you forged or faked your age, you must do the necessary restitution. God will save and deliver you, and you will not lose your job. And it is better to lose your job, than to end in Hell Fire!

Repentance from dead works is the foundation of Christianity. If you do any thing without repentance, you are heading to Hell Fire. No matter what the Lord may be gracious to give you, without repentance and holiness, you are heading to Hell Fire.

The bigger the ministry God may have for you, the stronger foundation you will need. Don't joke with your training period, and don't rush ahead of God, so that you will not crash in future.

Don't destroy yourself by competing with other Believers and ministries. If you cleanse and prepare yourself, you will become a vessel of honour, sanctified and useful for the Master, prepared for every good work (2 Tim. 2:20-22). Flee also youthful lusts; but pursue righteousness, faith, love, peace with sincere Believers.

Also, deal with faulty ancestral and parental foundations. This may require prayer and fasting, or the assistance of someone with a greater anointing. Even after Lazarus was raised from the dead, he was still bound, until Jesus Christ said, "Lose him, and let him go" (Jn 11:44). A daughter of Abraham was bound for eighteen years (Lk. 13:10-16). Be wise!

DIVINE PROTECTION

There is security and protection in God. Everyone wants to be secure and protected. People look for protection from different means and places. Some go to witch-doctors for protection; some have joined cults and secret societies for protection. Some use the army, the police, and other security agencies for protection. But there is absolute protection and security in God.

The Bible says that if you dwell in the Secret Place of the Most High, you will abide under the Shadow of the Almighty (Psa. 91:1). The secret place is the place fellowship with God. It is the place of prayer. The Blood of Jesus is for our covering and protection. The Name of Jesus Christ, which is the Name above all names, is a strong tower in which we are safe when we call on that Name (Prov. 18:10; Rom. 10:13).

The angels of God and the host of Heaven are with us and for us. What is more? The Holy Spirit of the Living God is in us (1 Jn 4:4). No devil will come near the Fire of the Holy Spirit. God builds walls and hedges of protection around us (Job 1:10).

As a Christian, don't be afraid, for there is absolute safety in God your Father. When you are born again, you become God's Property and child. He cares for you, and He will not let evil befall and overcome you. But learn to be prayerful, to engage the service of angels, and to apply the Blood and the Name of Jesus Christ.

Don't put your trust on devils, for the devil has no good intention for you. Don't put your confidence on men, because vain is the help of man. Man is flesh and can disappoint you. Put your absolute trust in God. He loves us, and He cares for us.

When God told Jacob to go up to Bethel, Jacob spoke to those who were with him, saying, "Put away the foreign gods that are among you, purify yourselves, and change your garments." When they purified themselves, they journeyed, and the Terror of God was upon the cities that were all around them, and they did not pursue the sons of Jacob (Gen. 35:2,5).

His sons had deceitfully told the people of King Hamon to get circumcised, so that they can intermarry with them. As they were in pains from the circumcision, the sons of Jacob came upon their land, slew, and plundered them. Jacob was afraid that the neighbouring countries will attack them; but God protected and saved them

If you want to enjoy total protection from God, then you must be pure and holy. Sin, unrighteousness, and disobedience can create a loophole through which the devil can attack you. And the Bible tells us not to give any place to the devil (Eph. 4:27).

Whoever breaks the hedge will be beaten by the serpent. Satan, speaking to God about Job, said, "Have You not made a hedge around him, around his household, and around all that he has on every side? You have blessed the work of his hands, and his possessions have increased in the land" (Job 1:10).

Job was blameless and upright, and one who feared God and shunned evil. Without God's Permission, nothing can happen to you. Why didn't Job's neighbours plunder his possessions? It was because there was a hedge around him. Though they envied him, yet no one attacked him to dispossess him.

But when God permitted the devil to touch his property, then, all of a sudden, the Sabeans raided the oxen and the donkeys and took them away, fire fell from heaven and burned up the sheep and the servants, the Chaldeans raided the camels and took them away, and house fell on his children and killed them.

But thanks be to God that Job was not the kind of person who valued the blessings more than the Blesser. He loved God more than the things of this world. And Job proved to satan that

God was right. And after everything, God restored his losses, so that his latter end was by far better than the first.

The Word of God which lives and abides forever declares: "In righteousness you shall be established; you shall be far from oppression, for you shall not fear; and from terror, for it shall not come near you. Indeed they shall surely assemble, but not because of Me. Whoever assembles against you shall fall for your sake.

'Behold, I have created the blacksmith who blows the coals in the fire, who brings forth an instrument for his work; and I have created the spoiler to destroy. No weapon formed against you shall prosper, and every tongue which rises against you in judgment you shall condemn. This is the heritage of the Servants of the Lord, and their righteousness is from Me,' says the Lord" (Isa. 54:14-17).

No assassin or terrorist can kill you without God's Permission. No gun, sword, axe, or bomb can kill or destroy you, except God says, "Yes". It doesn't matter what the devil may plan against you: God's angels will protect you. No poison or snake's bite can kill your body, which is the Temple of God.

The Bible says, "Now it shall come to pass, if you diligently obey the Voice of the Lord your God, to observe carefully all His Commandments which I command you today, that the Lord your God will set you high above all nations of the earth.

"The Lord will cause your enemies who rise against you to be defeated before your face; they shall come out against you one way and flee before you seven ways. Then all peoples of the earth shall see that you are called by the Name of the Lord, and they shall be afraid of you (Deut. 28:1,7,10).

When the king of Syria sent his army to capture Elisha, one would have thought that the end has come for Elisha. But instead of those assassins to get you, police will catch them along the road before they reach where you are. Instead of them to kill you, their car will have accident along the way.

This is because you are the apple of God's Eyes, and whoever touches you touches Him (Zech. 2:8). Thus says the Lord, Who redeemed you, O Believer in Christ Jesus, "Fear not, for I have redeemed you; I have called you by your name, you are Mine.

"When you pass through the waters, I will be with you; and through the rivers, they shall not overflow you. When you walk through the fire, you shall not be burned, nor shall the flame scorch you. For I am the Lord your God. Since you are precious in My Sight, you have been honoured and I have loved you; therefore I will give men for you, and people for your life" (Isa. 43:1-4).

The fiery flames of Nebuchadnezzar's fire refused the bodies of Shadrach, Meshach, and Abed-Nego. Lions couldn't touch the flesh of Daniel. God has not changed, and He is still the same today. The psalmist said, "The Lord is my Shepherd; I shall not want. He makes me to lie down in green pasture;

"He leads me beside the still waters. He restores my soul; He leads me in the paths of righteousness for His Name's sake. Yea, though I walk through the valley of the shadow of death, I will fear no evil; for You are with me; Your Rod and Your Staff, they comfort me.

"You prepare a table before me in the presence of my enemies; You anoint my head with oil, my cup runs over. Surely goodness and mercy shall follow me all the days of my life; and I will dwell in the House of the Lord forever" (Psa. 23). Isn't this wonderful? Whether the attack is spiritual or physical, it will not get at you!

The king of Syria sent horses and chariots and a great army to catch Elisha, and they came by night and surrounded the city. And when the servant of the man of God arose early and went out, there was an army, surrounding the city with horses and chariots.

And his servant said to him, "Alas, my master! What shall we do?" So he answered, "Do not fear, for those who are with us are more than those who are with them." And Elisha prayed, and said, "Lord, I pray, open his eyes that he may see." Then the Lord opened the eyes of the young man, and he saw. And behold, the mountain was full of horses and chariots of fire all around Elisha.

Elisha prayed to God, and God struck them with blindness. Elisha led them into the city of Samaria, the capital of Israel. He arrested those who came to arrest him by the demonstration of the Power of God. Elisha knew that there were angels who guarded him. He fed his enemies and let them go, and they stopped coming to Israel (2 Kgs 6:14-23).

When Sennacherib, the king of Assyria, came to Jerusalem with his army and wanted to capture Jerusalem, he thought that the end had come for Jerusalem. But an angel of the Lord went out, and killed in the camp of the Assyrians one hundred and eighty-five thousand, and when people arose early in the morning, there were corpses – all dead (Isa. 37:36).

Why are you afraid, when God is for us, in us, and upon us? Why do you tremble, when the angels of the Lord encamp around those who fear the Lord? Why are you afraid of that cultist, when one of us shall chase a thousand and two of us chase ten thousand? But, be strong in the Lord, put on the whole Armour of God, and keep close relationship with the Almighty.

The Word says that we shall cast out demons; we shall take up serpents without being harmed; and if we drink anything deadly (chemical, biological, or witchcraft poison), it shall not hurt us (Mk 16:17-18). We have been given the authority and power to trample on serpents and scorpions, and over all the power of the enemy, and nothing shall by any means hurt us (Lk. 10:19).

He who dwells in the Secret Place of the Most High shall abide under the Shadow of the Almighty. I will say of the Lord "He is my Refuge and my Fortress; my God, in Him I will trust." Surely He shall deliver you from the snare of the fowler and from the perilous pestilence. He shall cover you with His Feathers, and under His Wings you shall take refuge; His Truth shall be your shield and buckler.

You shall not be afraid of the terror by night, nor of the arrow that flies by day, nor of the pestilence that walks in darkness, nor of the destruction that lays waste at noonday. A thousand may fall at your side, and ten thousand at your right hand; but it shall not come near you. Only with your eyes shall you look, and see the reward of the wicked.

Because you have made the Lord, Who is my Refuge, even the Most High, your Dwelling Place, no evil shall befall you, nor shall any plague come near your dwelling.

He shall give His angels Charge over you, to keep you in all your ways. In their hands they shall bear you up, lest you dash your foot against a stone. You shall tread upon the lion and the cobra, the young lion and the serpent you shall trample underfoot.

Because you have set your love upon God, therefore He will deliver you, He will set you on high, because you have known His Name.

You shall call upon Him, and He will answer you. He will be with you in trouble: He will deliver you and honour you. With long life He will satisfy you, and show you His Salvation.

ANGELS SURROUND US!

The Bible says that the angel of God encamps all around those who fear Him, and delivers them (Psa. 34:7). There are angels who encamp around us! If you had been thinking that they live only in Heaven, you had been making a great mistake. Yes, there are angels in Heaven; but God has got so many of them, and they are here with us to protect us.

An angel of God must have supervised the movement of the ark in which Noah and his family were. Angels ministered for Abraham, Isaac, and Jacob. Angels ministered to the Israelites in their journey through the wilderness into the promised land.

When the armies of Syria came by night, and encamped around the city where Elisha dwelt to capture him, the servant of the man of God saw that the mountain was full of horses and chariots of fire all around Elisha. Those angels were there protecting the man of God. And they are with us – children of God.

When Sennacherib, the King of Assyria, came to Jerusalem to capture the city, an angel of God went out into the Assyrian camp, and killed one hundred and eighty-five valiant warriors of Assyria in one night. When they woke up, they had no option than to depart to their place.

Angels of God have fought many battles for you, even without your knowledge. The Word says that the Lord God will give His angels Charge over us to keep us in all our ways. They will bear us up in their hands, lest we dash our feet against stones. Angels are swift enough to stop the plans of the devil from coming to pass in our lives.

When Daniel was thrown into the lion's den, nothing happened to him, because, "My God sent His angel and shut the lions' mouths, so that they have not hurt me…" (Dan. 6:22). One would have expected that the end had come for Prophet Daniel; but God said, "Son, I am here with My angel!" And he lived, contrary to the expectations of his enemies.

The apostles were arrested by the Jews; and they put them together in a common prison. But what happened? In the night, an angel of God opened the prison for them and told them to continue preaching the Gospel that they had been preaching. The same thing happened to Apostle Peter, when King Herod might have beheaded him, as he did to Apostle James.

It was an angel of the Lord, Whose Apostle Paul was, that appeared to Apostle Paul and encouraged him when all hope that they would be saved was lost. They had been entrapped in the sea for many days; but God saved them through the angelic ministry. God directed their ship to the Island of Malta by the angelic ministry.

Angels also protect us by directing us, as Joseph was directed by an angel to take Jesus Christ and Mary to Egypt. Herod had wanted to kill the Baby. You have got to know that many of the dreams you have had were programmed by angels to warn you against impending danger. The Word of God says that angels are ministering spirits sent forth to minister for the heirs of salvation – us (Heb. 1:14).

God makes His angels spirits and His ministers a flame of fire (verse 7). The warring angels are fiery, and demons run from them when they come to war and fight for us. The forces of darkness cannot overpower them, because our God has strengthened (and strengthens) them.

They that are with us are more than they that are against us. No matter what the devil may do, whatever God has not permitted to happen will not happen; angels make sure that the Will and Commandment of God is carried out. Angels of God obey the Word of God promptly.

Therefore, stop fearing the devil, but concentrate on pleasing God and obeying His Word, and the plans of the devil will not come to pass in your life. Of course, the Bible tells us to resist the devil ourselves; but even while doing this, don't fear him, because he is under your foot.

Jesus Christ has defeated him for us, and He gave us the power and authority that destroys the works of the devil.

The Word says, "Because you have made the Lord, Who is my Refuge, even the Most High your Dwelling Place, no evil shall befall you, nor shall any plague come near your dwelling; for He shall give His angels Charge over you, to keep you in all your ways. In their hands they shall bear you up lest you dash your foot against a stone" (Psa. 91:9-12).

When Hagar was running away from Sarah, the Angel of the Lord met her and told her to go back and submit to Sarah, and she said, "Have I also here seen Him Who sees me?" (Gen. 16:13). God sees you in your afflictions, and He will send His angel to see you through. God promised to send His Angel before Moses and the Israelites; He protected them and fought for them by His Angel.

Elijah had been afraid of the threat which Jezebel had made against him and ran away for his life. However, an angel of the Lord met him along the way and fed him twice. In your weakness, the Lord will be with you and strengthen you by His angel. Therefore be encouraged in the Lord your God!

After the Lord had been crucified and buried, His enemies went and made the tomb secure, sealing the stone and setting the guard. They thought that they had achieved their purpose. Some people want to destroy you and make your memory to be forgotten. But they are wrong, because the Lord God Almighty is watching.

What happened? The Bible says, "And behold there was a great earthquake; for an angel of the Lord descended from Heaven, and came and rolled back the stone from the door, and sat on it. His countenance was like lightning, and his clothing as white as snow. And the guards shook for fear of him, and became like dead men" (Matt. 28:2-4).

An angel directed Philip to go towards the south along the road which goes down from Jerusalem to Gaza. That was where he saw the Ethiopian eunuch, and after being preached to, the man received Jesus Christ. An angel also directed Cornelius to send for Peter who would tell him what he must do to be saved. Angels help us in the preaching of the Gospel.

When the angels of the Lord went to destroy Sodom, the men of Sodom came to Lot's house and wanted to force their way into Lot's door, but the angels reached out their hands and pulled Lot into the house with them, and shut the door. And they struck the men who were at the doorway with blindness, both small and great, so that they became weary trying to find the door.

The angels of God ministered to Jesus Christ in the wilderness during His Fasting period of forty days and forty nights. You are not alone; the Lord has sent His angels to encourage and help you. Even before His Death, as He prayed at Gethsemane, an angel of the Lord appeared to Him and strengthened Him. Angels surround us!

NO WEAPON FORMED AGAINST YOU SHALL PROSPER

No weapon formed against you shall prosper. Wherever they are formed, and however they are formed, they shell not prevail. Whether they are spiritual or physical weapons, because you are a Christian and God's Property, it shall not prevail or prosper against you.

God did not say that you may not feel it: He said that the weapon shall not prevail against you. There is something about the word – prevail; for something to prevail over another is for the thing to win over the other after a time. And this does not mean that the weapon will affect you, because it will not affect you.

But even if the weapon affects you, yet it will not prevail over you, because your Lord is the King of kings and Lord of lords. Trials and wilderness experiences are weapons; though you will feel the pain, yet they will not overcome you. And the Lord has stated that He will not allow any temptation that is greater than you to come your way (1 Cor. 10:13).

Symptoms of sicknesses or diseases are weapons of the enemy; but they will not prevail over you, because by the Stripes of Jesus Christ, you were healed (1 Pet. 2:24). He Himself carried our sicknesses and bore our infirmities (Matt. 8:17). Therefore, resist the devil by speaking according to the Word of God, and he will flee from you.

We are overcomers, because He Who is in us (the Holy Spirit) is greater than the devil. When they see us, they see fire. When they come near us, the Blood of Jesus Christ separates us from them. When they want to intrude to cause any havoc, the angels of God will block them. What a great reinforcement we have!

Your life is hidden with Christ in God. The hairs of your head are all numbered. God, Who protects the sparrows, will much more protect you. You need not fear him who can only touch the body, but have no power over the soul. Even the one carrying a gun or a bomb is a flesh, and his weapons are man-made.

Because of you, that gun will not shoot, and that bomb will not explode. And even if they shoot and explode, God will give you a supernatural bullet-proof, so that no harm will touch you. We have a great heritage in Christ Jesus. We are blessed, because the Lord redeemed us with His Blood.

This is why the Lord Jesus says, "I saw satan fall like lighting from Heaven. Behold, I give you the authority to trample on serpents and scorpions, and over all the power of the enemy, and nothing shall by any means hurt or harm you" (Lk. 10:19).

Because you believe in Christ Jesus, in His Name, you will cast out demons; you will take up serpents; and if you drink any deadly thing (whether chemical or witchcraft poison), it will not hurt or harm you (Mk 16:17-18). Do you know that you are a super-human? No wonder the Word declares that you are a god (Psa. 82:6). You are a god because you are a child of the Most High God.

In righteousness you shall be established; you shall be far from oppression, for you shall not fear; and from terror, for it shall not come near you. Indeed they shall surely assemble, but nor because of God. Whoever assembles against you shall fall for your sake.

Behold, God has created the blacksmith who blows the coals in the fire, who brings forth an instrument for his work; and He has created the spoiler to destroy. No weapon formed against you shall prosper, and every tongue which rises against you in judgment, you shall condemn.

This is the heritage of the Servants of the Lord, and their righteousness is from Him (Isa. 54:14-17). God tells us that we shall be far from oppression and terror. Therefore, whoever oppresses or terrorizes you makes himself an enemy of God. Though it may look like the Lord is not seeing them, yet He sees and knows everything.

And if they don't repent, God's Judgment will fall on them. God is merciful and slow to anger, but He will not leave the unrepentant sinner go unpunished. God gives people time to repent of their evil doings, because He does not take delight in the death of the sinner. But, if he refuses to repent, then the soul that sins shall die.

The Book of Psalms, number ninety-one tells us much about our security and victory in Christ Jesus, our Lord. It says, "He who dwells in the Secret Place of the Most High shall abide under the Shadow of the Almighty. I will say of the Lord, 'He is my Refuge and my Fortress; my God, in Him I will trust.'

"Surely He shall deliver you from the snare of the fowler and from the perilous pestilence. He shall cover you with His Feathers, and under His Wings you shall take refuge; His Truth shall be your shield and buckler.

"You shall not be afraid of the terror by night, nor of the arrow that flies by day, nor of the pestilence that walks in darkness, nor of the destruction that lays waste at noonday. A thousand may fall at your side, and ten thousand at your right hand, but it shall not come near you.

"Only with your eyes shall you look, and see the reward of the wicked. Because you have made the Lord, Who is my Refuge, even the Most High your Dwelling Place, no evil shall befall you, nor shall any plague come near your dwelling; for He shall give His angels Charge over you, to keep you in all your ways.

"In their hands they shall bear you up, lest you dash your foot against a stone. You shall tread upon the lion and the cobra, the young lion and the serpent you shall trample underfoot. 'Because he has set his love upon Me, therefore I will deliver him; I will set him on high, because he has known My Name.

'He shall call upon Me, and I will answer him; I will be with him in trouble; I will deliver him and honour him. With long I will satisfy him, and show him My Salvation" (Psa. 91). You are protected from the plans, devices, and works of the enemy.

Jesus Christ says that nothing shall by any means harm or hurt you. It may pain you, but it will not harm or hurt you. Believe the Word of God instead of believing the symptoms of the enemy's projections. Accept the Word of God instead accepting what men or circumstances say.

We have mighty reinforcements from the Almighty God. The devil, speaking to God about Job, said, "Have You not made a hedge around him, around his household, and around all that he has on every side? You have blessed the works of his hands, and his possessions have increased in the land" (Job 1:10). God protects you more than you know of.

No enchantment from any witch or wizard will succeed on your head. You are above destruction; and nothing can happen to you without God's Permission. When Balak hired Balaam to curse the children of Israel, God used the opportunity to cause Balaam to speak well of them instead.

We have the Name of Jesus Christ as our weapon of mass destruction, with which we destroy the works of the devil and his hosts. The Blood of Jesus Christ covers us, and protects us from the attacks of the enemy. When we call on the Fire of the Holy Ghost, the devil, his devils, their agents, and their works cannot stand it.

The Word of God says, "Finally, my brethren, be strong in the Lord and in the power of His Might. Put on the whole Armour of God, that you may be able to stand against the wiles of the devil. For we do not wrestle against flesh and blood, but against principalities, against powers, against the rulers of the darkness of this age, against spiritual host of wickedness in the heavenly places.

"Therefore take up the whole Armour of God, that you may be able to withstand in the evil day, and having done all, to stand.

"Stand therefore, having girded your waist with truth, having put on the breastplate of righteousness, and having shod your feet with the preparation of the Gospel of Peace; above all, taking the shield of faith with which you will be able to quench all the fiery darts of the wicked one.

"And take the helmet of salvation, and the Sword of the Spirit, which is the Word of God; praying always with all prayer and supplication in the Spirit, being watchful to this end with all perseverance and supplication for all the Saints" (Eph. 6:10-18).

THE POWER-FILLED LIFE

Christianity is the life that is full of power – the power of the Living God. Christ, the Messiah, was anointed as He came out to fulfil the Father's Plan for Him. Jesus Christ, our Lord, operated in the Anointing and Power of the Holy Spirit. As a Man, even though He was the Son of God, He depended on the Empowerment of the Spirit of God to fulfil God's Assignment for Him.

The Word of God says that Jesus Christ emptied Himself of His Great Divine Power before coming to this world in the form of Man. It is not recorded in the Bible that He performed any miracle before His Infilling of the Holy Ghost. It was when He was filled with the Holy Ghost and endued with power that He came back in the Power of the Holy Ghost (Lk. 4:1,14).

Having been endued with power, He began to perform mighty signs and wonders. The miracles He did were so spectacular that News about Him spread throughout the region He ministered. When your life is full of power – God's Power – you will be known as one who stands for God. You will be sought after if people notice the demonstration of God's Power in your life.

As a matter of fact, people desire for God to meet their needs, they want their problems to be solved. Have you ever wondered why people go to witch-doctors and occult ministers in search of solution to their problems? It is because they have heard that people's problems have been solved through them; it is because they have been promised solutions to their pressing problems.

It is a pity to note that many negative solution-givers are more serious and committed than many real positive solution-givers. Many ministers of the Gospel, not to talk of laymen (as we call them), are either powerless or not filled with power. When you can't drive out demons, it has to do with lack of the needed power.

When you pray for the sick and nothing happens (of course, some healings are not instant), work on yourself for power. The Word of God says that Believers speak in new tongues; they cast out devils and administer healings by the laying on of hands. It goes on to tell us that neither snake nor poison can harm us. These abilities have to do with the presence of God's Power in our lives.

As many as received Jesus Christ as Saviour and Lord, to them gave He the power to become children of God. People of God are people of power; but there are levels of spiritual empowerment. However, it is the same Spirit of God that empowers us. You have a level of power when you are born-again and become a child of God.

However, the Power of God in your life will be multiplied by very many folds when you are filled with the Holy Spirit. It is when you are filled with the Holy Spirit that the Spirit of anoints you to varying degrees, depending on your obedience, commitment, diligence, faithfulness, and other factors. When the Power of God is in your life, people will see it and recognize it.

One way to increase the Power of God in your life is to be prayerful; another is by the reading and study of the Word of God. Fasting and waiting on God will increase your anointing beyond your imagination. Learn to obey the Word of God and the Voice of the Spirit of God. God cannot lie nor fail; if He says this thing is this way or will happen this way, it will come to pass.

A Believer who wants to see his life full of power, the Believer who wants to see God's Power demonstrated through his hand life must move out. That Believer will have to go out and

THE POWER AND AUTHORITY OF THE BELIEVER

preach, for it was when they move out and preached everywhere that the Lord worked with them, confirming their Words with signs following (Mk 16:20).

The Lord God confirms the Word of His that you speak. God's Word represents God, and God can neither lie nor fail to perform His Word. But if you don't have time to be in His Presence before preaching His Word, you will speak without the Anointing of the Holy Spirit that should have accompanied the Word, for the Word to produce the required results. You can't do it by the power of the flesh, but by God's Spirit; so depend on the Holy Spirit of the Living God, Whose Word you are preaching.

And the Holy Spirit will not anoint you when you are busy running around for God, and going about the things of this life, without spending time with God. Man was created to fellowship with God; God longs for that fellowship with every child of His. Pursue after God, and He will use you to minister both to the Believers and to the unbelievers.

When your life is full of power, your life will not remain the same. People will seek after you; devils will be afraid of you, and will summit to your command in the Name of Jesus Christ. When your life is full of the Power of God, God will be pleased with you, for you will work with Him to bring His Will come to pass in the lives of men.

Think about the power demonstrated by the Lord Jesus Christ in His Earthly Ministry: He opened blind eyes; He healed the deaf and dumb; He cleansed the lepers; He raised the death; He cast out demons; He walked on water; He multiplied small food to feed many people; He calmed the raging storm and sea; and He made Peter have a miraculous catch of fish.

Even when they came to arrest Him, when He said, "I am He," the people that came to arrest Him went back with force and fell to the ground. But because He came to die for us, He still allowed Himself to be arrested by them and crucified. And when He said, "It is finished," and bowed His Head, the centurion, seeing how He died said, "Of a truth, this was the Son of God."

Think about the power demonstrated by the Old Testaments prophets and men of God! Joseph and Daniel interpreted dreams that the magicians, sorcerers, and astrologers couldn't interpret. Moses did great signs and wonders in the land of Egypt. He divided the Red Sea, so that the Israelites passed the sea on dry land. He struck the rock, and water came out.

Joshua spoke to sun, and it stood still, thereby elongating the period of daylight for a long time. Sampson killed a lion with bare hands. He also pushed down a big building. Elijah called fire down from Heaven. He stopped rainfall for about three and half years; and later brought it back. In fact, this very prophet was caught up alive to Heaven.

Prophet Elisha divided the River Jordon, and passed through the ground of the river, having watched his master, Elijah, do the same. Elisha cursed people that reviled him, and two female bears came out and killed forty-two of them. He raised the dead back to life. He also multiplied food to feed many people, as Jesus Christ did. Even at death, his bones brought a dead man back to life.

Isaiah, Jeremiah, Ezekiel, and others prophesied and revealed what will come to pass many years later. Daniel, Shadrach, Meshach, and Abed-Nego were ten times wiser than the magicians and astrologers of Babylon. Fire and lions couldn't touch them, but refused their flesh Babylon; and the whole world were forbidden from speaking against God because of these people.

And the story was the same in the early New Testament time. Peter healed a lame man. The anointing in the life of Apostle Peter was so great and enormous that his shadow could heal the sick. Peter raised the dead, having watched his Master do the same. Stephen, filled with the

Holy Spirit, did mighty signs and wonders among the people. And his opponents could not resist the wisdom with which he spoke.

Philip did great signs and wonders at Samaria, so that Simon, the sorcerer, was puzzled. Apostle Paul spoke to Elymas, and he became blind. He cast out devils. He raised the dead. He was used by God to write many inspired Letters and Books to churches and persons, which we use now. In fact, the anointing in his life was so great that handkerchiefs taken from his body could heal the sick and drive out demons.

The Power of God has not changed; the Anointing of the Holy Spirit remains the same today. And God expects us to do the same things that they did, because we are in the same dispensation. And because the glory of the latter days shall be greater than that of the former, we are to do greater works.

The Bible says that the Kingdom of God is not in word but in power (1 Cor. 4: 20). Apostle Paul said, "And I, brethren, when I came to you, did not come with excellence of speech or of wisdom declaring to you the Testimony of God. For I determined not to know anything among you except Jesus Christ and Him crucified.

"I was with you in weakness, in fear, and in much trembling. And my speech and my preaching were not with persuasive words of human wisdom, but in demonstration of the Spirit and of power, that your faith should not be in the wisdom of men but in the Power of God" (1 Cor. 2: 1-5). Isn't this a wonderful testimony? Certainly, it is. Can you give that type of testimony?

Writing to the Thessalonians, he said, "For our Gospel did not come to you in word only, but also in power, and in the Holy Spirit and in much assurance, as you know what kind of men we were among you for your sake" (I Thes. 1:5). That means that it didn't happen in one church only, but in other churches too.

Concerning his ministry, Apostle Paul wrote, "For I will not dare to speak of any of those things which Christ has not accomplished through me, in word and deed, to make the Gentiles obedient – in mighty signs and wonders, by the Power of the Spirit of God, so that from Jerusalem and round about to Illyricum I have fully preached the Gospel of Christ" (Rom. 15:18-19).

We are a Kingdom of power demonstrators. We demonstrate the Power and Anointing of the Holy Spirit of the Living God. If you have not started demonstrating that power, then you have to start now. You have the authority of a child of God. And if you have been filled with the Holy Spirit, you have the very Power of God.

This is why the Lord Jesus Christ said, "Behold, I send the Promise of My Father upon you; but tarry in the city of Jerusalem until you are endued with power from on High" (Lk. 24:49). Just before He left, He said, "But you shall receive power when the Holy Spirit has come upon you; and you shall be witnesses to Me…to the end of the earth" (Acts 1:8).

God has not changed. Jesus Christ is the same yesterday, today, and forever. God bears witness to Message of the Gospel both with signs and wonders, and with various miracles, and the Gifts of the Holy Spirit, according to His Own Will (Heb. 2:4). There are many people who will not believe the Gospel that we preach, until they have seen the demonstration of power. When Power jam power, the lesser power will bow to the Superior Power!

The Almighty does not intend that we beg the devil or dialogue with him. As a matter of fact, you will be wasting your time begging the devil, because he has no mercy for the human race, not to talk of having one for the Believer in Christ Jesus. Demonic and satanic works need confrontation with Divine Power to remove and destroy them.

The Word of God says, "It shall come to pass in that day that his burden will be taken away from your shoulder, and his yoke from your neck, and the yoke will be destroyed (or broken) because of the anointing" (Isa. 10:27). God has spoken once, twice I have heard this: that power belongs to God (Psa. 62:11).

The enemies of God shall submit themselves to Him through the greatness of His Power (Psa. 66:3). God put us here as His representatives, and we must represent Him well. God wants to prove to the devil, through us, that he is nothing before Him. The Bible says, "To the intent that now the Manifold Wisdom of God might be known by the Church to the principalities and powers in the heavenly places" (Eph. 3:10).

To be sincere with you: people like power. People like signs, wonders, and miracles. And God has put us here to give them to the people. Furthermore, the devil is against God and us; therefore, we need God's Power to put him down. The power of the devil is powerless before the Power of the Almighty God – the Power and Anointing of the Holy Ghost!

Never Say That God Said What He Did Not Say!

GREAT POWER GIVEN TO MEN

God has given great power unto men. When God anoints and empowers someone by the Holy Spirit, the person receives the ability to represent God and do what God would have done. The Bible says that we have been made partakers of the Divine Nature. This is talking about our having received the God-Nature. No wonder the Word of God says that God has given those that believe on and accepted His Son, Jesus Christ, the power to become the sons of God (Jn 1:12).

Do you know what it means to be a son of God? That means that you proceeded from God. The Bible says that we are gods. We are the representatives of Jesus Christ. Jesus Christ rose up and collected all authority and all power in heaven and earth. He handed the authority and the power to us and went back to Heaven. That was the dominion that the devil collected from Adam when Adam sinned.

Jesus Christ restored the dominion and told us that we will do the works that He did, even greater works than His (Jn 14:12). We have the power and ability to heal the sick, to cast out devils, to raise the dead, and move mountains. This privilege and power God has given us is because of His Grace, and not because we merited it.

When God gives us different ministries, He chooses us sovereignly. When the Holy Spirit shares His Gifts among Believers, He shares them as He wills. Even though our faithfulness in one area can lead to His increasing our responsibilities and the gifts He gives, yet it is still because of His Grace and His Love for us.

When the Lord Jesus Christ performed mighty miracles, the people were stunned and puzzled. When ordinary people, the apostles and the Disciples, did mighty things among the people, the people's mouths fell open, and they feared them. That same power is still available today for us Believers in Christ.

Remember that the Lord said that the signs will follow the Believers (Mk 16:17). He was not talking about the apostles, the prophets, the evangelists, the pastors, and the teachers. He was talking about the Believers; the Believers are the clergy as well as the laity. If you are a Christian, this is for you. If you have been filled with the Holy Ghost, you have been filled with power to do exploits.

Even Paul's handkerchiefs could heal the sick and drive out demons (Acts 19:12). Peter's shadow worked wonders (Acts 5:15). Jesus Christ's Words produced tangible results. We have the same ability these days, and we must not fail to exercise the authority and power we have received from God. God is watching us, and He will greatly reward the faithful.

We are children and sons of God; we are God's Offsprings, and we partake of the Divine Nature. We were Born of God, and we have the Nature and Life of God inside us. Because we have the Holy Spirit of God dwelling and living inside of us, we have the Power and Ability of God resident in us. We are heirs of God and joint-heirs with Christ. The things that God has provided for us in Christ Jesus our Lord are great. Behold, what manner of love the Father has bestowed on us, that we should be called the children of God.

And the Word of God says, "As His Divine Power has given to us all things that pertain to life and Godliness, through the Knowledge of Him Who called us by glory and virtue, by which have been given to us exceedingly great and precious promises, that through these you may be partakes of the Divine Nature, having escaped the corruption that is in the world through lust (2 Pet. 1:3-4). It is through the exceedingly great and precious promises that God gave us that we partake of the Divine Nature.

And the Word says, "Behold, I give you the authority (power) to trample (tread) on serpents and scorpions, and over all the power of the enemy, and nothing shall by any means hurt you. No weapon formed against you shall prosper and every tongue which rises against you in judgment you shall condemn. This is the heritage of the Servants of the Lord, and their righteousness is from Me."

First paragraph it is through.

We are called the children of God because we were Born of God. Whoever is Born of God has the Nature of God in him, at least to an extent, even though that nature may be suppressed from manifesting because of unrenewed mind and the body that is not brought into subjection to the born-again spirit.

The Bible says that that which is Born of the Spirit of God is the spirit of man (Jn 3:6). Actually, it is our spirit that has the Nature of God in him. God is a Spirit, and when the Bible says that we were made in the Likeness and Image of God, it is saying, in part, that we are spirit beings, though we have souls and live in bodies.

God has commanded us to renew our minds and thinking with the Word of God so that we can start thinking as God thinks! We are also admonished to put our bodies under subjection to our spirits because our spirits will want to please God, but the body, naturally, will object to pleasing God! The spirit is opposed to the flesh.

The Nature of God is the nature of power; it is the nature of holiness. As our spirit has God's Nature in him; he will want to please God. Sickness flees from the Presence of God; therefore, we should enjoy Divine Health, and be healed of any sickness trying to afflict our bodies. An unbeliever may want to do God's Will, but he does not have the in-built ability to please God instead of the devil.

Even though we have the Divine Nature in us, we may allow things that should not afflict us to afflict us because of sin, ignorance, and unbelief. But God expects us to take our stand and resist the devil, and he will flee from us. The Power of the Holy Spirit will help us in our Christian endeavours.

Jesus Christ says that He came to give us life and more abundant life (Jn 10:10). The Divine Life we have in Christ Jesus is the life of the miraculous; and it pleases God. We should not live a defensive life, just dodging the devil. We can move in the Power of the Spirit, do the Works of Jesus Christ, and destroy the works of the devil. The devil has no good thought for us, and we should never co-operate with him.

And the Words says, "As His Divine Power has given to us all things that pertain to life and Godliness, through the Knowledge of Him Who called us by glory and virtue, by which have been given to us exceedingly great and precious promises, that through these you may be partakers of the Divine Nature, having escaped the corruption that is in the world through lust.

"But also for this very reason, add to your faith virtue, to virtue knowledge, to knowledge self-control, to self-control perseverance, to perseverance Godliness, to Godliness brotherly kindness, and to brotherly kindness love. For if these things are yours and abound, you will neither be barren nor unfruitful in the Knowledge of our Lord Jesus Christ.

"For he who lacks these things is shortsighted, even to blindness, and has forgotten that he was cleansed from his old sins. Therefore, brethren, be even more diligent to make your call and election sure, for if you do these things you will never stumble; for so an entrance will be supplied to you abundantly into the Everlasting Kingdom of our Lord and Saviour Jesus Christ" (2 Pet. 1:3-11).

But the Bible says, "Now I say that the heir, as long as he is a child, does not differ at all from the slave, though he is a master of all" (Gal. 4:1); and, "I said, 'You are gods, and all of you are the children of the Most High. But you shall die like men, and fall like one of the princes'" (Psa. 82:6-7).

We can see that though we are partakers of the Divine Nature, because of immaturity, many of us do not live the good and victorious life that God has given to us. The Word says that many of us die like ordinary men, though we are gods, and fall like one of the princes. Can you see that your position is, by far, higher than that of a prince?

God's people perish because of ignorance; and ignorance is not an excuse to the devil, who thrives in ignorance to steal God's Provisions from God's people. But we must refuse ignorance and lukewarmness, and grab all that the Father has provided for us in Christ Jesus!

Never Say That God Said What He Did Not Say!

YOU ARE GODS

The Word of God records in the Book of Psalms that God's children are gods (Psa. 82:6). Jesus Christ referred to this statement when He was accused of blasphemy because He said that He is the Son of God. Jesus Christ told them not to believe Him if He does not do the Works of God. This implies that the sons of God, who are gods, should do the Works of God.

A born again Christian is Born of the Spirit of God (Jn 3:5). He is born of God (1 Jn 5:4), and so came out from God. Whoever is Born of God is an Offspring of God, and is a son of God. Children have the trait of their parents. The sons of God have the Nature of God inside of them. The Nature of God is a Godly nature, and it is a supernatural Divine Nature.

The sons of God are supernatural beings, and they do the Works of God. Moses showed us what it means to do the Works of God; his rod swallowed up all the rods of Pharaoh's magicians. God always tops satan in everything.

Preachers who go to look for powers outside God so that their congregation will increase are faithless and ignorant people. If they know that God's Power always tops satan's power everywhere, every time, and anyhow, they would have patiently sought God for His Power.

God may not give you the power you want immediately, because He wants you to develop and mature spiritually. Just because you fasted for seven, fourteen, twenty one, or forty days does not mean that you have matured. God will want you to get trained, experienced, tested, and matured before giving you the power, so that power will not destroy you.

A 15-amperes current will blow the fuse of a 13-amperes socket. Shallow foundations are not made for 50-storey buildings. God may have to wait, even for years sometimes, for you to mature.

Of course, your faithfulness in your preparation can affect the time you mature. Therefore, be faithful in prayers and in the study of God's Word. Take some time to fast as the Spirit leads you.

God is ever faithful, and He is not unjust. He loves you, and that is why He waits for you to mature. It is the devil that gives his power to novices and the immature. They always end up abusing it. Do you know that power can be abused? Pride can destroy a minister of the Gospel. Ignorance can make a child of God to perish.

Jesus Christ showed us an example of what it means to be a god, what it means to be a son of God. He did the Works of God and tells Believers that they can do the same works that He did, even greater works.

Why did He do them? Because He was anointed, empowered, and trained by the Holy Spirit. If we allow ourselves to be anointed and trained by the Holy Spirit, we will operate in the power that Jesus Christ operated on.

Jesus Christ did good works: he healed the sick, cast out devils, and raised the dead. He did mighty and amazing deeds, for God was with Him (Acts 10:38). We are Christians, the anointed ones, and we are to do the Works of Christ. All the glory must go to God; we should not share in God's Glory, for we are just Servants.

Even as a god, you can die as a mere man (Psa. 82:7). Jesus Christ has given us authority and power over the devil, his cohorts, and their works. Yet, we must apply that authority and power in order to destroy the works of the devil in our lives and in others' lives. Ignorance of God's Word and Promises can keep us from receiving God's Best and Promises for us.

From this day onwards, live in the consciousness that you are a god, a son of God. Operate in that level and fear nothing. God wants to show the devil and his devils his manifold wisdom and power through His Church, and you are part of the Church (Eph. 3:10). Stop making the devil rejoice over you; let God rejoice and be glad always for your life as a Christian and as a minister.

God hates barrenness and unproductiveness. God wants us to be fruitful, and to produce the expected results. One area we should be fruitful in is in winning of souls. Jesus Christ is the True Vine and we are the branches. The Father, Who is the Vine-dresser, takes away every branch that does not bear fruit.

However, He prunes the branches that bear fruit, that they may bear more fruit. We are in Jesus Christ, and just as Jesus Christ bore Fruit by getting Followers and pleasing the Father, we too ought to win souls and please God.

Abide in Jesus Christ, and let Him abide in you. As the branch cannot bear fruit of itself, unless it abides in the vine, neither can you, unless you abide in the Lord. He who abides in Him, and He in him, bears much fruit; for without Him, you can do nothing.

Anyone who does not abide in Him is cast out as a branch and is withered and burnt. The Father is glorified when we bear much fruit, so as to confirm that we are Jesus Christ's Disciples.

If we abide in Him and His Words abide in us, we will ask what we desire, and it shall be done for us. If we keep His Commandment, we will abide and remain in His Love, just as He kept His Father's Commandments and abides in His Love.

We are His Friends if we do whatever He commands us. We did not choose Him, but He chose us and appointed us that we should go and bear fruit, and that our fruit should remain, that whatever we ask the Father in His Name He may give us (Jn 15).

For us to be fruitful and productive requires that we have patience, endurance, and longsuffering. Just as different crops and trees take different periods to mature and produce fruits, so is the Christian life and the ministry.

Therefore be patient, brethren, until the Coming of the Lord. See how the farmer waits for the precious fruit of the earth, waiting patiently for it until it receives the early and the latter rain (Jas 5:7).

Jesus Christ says that if we are ashamed of Him and His Word, especially before this sinful and adulterous generation, He Himself will be ashamed of us before His Father (Mk 8:38). If we confess Him before men, He will also confess us before His Heavenly Father and before the holy angels (Matt. 10:32-33).

Those who are wise shall shine like the brightness of the firmament, and those who turn many to righteousness like the stars forever and ever (Dan. 12:3). We must strive to win souls for the Lord no matter the cost.

Giving all diligence, add to your faith virtue, to virtue knowledge, to knowledge self-control, to self-control perseverance, to perseverance Godliness, to Godliness brotherly kindness, and to brotherly kindness love.

For if these things are in you and abound, you will be neither barren nor unfruitful in the Knowledge of our Lord Jesus Christ. For he who lacks these things is short-sighted, even to blindness, and has forgotten that he was cleansed from his old sins.

Therefore, brethren, be even more diligent to make your call and election sure; for if you do these things, you will never stumble; for so you will be abundantly allowed to enter the Kingdom of Christ (2 Pet. 1:5-11).

Apostle Paul, writing to the Galatians, spoke of what Apostle Peter said in another way. The Book of Galatians speaks of what the Bible translators translated as the Fruit of the Spirit (Gal. 5:22), even though it is actually 'the fruit of the spirit (the human spirit).'

It is talking about what the recreated human spirit (by the Help of the Holy Spirit) produces. The fruit of the human spirit by the Holy Spirit is love, joy, peace, longsuffering, kindness, goodness, faithfulness, gentleness, self-control. Against such there is no Law (Gal. 5:22-23).

As you were once darkness, but now you are light in the Lord, walk as children of light (for the Fruit of the Spirit is in all goodness, righteousness, and truth), finding out what is acceptable to the Lord.

And have no fellowship with the unfruitful works of darkness, but rather expose them (Eph. 5:8-11). And those who are Christ's have crucified the flesh with its passions and desires. If we live in the Spirit, let us also walk in the Spirit (Gal. 5:24-25).

Father Abraham started as one person; God called him and as he believed God and obeyed Him, God multiplied him into a multitude as innumerable as the stars and as uncountable as the sand by the sea-shore (Heb. 11:12).

And today we are part of the offspring of Abraham through Jesus Christ. God will make great things out of anyone who trusts Him and does His Will.

Jesus Christ came alone, He followed God's Plan for His Life, and before He left for Heaven, He had got the twelve apostles and many other strong Disciples. Today, we are part of the Believers in Him; we are part of His Body (the Church) and the number of the sons brought to glory increases day by day.

This was made possible because He laid down His Life for the salvation of many. When you sacrifice for the Lord, and deny your body of its pleasures (as the Spirit leads), you can't be an ordinary person.

The early apostles and Disciples multiplied greatly, and that was God's Will for them. Apostle Peter's first preaching brought about three thousand souls to the Lord Jesus Christ. Another preaching brought more souls (in thousands) to repentance (Acts 2:41; Acts 4:4).

The story became the same as the days went by and the number of the Disciples multiplied greatly in Jerusalem and many of the priests were obedient to the faith (Acts 6: 7). Even when serious persecutions came, the Disciples preached wherever they went.

You must preach the Word (the Gospel), in season and out of season; reprove, rebuke, exhort with all longsuffering and Doctrine (2 Tim. 4:2). If you are ashamed of Jesus Christ and His Gospel, He will also be ashamed of you.

If you confess Him before men, He also will confess you before His Father and before the holy angels (Lk. 9:26). God will reward you abundantly if you win souls, because Jesus Christ gave up His Life for that purpose.

In every area of your life, be fruitful and productive. Be fruitful and productive: spirit, soul, and body. God told Adam to be fruitful and multiply and replenish the earth.

That is still His Will for today: in finance, in health, in academics, in job, in ministry. Once you have found out God's Perfect Will for your life, work towards it and show God that He has not invested in you in vain, and He will be glad.

Fight the good fight of faith, lay hold on Eternal Life. Flee evil things and pursue righteousness, Godliness, faith, love, patience, gentleness (1 Tim. 6:11-12).

Let no one despise you, but be an example to the Believers in word, in conduct, in love, in spirit, in faith, in purity. Do not neglect the gift that is in you. Meditate on these things; give yourself entirely to them, that your progress may be evident to all.

Take heed to yourself and to the Doctrine. Continue in them, for in doing this, you will save both yourself and those who hear you (1 Tim. 4:12-16).

You must discipline your body and bring it to subjection in order to obey God and fulfil His Purpose for your life. Run so as to obtain: if people who take part in games train hard to excel, how much more you whose engagement and investment is eternal?

Love not the world or anything in the world. Without holiness, no eye shall see the Lord (Heb. 12:14). God is of a Purer Eyes than to behold iniquity (Habk. 1:13); and only the pure in heart shall see Him.

If God turned His Face away from Jesus Christ, as He hung on the Cross carrying the sins of the whole world, who are you that God will compromise His Standards? Be holy for the Lord is holy.

And if you call on the Father, Who without partiality judges according to each one's work, conduct yourselves throughout the time of your stay here in fear (1 Pet. 1:16-17). Work out your salvation with fear and trembling, for God is no respecter of persons.

Daniel and his friends feared God and God promoted them and delivered them. The Eyes of the Lord run to and fro the face of the earth to show Himself strong on behalf of anyone, who will believe Him, obey Him and cooperate with Him. With God, nothing shall be impossible.

The Church is marching on and the gates of Hades shall not prevail against it. The Letters that the Lord wrote to the seven Churches tell us what He expects from us, how some of us are, and the reward He has for us.

Break up your fallow ground, and do not sow among thorns. Stop procrastination and do what you are supposed to do now. Don't wait for tomorrow, for you don't know what tomorrow will bring forth.

We are a generation of blessings. We have been blessed, and empowered to bless others. Bless and do not curse; bless those who curse you! Leave vengeance to the Lord; the Lord will avenge you.

Of course, there are times you will need to cause someone to submit to the Gospel and the Lord by God's Power as Apostle Paul did to Elymas who was distracting Sergius Paulus. There are times that you will need to put the fear of the Lord into people and judge hardened sinners (as God leads) as Peter did to Ananias and Sapphira

Prosperity is the Will of God for all of His children. God wants His children to prosper in every area of their lives. They are to prosper spiritually, mentally, emotionally, and physically.

God's children should prosper ministerially, financially, academically, materially, health-wise, in business, and in every other area they may find themselves, according to the Will of God for their individual or collective lives.

Hence Apostle John prayed that Elder Gaius might prosper in all things and be in health just as his soul prospered (3 Jn 1:2).

That is God's Will for all of His children, even till date. However, we see many of Gods' people who are not prospering in many areas of their lives. There are many reasons why this can be so.

How can a child of God not prosper when the earth is the Lord's and the fullness of it? Why do many Christians not prosper when silver, gold, and the cattle belong to God? What makes them to fail when the Lord God can do all things?

Jesus Christ is the Door to God and His Blessings. He is the Way, the Truth, and the Life. Speaking to the Church at Philadelphia, Jesus Christ said, "See, I have set before you an open door, and no one can shut it...."

He is the Door, and the Way through the Door. He holds the key of David. When He opens, no one can shut; and when He shuts, no one can open (Rev. 3:7-8).

If you are willing and obedient, you shall eat the good of the land (Isa. 1:19). You must be willing to prosper in order to prosper. Any area you are unwilling to prosper will not go smoothly for you. You may prosper in one area and not prosper in the other.

However, God will sustain you as His child in any area, though you may not prosper in that area. Someone said that he neither wants riches nor poverty, but God's Provisions and Sustenance (Prov. 30:8).

In the scale of wealth, you have: the poor, the comfortable, the rich, the wealthy, and the flourishing. To flourish is the highest level of wealth, and the righteous shall flourish (Prov. 11:28).

Those that flourish lend to many nations and don't need to borrow from any. But you must be willing to flourish to flourish, and you can flourish in any area of your life and ministry.

However, always have it in mind that life does not consist in the abundance of what you have. This is why the Lord tells us to beware of covetousness. If you have all the money, wealth, fame, power, certificate, etc, and you don't please God, or you end in Hell, you gained nothing.

It will be better for you to be poor and wretched in this world and make Heaven at last, than to be the richest, most famous, powerful, and educated person, and be cast into Eternal Punishment.

Also, you must be obedient to prosper. Any prosperity (in human eyes) that is achieved through the life of sin and disobedience has a comma and a question mark. Obedience, righteousness, and holiness will bring true prosperity to you.

"But, what of unbelievers or unfaithful Believers that prosper?" you may ask. In the first place, you are talking of material prosperity, for you cannot prosper spiritually in sin and disobedience. In the second place, that is in the eyes of the natural man.

Any prosperity that leads you to Hell Fire is no prosperity at all. What shall it profit a man if he gains the whole world and loses his own soul?

Also, people see people with flashy cars and of high social status, but they don't know what those people pass through. Many of them will find it very difficult to sleep for two hours a day because of fear and anxiety; others have different health problems that keep them sad, internally.

Still, others have made different sacrifices and commitments that have brought heavy losses to them. Some used their body parts or family members to sacrifice to the spirits that gave them money.

Others are involved in gross corruption and bribery, and because of their practices, they are always afraid. But the Blessings of the Lord make rich and add no sorrow to the blessed.

Spiritual prosperity requires a good knowledge of the Word of God and being prayerful. It involves faith and spiritual exercise.

Spiritual prosperity affects, to a great extent, other areas of life, for the spiritual controls the physical. How you prosper spiritually will affect you health-wise, maritally, and financially.

I know there are people who prosper spiritually but not financially: many of them are unwilling, because they think financial prosperity will lead them into sin and compromise.

Financial prosperity comes from God. In fact, no matter what you do, if God has made up His Mind that you will never prosper financially, you cannot prosper financially.

If you like, go to the strongest secret society or witch-doctor, if God says you will die today, you cannot see tomorrow. Even, all the things satan boasts of cannot be if God says, "Enough is enough."

He who trusts in the devil or in man is a fool. He who says that the Lord does not see has no understanding.

Financial prosperity is a product of obedience, faith, hardwork, giving, and diligence. You cannot maintain these five virtues permanently and not prosper financially.

Faith will bring what does not exist to existence. Obedience will make you follow God's Plan for your life and to obey His Word.

Hardwork will make you invest your resources and energy to the cause you are pursuing; Giving will bring multiplication and increase to your seed and offerings; and diligence will produce consistency.

Physical prosperity is a function of Divine Intervention and obedience to physical laws. God's Word is medicine to your body. He sends forth His Word, and His Word heals the sick.

By the Stripes of Jesus Christ, we were healed. No matter the type of sickness (even when medical science has no solution for it), God can heal you if you believe.

But to pass from the level of healing to the level of health, you must feed on God's Word and meditate on it; you must be prayerful; you must maintain a healthy eating-habit; you must exercise bodily; and you must have adequate rest.

A student who wants to do well in his academics must be studious and diligent. The lazy man, no matter how he wants good things, will not have them, except someone gives him by charity. An idle mind is the devil's workshop.

The reason many students go into cultism is because many of them are not very committed to their studies. Others go into it because of bad friends, fear, and threats. But why should a hardworking student be a friend to a lazy and uncommitted student?

Do not be deceived, evil communication (wrong company) corrupts good manners. Influence is stronger than information. This is why a boy that was brought up in a Christian home can change into something else when he starts associating with bad friends.

Emotionally, many are disorganized and not stable because of fear, disappointment, and anxiety. Why worry about your life or tomorrow? God is faithful and He will bring His Will to pass in your life.

Commit your cares to Him, for He cares for you (1 Pet. 5:7). Get rid of pondering on past disappointments, because God has a brighter tomorrow for you.

Do not be afraid of him who can touch the body but not the soul. Worry and anxiety cause physical sicknesses. Get rid of bitterness, hatred, and unforgiveness from your heart.

No matter how your marital life may be, commit it to God and He will bring peace and joy to your family. God can change your husband, wife, children, mother, sister, and brother. The problem with us is that we try to please people without pleasing God first.

If you spend enough time with God in prayer and listening to Him, He will remove satanic barriers and obstacles along your way, and He will give you directions on how to relate with your family members, and you will find happiness.

No matter how hopeless the ministry God has given you may look like, the Lord that commissioned it will prosper it. No matter how the devil fights your ministry, God's Spirit and His angels will fight for you. You only have to be faithful in what the Lord called you to do.

Find out exactly what He wants you to do so that you will not run along the wrong track. God is committed to His Cause, and the gates of Hades will not prevail against the Church of Jesus Christ.

If you do not let the Word of God depart from your mouth, but you meditate on it day and night, and do what it says, your way will be made prosperous, and you will have a good success (Josh. 1:8).

God is the Source of the security and protection that you need; don't go after strange gods, and even if you use police or military escort (Apostle Paul used in Acts 23:12-32 and Acts 28:16), don't put your trust on them, because if God leaves you, a bomb can destroy you along with those security men.

Poverty is not good. However, each person has or will go through lack, hardship, and adversity. God allows those things for different purposes. Some people will not pay attention to God's Leading or Prompting until they enter into hard and difficult situations, and then they will seek God like never before.

The Lord has declared that if you are willing and obedient, you shall eat the good of the land. Two things are involved here: willingness and obedience. If you conform to two of them, you will enjoy the good things that the Lord has provided for you.

To be successful in life is to fulfill God's Purpose and Plan for your life. This is why the Lord says that life is not in the abundance of what a man possesses (Lk. 12:15).

This is why the poor members of the Church of Smyrna were told by the Lord that they were rich (Rev. 2:9), and the rich members of the Church of the Laodiceans were told that they were poor and wretched (Rev. 3:17).

God sees differently from how men see. Do you know that, even as a minister, you can have the largest church and organize the biggest crusade, and still not be following God's Plan for your life?

What people call 'success' is no success at all. If you become the wealthiest, richest, most famous, most powerful, or most educated person of all ages, and you lose your soul in Hell at last, you were very unsuccessful.

Material blessings, academic blessings, marital blessings, ministerial blessings, and many others are good and necessary; after all, without money, how can the Gospel go to the ends of the earth?

But let me tell you the truth, true success is obedience to the Word of God, and the achievement of God's Purpose for your life.

Abraham was successful in life, even though he had only one son after many years (apart from the son of the bondwoman – Ishmael). Moses was successful; even though he did not make it to the land of Canaan, he made it to Heaven.

Joshua and Caleb were successful; of all the adults that left Egypt, only two of them made it to Canaan, and they fulfilled God's Purpose for their lives. Samuel, David, Isaiah, Daniel, Jesus Christ, Peter, Paul, and many others were successful. David was rich and Daniel was famous, but all of them fulfilled God's Plans for their lives.

Most of the adults that left Egypt at the exodus of the Israelites did not make it to Canaan, and to Paradise. Sampson lost his ministry and his eyes due to irresponsibility.

Solomon lost the kingdom of Israel after his death, because his heart was estranged from God, though he was very wise and rich. Judas Iscariot fell by the way. King Asa did not end well. These and many others were unsuccessful in life. They displeased God and lost their missions.

What does it mean to be successful in life? The word 'success' means the achieving of something you have been trying to do, with a good result. If you do very well in what you want to do or in what you are to do (like your Christian life, your ministry, or your job), you are a success.

However, Godly success is not always the same with human success. What humans regard as success may be seen by God as destruction. What humans may regard as foolishness may be seen by God as success.

Concerning success, I will like to speak about Apostle Paul. This holy and fiery apostle of the Almighty God had a great success in his ministry. This is not to say that he did not make mistakes; of course, he made some mistakes.

This holy apostle and prophet of Jesus Christ suffered dearly in the ministry. He traveled by foot and by ship; he was stoned and beaten with rod and whips; he suffered hunger and rejection. Nevertheless, he called all those things, and many more, light afflictions (2 Cor. 4:17).

Apostle Paul wanted and desired to succeed in the ministry and be faithful to the Lord that he despised the pains and the shame he encountered, and pressed for the prize of the High Call of God.

He did not have internet services, aircraft, cars, duplexes, cathedrals; yet he decided to preach the Gospel where Christ had not been named. He did not collect tithes and offerings to enrich himself, and keep a lot in store.

He used what he collected for the Work of God. Today, many have removed their focus from Jesus Christ, Heaven, and souls; they are interested in money.

Let me talk about other areas of success before I go back to the real success – spiritual success. But the spirit-realm controls the physical realm; therefore, spiritual success is supposed to show physically.

However, if you are not rich yet, it does not necessarily mean that you have a problem spiritually, even though you may have to check your life of obedience and faith; your unwillingness to get rich will affect God's Supply for you (Isa. 1:19). God's Divine Power has given us all things we need for life and Godliness.

Also, God's people suffer due to ignorance (Hos. 4:6). Some don't even know that it is God's Will for them to prosper materially and financially. The earth is the Lord's and the fullness of it (Psa. 24:1).

Silver and gold is God's; a thousand cattle by the hill are His (Psa. 50:10). God did not create these things for the devil and his children, but for God's people, even though Adam sold out his inheritance to the devil when he disobeyed God and sinned against Him.

Thus satan became the god of this world (2 Cor. 4:4). But Jesus Christ came to bring that inheritance back to us and we are gods and kings of the Great God and King (Psa. 82:6; Rev. 1:6).

Jesus Christ became poor so that through His poverty, we might be made rich (2 Cor. 8:9). It is God's Will for us to prosper in material things. Of course, many of the early apostles, prophets, and Disciples were not rich materially.

One reason this was so is because they were committed to winning souls: we must be committed to winning souls like them; they won souls in the face of fierce persecutions. We live more peaceably now.

Another reason is that many of them were ignorant of God's Will in this area. They didn't have the entire Bible as we have today; we can compare one part with another. Nevertheless, they pursued the substance, and today many of us seem to be pursuing the shadows – riches and material blessings.

No wonder they were more spiritual than many today. However, never set your mind on temporal things, things that perish and do not have eternal value. Riches and wealth have eternal value when used for God's Glory.

Physical prosperity or success is very necessary. I am speaking of health and healing here. No matter how much you have, if you are sick and can't work or stand, it is a very big problem. In that case, you wouldn't even enjoy your meals.

But God has provided health and healing for us. Jesus Christ carried our sicknesses and diseases, and it is God's Will for us to be healthy. If you choose to be sick, you are just giving the devil a place in your life. God is not responsible for it.

Abraham was very rich in cattle, in silver, and in gold (Gen. 13:2). He had 318 trained servants, and more than that, for he couldn't have used all for the war he fought (Gen. 14:14). The Lord blessed Abraham in all things (Gen. 24:1).

Isaac reaped a hundred-fold of what he planted. He waxed great, and went forward, and grew until he became very great (Gen. 26:12-13). Isaac had possession of flocks, and possession of herds, and great store of servants: and the Philistines envied him (Gen. 26:14).

Jacob increased exceedingly, and had much cattle, and maidservants, and menservants, and camels, and asses (Gen. 30:43). Job was blameless and upright, and one who feared God and shunned evil. He had so much that he was the greatest of all the people of the east (Job 1:1-3).

David was righteous and feared God, yet he was a king and prepared for the House of the Lord a hundred thousand talents of gold, and a thousand talents of silver, and of brass and iron without weight for it was in abundance: timber also and stone he prepared (1 Chron. 22:14).

Even in the New Testament, people of God were rich. That is why Apostle Paul told Timothy to charge the rich to do good (1 Tim. 6:17). Talking of promotion and power, Daniel and his three friends were high in positions in the Babylonian government.

They were blessed academically also, for they were ten times wiser than the others. God blessed them in appearance also. (Dan. 1:15,19-21; Dan. 3:29-30; Dan 6:1-3). Mordecai was highly promoted and honoured by God (Esth. 6:1-14). God delivered the Israelites with a strong hand (Exo. 12:29-33). Joseph was the prime minister of Egypt for God was with him (Gen. 41:38-44).

But, Brethren, do not love the world or anything in the world. The love of money is the root of all evil. He who loves silver will not be satisfied with silver. Whatever God gives you, use it for His Glory and to expand the Church on earth.

Heaven should be your main goal, and you must strive to please God. The Word of God shall not depart from your mouth, but you shall meditate on it day and night, that you may do all His Word. For then you will make your way prosperous, and then you will have good success (Josh. 1:8).

Curses and spiritual attacks can hinder somebody's progress in life. Be sensitive to the Spirit, because He will give you a signal, by any way He chooses, of the existence of any of them in your life. Then, break them in the Name of Jesus Christ.

God has given you the power to decree a thing and it will be established. Whatever you decree will come to pass; don't doubt. You may need to add fasting to your prayer.

The Power, Presence, and Favour of God bring increase and multiplication in all areas of life: spiritual, mental, physical, and otherwise. God is a Good God!

Many have not realized the power of the tongue. This is why many of them speak the way they do. If people realize the importance, the value, or the power of the tongue, they will be careful and weigh their words before they speak.

Unfortunately, even those who have been taught along this line have offended in words, at one time or the other, and have reaped the negative impacts of their negative words.

The Bible says that life and death are in the power of the tongue (Prov. 18:21). Words, even words spoken by them, have killed many, more than we have realized.

When someone feels some symptoms of sickness or disease, and speaks with his own mouth, saying, "I am sick," that person is accepting the sickness or disease that the devil wants to bring upon him.

The spiritual controls the physical. But someone may ask, "What of when I already have the sickness?" or, "What of when I have the symptoms?"

When you are tempted to steal, have you stolen simply because the thought came to your mind? No, you steal when you take that thing or when you have made up your mind to take it, and you are waiting for an opportunity or when you will not be caught.

In the later case, even when you have not touched that thing, God sees you as a thief; but the simple thought or temptation does not make you a thief.

The same is applicable to sickness, even though you may not see it that way. The devil will throw an arrow of sickness at you; you must reject that sickness, and confess health in the Name of Jesus Christ.

By the Stripes of Jesus Christ we were healed (not that we shall be healed) (1 Pet. 2:24). He carried our sicknesses and diseases (Matt. 8:17). Learn to speak according to the Word of God: this is faith.

But the problem is that many people want sympathizers. Those people that sympathize with you are not God, and if you want sympathy, it will destroy your faith.

In fact, the devil will use the words of those sympathizers to keep your eyes off Jesus Christ, the Author and Finisher of our faith, and keep you looking at the problems.

And if you look at the problems and you look away from your God, you will sink as did Peter. When he saw the wind boisterous, he began to sink (Matt. 14:30), and if not because he cried for help, he might have sunk, got drowned, and died.

Jesus Christ tells us that for every idle word men may speak, they will give account of it in the Day of Judgment. For by your words you will be justified; and by your words, you will be condemned (Matt. 12:36-37).

Your words can justify you, and it can also condemn or mar you. You can receive healing, financial breakthrough, marital well-being, and spiritual success by your words; and those areas of life can be cursed by your words.

Many people speak too much; they speak when it is not necessary. The Word says that sin is not absent in the multitude of words (Prov. 10:19).

Do you want to be perfect in words? Then learn when to speak and when not to speak. We should be quick to hear and slow to speak. Be slow to anger as well (Jas 1:19-20). Man's anger or wrath does not work out the Righteousness of God.

When you want to defend yourself, you will speak too much. I am not saying that you should not defend yourself, but know what to say to defend yourself when necessary, and learn to leave the rest to God.

Even Jesus Christ was criticized; who are you not to be criticized? Even when men may not believe you, God will justify you. Anyway, God is the Final Judge and not any man. Learn to be quiet and leave things to God (1 Thes. 4:11).

The Bible says that those who love the tongue, those who don't mind what they say, will reap the fruit of their work or word (Prov. 18:21). There are spiritual laws, just as they are natural laws.

When you speak against someone who is greater than you or who has authority over you, the person may punish you, and that will be your reward. If you curse someone who is on a higher spiritual level than you, the curse may return to you. When you say good or bad things about yourself, good or bad things will come to you.

The Bible says that the Servant of God must not quarrel (2 Tim. 2:24). I know, from experience, that if you make up your mind not to quarrel, the enemy will bring so much pressure and many temptations to lure you to quarrel, so that you will say bad things and offend God.

But, thanks to God that the devil will not have any place in your life, unless you let him, and he is not going to seize your mouth and speak with it. Hold fast to that which is good without wavering.

Some people say things that they neither understand nor are convinced of. People even affirm things they are not sure of, and this is not good. Reject profane and old wives fables. Do not rebuke an older man and an elder, but exhort him as a father.

Don't be a busybody in other people's affairs, or a gossip, saying things you should not say. Avoid the profane and idle babblings, and contradictions of what is falsely called knowledge. Speak evil of no man.

Do not strive about words to no profit, to the ruin of the hearers; shun profane and idle babblings, for they will increase to more ungodliness. Avoid foolish and ignorant disputes, knowing that they generate strife.

Beware of pride and boasting, shun blasphemy and slander. Speak the truth in love; let each one of you speak truth with his neighbours. Let no corrupt word proceed out of your mouth, but what is good for necessary edification, that it may impart grace to the hearers.

Let all bitterness, wrath, anger, clamour, and evil speaking be put away from you, with all malice. Refuse filthiness, foolish talk, and coarse jesting, which are not fitting, but rather giving of thanks. Remove filthy language out of your mouth.

Avoid foolish disputes, genealogies, contentions, and striving about the Law, for they are unprofitable and useless (Tit. 3:9). Do not allow negative confession out of your mouth, no matter how the situation may look like.

Speak the things which are proper for Sound Doctrine (Tit. 2:1). Speak sound speech which cannot be condemned. If any man does not stumble in word, he is a perfect man, able also to bridle the whole body. Bits in horses' mouths make them obey men, and men can turn their whole body.

Even though ships are very big, and are driven by fierce winds, they are turned by a very small rudder wherever the pilot desires. A forest is set on fire by a little fire. And the tongue is a fire, a world of iniquity.

No man can tame the tongue. It is an unruly evil, full of deadly poison. Don't bless God with your tongue and curse men with it also. Let the Spirit direct your tongue.

Use your tongue for effective prayer. Many will rather go about visiting and gossiping than pray. Preach and teach the Word of God, as God enables you. Don't be ashamed to speak of Jesus Christ.

Declare the Gospel in the public: blow the horn, let all men hear it! The Great Commission or world evangelism is still a priority with God and with us His children. Men, and not angels, are sent to preach the Gospel.

The tongue is so powerful that God created the heavens and the earth by His Words. God calls those things that do not exist by name as though they existed, and when He calls them, they come to existence. You are a god (Psa. 82:6).

Therefore, speak the Way God speaks, and you will see great results that will blow your mind. Maintain the profession or confession of your faith without wavering. If you believe, speak out what you believe, because it is the speaking that brings the physical manifestation!

TAKING IT BY FORCE

The Word of God says that from the days of John the Baptist until now the Kingdom of Heaven suffers violence, and the violent take it by force (Matt. 11:12). Who is the violent; and what does it mean to take something by force? The violent is the aggressive; and to take something by force is to take something aggressively. God expects us to obey Him wholeheartedly and completely. We shall be able to punish every act of disobedience when our own obedience is complete (2 Cor. 10:6).

The Lord Jesus Christ tells us that He hates lukewarmness (Rev. 3:15-16). People will not want to be cold, but they will prefer being lukewarm to being hot. They think they will be called fanatics and zealots if they are hot. They reason that life will not be easy for them if they give themselves wholly to God. God can tell you to do a difficult thing but never an impossible thing.

By the way, was it very easy for Jesus Christ when He left His Throne in Heaven, came into this world and suffered, and finally died on the Cross? The Bible says that Jesus Christ suffered for us and left us an Example that we should follow His Footsteps (1 Pet. 2:21). People think that many will dissociate themselves from them if they become fully committed to the Lord. Well, they dissociated themselves from Jesus Christ; and more people than those who hated Him followed Him.

God say that anything you lose, for His Sake will be returned to you many folds. If people resent you, more people will like you. If people persecute you, more people are for you. Encourage yourself. David encouraged himself in the Lord when the situation looked hopeless for him. What happened later? He pursued, overtook, and recovered all. That will be your portion in Jesus Christ's Name!

God has promised many things to the members of His Kingdom, but those things must be taken violently by force by the violent. God admonishes us to give no place to the devil (Eph. 4:27).

If we keep quiet, the devil will hold some of our blessings. But if we use the power and authority that God has given us, and declare what we want by faith, God is faithful to bring it to pass.

Many are pressing into the Kingdom of God. Don't be left out. Many are receiving God's Provisions for their lives. Join the band-wagon of the faithful and the violent, who will take the Kingdom by force. The devil is no friend of yours; he will do everything to deprive you of God's Blessings. But you must never allow it. Be violent and determined in your prayers; take some time to fast to subdue your flesh and strength your spirit.

Fear not, my brethren, it is the Father's Will to give you the Kingdom. The angels of God are with you. Though satan will put obstructions to stop you, know that greater is the One that is in you. The Lord Jesus Christ is with you and the Holy Spirit of the Living God is in you and upon you. Rise up in this power of yours that the Almighty has given you!

Whether it is spiritual, take it by force! If it is mental or emotional, take it by force! Is it physical? Then take it by force! Whether it is academic, financial, health-wise, or marital, still take it by force! We are a people of power. We are more than conquerors through the Lord Jesus Christ.

And the Word of God says, "Finally, my brethren, be strong in the Lord and in the power of His Might. Put on the whole Armour of God, that you may be able to stand against the wiles of the devil. For we do not wrestle against flesh and blood, but against principalities, against powers, against the rulers of the darkness of this age, against spiritual hosts of wickedness in the heavenly places.

"Therefore take up the whole Armour of God, that you may be able to withstand in the evil day, and having done all, to stand. Stand therefore, having girded your waist with truth, having put on the breastplate of righteousness, and having shod your feet with the preparation of the Gospel of Peace;

"Above all taking the shield of faith with which you will be able to quench all the fiery darts of the wicked one. And take the helmet of salvation, and the Sword of the Spirit, which is the Word of God; praying always with all prayer and supplication in the Spirit, being watchful to this end with all perseverance and supplication for all the Saints" (Eph. 6:10-18).

For though we walk in the flesh, we do not war according to the flesh. For the weapons of our warfare are not carnal but mighty in God for pulling down strongholds, casting down arguments and every high thing that exalts itself against the Knowledge of God, bringing every thought into captivity to the Obedience of Christ (2 Cor. 10:3-5).

Since Christ Jesus has defeated the devil and his host, and has given us authority and power over the devil and his works, we have to exercise the authority and power we received against the activities of the enemy. The Lord is on our side, and we have Divine Protection from the Almighty God. Therefore, let us possess our inheritance in Christ Jesus actively in faith and not allow the devil steal our blessings. Let us also take the souls of men by the preaching of the Gospel, and the demonstration of the Spirit and power.

THE WEAPONS AND ARMOUR OF OUR WARFARE

Weapons are instruments or devices used for attack or defence. Armour is any covering that serves as a protection or defence. The Bible commands us to put on the whole Armour of God, so that we can withstand evil in the evil day (Eph. 6:13). God is a Wise God, and He has made adequate provision to us in our warfare.

The weapons of our warfare are neither carnal nor man-made; rather they are spiritual (2 Cor. 10:4). God does not want us to fight carnally or according to the flesh. We don't fight by slander, criticism, fighting, and quarreling.

Even though I am not saying that police is evil (police is good for the peace and security of life and property in a state or community), if you decide to fight using police and law-court, you may lose. If someone else takes you to the police or the law-court, God will deliver you; but know that if you go that way yourself, the other party may bribe them; and what will you do then?

Our method is spiritual and the spirit-realm controls the physical realm. Things you have settled spiritually will be settled physically. Do you remember how an angel destroyed one hundred and eighty-five thousand Assyrian soldiers in one night for the children of Israel?

Remember how the wall of Jericho fell down, after the children of Israel had encircled it seven days! After God demonstrated His Power in Egypt, the king of Egypt, Pharaoh, had no choice but to let the children of Israel go.

Our enemies are spirit-beings. The person you may regard as your enemy may not be the real enemy. The real enemy, a spirit-being, is just using the person to carry out its purpose. If you deal with the real enemy, the physical servant will bow.

An example of this is seen in the fact that though Herod and Pilate had been enemies before, when the devil wanted to kill Jesus Christ, he removed the enmity between them and they became friends that day (Lk. 23:12).

The Bible says that we wrestle not against flesh and blood, but against powerful wicked spirits (Eph. 6:12). However, God has given us the authority and power to overcome the devil and his host of evil powers. We can destroy the works of the devil, personally and collectively. We can bind the strong man and loot his house, and we can put the angels of God in action by declaring what we want.

In Ephesians 6:14-18, the Bible lists some of our armour, using the example of a Roman soldier. We see the helmet of salvation, the breastplate of righteousness, the belt of Truth, the shoe of the Gospel of Peace, the shield of faith, the Sword of the Spirit (which is the Word of God), and prayer, which binds all of them together.

Do you know that soldiers used spears and bows and arrows in the olden days, apart from swords? In this current age, they use gun and bomb; even bombs are of different kinds.

We have the armour of the Blood of Jesus Christ. The Blood of Jesus Christ is so powerful that it can seal you up without any enemy's penetration. We have the weapon of speaking in tongues. Do you know that the devil gets confused and afraid when we speak in tongues, because he wonders what we may be asking God for? Speaking in tongues puts angels of God to work for you, even without your knowledge. We decree and establish different things, even without our knowledge.

Another weapon of mass destruction is the Name of Jesus Christ. At His Name, every knee should bow (Phil 2:9-11). The Fire of the Holy Ghost is another weapon that destroys massively. No devil can stand this fire, but they must flee or be consumed. The Fire of the Holy Ghost knows nothing that is incombustible; it consumes whatever is to be consumed.

The Anointing of the Holy Spirit is another weapon of mass destruction. The anointing breaks yokes and bondages, and works in different ways. It can work by waving of hands, for instance. The Gifts of the Holy Spirit are for our warfare also. The inspirational or vocal gifts build us up; the revelation gifts give us insight into the enemy's plans; and the power gifts help us destroy the works of satan.

But, we are victorious in Christ Jesus. The Lord has got the victory for us. He has conquered the devil for us and given us the authority and power over the devil, his devils, and their works. God has given us adequate armour and weapons, and our victory is sure when we apply the full Armour of God and the weapons of our warfare.

Never Say That God Said What He Did Not Say!

I GIVE YOU DOMINION

To have dominion over something is to have authority, power, and control over the thing. Man was created to have dominion over the fish of the sea, over the birds of the air, and over every living thing that moves on the earth (Gen. 1:28).

Having overcome the devil, the Lord Jesus Christ came up and said "All authority has been given to Me in heaven and on earth. Go therefore and..." (Matt. 28:18-19). The authority and power that the devil collected from man, when he disobeyed God's Command at the Garden of Eden, is what the Lord got back for us, gave to us, and said, "Go therefore and...."

What Jesus Christ came for was to restore man from his fallen state to the glorious state that God had for man before Adam fell. But God added extra things that Adam didn't have. He will even remove this body and give us a glorious body, so that we may live with Him forever in His Kingdom.

The Word says, "Behold, I give you the authority to trample on serpents and scorpions, and over all the power of the enemy, and nothing shall by any means hurt you" (Lk. 10:19). We have authority and power over the devil, his devils, and their works. We have overcome, because He that is in us is greater than the devil that is in the world.

If God is for us, who can be against us? He Who did not spare His Own Son, but delivered Him up for us all, how shall He not with Him also freely give us all things? We are more than conquerors through Him Who loved us. Neither death nor life, nor angels nor principalities nor powers, nor things present nor things to come, nor height nor depth, nor any other created thing, shall be able to separate us from the Love of God which is in Christ Jesus our Lord.

Whether the devil comes spiritually or physically, God has reinforced and protected us. This is why the Word of God says, "In righteousness you shall be established; you shall be far from oppression, for you shall not fear; and from terror, for it shall not come near you.

"Indeed they shall surely assemble, but not because of Me. Whoever assembles against you shall fall for your sake. Behold, I have created the blacksmith who blows the coals in the fire, who brings forth an instrument for his work; and I have created the spoiler to destroy.

"No weapon formed against you shall prosper, and every tongue which rises against you in judgment you shall condemn. This is the heritage of the Servants of the Lord, and their righteousness is from Me" (Isa. 54:14-17). Did you notice that you have also been protected from gunshots and bombs?

The psalmist wrote: "O Lord, our Lord, how excellent is Your Name in all the earth, Who have set Your Glory above the heavens! Out of the mouth of babes and nursing infants You have ordained strength, because of Your enemies, that You may silence the enemy and the avenger.

"When I consider Your heavens, the work of Your Fingers, the moon and the stars, which You have ordained, what is man that You are mindful of him, or the son of man that You visit him? For You have made him a little lower than the angels, and you have crowned him with glory and honour.

"You have made him to have dominion over the works of Your Hands; You have put all things under his feet, all sheep and oxen – even the beasts of the field, the birds of the air, and the fish of the sea that pass through the paths of the seas. O Lord, our Lord, how excellent is Your Name in all the earth" (Psa. 8).

God is mindful of us because of His Great Love and Mercy. He made us in His Own Image to have dominion over the works of His Hands. When we were born again, we were raised up together with Jesus Christ, and sitted with Him at the Right Hand of God, far above all thrones, powers, or dominions.

THE LIGHT AND SALT OF THE WORLD

Jesus Christ has said that His people, the Christians, are the light of the world. Of course, Jesus Christ is the Light of the world; without Him, the world is in darkness. Without the Lord Jesus Christ, the world is in darkness of sin, sickness, poverty, demonic oppression, and things like them. But when Christ Jesus comes into the life of anyone, He brings light; and that light is forgiveness for sins, holiness, health, healing, success, prosperity, freedom from demons, and such-like things.

We are Christians and representatives of Christ. The Bible says that Believers are to do the same works that Jesus Christ did, even greater works (Jn 14:12). We are the light of the world. A city on a hill cannot be hidden. Men do not light a candle and put it under a basin; they put it where it can give light to people (Matt. 5:14-5).

We are supposed to bring hope to the world. The world is in pains, and the people don't know where they are heading to. They are going to Hell without their knowledge. We must give them the Gospel of Salvation, the Good News of Jesus Christ, which alone can save them if they believe in it.

We must not hide our faith, but declare it at all cost, individually and collectively, to one person and to groups of people. The Gospel, which is the Word of God, is what will give them light and deliver them from the bondage and captivity of the devil.

If we fail to preach the Gospel, God will hold us responsible. The sinner who did not believe and repent will die for his sins; but God will hold the preacher that should have warned him responsible (Ezek. 33:6).

Multitudes of people are trooping into Hell, and we cannot keep quiet; we must preach, in season and out of season (2 Tim. 4:2). We must warn the people of impending punishment and danger. We must not allow our personal commitments to stop us from doing God's Work.

We have been anointed by God, and we must use the authority and power which God has given us to set people free from demonic oppressions and diseases. We have the ability to cast out devils in the Name of Jesus Christ (Mk 16:17). Let's put our authority and power to work, so that the works of the devil in people's lives will be destroyed.

The Bible says that we are the salt of the earth. What will salt be used for if it loses its taste? (Matt. 5:13). Salt adds good taste to our food. Therefore, the presence of Christians on this earth should bring happiness to the people of the world. We should do good deeds to all, especially those of the Household of Faith (Gal. 6:10).

Salt is also used as a preservative for preserving things. But for the presence of Christians in this world and God's Programme for the earth, God would have destroyed this world. But a time will come when He will burn this earth with fire; by then, the Christians will have been gone.

The Bible says that God's Name is blasphemed among sinners and unbelievers because of God's people. When we don't represent God well, in character, life, blessing, and power, the unbelievers take the Name of the Lord for granted, and they despise Him. But instead of bringing shame to the Name of our God, we should bring praise and glory to His Glorious Name.

Our lives will have something to do with how readily the people will submit to the Gospel of our Lord Jesus Christ. We should not be hypocrites and live the opposite of what we profess. We have the ability to stand as priests and mediators between God and men; and we can stand in the gap, so that God will not pour out His Wrath on people.

We can also prevent the devil from carrying out his plans on people. We are the light of the world through Jesus Christ our Lord. And we are the salt of the world by the Holy Spirit of the Living God.

THEY THAT KNOW THEIR GOD

The Bible says that they that know their God shall be strong and do exploits (Dan. 11:32). That is wonderful; isn't it? They that know their God shall be strong. Why? Because their God is the Strongest of all.

They that know their God shall do exploits. Why will they do exploits? Because their Lord Jesus Christ is the Maker of all things. They will do exploits, because the Spirit of God Who dwells in them, and is upon them, brought everything into existence.

Why will this happen? This will happen, because their Father is the Beginning and the End of all things, the Almighty Jehovah is His Name. We are on the winning side. If you are not on God's Side, you are on the losing side: change your side now!

For you to know God, God will have to know you first. If you are not born again, God doesn't know you as His child. If you are walking in disobedience to the Word of God, if you are living in the pleasures of sin, God doesn't know you.

The Bible says that in the Day of Judgment, many will tell the Lord that they did this or that in His Name; and He will tell them that He never knew them (Matt. 7:21-23). What a disappointment!

Why will you be working in the Vineyard of the Lord, when the Lord doesn't know you? Some are in the ministry today, when God did not call them. Some are holding one position or the other in churches today; and they are not even born again.

Some are working in churches today with occult and devilish powers. The worst part is that many of them started well; but because of sin, pride, women, or money, they lost the Anointing of God, and sought for negative powers to keep going, instead of repenting.

Well, the Word has declared that we will be strong and do exploits. We are not those who call on the Lord Jesus Christ saying, "Lord, Lord," but don't do what He says (Lk. 6:46). We are those who believe in the Lord Jesus Christ and obey His Word.

What are the exploits that we will do? The Lord tells us in His Word that the works that He did, we will do. We are to do even greater works than He did. Jesus Christ preached, taught, cast out demons, and performed signs, wonders, and miracles.

God anointed Jesus Christ of Nazareth with the Holy Spirit and with power, Who went about doing good and healing all who were oppressed by the devil, for God was with Him (Acts 10:38). Going through the Books of Matthew, Mark, Luke, and John, we see that the exploits that Jesus Christ did were great.

When the Lord was about to leave this world, He told the apostles that there are signs that will follow the generation of those who believe in Him. In His Words, "Go into all the world and preach the Gospel to every creature. He who believes and is baptized will be saved; but he who does not believe will be condemned.

"And these signs will follow those who believe: In My Name they will cast out demons; they will speak with new tongues; they will take up serpents; and if they drink anything deadly, it will by no means hurt them; they will lay hands on the sick, and they will recover."

So then, after the Lord had spoken to them, He was received up into Heaven, and sat done at the Right Hand of God. And they went out and preached everywhere, the Lord working with them and confirming the Word though the accompanying signs (Mk 16:15-20).

But you need to be anointed in order to do the exploits that God expects from you. We saw that Jesus Christ was anointed with the Holy Spirit and with power. The Word tells us that we receive power when the Holy Spirit comes upon us. That power enables us to do exploits. The exploits we do confirm us as witnesses (proof-providers) to the Lord (Acts 1:8).

THE POWER AND AUTHORITY OF THE BELIEVER

After being born again, you need to be baptized in the Holy Spirit. Be filled with the Holy Ghost, so that you can do the works that the Lord says we will do. You need to follow the Leading of the Holy Spirit, so that He will anoint you with greater levels of the anointing.

There are different levels of the anointing; and it is the anointing that breaks the yokes and bondages of the devil. Prophet Ezekiel was shown this reality when he had the vision of which he wrote: "And the man went out to the east with the line in his hand, he measured one thousand cubits, and he brought me through the waters; the waters came up to my ankles.

"Again he measured one thousand and brought me through the waters; the water came up to my knees. Again he measured one thousand and brought me through; the water came up to my waist.

"Again he measured one thousand, and it was a river that I could not cross; for the water was too deep, water in which one must swim, a river that could not be crossed. He said to me, 'Son of man, have you seen this?'" (Ezek. 47:3-6).

What do you think would have happened to the prophet if he had not obeyed and followed the angel? Certainly, he would have not experienced the different levels of the Lord's Provision. He would have been at the bank of the river, observing but not experiencing the different depths of the anointing.

Even today, many just stay outside the anointing, observing it in the lives of others. They are not ready to pay the price of obedience to the Word and the Spirit of God. They don't want to deny their flesh of anything.

Brother, if you must experience the overwhelming anointing (the river that could not be crossed without swimming), you must learn to pray. To experience higher levels of the anointing consistently, you must learn to fast. And you must know the Word of God, for faith comes by the Word of God.

God likes faith; and without faith, it is impossible to please God. Shadrach, Meshach, and Abed-Nego believed God so much that they declared that their Lord could deliver them from the fiery furnace of King Nebuchadnezzar. Because they trusted the Lord, the Lord God Almighty showed Himself strong, and delivered them from the heat and effect of the fiery furnace (Dan. 3).

They that know their God shall be strong and do exploits. No wonder Prophet Moses performed so many signs and wonders in the land of Egypt that the Egyptians had to beg the Israelites to go; because they became a terror to them. Moses did those things, because he encountered God and knew Him.

Sampson – that one-man army – killed one thousand Philistines with a jawbone. He killed a lion with bare hands. He pulled down a mighty building with his hands. He did those things by the anointing that empowered him.

King David killed a lion and a bear, because the anointing empowered and emboldened him. He killed the giant – Goliath of Gath – and cut off his head, after the man had frightened the armies of Israel for forty days. A single stone, empowered by the Holy Ghost, struck the man in his forehead and sunk inside his head, so that the giant fell down flat.

Prophet Elijah stunned Israel when he prayed and God brought down visible fire from Heaven to consume his prepared sacrifice. The man prayed, and it did not rain in the land for three and half years; when he prayed afterwards, rain came back.

Prophet Daniel knew his God; and when he prayed, God revealed the dream that Nebuchadnezzar had to him. This is what all the magicians and astrologers of Babylon could not do. But there is no impossibility with our God. Our God reveals secrets.

The early apostles and Disciples did so many exploits, in signs, wonders, and miracles, that it staggered the mentality of those that opposed them. Even though they used soldiers and officers against them, yet they multiplied greatly in Jerusalem, that many priests became obedient to the Faith.

Shall we talk of the fiery Apostle Paul? Apostle Paul desired to fulfil God's Purpose for his life. He despised shame, and did not count his life dear to him, that he might gain Christ. He wanted to know Christ, the power of His Resurrection, and the fellowship of His Suffering, if by any means, he could attain to the Resurrection of the dead.

Apostle Paul preached and taught the Gospel – the Word of God about man's salvation and God's Provisions for man. He brought the dead back to life; his handkerchiefs and aprons could heal the sick and drive out demons. Even when he was attacked by a viper, he sustained no ailment or harm. Our God is great!

THE NAME OF JESUS CHRIST

There is a Name that is above all other names; and that Name is the Name of Jesus Christ, at Whose Name, every knee should bow, of things in heaven, of things on earth, and of things under the earth (Phil. 2:9-10). The Name of Jesus Christ was given to Him because He humbled Himself and became obedient to God, even unto death.

The Name of Jesus Christ in the mouth of the Believer is an atomic bomb in the spiritual realm. The Name causes explosion, and precipitates the Presence of Jesus Christ to where it is mentioned and required. For whoever calls on the Name of the Lord Jesus Christ shall be saved (Rom. 10:13).

There is great power and authority vested on the Name of Jesus Christ. It is by His Name that we receive answers to our prayers from God. It is by this Name that we destroy the works of Satan. By that Name, we declare what we want done; and it is done.

The all-powerful Name of Jesus Christ even works for unbelievers. When an unbeliever in distress calls on the Name of Jesus Christ, the Lord can save him. However, there is a difference between being delivered, because you called on the Lord, and making Him your Lord and Saviour, which alone can save you and take you to Heaven.

You might be in sin now; repent and call on Jesus Christ, and He will help you. Whether the problem you have found yourself in is spiritual, mental or physical, call on His Name, and He will deliver and liberate you. The Eyes of the Lord move to and fro the earth, to see whom He might show mercy to and make Himself strong among men (2 Chron. 16:9).

Jesus Christ got the Name by inheritance, by obedience, and by conquest. When He was born, God commanded the angels to worship Him. He obeyed God even when it involved His Life. The Lord Jesus Christ, the King of kings and Lord of lords, conquered the devil in the grave and rose up on the third day, taking with Him all authority and power (Matt. 28:18).

There is so much great ability in the Name of Jesus Christ, much more than we have realized. The Name of Jesus Christ can remove mountains; it can separate seas; it can change the course of nature. There is life in the Name of Jesus Christ. On this Name we stand!

When Jesus Christ was laid in the tomb, soldiers were hired to guard the tomb to prevent Him from rising, and from His Body being carried away by His Disciples. How many devils and forces have come against you to prevent you from having what God ordained for you? Focus on the Power of your God, and not on those small devils.

But did the plan of the enemies against our Lord succeed? Behold, there was great earthquake; for an angel of the Lord descended from Heaven, and came and rolled back the stone from the door of the tomb, and sat on it. His countenance was like lighting and his clothing as white as snow.

And the guards shook for fear of him, and became like dead men (Matt. 28:2-4). A single angel from the Presence of the Lord God Almighty so terrified the guards that they had no potion but to bow out. If you keep looking at Jesus Christ and believing the Word of God, no demon from Hell, no matter how deadly it is, can stop you!

When an angel was sent to deliver message to Prophet Daniel, the angelic messenger was withstood twenty-one days by the prince of Persia. On the twenty-first day, an angelic intervention of a warring angel – Michael – was ordered by God. And this gave the obstructed angel access to Daniel to deliver his message. We need not fear any devil of any sort.

We have been given the great Name of Jesus Christ. And in this mighty Name of His, we do exploits for our God. In His Name, we cast out demons; in His Name, we speak with new tongues; in His Name, we take up serpents; in His Name, if we drink anything deadly, it will by no means hurt us; and in His Name, when we lay hands on the sick, they will recover (Mk 16:17-18).

DECREE A THING TO BE ESTABLISHED

There is power in your saying or decreeing something. Speaking out your mind, will, and thought is powerful. By your speech, we can know what is in your mind. By your word, you also set in motion spiritual force(s) to work for or against you. This is why the Bible says that life and death are in the power of the tongue (of words).

Jesus Christ, wanting to get fruits from a fig tree, found none on it. In response, He said to it, "Let no one eat fruit from you ever again." And His Disciples heard what He said. As they passed by the tree the following morning, they saw the fig tree dried from the roots. When this surprised the Disciples, He spoke to them, saying, "Have faith in God.

"For assuredly, I say to you, whoever says to this mountain, 'Be removed and be cast into the sea,' and does not doubt in his heart, but believes that those things he says will be done, he will have whatever he says. Therefore I say to you, whatever things you ask when you pray, believe that you receive them, and you will have them" (Mk 11:22-24).

In effect, He says that if you believe and doubt not, you can decree what you want, and you shall have it; the thing will be done according to your decree. And notice that the believing comes before the receiving. Also, notice that Jesus Christ didn't tell the tree to dry up, but that no one would eat from it again. For no one to eat from it again, it had to dry up; and the drying up happened fast. For God to establish what you say or decree, He may do other things you didn't say directly; but they are needed for you to have your desire.

This is one reason why you have to be careful of what comes out of your mouth. Speaking negative words can empower devils to work against you, and you will have what you never consciously bargained for. Be cautious while speaking about yourself or to others, so that the devil will not gain advantage over you; for we are not ignorant of his devices. Give no place to the devil!

According to Matthew's report, He said, "Let no fruit grow on you ever again." When the Disciples marveled, He said, "Assuredly, I say to you, if you have faith and do not doubt, you will not only do what was done to the fig tree, but also if you say to this mountain, 'Be removed and be cast into the sea,' it will be done. And whatever things you ask in prayer, believing, you will receive" (Matt. 21:21-22).

Notice that He says that you will receive whatever you ask in prayer. It is whatever you ask, as far as it is not contrary to the Word of God. But the devil himself will want to give you whatever you say that is contrary to God's Will. The Word says that we should decree a thing to be established. In the beginning, after God had made the heavens and the earth, the earth was void and without form, and darkness covered the surface of the deep (waters). Then God decreed that many things would be, and they came to be. And we were made in God's Image and Likeness.

Therefore, we are to decree, declare, and speak out what we want to be, according to the Will of God, so that we can have what we want to be. As the Bible puts it, "You will also declare a thing, and it will be established for you, so light will shine on your ways" (Job 22:28). What you say or declare will be done for you by God; and when God does them, light will shine on you (you will rejoice for receiving your desire).

Having what you want from God by decreeing it, is God's Way and Mind concerning His children. To this end, He says, "Ask Me of things to come concerning My sons; and concerning the works of My Hand, you command Me" (Isa. 45:11). This is applicable individually or collectively.

This is why our Lord Jesus Christ says "Assuredly, I say to you, whatever you bind on earth will be bound in Heaven, and whatever you loose on earth will be loosed in Heaven. Again I say to you that if two of you agree on earth concerning anything that they ask, it will be done for them by My Father in Heaven. For where two or three are gathered together in My Name, I am there in the midst of them" (Matt. 18:18-20).

This declaring or decreeing of things to be, has to do with praying, asking, speaking out, and confession. And we have been given the all-powerful Name of Jesus Christ to use in our praying, asking, decreeing, and declaring. God does what we ask for in the Name of Jesus Christ. When we ask in His Name, we stand in His Place; and we are His Body through which He works on earth.

The Word of God says, "And whatever you ask in My Name, that I will do, that the Father may be glorified in the Son. If you ask anything in My Name, I will do it" (Jn 14:13-14). The Name of Jesus Christ has been given to us to use in praying to God, speaking out what ought to be, casting out demons and destroying their works, healing the sick, taking up serpents without being harmed, taking deadly things without being hurt, etc.

Confession brings possession. What you confess is what you will have, just as you reap what you sow (Gal. 6:7). Life and death, riches and poverty, holiness and sinfulness, etc are in the power of the tongue; they depend on what you say (Prov. 18:21). The Bible says that salvation is in your mouth (Rom. 10:10). The Word of Faith, the Word that delivers and saves you, is in your mouth.

The Lord Jesus Christ says that if you speak to a mountain with your mouth without doubt in your heart, the mountain will obey you. The Lord says that you will have what you say (Mk 11:23). Therefore, speak positive things into your life and your environment, and they will receive positive things. Your world can be changed for good by your mouth.

Some people say they are suffering, and they continue to suffer. Others say that it is just this their sickness, and they continue to have that sickness. When you confess that you are like a fish in a river that cannot leave water, you will continue to sin. The same thing applies to poverty; if you confess poverty, it will follow you. Be careful of what you say with your mouth.

Don't say that your wife is a fool, for you will not enjoy it if she becomes one. Don't say that your husband doesn't love you, for that may open a door for the devil to come in. Don't say that your children are stubborn, because they shouldn't be.

If your children behave stubbornly and you want to report it, you can say something like, "Johnson behaved stubbornly"; or, if it has been a continual behaviour, you can say, "Johnson had been behaving stubbornly." Pray over them, and break the power of the devil over their lives, because the devil is working through them to frustrate you.

Beware of self-inflicted curses! Don't curse yourself with your own mouth. Make up your mind to speak only positive things, no matter the circumstance or condition. God will reward your positive words. Put your angels to work on your behalf for good by speaking positive and Biblical words.

God told Moses to send men to spy out the land of Canaan. Moses sent twelve men from twelve tribes of Israel. After they had spied out the land, they came back. When they came back, they said, "We went to the land where you sent us. It truly flows with milk and honey, and this is its fruit. Nevertheless the people who dwell there are strong;

"The cities are fortified and very large; moreover we saw the descendants of Anak there." Then Caleb quieted the people before Moses, and said, "Let us go up at once and take possession, for we are well able to overcome it." But the men who had gone up with him said, "We are not able to go up against the people, for they are stronger than we" (Num. 13).

Think of this! God performed great signs and miracles in the land of Egypt on their behalf, and also divided the Red Sea for them to pass on a dry land. Yet they were so full of unbelief that they gave such disheartening and doubtful report.

They said, "We are not able to go up against the people, for they are stronger than we." Who told them that the Canaanites were stronger than they? They were looking at themselves, and forgot their Great and Almighty God. But have many of us not done the same thing in many areas of our lives?

God spoke to Moses, saying, "Send men to spy out the land of Canaan, which I am giving to the children of Israel…." If God, after performing all the great signs and wonders in their sight, said again, "I am giving you the land of Canaan," why didn't they believe God? And why don't many Christians believe God and His Word these days?

In order to dishearten the people and contradict Caleb's words, they said, "The land through which we have gone as spies is a land that devours its inhabitants, and all the people whom we saw in it are men of great stature. There we saw the giants (the descendants of Anak came from the giants); and we were like grasshoppers in our own sight, and so we were in their sight." I wonder why they decided to give such a report!

So all the congregation of Israel lifted up their voices and cried, and the people wept that night. And all the children of Israel complained against Moses and Aaron, and the whole congregation said to them, "If only we had died in the land of Egypt! Or if only we had died in this wilderness! Why has the Lord brought us to this land to fall by the sword, that our wives and children should become victims? Would it not be better for us to return to Egypt?"

So they said to one another, "Let us select a leader and return to Egypt." Can you imagine this? God gave them a leader, Moses, to fulfil His Word, and they themselves wanted to select another leader out of their will, reasoning, and flesh to return to Egypt, thereby achieving their anti-God and selfish desires. But unknown to them (maybe), God was hearing what they were saying. They thought that they were speaking to Moses and Aaron, but they were speaking against God.

Be careful, because God sees your thoughts and reasoning, and He hears your words. Be careful of idle and careless words. Don't joke with holy things! Revere and fear the Almighty God in your thoughts, words, and actions. Consider that the Word of God cannot fail. Whether it is what He said in the Bible, or what He told you specifically, it cannot fail. He is both faithful and able!

Moses and Aaron fell on their faces before all the assembly of the congregation of the children of Israel. But Joshua the son of Nun and Caleb the son of Jephunneh, who were among those who had spied out the land, tore their clothes, and they spoke to all the congregation of the children of Israel, saying: "The land we passed through to spy out is an exceedingly good land.

"If the Lord delights in us, then He will bring us into this land and give it to us, 'a land which flows with milk and honey.' Only do not rebel against the Lord, nor fear the people of the land, for they are our bread, their protection has departed from them, and the Lord is with us. Do not fear them." Joshua and Caleb knew and trusted the Lord. Notice that the protection (army or spiritual) of their enemies were departed from them.

The congregation of the children of Israel wanted to stone Joshua and Caleb who wanted to strengthen their faith in God. God was so angry with them that He wanted to wipe them out. God said He would strike them with the pestilence and disinherit them, and He would make of Moses a nation greater and mightier than them. But Moses pleaded for them before God.

God heard the prayer of Moses and said, "I have pardoned, according to your word." And God said that those of them who saw His Glory and the signs which He did in Egypt and in the wilderness, and had put Him to test, not heeded His Voice, and rejected Him, will not see the land of Canaan.

He said "But My Servant Caleb, because he has a different spirit in him and has followed Me fully, I will bring into the land where he went, and his descendants shall inherit it." God told Moses to lead them into the wilderness again, to turn with them by the way of the Red sea.

He said, "Say to them, 'As I live,' says the Lord, just as you have spoken in My Hearing, so I will do to you." They had said that they preferred to die either in the wilderness or in Egypt. God chose their dying in the wilderness. God said that apart from Joshua and Caleb, any of them from twenty years and above will die in the wilderness (Num. 14).

Though He forgave them by relenting from wiping them out, He made an alternative plan to destroy the matured among them through a period of forty more years. When they knew what God had said, they decided to go up to the promised land, admitting that they had sinned. Moses told them not to go up, for they would be defeated before their enemies, because the Lord would not be with them. They went, and they were attacked and driven by the Amalekites and the Canaanites.

We may blame the children of Israel; but how many of us have done the same things, because of unbelief, doubt, sin, compromise, and disobedience? God is no respecter of persons. Even though He bears with us in longsuffering, we must not take His Patience and Longsuffering in vain.

KINGS AND PRIESTS

We, the people of God, are kings and priests. The Bible says, "For if by one man's offence death reigned through the one, much more those who receive abundance of grace, and of the gift of righteousness will reign in life through the One, Jesus Christ" (Rom. 5:17). We have been made kings by our Lord and Master; and we will reign through Him also.

John wrote: "John, to the seven churches which are in Asia: Grace to you and peace from Him Who is and Who was and Who is to come, and from the Seven Spirits Who are before His Throne,

"And from Jesus Christ, the Faithful Witness, the Firstborn from the dead, and the Ruler over the kings of the earth. To Him Who loved us and washed us from our sins in His Own Blood,

"And has made us kings and priests to His God and Father, to Him be glory and dominion forever and ever. Amen" (Rev. 1:4-6). Having washed us from our sins, He made us kings and priests.

This is confirmed again in the account of the opening of the scroll that is sealed with seven seals. The Bible says, "And I saw in the Right Hand of Him Who sat on the Throne a scroll written inside and on the back, sealed with seven seals.

"Then I saw a strong angel proclaiming with a loud voice, 'Who is worthy to open the scroll and to loose its seals?' And no one in Heaven or on the earth or under the earth was able to open the scroll, or to look at it.

"So I wept much, because no one was found worthy to open and read the scroll, or to look at it. But one of the elders said to me, 'Do not weep. Behold, the Lion of the tribe of Judah, the Root of David, has prevailed to open the scroll and to loose its seven seals.'

"And I looked, and behold, in the midst of the Throne and of the four living creatures, and in the midst of the elders, stood a Lamb as though it had been slain, having seven horns and seven eyes, which are the Seven Spirits of God sent out into all the earth.

"Then He came and took the scroll out of the Right Hand of Him Who sat on the Throne. Now when He had taken the scroll, the four living creatures and the twenty-four elders fell down before the Lamb, each having a harp, and golden bowls full of incense, which are the prayers of the Saints.

"And they sang a new song, saying: 'You are worthy to take the scroll, and to open its seals; for You were slain, and have redeemed us to God by Your Blood out of every tribe and tongue and people and nation,

"And have made us kings and priests to our God; and we shall reign on the earth" (Rev. 5:1-10). Having been redeemed by the Blood of Jesus Christ, our Lord and Christ made us kings and priests to our God; and we shall reign on earth.

Speaking of our priesthood, the Word of God says, "You also, as living stones, are being built up a spiritual house, a holy priesthood, to offer up spiritual sacrifices acceptable to God through Jesus Christ.

"But you are a chosen generation, a royal priesthood, a holy nation, His Own special people, that you may proclaim the Praises of Him Who called you out of darkness into His Marvelous Light" (1 Pet. 2:5,9). We are built up a spiritual house, a holy priesthood, to offer up spiritual sacrifices acceptable to God through Jesus Christ.

We are a kingdom of kings and priests under the Great King and Father, Who rules with His Son, upholding everything by the Power of His Holy Spirit and His Word. Jesus Christ, our Great High Priest, is the Kings of kings and Lord of lords.

The Father has highly exalted Him and given Him the Name which is above all other names. He has also put all thrones, dominions, powers, and principalities under the Foot of His Son.

As kings and priests, what are our functions? As priests, we are to offer up spiritual sacrifices to God and the Father. The Bible says, "Therefore, laying aside all malice, all deceit, hypocrisy, envy, and all evil speaking,

"As newborn babes, desire the pure milk of the Word, that you may grow thereby, if indeed you have tasted that the Lord is gracious.

"Coming to Him as to a Living Stone, rejected indeed by men, but chosen by God and precious, you also, as living stones, are being built up a spiritual house, a holy priesthood, to offer up spiritual sacrifices acceptable to God through Jesus Christ.

"Therefore it is also contained in the Scripture, 'Behold, I lay in Zion a Chief Cornerstone, elect, precious, and he who believes on Him will by no means be put to shame.'

"Therefore, to you who believe, He is precious; but to those who are disobedient, 'The Stone which the builders rejected has become the Chief Cornerstone,' and 'a Stone of stumbling and a Rock of offence.' They stumble, being disobedient to the Word, to which they also were appointed.

"But you are a chosen generation, a royal priesthood, a holy nation, His Own special people, that you may proclaim the Praises of Him Who called you out of darkness into His Marvelous Light; who once were not a people but are now the people of God, who had not obtained mercy but now have obtained mercy.

"Beloved, I beg you as sojourners and pilgrims, abstain from fleshly lusts which war against the soul, having your conduct honourable among the Gentiles, that when they speak against you as evildoers, they may, by your good works which they observe, glorify God in the day of visitation.

"Therefore submit yourselves to every ordinance of man for the Lord's Sake, whether to the king as supreme, or to governors, as to those who are sent by him for the punishment of evildoers and for the praise of those who do good.

"For this is the Will of God, that by doing good you may put to silence the ignorance of foolish men – as free, yet not using liberty as a cloak for vice, but as Bondservants of God. Honour all people. Love the Brotherhood. Fear God. Honour the king (1 Pet. 2:1-17).

"Therefore by Him let us continually offer the sacrifice of praise to God, that is, the fruit of our lips, giving thanks to His Name" (Heb. 13:15). We are to proclaim the Praises of God, Who has called us and brought us into His Kingdom.

What are the functions of priests? Priests offer sacrifices on the altar to God. And we have seen that we are to offer sacrifices of praises – the fruits of our lips – to God.

Furthermore, priests make intercession for the people. We are to pray for people. We are to pray for both Believers and unbelievers.

The Word of God says, "Praying always with all prayer and supplication in the Spirit, being watchful to this end with all perseverance and supplication for all the Saints (Eph. 6:18). Here, we are told to persevere and make supplication for all the Saints – the people of God.

Writing to Timothy, Apostle Paul said, "Therefore I exhort first of all that supplications, prayers, intercessions, and giving of thanks be made for all men, for kings and all who are in authority, that we may lead a quiet and peaceable life in all Godliness and reverence.

"For this is good and acceptable in the Sight of God our Saviour, Who desires all men to be saved and to come to the knowledge of the Truth. For there is One God and One Mediator between God and men, the Man Christ Jesus, Who gave Himself a Ransom for all, to be testified in due time" (1 Tim. 2:1-6).

Jesus Christ gave Himself a Ransom for all men. And it is not the Will of God that any soul should perish, but that all men should come to repentance and accept the Son of His Love – the Lord Jesus Christ – into their lives as their personal Lord and Saviour.

The Word of God says, "Then Jesus went about all the cities and villages, teaching in their synagogues, preaching the Gospel of the Kingdom, and healing every sickness and every disease among the people.

"But when He saw the multitudes, He was moved with compassion for them, because they were weary and scattered, like sheep having no shepherd.

"Then He said to His Disciples, 'The harvest truly is plentiful, but the labourers are few. Therefore pray the Lord of the harvest to send out labourers into His Harvest'" (Matt. 9:35-38).

It is part of your ministry, in pursuit of the salvation of men, to pray to God to send labourers, workers, preachers, evangelists, and ministers into the field. Workers and labourers are needed, both in the Church of Jesus Christ and outside the Church.

Priests stand in the gap between God and men. This will help prevent the Wrath of God from falling on them, as Moses' intercession and prayer for the Israelites prevented God from wiping them out from the face of the earth, when they provoked Him to anger, as He had intended to do.

The Bible says, "'The people of the land have used oppressions, committed robbery, and mistreated the poor and needy; and they wrongfully oppress the stranger. So I sought for a man among them who would make a wall, and stand in the gap before Me on behalf of the land, that I should not destroy it; but I found no one.

'Therefore I have poured out My Indignation on them; I have consumed them with the fire of My Wrath; and I have recompensed their deeds on their own heads,' says the Lord God (Ezek. 22:29-31).

"I have set watchmen on your walls, O Jerusalem; they shall never hold their peace day or night. You who make mention of the Lord, do not keep silent, and give Him no rest till He establishes and till He makes Jerusalem a praise in the earth" (Isa. 62:6-7).

As kings, we have been given authority to trample on serpents and scorpions, and over all the power of the enemy; and nothing shall by any means hurt/harm us (Lk. 10:9).

Where the word of the king is, there is power. When we give commands in the Name of Jesus Christ, the Power of God and the host of Heaven back our commands. The Word of God says, "Have faith in God.

"For assuredly, I say to you, whoever says to this mountain, 'Be removed and be cast into the sea,' and does not doubt in his heart, but believes that those things he says will be done, he will have whatever he says.

"Therefore I say to you, whatever things you ask when you pray, believe that you receive them, and you will have them (Mk 11-22-24).

"And you He made alive, who were dead in trespasses and sins, in which you once walked according to the course of this world, according to the prince of the power of the air, the spirit who now works in the sons of disobedience,

"Among whom also we all once conducted ourselves in the lusts of our flesh, fulfilling the desires of the flesh and of the mind, and were by nature children of wrath, just as the others.

"But God, Who is rich in mercy, because of His Great Love with which He loved us, even when we were dead in trespasses, made us alive together with Christ (by grace you have been saved),

"And raised us up together, and made us sit together in the Heavenly places in Christ Jesus, that in the ages to come He might show the exceeding riches of His Grace in His Kindness towards us in Christ Jesus" (Eph. 2:1-7).

Kings rule effectively by wisdom, knowledge, and understanding. Therefore, as kings, we have to seek after wisdom, knowledge, and understanding, in order to do what we are supposed to do well.

The Bible says, "Does not wisdom cry out, and understanding lift up her voice? She takes her stand on the top of the high hill, beside the way, where the paths meet.

"She cries out by the gates, at the entry of the city, at the entrance of the doors: 'To you, O men, I call, and my voice is to the sons of men. O you simple ones, understand prudence, and you fools, be of an understanding heart.

'Listen, for I will speak of excellent things, and from the opening of my lips will come right things; for my mouth will speak Truth; wickedness is an abomination to my lips. All the words of my mouth are with righteousness; nothing crooked or perverse is in them.

'They are all plain to him who understands, and right to those who find knowledge. Receive my instruction, and not silver, and knowledge rather than choice gold; for wisdom is better than rubies, and all the things one may desire cannot be compared with her.

'I, wisdom, dwell with prudence, and find out knowledge and discretion. The Fear of the Lord is to hate evil; pride and arrogance and the evil way and the perverse mouth I hate.

'Counsel is mine, and sound wisdom; I am understanding, I have strength. By me kings reign, and rulers decree justice. By me princes rule, and nobles, all the judges of the earth.

'I love those who love me, and those who seek me diligently will find me. Riches and honour are with me, enduring riches and righteousness. My fruit is better than gold, yes, than fine gold, and my revenue than choice silver.

'I traverse the way of righteousness, in the midst of the paths of justice, that I may cause those who love me to inherit wealth, that I may fill their treasuries.

'The Lord possessed me at the beginning of His Way, before His Works of old. I have been established from everlasting, from the beginning, before there was ever an earth.

'When there were no depths I was brought forth, when there were no fountains abounding with water. Before the mountains were settled, before the hills, I was brought forth; while as yet He had not made the earth or the fields, or the primal dust of the world.

'When He prepared the heavens, I was there, when He drew a circle on the face of the deep, when He established the clouds above, when He strengthened the fountains of the deep,

'When He assigned to the sea its limit, so that the waters would not transgress His Command, when He marked out the foundations of the earth, then I was beside Him as a master craftsman; and I was daily His Delight, rejoicing always before Him, rejoicing in His inhabited world, and my delight was with the sons of men.

'Now therefore, listen to me, my children, for blessed are those who keep my ways. Hear instruction and be wise, and do not disdain it. Blessed is the man who listens to me, watching daily at my gates, waiting at the posts of my doors.

'For whoever finds me finds life, and obtains favour from the Lord; but he who sins against me wrongs his own soul; all those who hate me love death'" (Prov. 8:1-36).

Just as kings want to extend their kingdoms we should devote our wisdom and energy to expanding the Kingdom of God. It may be stressful and difficult; but God will reward us abundantly!

FULL OF THE WORD AND THE SPIRIT OF GOD

As a child of God, you should be full of the Word of God. There are many advantages to being full of the Word of God; but many Believers don't spend enough time to either read or study the Word of God.

The Word of God is God. The Word of God reveals the Mind of God to us. God works through and by His Word. The Word and the Spirit agree (1 Jn 5:8), for the holy men of God who wrote the Scriptures were moved by the Holy Ghost (2 Pet. 1:21).

All Scripture is God-breathed, is inspired by God; and is profitable for Doctrine, for reproof, for correction, for instruction in righteousness, that the man of God may be complete, thoroughly equipped for every good work (2 Tim. 3:16-17).

We are to fight the good fight of faith. The fight of faith is to contend earnestly for the faith once delivered to the Saints; the fight of faith is to strive to see that the Word and Will of God comes to pass in our lives, and in the lives of others, for faith comes by hearing the Word of God.

We must also grow from faith to faith. The Bible commands us to let the Word of God, of Christ, dwell in us richly in all wisdom (Col. 3:16). That means that we are to get soaked in the Word of God. When a sponge is soaked in water and brought out, any side of the sponge you touch, water sticks on you.

The same thing applies when we are full of the Word of God. Whatever trial, temptation, or situation we may find ourselves in, we have solution in the Word available to us, and we will overcome and succeed.

Search the Scriptures as you would search for hidden treasures, for they are costlier than gold, silver, and diamond. The place we read says that the Word of God should dwell in us, not just in any measure, but in a rich measure, in a full measure, preferably. Also, in the rich measure, it must be in all wisdom.

This is why the Bible speaks of rightly dividing the Word of Truth (2 Tim. 2:15). To divide the Word of God aright is to apply it wisely and to interpret it the right way. This is why you have to compare Scripture with Scripture (you have to compare spiritual things with spiritual things) (1 Cor. 2:13).

You must study the Word of God to show yourself approved to God, a workman who does not need to be ashamed, rightly dividing the Word of Truth. Be diligent to present yourself approved to God (2 Tim. 2:15).

It is the Word of God in your heart and mouth that will help you succeed in life and Godliness, and overcome temptations. Make every effort to hear, read, study, meditate on, believe, and confess the Word of God.

When the devil tempted Jesus Christ, he used the Scripture, by quoting it to Jesus Christ. But he misapplied the Word, and Jesus Christ, being full of the Word of God, quoted the appropriate Word, and the devil was put to shame.

If you don't know the Word of God, the devil will deceive you, misapplying it to you; and you will fall into temptations. The devil has no mercy. If you don't know and apply your rights and authority in Christ, he will keep you miserable.

The Word of God is spirit and life. It will quicken your human spirit and wage your spiritual wars; it will also give life to your body and soul. The Word that you hear is spirit and it is life (Jn 6:63).

The Word of God cleanses you: spirit, soul, and body (Jn 15:3). It will build your spirit and get it to be strong spiritually. The Word is the food of the human spirit that gets him grow and matured. Desire the Word of God (1 Pet. 2:2).

The Word of God is fire that burns all things that are ungodly and satanic; it is the hammer that breaks to pieces all obstacles and hindrances (Jer. 23:29). It is the water that purifies you daily. It is truth, and God's Truth sanctifies you to holiness, blamelessness, and spotlessness (Jn 17:17).

Go for the Word of God, because all things that you ever need in your life are in it. The source of God's Blessings is the Word and the Manifester of the Blessings of God is the Holy Spirit.

When the deacons were to be appointed, the apostles declared that anyone to be appointed must be full of wisdom, and the Wisdom of God is in His Word. That was why Stephen, who was full of faith and the Holy Spirit, was selected (Acts 6:5).

To be full of faith is to be full of the Word, because faith comes by hearing and studying the Word of God (Rom. 10:17). If you have problem with faith, just take enough time to fill yourself with the Word, and you will see faith spring up from within you with great force, frequency, and magnitude.

The Word says that the Word that goes out of the Mouth of God will not go back to Him without accomplishing the purpose for which He sent it (Isa. 55:11). Instead of His Word to fail, heaven and earth shall pass away (Matt. 24:35).

God is not a man to lie, and He cannot change His Mind (Num. 23:19). Except the condition under which He said something is changed by men, He cannot change what He said for that circumstance.

God's Thoughts are higher than our thoughts and His Ways than our ways (Isa. 55:9). Don't be wise in your own eyes, trust in the Lord, and do the right (Prov. 3:7).

If what God told you has not come to pass, don't doubt Him, but be patient in believing, for the vision is yet for an appointment time: it will come to pass and will not tarry (Habk. 2:3).

If God delays His Judgment, it is because He is full of mercy and does not want anyone to perish. However, when He casts His Judgment, He does not respect anybody.

The Word of God says that we are to prove all things, and hold on to that which is true and good (1 Thes. 5:21). Do not believe every spirit, but test the spirits whether they are of God, for many false teachings, ministries, and ministers are in the world today (1 Jn 4:1).

The litmus paper is an indicator that you can easily use to distinguish an acid from an alkali. In the same vein, judging by the Word of God is a good litmus-test for the good and the evil, the Godly and the ungodly. Don't be wise in your own eyes and mind. Even prophecies are to be judged (1 Cor. 14:29).

The people of God perish and suffer because of ignorance or lack of the knowledge of the Word of God (Hos. 4:6). Even though God will want to protect you, know that the devil that is fighting against you has no mercy.

God even said that He will reject some people from being His Original Intention or Plan for them, because they rejected knowledge (Hos. 4:6). If you reject Divine Knowledge, you are heading to disaster.

Don't leave the Word to serve tables (Acts 6:2). The apostles refused to do that. But preach and teach the Word of God, in season and out of season. Convince, rebuke, exhort with all longsuffering and teaching.

For the time has come when they do not endure Sound Doctrine, but according to their own desires, because they have itching ears, they have heaped up for themselves teachers, and they turn their ears away from the truth, and are turned aside to heresies (2 Tim. 4:1-5).

The Word of God says that those that preach the Gospel should live by the Gospel (1 Cor. 9:14). Notice that it did not say that they must live by the Gospel; hence, Apostle Paul said that he did not use that right. But we know, from the Epistles of Paul that some churches and brethren supported him materially and financially.

Even though Apostle Paul worked, part-time, to support himself, that was God's Permissive Will and human thinking, because he said that it was better for him to die than anyone should deny him of his boasting (or self-dependence).

I know many people use Apostle Paul's approach as an excuse, but do they even ask themselves why they are not as effective as Apostle Paul was? The man did not labour to accumulate any wealth, for he went from places to places.

If your church or ministry can sustain you, it is best to commit your whole spirit, mind, and body to the Gospel. If you must work, let it not take too much of your time. But God will sustain you!

Jesus Christ did not work, but showed us an example that even if you are a missionary without definite sponsorship, God will feed and clothe you (and give you other needs, even wants).

Hence the Lord says that the worker is worthy of his pay, and you should carry no extra purse (Matt. 10:7-10). Yes, He told us to carry, just before He was crucified (Lk 22:35-36). The problem is that many ministers are lazy in the ministry and they do not do the Works of Jesus Christ (Jn 14:12; Matt. 10:8).

Many times, Jesus Christ spoke to the people in parables, some of which were actual stories (because sometimes He said, "There was a certain..."). There are many things we can learn from the parables.

Martha was worried with too much serving when Jesus Christ visited her, but Mary was at the Feet of Jesus Christ listening to Him. When Martha wanted Mary to leave listening to Jesus Christ in order to help in the serving, Jesus Christ told Martha that Mary had taken that one thing which is needful, and it will not be taken away from her.

Receiving the Word of God and keeping it is more important than sacrifices. Also, half-obedience is disobedience in the Sight of God. Don't be hearers only, but be doers of the Word you hear.

The Word of God is forever settled in Heaven. God is not a man to lie, and He is not a son of man to change His Mind. Has He spoken and shall He not bring it to pass? Instead of one Word from God to fail, heaven and earth shall pass away.

People try to change the Word of God to suit their desires. They use the Bible to defend themselves, when it is actually the devil that is quoting the Scripture to them wrongly, as he did to Jesus Christ. But God cannot be mocked; whatever you sow, that you will reap.

Brethren, contend earnestly for the faith which was once for all delivered to the Saints. For certain men have crept in unnoticed who long ago were marked out for this condemnation, ungodly men who turn the Grace of our God into lewdness, and deny the only Lord God and our Lord Jesus Christ.

But remember that the Lord, having saved the people out of the land of Egypt, afterward destroyed those who did not believe.

All the fathers of the Israelites were under the cloud, all passed through the sea, all were baptized into Moses in the cloud and in the sea, all ate the same spiritual food, and all drank the same spiritual drink.

But with most of them, God was not well-pleased, for their bodies were scattered in the wilderness. Now, these things became our examples, to the intent that we should not lust after evil things as they also lusted.

And do not become idolaters, as were some of them. Nor let us commit sexual immorality, as some of them did, and in one day twenty-three thousand fell; nor let us tempt Christ, as some of them also tempted, and were destroyed by serpents; nor complain, as some of them also complained, and were destroyed by the destroyer.

Now all these things happened to them as examples, and they were written for our admonition, upon whom the ends of the ages have come. Therefore, let him who thinks he stands take heed lest he fall.

No temptation has overtaken you, except such as is common to man; but God is faithful, Who will not allow you to be tempted beyond what you are able, but with the temptation will also make the way of escape, that you may be able to bear it (1 Cor. 10:1-13).

Therefore, we must give the more earnest heed to the things we have heard, lest we drift away. For if the Word spoken through angels proved steadfast, and every transgression and disobedience received a just recompense or reward, how shall we escape if we neglect so great a salvation;

Which at the first began to be spoken by the Lord, and was confirmed to us by those who heard Him. God also bearing witness both with signs and wonders, with various miracles, and Gifts of the Holy Spirit, according to His Own Will? (Heb. 2:1-4).

Beware, brethren, lest there be in any of you an evil heart of unbelief in departing from the Living God, but exhort one another daily, while it is called "Today," lest any of you be hardened through the deceitfulness of sin.

For we have become partakers of Christ, if we hold the beginning of our confidence steadfast to the end, while it is said "Today, if you will hear His Voice, do not harden your hearts, as in the rebellion." For who, having heard, rebelled? Indeed, was it not all who came out of Egypt, led by Moses?

Now, with whom was He angry forty years? Was it not with those who sinned, whose corpses fell in the wilderness? And to whom did He swear that they would not enter His Rest, but to those who did not obey?

So we see that they could not enter in because of unbelief. Therefore, since a promise remains of entering His Rest, let us fear, lest any of you seem to have come short of it. For indeed, the Gospel was preached to us, as well as to them;

But the Word which they heard did not profit them, not being mixed with faith in those who heard it. For we who have believed do enter that rest (Heb. 3:12-4:3).

The angels who did not keep their proper domain, but left their own abode, He has reserved in everlasting chains under darkness for judgment of the Great Day. For God did not spare the angels who sinned, but cast them down to Hell; and delivered them into chains of darkness to be reserved for judgment.

God did not spare the ancient world, but saved Noah, one of eight people, a preacher of righteousness, bringing in the Flood on the worlds of the ungodly.

As Sodom and Gomorrah, and the cities around them, in a similar manner to these, having given themselves over to sexual immorality and gone after strange flesh, are set forth as an example, suffering the vengeance of Eternal Fire.

God turned the cities of Sodom and Gomorrah into ashes, condemned them to destruction, making them an example to those who afterward would live ungodly; and delivered righteous Lot, who was oppressed by the filthy conduct of the wicked (for that righteous man, dwelling among them tormented his righteous soul from day to day, by seeing and hearing their lawless deeds).

These dreamers defile the flesh, reject authority, and speak evil of dignitaries. They speak evil of whatever they do not know; and whatever they know naturally, like brute beast, in these things they corrupt themselves. Woe to them!

This is because they have gone into the way of Cain, have turned greedily in the error of Balaam for profit, and perished in the rebellion of Korah.

These are spots in your love-feasts, while they feast with you without fear, serving only themselves. They are clouds without water, carried about by the winds; late autumn trees without fruit, twice dead, pulled up by the roots.

These are raging waves of the sea, foaming up their own shame; wandering stars for whom is reserved the Blackness of Darkness forever.

Behold, the Lord comes with ten thousand of His Saints, to execute judgment on all, to convict all who are ungodly among them of all their ungodly deeds, which they have committed in an ungodly way, and of all the harsh things which ungodly sinners have spoken against Him.

These are grumblers, complainers, walking according to their own lusts; and they mouth great swelling word, flattering people to gain advantage. Many walk according to their own ungodly lusts. These are sensual persons, who cause divisions, not having the Spirit.

But you beloved, building yourselves up on your most holy faith, praying in the Holy Spirit; keep yourselves in the Love of God. On some have compassion, making a distinction, but others save with fear, pulling them out of fire.

There were false prophets among the Israelites of Old, just as they are false teachers among the Church today, who secretly bring in destructive heresies, even denying the Lord Who bought them, and bring on themselves swift destruction.

And many follow their destructive ways, because of whom the way of truth is blasphemed. By covetousness, they exploit you with deceptive words. The Lord knows how to deliver the Godly out of temptations and to reserve the unjust under punishment for the Day of Judgment.

The Lord will judge those who walk according to the flesh in the lust of uncleanness and despise authority. They are presumptuous, self-willed. They are not afraid to speak evil of dignitaries.

They speak evil of the things they do not understand, and will utterly perish in their own corruption, and will receive the wages of unrighteousness.

They are spots and blemishes, carousing in their own deceptions while they feast with you, having eyes full of adultery and that cannot cease from sin, enticing unstable souls.

They have a heart trained in covetous practices, and are accursed children. They have forsaken the right way and gone astray. While they promise them liberty, they themselves are slaves of corruption; for by whom a person is overcome, by him also he is brought into bondage.

For if after they have escaped the pollutions of this world through the knowledge of the Lord and Saviour Jesus Christ, they are again entangled and overcome, the latter end is worse for them than the beginning.

For it would have been better for them not to have known the way of righteousness, than having known it, to turn from the Holy Commandments delivered to them (Jude 1 and 2 Pet. 2).

God cannot change His Word and Standard for anyone. God is of Purer Eyes than to behold sin, disobedience, unrighteousness, and iniquity.

If God could turn His Face away from Jesus Christ Himself when He was carrying the sins of the world on the Cross of Calvary, who are you that God will allow you into His Kingdom with sin? All the ungodly, the unrighteous, and sinners will be cast into the Lake of Fire, Hell Fire.

God can never lie nor fail to fulfil His Word. God has promised that He will provide all that you need. He has also promised to protect you. Therefore, do not worry; do not be anxious for anything. Anyway, worrying will not solve the problem. Commit your cares to the Lord for He cares for you.

By the Stripes of Jesus Christ you have been healed. The Bible says that you were healed by the Stripes of Jesus Christ (1 Pet. 2:24). That means that even when you may be feeling the symptom of the sickness, you were healed.

Learn to walk by faith, and don't accept the package of the devil. Speak according to the Word of God, and believe the same, and the plans of the devil will fail to come to fruition in your life. The Promises of the Almighty can never fail; hold on to anything He has promised you.

Preach and teach the Gospel of the Kingdom of God. Don't preach or teach human wisdom and reasoning. Don't preach psychology, philosophy, or faithlessness. God's Word can never fail, and if you preach and teach it, you will see outstanding results of it, both in your life and in the lives of those who hear you.

The Holy Spirit is the Source of the Power of God. And without Him, you are powerless. You cannot do God's Work effectively with human strength. Yes, you have to use your strength to serve God, but His Work is done effectively by the Power of the Holy Spirit.

When the apostles needed deacons, who were to help them in taking care of the Disciples, they required that the people to be appointed had certain qualifications. They were to be people of good reputation, full of the Holy Spirit, and wisdom.

However, in many churches, many people are appointed deacons and elders, and they do not have these qualifications. Many are appointed to positions of authority in churches based on their fame, financial power, contributions to the church, age, and other human judgments.

Christians have a Wonderful Inheritance Who is the Holy Spirit. The Lord Jesus Christ did not leave us helpless, He sent the Holy Spirit to us (Jn 16:7). The Lord Jesus Christ baptizes with the Holy Spirit and fire.

The Holy Spirit of God is the Manifester of God's Power. In the beginning, when darkness covered the surface of the deep (water), the Spirit of God moved upon the face of the water, and when God declared that anything be on earth, His Spirit brought it to pass.

Some say that the Holy Spirit is the Power of God. That is true and untrue, depending on what you mean. The Holy Spirit is a Personality; He is the Third Person in the Holy Trinity, the Three in One.

Many don't believe in the Trinity, but the Bible teaches so. Jesus Christ told the apostles to baptize the Believers in the Name of the Father and of the Son and of the Holy Spirit (Matt. 28:19).

Apostle Paul prayed that the Grace of the Lord Jesus Christ, the Love of God, and the Communion of the Holy Spirit be with the Corinthian Christians (2 Cor. 13:14). For through Him (Jesus Christ), we both have access by one Spirit (the Holy Spirit) to the Father (Eph. 2:18).

The Lord (Jesus Christ) began the Message of Salvation which God (the Father) bears witness to with signs and wonders, and the Gifts of the Holy Spirit (Heb. 2:3-4).

There are Three that bear witness in Heaven: the Father, the Word (Jesus Christ), and the Holy Spirit; and these Three are One. (1 Jn 5:7). These Scriptures and others speak of the Trinity.

Believers receive power when the Holy Spirit comes upon them, so as to be witnesses to the Lord in their area and to the ends of the earth (Acts 1:8). This is why the Lord Jesus Christ told His apostles not to leave Jerusalem until they are endued with power from on High (Lk. 24:49).

But many try to do the Lord's Work without being filled with the Holy Spirit, and the powerlessness in their lives and ministries is the testimony they may not even be aware of. Will a policeman, who either carries no gun or have a mark 4 gun, put fear to well-armed robbers?

When you are baptized with the Holy Spirit and filled with Him, you have all the potential power that you will ever need, and He will release His Power in your life more and more as you obey Him, control yourself, and please God.

There are levels of anointing, and the Holy Spirit will anoint you with greater anointing as you follow His Leading and increase in your knowledge of the Lord God Almighty. Fasting will be useful.

Baptism in the Holy Spirit will be evidenced by speaking in tongues as in the Early Church. Many, instead of taking up the responsibility, instead of finding out why they have not been baptized and spoken in tongues, settle for a lower Christian life and say that everybody must not speak in tongues.

I could have settled for that also after seeking the baptism for a very long time and not receiving; but thanks to God for His Grace.

You can preach Jesus Christ, but to prove Him with the required signs and wonders, you must be filled with the Holy Spirit.

Note that the apostles and the Disciples had done marvelous things (signs and wonders) when the Lord imparted His Own Anointing on them, and yet, they were to wait for the Promise of the Father (Lk. 10:1-20).

Even though the Name of Jesus Christ in your mouth, as a Believer, can work miracles and wonders, there is a great difference when the anointing is resident on you.

Peter received the revelation of Whom Jesus Christ was when he was not yet filled with the Holy Spirit (Matt. 16:13-20). That you received a revelation, a vision, or that you prayed and God answered the prayer does not mean that you have been filled with the Holy Ghost.

You can only be full of the Power of the Holy Spirit after you must have been filled with the Person of the Holy Spirit (Acts 10:38; 1 Cor. 2:4; 1 Thes. 1:5). There is no other way, your title or position notwithstanding.

Being full of the Holy Spirit is the door to the Spiritual Gifts of the Holy Spirit (1 Cor. 12:1-11). After being baptized with the Holy Spirit, you must maintain the full measure of the Holy Spirit to keep on operating in His Power the way you should.

The Ephesian Christians were told to be filled (literally, be being filled) with the Holy Spirit (Eph. 5:18). The Roman Christians were told to be fervent in spirit (be on fire in the Spirit, maintain the Glow of the Holy Spirit) (Rom. 12:11).

When you are filled with the Holy Spirit, you will speak in tongues and to maintain the fullness of the Spirit, you will continue to speak…. This is a Biblical way, and any other way is not Biblical and cannot work.

This does not mean that God cannot use you if you are not filled with the Holy Spirit. The Disciples were filled with the Holy Spirit on the day of Pentecost and they spoke in other tongues as the Spirit gave them utterance (Acts 2:4).

Apostle Peter said that the Gift of the Holy Spirit is for every Believer (Acts 2:38-39). The Ephesian Believers that Apostle Paul found, even though they were Disciples, had not been filled with the Holy Spirit.

Thanks to God that they were filled with the Holy Spirit when hands were laid on them. Note that they spoke in tongues and prophesied (Acts 19:1-7).

Cornelius and his household only listened and believed Apostle Peter's message, and they were filled with the Holy Spirit and spoke in other tongues (Acts 10:44-48; Acts 11:13-15).

Saul (later known as Paul) was saved when he met Jesus Christ on his way to Damascus. Apostle Paul was filled with the Holy Spirit when Ananias laid hands on him (Acts 9:1-22), and he spoke in tongues (1 Cor. 14:18).

Apostle Paul encouraged Christians to speak with tongues in their individual prayers (1 Cor. 14:4,14; Jude 1:20). Speaking in tongues helps you pray for what you and others may not know about (Rom. 8:26). Speaking in tongues will help you tame the tongue (Jas 3:8).

Don't be afraid of receiving the wrong spirit, if you are born again and God is your Father. If our earthly parents will not give us fake or dangerous things, how much more will the Good, Loving, and Faithful Almighty God give us all good things? (Lk. 11:9-13).

Speaking in tongues is not the evidence of being born again, but of being baptized and filled with the Holy Spirit. The qualification for going to Heaven is being born again, and not speaking in tongues.

When you are born again, you receive a measure of the Holy Spirit to keep you going on in your Christian life, but when you are baptized and filled with the Holy Spirit, you are filled with the Holy Spirit to overflowing and this leads to power for witnessing for Jesus Christ.

The purpose of being filled with the Holy Spirit is to be a witness for Jesus Christ. It is to produce proofs and evidence that Jesus Christ is the Son of God, and He is alive. No wonder the Lord says that Believers will do the works that He did, even greater works than them (Jn 14:12).

The Holy Spirit will lead you into all truth and show you things to come. He will remind you of what you had heard and read (Jn 16:13; Jn 14:26).

There is no substitute for the Holy Spirit. He is in-charge of the world today, and as the Christians co-operate with Him, in obedience and prayer, He will bring the Will of God to pass on the earth.

Personality, learning, certificate, title, position, fame, and money cannot substitute the Holy Spirit, because it is not by power, nor by might, but by the Spirit of the Living God (Zech. 4:6). We must live and walk in the Spirit.

There is a Pentecostal mentality. Some assume that because they go to churches that are called Pentecostal churches, they have more power or gifts in them than others, but that is not the yardstick of measurement of the Power and Gifts of the Spirit.

Some assume that because they speak in tongues, they have arrived in the Things of the Spirit, but there is so much more to the Things of the Spirit. Then some others may assume that if you are not baptized in the Holy Spirit you will not go to Heaven, but this is far from the truth.

When you are full of the Holy Spirit, and you are obedient to Him, you will be full of the Mighty Power of God. Then you will affect your generation in a mighty way and bring much glory and praise to the Almighty God. Amen.

Before the Lord Jesus Christ left, He told the apostles and the Disciples that they will receive power, after that the Holy Ghost has come upon them; and they shall be witnesses to Him from their place to the ends of the world (Acts 1:8).

This Statement is applicable to us also for we are in the same dispensation. Even though the world needed to be evangelized quickly, He told them to tarry in Jerusalem until they are endued with power from on High (Lk. 24:49).

When the power came upon them, they went out and preached everywhere, the Lord working with them and confirming the Word through signs and wonders (Mk 16:20).

We are called as fishers of men, and we must occupy till the Lord Jesus Christ comes. We are labourers together with God.

We cannot expect to preach the Gospel any other way, for Apostle Paul declares that the Kingdom of God is not in word but in power (1 Cor. 4:20).

No wonder when he preached to the Corinthians, he did not go with excellence of speech or of wisdom, declaring to them the Testimony of God.

He was with them in weakness, in fear, and in much trembling, having decided to know nothing among them except Jesus Christ and Him crucified.

And his speech and his preaching were not with persuasive words of human wisdom, but in demonstration of the Spirit and of power, that their faith should not be in the wisdom of men but in the Power of God (1 Cor. 2:1-5).

This happened wherever he went, for, concerning the Thessalonians, he said, "For our Gospel did not come to you in Word only, but also in power, and in the Holy Spirit, and in much assurance, as you know what kind of men we were among you for your sake" (1 Thes. 1:5).

Jesus Christ drew people's attention more by the miracles He performed than by His Teachings and Preachings. I am not saying that miracles are greater than the Word of God.

As a matter of fact, the Word of God is greater than signs, wonders, and miracles; but it is the signs, wonders, and miracles that will draw people to you so that they can receive the Word.

After Jesus Christ was filled with the Holy Spirit, the Spirit led Him into the wilderness, being tempted for forty days by the devil. And in those days He ate nothing, and afterward, when they had ended, He was hungry. Now when the devil had ended every temptation, he departed from Him until an opportune time.

Then Jesus Christ returned in the Power of the Spirit to Galilee, and News of Him went out through the entire surrounding region. And He taught in their synagogues, being glorified by all (Lk. 4).

The miracles and healings He performed attracted the attention of the people so that they themselves advertised for Him (they advertised His Ministry) throughout the entire surrounding region. When He went down to Capernaum, they were astonished at His Teaching, for His Word was with authority.

When you are full of the Holy Spirit and the Word of God, when you are filled with power, people will notice a recognizable difference and authority in your preaching and teaching.

As He was in their synagogue, a man with an unclean spirit cried out with a loud voice. But Jesus Christ rebuked the demon, saying, "Be quiet, and come out of him!" The demon came out immediately. That is power and authority.

He did not spend hours or days trying to cast out the same devils. He did not even want to know from the people whether it was a generational or an ancestral spirit. The anointing, the liquid-fire anointing, knows of no yoke that cannot be broken.

The people there were all amazed and spoke among themselves, saying, "What a Word is this! For with authority and power He commands the unclean spirits and they come out." I like that! The problem is that many move out without the power.

However, this is not to say that you have to wait for your whole life for the power. Some pray and wait too long. It took Jesus Christ forty days. Your own may last for only three days, because the Lord has conquered the devil for us. We operate in His Name!

Once you are filled with the Holy Spirit, and you are obedient to God and prayerful, devils and their works will yield to your commands.

Of course, there are levels of the anointing, but start with the one you have, and as you are faithful in the little you have, the Lord will increase the anointing in your life. You wouldn't have all at the same time.

The Report about Him went out into every place in the surrounding region. As He stood over Simon's wife's mother and rebuked the high fever she had, it left her. And immediately she arose and served them.

When the sun was setting, all those who had any that were sick with various diseases brought them to Him; and He laid His Hands on every one of them and healed them (verse 40). Many demons also left.

The people tried to keep Him there, but He told them that He must preach the Kingdom of God to other cities also. He did not settle down to establish a church and pastor it against God's Will for Him!

The story was the same throughout His Ministry. He operated supernaturally. After using Peter's boat to preach to the multitude, He told Peter to launch out for a catch. When Peter did, they caught a great number of fish, and their net was breaking.

Peter had said, "Master, we have toiled all night and caught nothing; nevertheless at Your Word I will let down the net." What you have toiled for the past twenty years, God can give it to you in an hour.

He healed the leper. He healed the paralyzed. He restored the withered hand of a man. He raised the dead. He did all manner of healings.

He fed five thousand people with five loaves of bread and two small fish. The people were so much amazed that had it been that Jesus Christ did not leave them, they would have taken Him by force to make Him king. The people kept on looking for Him, and even used boat, seeking for Him.

Don't say, "That was Jesus Christ the Son of the Living God." Yes, He was, but Jesus Christ Himself said, "Most assuredly, I say to you, he who believes in Me, the works that I do he will do also, and greater works than these he will do, because I go to My Father (Jn 14:12).

What happened after Apostle Peter had healed the lame man at the gate of the Temple called Beautiful? As the man held on to Peter and John, all the people ran together to them, greatly amazed. Peter used that opportunity to preach to them, and they listened to him attentively.

Even though their opponents came upon them and arrested them, many of those who heard the Word believed; and the number of the men came to be about five thousand. God has not changed. It is the Believers that doubt God (Acts 3).

The eight chapter of the Book of Acts gives us a story that will convince the 'doubting Thomas' of the need for the demonstration of the Power of the Holy Spirit through the Believers.

This story will convince you that even witches and wizards will leave their witchcraft practices and come after your Jesus Christ when the power in your life is strong enough. Philip, who was not even one of the apostles, went down to Samaria and preached Christ to them.

The Bible says, "And the multitudes with one accord heeded the things spoken by Philip, hearing and seeing the miracles which he did.

"For unclean spirits, crying with a loud voice, came out of many who were possessed; and many who were paralyzed and lame were healed. And there was great joy in the city.

"But there was a certain man called Simon, who previously practiced sorcery in the city and astonished the people of Samaria, claiming that he was someone great, to whom they all gave heed, from the least to the greatest, saying, 'This man is the Great Power of God?'

"And they heeded him because he had astonished them with his sorceries for a long time. But when they believed Philip as he preached the things concerning the Kingdom of God and the Name of Jesus Christ, both men and women were baptized.

"Then Simon himself also believed; and when he was baptized he continued with Philip, and was amazed, seeing the miracles and signs which were done." Even the sorcerer, Simon, wanted that power and authority, because he had seen something that was greater than his sorcery.

When power jam power, the lesser power will bow! I know there are people whose hearts have been hardened to the extent that even when they know the truth, they would rather die than serve Christ. But God can deliver them from that hardened state.

Jesus Christ is the same yesterday, today, and forever (Heb. 13:8). He has not changed and He still works with His people to expand the Kingdom of God on earth. The Lord God Almighty does not change (Mal. 3:6).

God cannot lie and He cannot disappoint His people. It is not possible for God to fail to fulfill His Word. Jesus Christ came to destroy the works of satan and save men.

In preaching the Gospel of our Lord Jesus Christ, you must remove shame, fear, and timidity. If you are ashamed of the Lord before sinners, He will be ashamed of you before His Father and the holy angels.

Do not be afraid of him who only has power to kill the body; rather fear God, Who has power to destroy both the body and the soul in Hell. Only Jesus Christ is the Light of the world, and He has made us the light of the world, as His representatives and brethren.

We have been given the ministry of reconciliation, and we must not fail in this task. Jesus Christ came to reconcile men to God and we are labourers together with Him. Jesus Christ came to seek those who were lost in order to save them. We must seek the lost and get them saved.

WE ARE MORE THAN CONQUERORS

We are more than conquerors; we are overcomers in this world. We have been made victorious by the Blood of Jesus Christ, the Son of the Living God, Who died for our sins, and was resurrected from the dead for our justification.

We are soldiers of Christ. We are a triumphant people who are to enforce the victory Jesus Christ already got for us. Do not be afraid; do not be dismayed: the Lord God Almighty is our God.

Rejoice in the Lord always; no matter the circumstance or condition you may find yourself in, rejoice in the Lord your God. We are heirs of God and joint-heirs with Christ. The Presence of God goes with us; we have the Power of the Spirit! Great power has been given to us.

Realizing that you are more than conquerors is a step to entering God's Rest. You can do all things through Christ Jesus. All things are possible by the Spirit of God.

It is not by might nor by power, but by the Holy Spirit. Whatever you bind on earth is bound in Heaven, and whatever you loose on earth is loosed in Heaven.

If God is for us, who can be against us? He Who did not spare His Own Son, but delivered Him up for us all, how shall He not with Him also freely give us all things? Who shall bring a charge against God's Elect? It is God Who justifies.

Who is He who condemns? It is Christ Who died, and further more has also risen, Who is even at the Right Hand of God, Who also makes intercession for us.

Who shall separate us from the Love of Christ? Shall tribulation, or distress, or persecution, or famine, or nakedness, or peril, or sword? Yet in all these things we are more than conquerors through Him Who loved us.

For I am persuaded that neither death nor life, nor angels nor principalities nor powers, nor things present nor things to come, nor height nor depth, nor any other created thing, shall be able to separate us from the Love of God which is in Christ Jesus our Lord (Rom. 8:31-39).

In righteousness you shall be established, you shall be far from oppression, for you shall not fear; and from terror, for it shall not come near you.

Indeed they shall surely assemble, but not because of God. Whoever assembles against you shall fall for your sake. Behold, God created the blacksmith who blows the coals in the fire, who brings forth an instrument for his work; and He created the spoiler to destroy.

No weapon formed against you shall prosper, and every tongue which rises against you in judgment you shall condemn. This is the heritage of the Servants of the Lord, and their righteousness is from Him (Isa. 54:14-17).

We are in the New Testament which is established upon better promises than the Old Testament. In the Old Testament, the Lord demonstrated His Power to show that His people are more than conquerors.

When Jacob laboured for Laban, Laban cheated him; but the Lord intervened supernaturally, so that Jacob outsmarted Laban and God restored to him the years that the enemy had cheated him (Gen. 30)

In God's Plan, God told Abraham that his descendants will be slaves in a foreign land for four hundred years, and after that, they will come out. This came to pass in the land of Egypt where Israelites were held in bondage for hundreds of years.

When God sent Moses to Pharaoh to tell him to let the Israelites go, Pharaoh said, "Who is the Lord that I should obey Him?" As God brought different plagues to the Egyptians, Pharaoh was frightened, even though his heart was still hardened, and he gave conditions upon which they could go.

But when God slew all the firstborns of the Egyptians, they themselves had to beg the Israelites to go and the people of Israel plundered them. The enemy who stands by your way to stop you from having the inheritance that the Lord has provided for you will fall for your sake.

When the Lord told Joshua that He has given him and the people of Israel Jericho, many of the Israelites doubted the possibility of it, because they thought that they were not their match. The ten spies confessed that they saw giants in Jericho.

But thanks to God for Joshua and Caleb who believed God, and shunned the other ten spies, telling the people that they were well able to take Jericho. Can you speak differently, according to the Word of God, even when the surrounding circumstances say otherwise?

When Jericho had been circled seven times and the trumpets were blown, according to the Instruction of the Lord, the walls of Jericho crumbled, and the people captured it.

Even when the less powerful Ai defeated Israel because there was sin in their midst (make sure there is no sin in your life, for God is of Purer Eyes than to behold iniquity, and He is no respecter of persons), when they repented and removed sin from their midst, Ai fell to them.

It is only sin, disobedience, and unbelief that will hinder you from taking your inheritance in Christ Jesus. Therefore, strive to be holy, obedient, righteous, and full of faith.

Gideon had planned to go with several thousands to battle, but God told him that all he needed were three hundred men. When he went to the battle with only three hundred men, they won the battle, because the battle is the Lord's.

No wonder Sampson was a one-man army who could defeat the Philistines alone. The man's anointing functioned greatly that he could pull out the doors of the gate to the city with bare hands and carry them up a hill. One will chase a thousand, and two will chase ten thousand.

Even though Goliath had been a man of war for many years and was well armoured with offensive weapons of sword, spear, and javelin, David who had the Anointing of the Spirit of God (who had killed both a bear and a lion by that anointing), and did not have experience in warfare, used only stones and a sling to attack the mighty Goliath of Gath.

A single stone, empowered by the anointing, sank into his forehead, and the man fell flat. The Anointing of the Spirit of the Living God breaks every yoke of the devil and destroys his burdens (Isa. 10:27).

If you study the deeds and exploits of David's mighty men in 2 Sam. 23:1-39, you will come to understand that if God is for us, no man can be against us. How much more shall our exploits be when we live in the New Testament which is established upon better promises?

In the New Testament, God is for us, with us, in us, and upon us; what a great reinforcement! The hosts of Heaven are on our side.

No wonder Prophet Elisha prayed that the eyes of his servant be opened that he might know that they which were with them were more than they which were against them. The servant had only been looking at the situation from the physical point of view; but Elisha saw beyond the physical.

We are of God (we were Born of God and we belong to Him) and greater is He that is in us than he that is in the world (1 Jn 4:4). Have you been afraid before? Don't be again. Had you been doubting before? Remove doubt now, and grab your strong faith.

Faith, as little as the mustard seed, will remove mountains. Remove sin and disobedience, for they block the door to the supernatural; grab holiness and righteousness, for they open the door-way of Heaven!

Be anxious for nothing; but in everything, by prayer and supplication, with thanksgiving, let your requests be made known to God. And the Peace of God, which passes knowledge, will guard your hearts and minds through Christ Jesus.

When the storm and the sea raged and roared so much that the Disciples of Jesus Christ thought they were going to get drowned, they cried for help from Jesus Christ. The Lord rebuked their unbelief and fear.

Just as the Lord commanded and the storm ceased, you too can speak peace and calmness to your circumstances in the Name of Jesus Christ, and there will be peace and tranquility. Stand still and see the Salvation of the Lord your God, for the battle is not yours but the Lord's.

All you need to do is to speak the Word in faith, and see God turn your circumstances around for your good. Peace, be still!

If you consider the life of Elijah who stopped rainfall for three and half years, and after that brought it back; who brought down fire from Heaven on three occasions: to consume his prepared sacrifice and consume the captains the king sent to fetch him with their fifties, you will know that we are more than conquerors.

Prophet Elisha healed the water of a land and healed Naaman of his leprosy. Fire couldn't even set the dresses of Shadrach, Meshach, and Abed-Nego ablaze. Lions refused the meat of Daniel. God is powerful and miraculous!

God has sent, provided, and commissioned His angels to protect us. Angels are ministering spirits sent to minister for the heirs of salvation: us. You have got to learn how to put your angels to work.

Of course, there are duties of angels you don't have anything to do with. Your relationship with Jesus Christ, your life of obedience and holiness, your prayer-life and faith-life have a lot to do with how angels attend to your cause.

Considering the Life and Ministry of Jesus Christ, you will come to know that our God is too much, and we, His people, are a people of signs, wonders, and miracles!

Jesus Christ walked on water, raised the dead, cast out demons, brought calmness to a raging storm on the sea, opened the eyes of the blind, and did many other mighty works. Before He left, He told His Followers that He who believes on Him shall do the same works, and even greater works (Jn 14:12).

No wonder the lives of the apostles, prophets, and Disciples of the Early New Testament time were filled with signs and wonders. The early apostles and Disciples walked with God so much that their opponents became afraid of them, because they could not deny the miracles which they performed.

Apostle Peter healed a lame man so that he walked. It even got to the level whereby Peter's shadows could heal the sick and diseased. Apostle Paul's handkerchiefs could heal the sick and drive out demons (Acts 5:15; Acts 19:11-12).

Apostle Paul commanded an opposer of the Gospel and he did not see again for a period of time. Even when the people thought that he would swell from a viper's attack, nothing happened to him so that they changed their mind and said that he was a god. They were right because we are gods (Pas. 82:1,6; Jn 10:34-35).

We have been given the Name of Jesus Christ, the Name above every other name, and at the Name Jesus Christ, every knee should bow, of those, beings, or things in heaven, on earth, and under the earth, and that every tongue should confess that Jesus Christ is Lord, to the Glory of God the Father.

Use that Name, and you will see wonderful changes in your circumstances. The Name of Jesus Christ is stronger than your strength, and you can accomplished more in a minute by using the Name of Jesus Christ than you can accomplish in a year by using your human strength.

No witch or wizard has any power over you, except you give them an opportunity by sin, disobedience, and faithlessness. Jesus Christ says, "Behold, I give you power to tread on serpents and scorpions, and over all the power of the enemy, and nothing shall by any means hurt you" (Lk. 10:19).

He says that the purpose the Holy Spirit came upon you is to empower you to be a witness for Him. As His witness, you will have to give evidence and proof that He is alive by signs and miracles.

In this dispensation, the Lord God Almighty is for us, with us, in us, and upon us. We cannot fail because greater is the Holy Ghost that is in us than the satan that is in the world. Confront anything that confronts you, and it will certainly bow to the Name of Jesus Christ and the Anointing of the Holy Ghost.

Resist the devil yourself, and he will flee from you (Jas 4:7). Don't wait for God to do it, because God has appointed that assignment for you. Take it up! No weapon fashioned against you shall prevail over you, for the Lord is with you.

We have Jesus Christ Who is our Great Intercessor. Jesus Christ intercedes for us at the Right Hand of the Father, and His Intercession keeps us safe, protected, and free.

We must have the rugged mentality. The Kingdom of God suffers violence, and the violent take it by force. The Church is marching on and the gates of Hades shall not prevail.

We must advance by force, and take what belongs to us in Christ Jesus. We must advance into the kingdom of the devil and take souls from there for the Lord our God.

The devil will bring barriers, obstructions, mountains, rivers, fire, and other forms of persecutions, trials, and wilderness experiences across your path; but your God is the Mighty One in Battle. And He has given you power to overcome the devil and his works.

All things are possible to the Believer. Christians are Offsprings of God Himself. Since the days of John the Baptist, the Kingdom of God suffers violence, and the violent take it by force (Matt. 11:12).

Turn your conditions around for good, and obtain your rights, privileges, and inheritances in Christ by confronting your confrontations. The righteousness which is of faith speaks in this way, "Do not say in your heart, 'Who will ascend into Heaven?' (that is, to bring Christ down from Above) or, 'Who will descend into the deep?' (that is, to bring Christ up from the dead)."

But what does it say? "The Word is near you, in your mouth and in your heart" (that is the Word of Faith which we preach). That if you shall confess with your mouth…and shall believe in your heart…you shall be saved.

For with the heart man believes…and with the mouth confession is made…. Whoever believes on Him shall not be put to shame (Rom. 10:6-11).

We, having the same spirit of faith, according as it is written, "I believed, and therefore have I spoken"; we also believe, and therefore speak (2 Cor. 4:13). You have to confront your confrontations to receive your victory.

It is not God that will do the confrontation for us. If we wait for God, we may die waiting for Him. This is why the Scripture tells us to resist the devil so that he will flee from us (Jas 4:7).

You have to resist him steadfastly in faith (1 Pet. 5:9). Don't give any place to the devil (Eph. 4:27). The devil will have the place you give him, he will occupy that place.

But the mistake many people make is to sit back and wait for God to remove the obstacles the devil has brought along their ways. Your word of faith can break that barrier. This is why God gave us the responsibility to pray.

The Word of God is the Sword of the Spirit; use the Word actively, and see the Spirit of God change your circumstances for good, better, and best. Contend, earnestly, for the faith and the Word; the Promises of God are 'Yes', and 'Amen.'

No matter how long you might have been oppressed and confronted, you can still confront your confrontations and get free. Even generational curses and covenants will crumble if you confront them.

Believe the Word of God more than any person's story or idea. The Anointing of the Holy Spirit of the Living God destroys the yokes and lifts the burdens the enemy puts on people. Jesus Christ gives peace, abundant peace.

The Philistines gathered their armies together to battle with Israel. And a champion went out from the camp of the Philistines, named Goliath, from Gath, whose height was six cubits and a span (that is, 13 feet, 4 inches).

He had a bronze helmet on his head, and he was armed with a coat of mail, and the weight of the coat was five thousand shekels of bronze (about 194 1/2 ibs in weight). And he had bronze armour on his legs and bronze javelin between his shoulders.

Now the staff of his spear was like a weaver's beam, and his iron spearhead weighed six hundred shekels (about 23 1/2 ibs, counting 224 grains to the shekel); and a shield-bearer went before him.

Can you imagine this type of a devil? He was armoured very well. He had offensive weapons of javelin and spear. Bronze is an alloy metal which is very hard. Brass is a mixture of zinc and copper, while bronze is a mixture of zinc, copper, and tin. He had both well-made defensive and offensive weapons.

Added to that is that a shield-bearer went before him. If you were to fight with Goliath naturally, his shield-bearer (who could be taller than you: Goliath himself was a giant) would stop your arrow, spear, and sword, while Goliath will thrust you through with his spear or javelin.

But I don't care about the barrier, opposition, stronghold, or attack the enemy and his demons have brought along your way, to stop you from enjoying the full benefit of the inheritance you have in Jesus Christ; if you will withstand him, he will flee.

It may not take a minute, an hour, a day or a week to break that barrier and stop the attack, but if you withstand him steadfastly in faith and pray, he will bow.

There are cases and situations that you will have to add fasting to prayer for the devil's handiwork to be destroyed. The Word says that some demonic works will be broken only by prayer and fasting (Matt. 17:21).

This does not mean that you can't cast out a demon unless you are fasting, but if the anointing in your life (gained by former prayer and fasting) is not strong enough for confronting that demonic attack, then you must fast until you have a breakthrough.

However, demons bow to the Name of Jesus Christ. Sometimes, the fasting may have to take a long time of about three, seven or more days. Imagine what would have happened if Prophet Daniel had stopped praying and fasting the twentieth day.

The answer to his prayers, which was released the first day, might have not reached him. An angel who was not a high-ranking warring angel was sent to deliver the answer, but a stronger satanic spiritual wickedness in high places withstood him.

But thanks to God that Daniel did not give up, and on the twenty-first day, another angel was sent to help the other angel. This made it possible for him to deliver the answer to Daniel (Dan. 10).

Some say that fasting is not that important; well, can you explain what you mean? Jesus Christ fasted; Apostle Paul fasted; and (I don't want to go the Old Testament now) the early Disciples and Believers fasted.

The truth is that there is a level of anointing the Holy Spirit will not anoint you with if you don't fast. Whether partial fasting, fruit-fasting, juice-fasting, the fasted life, water-fasting, or dry fasting, you will fast. Of course, dry fasting or water-fasting may, sometimes, not take as long as partial fasting.

Goliath of Gath, the Philistine, intimidated Israel many days, and said, "I defy the armies of Israel this day, give me a man that we may fight together." When King Saul and all Israel heard these words of the Philistine, they were dismayed and greatly afraid. By this time, God had rejected Saul as a king, and the anointing that was upon him, had lifted.

Maybe, it was the same anointing that lifted from Saul that came upon David, because Saul was rejected by God in chapter fifteen, David was anointed king in chapter sixteen, and here comes Goliath in chapter seventeen.

But one thing we know is that the anointing had lifted from Saul, and God had anointed David as king, even though, physically, he had not become one. But what has been settled in the spiritual realm will certainly come to pass physically, because the spiritual realm is very real.

After Goliath had terrorized Israel for forty days, the youngest son of Jesse, who had been anointed with the Power and Boldness of the Spirit of God, came to the camp of Israel and heard that thrash from the mouth of Goliath. All the men of Israel, when they saw the man, fled from him, and were dreadfully afraid.

And David said, "Who is this uncircumcised Philistine, that he should defy the armies of the Living God?" Eliab, his oldest brother, heard him and was very annoyed with him. He would have thought in his mind, saying, "What can this proud small boy do?"

Do you know that people can judge you, and take you to be proud when you say what you can do by the Power of God through the Name of Jesus Christ? Apostle Peter said, "I give you what I have, and in the Name of Jesus Christ, rise up and walk" (Acts 3:1-11).

David told Saul that their hearts should not fail because of Goliath, and that he will go and fight him. Saul said, "You are not able to go against this Philistine to fight with him; for you are a youth, and he a man of war from his youth." David told Saul that he had killed a lion and a bear, and he will kill Goliath also.

You see why you shouldn't be afraid. The anointing that removed malaria, can also open the eyes of the blind! Just be dedicated to making God's Anointing stronger and stronger in your life. All you need are the anointing and the real faith.

David declared that the Lord will deliver him. The anointing emboldened him and moved him. Saul armoured David with his armour and gave him a sword, but David could not use them. Some think that it must be done the same old way, but this is not true.

Find out the direction and the strategy God has for you, and you will conquer when you obey God. David used stones and a sling. The Philistine looked at David and disdained him. He cursed David by his gods. But David was not moved; he knew the outcome.

David said, "You come to me with a sword, with a spear, and with a javelin. But I come to you in the Name of the Lord of Hosts…the Lord will deliver you into my hand, and I will strike you and take your head from you….

"That all the earth may know that there is a God in Israel…the Lord does not save with sword and spear; for the battle is the Lord's…."

David hurried, took out a stone, and slung it and struck the Philistine in his forehead. The Philistine died and the others fled. David and Israel overcame by their God (1 Sam. 17).

The spiritual controls the physical. Stand upon the Word of God without doubting, and act: you will overcome always! No devil, demon, witch, or thing should stop you, as a Christian and a minister. Don't make yourself stoppable.

If you are confronting your confrontations and it seems that you are not achieving your purpose, you may have to change your strategy or battle plan. That God worked a certain way to solve a problem does not mean He will always work that way. Find out from God always how you have to approach your difficult situations.

THE STRONG AND UNTOUCHABLE CHRISTIAN

Many people will readily believe that a Christian can be strong, but will wonder how a Christian can be untouchable. Many Believers use their experiences, and those of others, to explain the truth, instead of allowing the Word of God to tell them the truth.

We know that whoever is Born of God does not sin; but he who has been Born of God keeps himself, and the wicked one does not touch him. We know that we are of God, and the whole world lies under the sway of the wicked one (1 Jn 5:18-19).

Sin and disobedience is the basis through which the devil and his agents touch people. Without sin in your life, no devil nor demon, no witch nor wizard, no principal agent of the kingdom of darkness can touch you. Don't be ignorant of the devices of the devil.

It was when Adam disobeyed God that the devil touched him. The devil stole what God had given to Adam from him. And we know that the devil does not come except to steal, and to kill, and to destroy. Jesus Christ came that we may have life, and that we may have it more abundantly (Jn 10:10).

The purpose the Son of God was manifested is that He might destroy the works of the devil. Whoever has been Born of God does not sin, for His Seed remains in him, and he cannot sin because he has been Born of God (1 Jn. 3:1-10).

Children of God purify themselves as Jesus Christ is pure. Whoever commits sin also commits lawlessness, and sin is lawlessness. And you know that He was manifested to take away our sins, and in Him there is no sin. Whoever abides in Him does not sin. Whoever sins has neither seen Him nor known Him.

Let no one deceive you. He who practices righteousness is righteous, just as He is righteous. He who sins is of the devil. Whoever does not practice righteousness is not of God, nor is he who does not love his brother.

Other things that can give the devil an opportunity in your life are unbelief and doubt. When you don't believe the Word of God, doubt sets in. Doubt prevents the manifestation of the Word of God in your life.

The Word of God says that he who doubts is like the wave of the sea, tossed to and fro, and that person should not expect to get anything from God. But God can neither lie nor fail to perform His Promises.

As Christians, we are untouchable beings, when we abide in Christ and in His Word. But the problem is that many Christians open a hole for the devil in their lives, and when you give him a loophole or place in your life, he will come in. He who breaks the hedge will be beaten by the serpent.

Be sober; be vigilant; because your adversary the devil walks about like a roaring lion, seeking whom he may devour. Resist him, steadfast in the faith (1 Pet. 5:8-9).

Therefore submit to God. Resist the devil and he will flee from you. Draw near to God and He will draw near to you. Cleanse your hands, you sinners; and purify your hearts, you double-minded.

Lament and mourn and weep! Let your laughter be turned to mourning and your joy to gloom. Humble yourselves in the Sight of the Lord, and He will lift you up. God resists the proud, but gives grace to the humble (Jas 4:6-10).

The devil will bring different things across your path, but whatever he throws at you, resist him and he will flee. To flee is to run away with fear.

In righteousness you shall be established; you shall be far from oppression, for you shall not fear; and from terror, for it shall not come near you. Indeed they shall surely gather, but not by God.

Whoever gathers against you shall fall for your sake. Behold the Lord created the blacksmith who blows the coal in the fire, who brings forth an instrument for his work; and He created the spoiler to destroy.

No weapon formed against you shall prosper, and every tongue which rises against you in judgment you shall condemn. This is the heritage of the Servants of the Lord, and their righteousness is from Him (Isa. 54:14-17).

Do not fear, for the Lord is with you; be not dismayed, for His is your God. He will strengthen you, yes, He will help you, and He will uphold you with His Righteous Right Hand.

Behold, all those who were increased against you shall be ashamed and disgraced, they shall be as nothing, and those who strive with you shall perish. You shall seek them and not find them; those who contend with you shall be as nothing, as a non-existent thing (Isa. 41:10-12).

Fear not, for the Lord has redeemed you, He has called you by your name; you are His. When you pass through the waters, He will be with you; and through the rivers, they shall not overflow you. When you walk through the fire, you shall not be burned, nor shall the flame scorch you.

For the Lord is your God, the Holy One of Israel, your Saviour; He gave Egypt for Israel's ransom. Since you are precious in God's Sight, He will honour you, for He loves you. Therefore He will give men for you, and people for your life. Fear not (Isa. 43:1-5).

The ninety-first chapter of the Book of Psalms tells us what it means to be untouchable. He who dwells in the Secret Place of the Most High shall abide under the Shadow of the Almighty. I will say of the Lord, "He is my Refuge and my Fortress; my God, in Him I will trust."

Surely He shall deliver you from the snare of the fowler and from the perilous pestilence. He shall cover you with His Feathers, and under His Wings you shall find refuge; His Truth shall be your shield and buckler.

You shall not be afraid of the terror by night, nor of the arrow that flies by the day, nor of the pestilence that walks in darkness, nor of the destruction that lays waste at noonday. A thousand may fall at your side, and ten thousand at your right hand; but it shall not come near you.

Only with your eyes shall you look, and see the reward of the wicked. Because you have made the Lord Who is my Refuge, even the Most High, your Dwelling Place, no evil shall befall you nor shall any plaque come near your dwelling.

He shall give His angels Charge over you, to keep you in all your ways. In their hands they shall bear you up, lest you dash your foot against a stone. You shall tread upon the lion and the cobra, the young lion and the serpent you shall trample underfoot.

Because you have set your love upon God, therefore He will deliver you, He will set you on high, because you have known His Name.

You shall call upon Him, and He will answer you. He will be with you in trouble: He will deliver you and honour you. With long life He will satisfy you, and show you His Salvation.

The Lord delivered Shadrach, Meshach and Abed-Nego from the fiery furnace of King Nebuchadnezzar. The fire had been heated seven times more as commanded by the king in his rage. The king also gave them a second opportunity to bow to the image so that they will not be burnt.

However, they maintained their steadfastness in the Lord their God and the Lord God delivered them (Dan. 3).

Don't compromise your faith and stand because of threats, persecutions, and trials. Even if it involves your losing your life, do not love your life to death and you will have it back at the Appearing of the Lord Jesus Christ.

The Lord delivered Daniel from lions when he was put into the den of lions. The Lord closed the mouths of the lions so that they could not eat him up; when Daniel was brought out, it was found out that not only did the lions not touch him, there was also no wound on him (Dan. 6).

When the Jews wanted to push Jesus Christ down the cliff, the Lord turned and walked through them and passed, and they could not touch Him. An angel of the Lord came into the prison where Peter was being held and delivered him.

Paul and Silas were also delivered when they prayed and sang praises to the Lord their God. God delivered Paul from shipwreck so that he did not die through it.

Even now, the Christian who is obedient to God, who is holy, prayerful, full of the Holy Spirit, full of faith, and who is sensitive to the Leading of the Holy Spirit, is untouchable.

Neither the devil nor man can destroy him. He is above destruction; it is only by persecution, for the Sake of Jesus Christ, that he himself can decide to lay down his life for the Cause of Christ.

Witches and wizards are so afraid of that Christian that they tremble because of him. The Precious Blood of Jesus Christ protects us and speaks good things that work for our good. Dare to be untouchable!

Don't keep the things that belong to the devil with you, so that they will not attract the devil and his works to you. Don't live his life, so that you will not attract his presence into your life or suffer the same thing(s) God has apportioned for him!

Using contaminated things will invite the devil into your life. If you bring an accursed thing to your house, God will count your house as accursed and you will not stand before your enemies (Josh. 7:10-13). That God might have had mercy on you this far does not mean that it will always be like that. Remove the accursed thing before the devil destroys you.

That is the danger the people that carry chaplets and moulded things they call Jesus' and Mary's structures have fallen into. God said that you must not make for yourself a carved image of anything or anybody, and you shall not bow down to them (Exo. 20:4-5). That is idolatry!

Using things dedicated to the devil will contaminate you and bring heavy loss into your life. You girls and ladies that use another person's dress, powder, shoe, etc can get initiated into secret societies, especially the mermaid kingdom, by that simple act. Many of the people you see are not what they pose to be, even inside the church.

The devil walks around the clock. Many focus their minds on 12:00 a.m., 3:00 a.m., etc as when the devil will attack them; and they prepare to backfire at those times. Well, inasmuch as there are times of concentrated demonic works, know that the devil does not sleep.

Many times, just spending enough time with God will neutralize demonic works programmed against you, even without having prayed specifically against them. Yes, you will need to destroy the works of the devil, but don't give the devil three hours while you give God ten minutes.

As a matter of fact, devil's power is nothing before God's Power. If you spend two or three hours with God, only five minutes declaration after that can neutralize all the works of the devil against you. But many fear satan, demons, and witches more than they fear God. Sorry!

THE POWER AND AUTHORITY OF THE BELIEVER

When the Lord Jesus Christ rose up from the dead, He declared that all power in Heaven and on earth has been given to Him. Now, Jesus Christ is God, and has never lost power as God (though He emptied Himself of His Divine Power before coming to the earth).

God is Lord over the entire universe, including the earth, whether it is physical, spiritual, or any other realm. Even the devil is nothing before God, and cannot do anything without God's Permission.

When God was to send satan out of Heaven, He did not need to fight with the devil because that would have amounted to giving much credit to the devil: He only sent Archangel Michael to do the job.

All the things that the devil is doing today and all his plans, boastings, and pride are because God allowed him (God permitted him, even though He never commissioned him). When his time is up, God will put him into the Lake of Fire which burns with brimstone.

However when you (as a landlord) leases your house to somebody for a period of time, within that period of time, you don't intrude anyhow into the house, except with your tenant's permission.

This is what happened when God created man and gave him dominion over the earth and the things in it. The devil came and tempted Adam (the first man), and because Adam disobeyed God, Adam lost the dominion God gave him to the devil.

It is that dominion, and for the restoration of mankind that the Lord Jesus Christ came. You know, when man sinned, demons, pain, sicknesses, diseases, poverty, and things like them started to have effects on men.

But Jesus Christ triumphed over principalities and powers, and made a public show of them. He said, "Go therefore…." He meant that the restored man, the Church, should go in the power and authority that He collected from the devil (which was originally man's).

However, the devil will continue to operate and rule over people (except the Christians) until Adam's time is over, that is, at the Second Coming of Jesus Christ. This is why the devil is called the god of this world (2 Cor. 4:4).

It is only Christians that have power and authority over the devil. Christ delivered us from the power of darkness and translated us to His Kingdom, and the devil doesn't have power and authority over us.

Therefore, none of us should get entangled in sin and disobedience, so that the devil will not lord it over us. It is not a matter of who has power but who has the legal ground to use the power, because the devil's power is powerless before the Holy Spirit's Power (the Spirit that lives in us).

You will punish every act of disobedience when your obedience is complete (2 Cor. 10:6). A word is enough for the wise.

Some Believers wonder why the devil prevails over them, why they still suffer under him, contrary to the Will of God. I said, 'contrary to the Will of God,' because we will pass through persecutions, trials, tests, and temptations, and the devil is responsible for the persecutions, trials, and temptations.

However, many suffer what they shouldn't have suffered because they broke the hedge around them, and gave the devil and his demons openings.

"Behold I give to you power to tread on serpents and scorpions and over all the power of the enemy, and nothing shall by any means hurt you" (Lk. 10:19).

This is the Word of Jesus Christ the Son of the Living God, Who can neither lie nor fail to perform what He has said. Instead of His Word not to come to pass, heaven and earth shall pass away.

But why do the devil, his demons, and his human agents hurt and harm those who believe in Christ? It is a matter of breaking the defence.

You can let the devil have a place in you by carelessness, disobedience, compromise, unbelief, and sin. And the Word of God tells us to give the devil no place in our lives, even in the lives of our family members (Eph. 4:27).

That is why the Word says, "Believe in the Lord Jesus Christ, and you will be saved, you and your family" (Acts 16:31). You have authority over your family and you can command the devil, in the Name of Jesus Christ, to remove his hands from your family members.

The devil oppresses, obsesses, and possesses people through his demons. Demonic oppression involves afflicting your body with sicknesses, diseases, pains, etc. Demonic obsession involves influencing your mind so that you are pressed to feel or think a particular way. Demonic possession involves their taking over your spirit, soul, and body completely.

We have power over the devil and his works and the weapons of our warfare are not carnal but mighty in God for pulling down of strongholds, casting down arguments and every high thing that exalts itself against the knowledge of God, bringing every thought into captivity to the obedience of Christ (2 Cor. 10:4-5).

We have the power and authority to subdue things and beings that are not subject to God. God anointed Jesus Christ with the Holy Spirit and with power, and He went about doing good and healing all who were oppressed by the devil, for God was with Him (Acts 10:38).

And the Lord tells us that we will do the works that He did; we will do greater works than those He did. The Holy Spirit was sent to us when He went back to Heaven, and the Lord sits at the Right Hand of God, where He lives to make intercession for us. We are not alone!

The Holy Spirit of the Living God, Who lives in us, is our Helper, Advocate, Intercessor, Standby, Comforter, Strengthener, and Counselor. You have overcome because greater is He that is in you than he that is in the world.

The Believers will cast out demons in the Name of Jesus Christ; they will take up serpents and won't be harmed by them; if they drink deadly poison (witchcraft or chemical), it will not hurt them; and they will lay hands on the sick, and they will recover.

When the Lord sent out the twelve, they were empowered to preach the Gospel, heal the sick, cleanse the lepers, raise the dead, and cast out demons (Matt. 10:7-8). We are to do the same.

The Spirit of God that came upon you is not just for speaking in tongues. It is to preach the Good News of the Kingdom of God, to heal the broken-hearted, to proclaim liberty to the captives, and recovery of sight to the blind.

He came upon you to set at liberty those who are oppressed, and to proclaim the Acceptable Year of the Lord (Lk. 4:18-19). You carry the very Power of God!

Christians receive power when the Holy Spirit comes upon them, and they are made witnesses, who by signs and wonders, prove that Jesus Christ is the same yesterday, today, and forever. The anointing breaks every yoke and lifts every burden. The Kingdom of God is not in word but in power.

We ought to be so anointed that we can no more be yoked. We should give ourselves to consistent prayer-life, with self-discipline and self-denial, so that we will move well with the Holy Ghost.

Indeed they shall surely assemble, but not because of God. Whoever assembles against us shall fall for our sake. No weapon that is formed against us shall prosper, and every tongue which rises against us in judgment, we shall condemn.

This is the heritage of the Servants of the Lord, and their righteousness is from Him (Isa. 54:15,17). Live a holy and a righteous life, and no devil nor their works will hurt you! In Christ Jesus, you are secure and protected.

Surely the Lord shall deliver you from the snare of the fowler and from the perilous pestilence. He shall cover you with His Feathers, and under His Wings you shall take refuge; His Truth shall be your shield and buckler.

You shall not be afraid of the terror by night nor of the arrow that flies by day, nor of the pestilence that walks in darkness, nor of the destruction that lays waste at noonday.

A thousand may fall at your side and ten thousand at your right hand, but it shall not come near you. Because you have made the Lord your Refuge, no evil shall befall you, nor shall any plague come near your dwelling; for He shall give His angels Charge over you to keep you in all your ways.

In their hands they shall bear you up, lest you dash your foot against a stone. You shall tread upon the lion and the cobra. He will deliver you and set you on high. When you call on Him, He will answer you. He will be with you in trouble, deliver you, and honour you.

With long life He will satisfy you and show you His Salvation (Psa. 91). You need not fear death, for you cannot die except the Lord permits it.

The Lord has called us to contend with the forces of darkness, and pull down the strongholds of the enemy, the devil.

No matter what you may be going through, there is power to set you free, and that power and authority is available in Jesus Christ and His Holy Spirit. The Lord has sent us to preach deliverance to the captives. These days, seducing spirits and doctrines of devils abound.

The Anointing of God's Spirit on you breaks every yoke of the devil and lifts the burdens of the enemy. Therefore, learn to wait on the Lord to renew your strength and increase the anointing in your life so that you can accomplish what God wants to be accomplished through you.

When the anointing in your life is strong enough, witches and wizards will run away from you. You should walk in the mountain-moving faith.

When you walk that way, no arrow the devil throws at you will succeed. Faith is the shield which protects you from the fiery darts of the enemy. Just as Daniel stayed with the lions without being hurt, you too can stay where the power of the devil is concentrated, and yet nothing will harm you.

Learn to praise God always. Praise puts the enemy to the flight. Prayer is like throwing bomb to the camp of the enemy; they will run for their lives, and many will be destroyed thereby. However, praise brings down God's Presence, and they cannot escape God's Intention; God is fearful in praises.

The walls of Jericho fell down when God's people praised Him. In prayer, God sends angels; but in praises, God comes down to do the work by Himself. When God comes down, which devil will stand?

God will remove sicknesses and diseases from you, so that none of the diseases or sicknesses the enemy may throw at you will get you. But you must be obedient to God; you must keep a close and intimate relationship with God to be covered by Him always.

Don't be afraid while doing what the Lord has called you to do. God calls people and commissions them without leaving them helpless; rather, the Lord commissions us with power. It is the Power and Anointing of the Holy Spirit that will break every shackle, destroy every yoke, and lift every burden.

The Church is marching on, and the gates of Hades shall not prevail! Be strong in the Lord and in the power of His Might (Eph. 6:10). This is a Command which the Lord has given to us. If the Lord has commanded us to be strong in Him, then we must obey Him and do just that.

How do we get strong in the Lord? There are many ways to get strong in the Lord, but we will start with the way that is given to us in the same chapter, and that is by putting on the whole Armour of God.

Armour is a defensive weapon; this is why we talk of armoured cars or vehicles in warfare. But looking at the armour we are given, we notice that one of them is an offensive weapon, and that is the Word of God, which the Bible calls 'the Sword of the Spirit' (Eph. 6:17).

There are many more offensive weapons we use and can use in our spiritual warfare. You know that we do not war against flesh and blood but against spiritual entities. The weapons we fight with are not carnal but mighty through God to the pulling down of strongholds (2 Cor. 10:4).

Other weapons (defensive and offensive) that we will consider include: the Name of Jesus Christ, the Blood of Jesus Christ, the Fire of the Holy Spirit, the anointing, speaking in tongues, praises, fasting, etc.

God showed me, by revelation, that certain situations require certain weapons; therefore, don't expect to use only particular ones and say that others are not necessary. I might have thought the same way, but God showed me otherwise.

One mighty weapon to use in our Christian life and spiritual warfare is the weapon of obedience. We will be able to punish every act of disobedience when our own obedience is complete (2 Cor. 10:6). Absolute obedience to God is holiness. Obedience is better than sacrifice and self-denial (1 Sam. 15:22).

According to the sixth chapter of the Book of Ephesians, we should be strong in the Lord and in the power of His Might. We should put on the whole Armour of God that we may be able to stand against the wiles of the devil.

For we wrestle not against flesh and blood, but against principalities, against powers, against the rulers of the darkness of this age, against spiritual hosts of wickedness in the heavenly places.

Therefore, take up the whole Armour of God, that you may be able to withstand in the evil day, and having done all, to stand.

We are to gird our waist with the belt of truth. It is the belt that holds your armour or wears together. The Word of God is the Word of Truth. The Word speaks of sanctification by the Word which is truth (Jn 17:17).

The Word of God cleanses us as we hear it (Jn 15:3). We are to rightly divide the Word of God (2 Tim. 2:15). To rightly divide the Word of Truth is to interpret the Word aright. It is to put Scripture where it belongs; and the Bible speaks of comparing Scripture with Scripture (1 Cor. 2:13).

Let the Word dwell in you richly in all wisdom (Col. 3:16). The belt of truth is a clear understanding of the Word of God.

Then, we should put on the breastplate of righteousness. The breastplate of righteousness protects your heart, your spirit, for your heart is located around your breast or chest. When we believed on the Lord Jesus Christ, we received the gift of righteousness from Him, which gave us a right-standing with God.

But the Bible says that he who does righteousness is righteous as Jesus Christ is righteous. If you commit sin, if you live in sin, you are of the devil (1 Jn 3:8). Righteousness is doing right; it is doing the good that you ought to do (Jas 4:17).

Then comes the shoeing of our feet with the preparation of the Gospel of Peace. It is the Gospel, the Good News of the Kingdom that brings peace to men; therefore, preach the Gospel, the Word of God, in season and out of season (2 Tim. 4:2).

Follow peace with all men (Heb. 12:14). Inasmuch as it lies with you, live peaceably with all (Rom. 12:18). Don't allow strife, envy, quarrels, and contentions into your life.

You must take the shield of faith with which you will be able to quench all the fiery darts of the wicked one. The devil throws many wicked arrows at us, and it is only faith that can protect us.

Faith is the assurance of things hoped for, the evidence of things not seen (Heb. 11:1). Faith comes by hearing and hearing by the Word of God (Rom. 10:17). Therefore, faith is being convinced of, being sure of the Word of God.

When you have faith, you are confident that your Almighty God will do for you what He says He will do for you.

Also, take the helmet of salvation. The Word speaks of the hope of salvation which shall be revealed in the Last Day (1 Thes. 5:8). It is the helmet that will protect your head; if your head is not protected, you may as soon become a dead man.

Many are walking around as Christians while they are already dead. In this age where evil abounds, it is your salvation, which is the hope of the Glory that shall be revealed when Christ comes, that will protect you.

Without such hope, your love will grow cold and you will backslide. But it is only those who endure to the end that shall be saved (Matt. 24:13).

Take the Sword of the Spirit which is the Word of God. The Sword of the Spirit is the offensive declaration and confession of the Word of God with your mouth.

As you speak the right Scriptures, in the spiritual realm, the Word you speak come out of your mouth as sword, piercing the devil. The Word of God comes out of your mouth as fire and as hammer (Jer. 23:29).

Then you are to pray always with all prayer and supplication in the Spirit, being watchful in prayer with all perseverance and supplication for all the Saints (Eph. 6:18).

Watch and pray that you may not fall into temptation. The spirit indeed is willing, but the flesh is weak (Matt. 26:41). Have you known that prayer is one of the things that Christians find very hard to do, even though it is indispensable and should be part of our lives?

Maintain a consistent prayer-life. Add fasting to your prayer, for fasting multiplies the power of prayer many times. If you say you can't fast, even till 12:00 p.m. or 4:00 p.m. because you are pregnant or sick, the day you may have miscarriage or die, you will judge for yourself whether you are wiser than God.

Other weapons include the Name of Jesus Christ. At the Name of Jesus Christ, every knee should bow, of things (beings) in heaven, and of things (beings) on earth, and of things (beings) under the earth, and every tongue should confess that Jesus Christ is Lord, to the Glory of God the Father (Phil. 2:9-11).

The Blood of Jesus Christ protects us from the attacks of the enemy. The Blood speaks better things than the blood of Abel (Heb. 12:24). Learn to plead the Blood of Jesus Christ; it is a good attitude. However, don't plead the Blood in fear, for the hosts of Heaven are for you and with you.

The Holy Ghost's Fire is a mighty weapon that is at our disposal. Many don't believe in it. However, inasmuch as there are ways people pray which I don't like, the Lord showed me the effectiveness of the Fire of the Holy Ghost in spiritual warfare (Matt. 3:11).

The anointing is another mighty weapon of spiritual warfare, and there are different kinds and levels of the anointing. The Anointing and Power of the Holy Spirit breaks every yoke (Isa. 10:27).

Speaking in tongues is another mighty weapon. When you speak in tongues, you speak mysteries (hidden things) to God, you confuse the devil, and you pray for what you don't know of, the right way (1 Cor. 14:2; Rom. 8:26).

Praise is a weapon that scatters devils and sets confusion into the kingdom of darkness. Use it always. The last weapon we will discuss is spiritual gifts. The Manifestation of the Spirit (spiritual gift) is given to everyone for the good of all (1 Cor. 12:7). Use your own spiritual gift(s) effectively.

But to put on any armour, you must be spiritually alive and strong. First, you must be born again. Then you should be filled with the Holy Spirit, for you are endued with God's Power when you are filled. Be sensitive to the Holy Spirit and let Him lead you.

Let the fruit of the recreated human spirit (or the Fruit of the Spirit, according to the King James Version and some other versions) be abundant in you (Gal. 5:22-23). Make every effort to stand so that you will not fall.

As Christians, we are supposed to be mighty in words and deeds. When people see us, they are supposed to see Jesus Christ. God does not expect us to remain as spiritual babies, but we are to grow and mature to the fulness of the Stature of Christ Jesus. Seek to know the Lord more than before; seek God more than anything else.

Learn to praise and worship God always. The angels in Heaven worship God always. They sing, "Holy, holy, holy, Lord God Almighty…" and they fear and bow down before the Lord. Worship the Lord in the beauty of holiness. The more you praise and worship God, the more satan will run away from you.

They that know their God shall be strong, and they shall do exploits. To know your God, you have to know His Word and also know Him personally and intimately in prayer.

Knowing God will lead to your doing exploits, in signs, wonders, and miracles. You shall do the works that Jesus Christ did, even greater works than them.

Don't live the normal life that everybody lives. Dare to live extra-ordinarily. That is God's Will for you: living the extra-ordinary life. That extra-ordinary life is the supernatural life, and it transcends natural laws. It is the life by the Spirit of God; it is living by faith, and not by sight.

If many Christians apply half of what they know now, satan, his demons, and his human agents will be so afraid of them, that they will relate with them from afar.

But the devil operates almost freely in the lives of many Christians without much fear. God has told and taught many people many things and yet they don't apply them. It is applied knowledge that brings results.

If you know all and apply nothing, instead of gaining, you will lose, because the Servant that knows His Master's Commands and does not do them will be beaten with more stripes (Lk. 12:47-48).

There is a level of lack of knowledge, and that is a more terrible level, because you will not apply the things you don't know. Hence, the Word of God says that God's people perish for lack of knowledge (Hos. 4:6). Ignorance of God, His Word and Ways, and the ways of the devil will lead to loss, death, and destruction.

Of course, no one knows everything about God or the devil, but you can increase your knowledge by the study and reading of the Bible and other Godly Christian materials.

Some people listen to their pastors or general-overseers only. Though that approach has a positive side of being in a better position to avoid error and intrusion of false teachings, yet it has the negative side of not receiving what God may want to pass to you through other ministers.

There are many people that the Lord has called, and they have different ministries, abilities, and areas of calling. All you need for your Christian life can never be passed to you by any one preacher.

However, as you listen to anybody or read their materials, be careful to follow God's Spirit and His Word. This is why you must be sensitive to the Anointing that teaches you all things (1 Jn 2:20,27).

And you must be full of the Word of God so that you can test and prove the teachings you hear. If you are sincere, God will lead you into the truth and lead you away from the spirit of error.

This is not to say that you must listen to everybody. Don't listen to those you are convinced (without bias) are not teaching the truth. Remember that a little leaven leavens the whole lump. Small error can cause great havoc to your Christian faith.

I am saying this because we know that there are many false prophets and false teachers who use the Bible and the Name of Jesus Christ to extend the thoughts, plans, and works of the devil. There are many false ministers.

However, we are speaking about knowing what to do and not doing it. Whoever knows the good he should do and does not do it, to him it is sin (Jas 4:17). God commands us to be doers of the Word, and not just hearers alone.

He tells us that if we hear and do not do what we hear, we are deceiving ourselves (Jas 1:22). But don't deceive yourself nor let another person deceive you. God can never be mocked.

God loves obedience, and doing His Word proves to Him that you love Him (Jn 14:15). Absolute complete obedience is holiness, and without holiness, no man can see the Lord.

Even when you might have not reached perfection, make up your mind that whatever you are sure God wants you to do, you will do. That state of mind is consecration and dedication to God, and it is holiness.

God will then increase your knowledge and help you do what you are to do in order to perfect holiness (2 Cor. 7:1). The grace and ability to obey Him is there; use it!

Prayer is one area people don't apply what they know. When they listen to good messages about prayer, they decide to be consistently prayerful, but many never make it, for they go back after few days.

Some go back because of discouragement, but you don't need to be discouraged; you only need to be persistent. Think about this: those that take part in games, train and discipline themselves in order to succeed; and many of them make mistakes and fail along the line.

But it is persistence and consistence that produce champions. A winner or a champion had made many mistakes before. Some principles of God's Word don't produce fruits overnight; and God doesn't always settle His Account with people every twenty-four hours.

Some principles take a very long time to mature and produce the needed fruits. Others may take a short or shorter time, but make up your mind to achieve the results.

The Word of God is a seed and you know that some seeds or trees (crops) produce within a year (annual crops); some produce within two years (biennial crops); and some produce after many years (perennial plants).

Even pregnancy among animals takes different lengths of time. Some can produce within a short period (like insects); others within nine months (like human beings); and others after more than a year (like elephants).

In building construction, the bigger and taller the building, the deeper and more solid the foundation (of course, the nature of the ground or soil matters a lot; rocky basement will require a shallower foundation than sandy or clayey soil). Some foundations can cost what you may use to finish a five-storey building, like foundations for sky-scrappers.

You must apply what you know and wait patiently to reap its results. The devil has no mercy, and ignorance is no excuse to him.

In fact, he will want you to be ignorant of him and his devices; but we are not ignorant of his devices, and he will not get an advantage over us. In battle, if you don't know of your enemy's strategy, you may be destroyed in a split-second.

How can you use a machete to attack someone coming against you with a gun? And why will you use a gun to fire someone throwing bombs on you from fighter-jets? Be wise as serpents and harmless as doves (Matt. 10:16).

Demonic works and strongholds need confrontation. You must confront demonic conditions with God's Power. It may require fasting, and you have to do it (as led by the Holy Spirit).

Only counseling will not do the work. That is why people are counseled often, and they remain in their problems. Of course, if someone submits to counseling under God's Word and Anointing, he will receive result because God's Word is anointed.

The five foolish virgins should have carried extra oil; but they didn't, either by ignorance or by carelessness, and missed the bridegroom (Matt. 25:1-13). Let this not be your portion in any area in the Name of Jesus Christ. Amen.

Renew your mind by the Word of God and think the Way God thinks, and you will do God's Will. You need more information from the Word of God to increase your faith and function more effectively.

Some don't apply what they know because of unbelief. There are two kinds of unbelief: unbelief that comes by lack of the knowledge of the Word of God, and the unbelief that exists, not because you don't know, but because you are not persuaded by the Word that you know.

The second one is what the other ten spies, apart from Joshua and Caleb, exhibited. God had told them that Jericho will fall for their sake, but because of what they saw with their physical eyes, they doubted the Word of God (Num. 13 & 14).

The secret of receiving what you want is obedience, and obedience is the application of what you know. It is the application that produces the results and not just the knowledge.

Science without technology amounts to nothing. Science is the finding and the knowledge, and technology is the application of scientific findings and knowledge to solve the existing needs. This is true in medical, biological, chemical, engineering, and agricultural fields.

The same is applicable in Christianity. God's Word is meant to solve needs. If you want people to believe in your God, then your God will have to solve their problems.

Many Christians wonder why unbelievers go to witch-doctors for this or that solution. Preach and teach the real Word of God and allow God manifest Himself through you; if you do, more souls will accept our Lord and Christ.

Abraham was told to leave his country, and he left in obedience to God's Voice. Noah was directed to build an ark, with specifications, and he did it. Moses was told to build the ark of covenant and the tabernacle exactly the way he saw them, and he did it so.

Jesus Christ followed God's Plan for His Life and succeeded in His Earthly Ministry. Follow God's Word and Leading for you, as an individual, and what you will see will blow your mind!

What have you lost in your life? What have you failed to receive from God, because of satanic and demonic interferences? What has the devil taken from your loved ones? As a church or a group of people, what have you lost?

A time came in David's life that the Amalekites invaded Ziklag, and burned it with fire, taking captives their women (wives), their sons, and their daughters.

David and the people that were with him lifted up their voice and wept, until they had no more power to weep. What a calamity! Have your sufferings reached that extent?

David's two wives were taken captive. And David was greatly distressed; for the people spoke of stoning him, but David encouraged himself in the Lord his God.

David enquired of the Lord, saying, "Shall I pursue after this troop? Shall I overtake them?" And He answered him, "Pursue, for you shall surely overtake them, and without fail recover all."

So David went, he and his men. But David pursued, even though some of them who were very weak stayed behind when they could not cross the Brook Besor.

Along the way, they found someone who had not eaten for three days and fed him. When he had got his strength back, he directed David and his men to where the invading troops were.

Then David attacked them and recovered all that they had taken away. What would have happened if David had not pursued and attacked them? He would have lost all.

What would have happened if he had not enquired of the Lord? He might have not had the courage to pursue and attack them. God knows of your losses and predicaments, and He will make a way for you.

Even the Amalekite's servant that fell sick so that his master abandoned him (he directed David) was in God's Plan for the whole thing (1 Sam. 30:1-20).

This was also demonstrated by Abraham when he recovered Lot. When Sodom and other cities were attacked, the invading army took all the goods of Sodom, and all their provisions, and went their way.

They also took Lot, Abraham's brother's son who dwelt in Sodom, and his goods and departed. Then one who had escaped came and told Abraham, the Hebrew. When Abraham heard that his brother was taken captive, he armed his men and pursued the captors.

Abraham armed his three hundred and eighteen trained servants, who were born in his own house, and went in pursuit as far as Dan. He divided his forces against them by night, and he and his servants attacked them and pursued them.

So he brought back all the goods, and also brought back his brother Lot and his goods, as well as the women and the people (Gen. 14).

After his return, he gave tithe to Melchizedek who blessed him and said, "Blessed be Abram of God Most High, possessor of Heaven and earth; and blessed be God Most High, Who delivered your enemies into your hand."

Abraham would have lost Lot if he had remained in his place comfortably and not pursued. But he refused to remain at ease, and chose rather to act; and when he acted, he brought glory to the Name of the Lord.

The Word of God says that we should occupy till the Lord comes (Lk. 19:13). To occupy is to take charge and control of what you have been given to oversee. It is to enter a place and keep control of it; for example, by a military force.

In this case, the Lord wants us to oversee and do what He has entrusted into our hands, and keep it from interference by an enemy.

Then, even if due to one reason or the other, an enemy invaded our ground and took away anything, we should pursue, overtake, and recover all. To occupy is to do the Father's Business (the Lord's Business).

Some reason that since their income is enough, they will be buying medicine to control the disease they are passing through, which might have been termed 'incurable.'

Some may say, "Since I have this church or ministry, even if it is not flourishing well, at least let me maintain it." Inasmuch as we should give thanks to God in any situation we find ourselves in, yet it is the Lord's Will that you enjoy the fullness of His Provisions for you.

However, we must recognize that some deprivations and harsh states are brought about or allowed by the Lord Himself for different purposes. What I am saying is that you should know when to pursue and when not to pursue. Even David enquired of the Lord and pursued when the Lord told him to pursue.

Some harsh conditions may be a test or a trial for you, and in that case, pursuing will not help matters, because it will not change it.

God told me that it is not every time that you have to bind and loose in prayers to correct a negative situation. He cited the case of Abraham whose wife was barren. Abraham prayed to God about the situation and God gave him a son, without binding and loosing (or dealing with demons).

If you study your Bible well, you will come to know that the prayer of binding and losing (or casting out demons) will not solve some undesirable conditions. For example, do you think that Prophet Jonah would have cast out that big fish that swallowed him?

His was a case of sin and disobedience, and what he needed to do to be free was repentance, confession, and mercy. Some will not come out of their conditions until their knowledge and wisdom have been developed to a level that God is satisfied.

Some will not come out until they learn humility and despise pride. You may not like the situation, but God allowed it for your own good, for your development and promotion.

There is a case in the Bible where the Israelites said, "The time has not come, the time that the Lord's House should be built." The Lord asked them, saying, "Is it time for you yourselves to dwell in your paneled houses, and this Temple to lie in ruins?"

The Lord went on, "Consider your ways! You have sown much, and bring in little; you eat but do not have enough; you drink, but you are not filled with drink; you clothe yourselves, but no one is warm; and he who earns wages, earns wages to put them into a bag with holes."

The Lord told them, "Consider your ways! Go up to the mountains and bring wood and build the Temple, that I may take pleasure in it and be glorified. You looked for much, but indeed it came to little; when you brought it home, I blew it away.

"Why? Because of My House that is in ruins, while every one of you runs to his own house. Therefore the heavens above you withhold the dew, and the earth withholds its fruit. For I called for a drought on the land and the mountains…on whatever the ground brings forth, on men and livestock, and on all the labour of your hands" (Hag. 1).

However, whatever the enemy, who comes not but to steal, kill, and destroy, might have taken away from you will be restored to you. But you have to pursue him and overtake him so that you can recover all.

When you believe, you speak and confess so that you can possess your possession. Confront your confrontations! Pray through; pray until you have a witness that you have prayed through.

Some prayers require fastings. You may have to do some days or weeks of night-vigils, maybe some three hours every night.

The violent takes his inheritance and possession by force. The Spirit of God lifts up a standard against the devil. Greater is He that is in you than he that is in the world. Confront the devil. God has not given you a spirit of fear, but of power and of love and of sound mind (2 Tim. 1:7).

The Lord is with you, and He will never leave you. They that are with you are more than they that are against you. One angel destroyed one hundred and eighty-five thousand Assyrian soldiers in one night (2 Kgs 19:35).

Be glad then, you children of Zion, and rejoice in the Lord your God; for He has given you the former rain faithfully, and He will cause the rain to come down for you – the former rain and the later rain in the first month.

The threshing floors shall be full of wheat, and the vats shall overflow with new wine and oil. So the Lord will restore to you the years that the swarming locust has eaten, the crawling locust, the consuming locust, and the chewing locust, His great army which He sent among you.

You shall eat in plenty and be satisfied, and praise the Name of the Lord your God, Who has dealt wondrously with you, and God's people shall never be put to shame. Then you shall know that He is in the midst of Israel. He is the Lord your God and there is no other. God's people shall never be put to shame (Joel 2: 23-27).

Learn to distinguish when to wait on God and when to pursue and overtake the invaders and spoilers.

We must understand the strategies of the enemy, so that he will not gain an advantage over us. God's people perish because of ignorance.

We should not even give him the opportunity to strike in the first place, to take away anything from us; however, if he succeeds in depriving us of anything, we must pursue him and recover all by force.

Are you possessing your inheritance in Christ Jesus the way you should? How will you feel, if when you get to Heaven, you realize that you deprived yourself of many things the Lord purchased and provided for you?

Whatever you have lost shall be found. Whatever the enemy has stolen or robbed from you shall be found and recovered. But you have your part to play; and you know that God cannot fail to fulfil His Own Part.

The Kingdom of God suffers violence, and the violent take it by force. Don't sit back and watch the devil deprive you of God's Blessings for you without doing anything. Pursue, overtake, and recover all!

SECRETS TO GOD'S MIRACLE-WORKING POWER

If you must walk in God's Miracle-working Power, you must have an intimate relationship with Him. I am speaking of walking in that power consistently. An intimate relationship with God will necessitate your knowing and understanding His Word.

His Word will tell you His Character and His Ability. From His Word, you will get to know your rights and privileges as a child of God; you will develop your faith, for faith comes by hearing the Word of God.

Let the Word of God dwell in you richly in all wisdom (Col. 3:16), and study to show yourself approved to God, a workman that needs not to be ashamed, rightly dividing the Word of Truth (2 Tim. 2:15).

When you study the Word well, and compare Scripture with Scripture, you will understand it clearly and put the Word of God where it belongs: you will not misapply the Word. The devil wanted Jesus Christ to misapply the Scripture when he quoted Scripture for the wrong purpose.

To walk in God's Miracle-working Power consistently requires that you maintain a consistent prayer-life. The Lord Jesus Christ communed with the Father daily and always when He was on this earth as a Man.

He rose up very early in the morning and prayed till daybreak. He spent whole nights or almost the whole praying sometimes. He prayed from daylight into the night. He prayed in the public, and he prayed in private.

Prayer is the master-key, and you can't do without it. The more consistent your prayer-life is, the more consistent will be the manifestation of the Power of God through you to people.

The early apostles and Disciples prayed. They prayed in group, and they prayed privately. Even buildings shook when they prayed and sang. Don't get too busy working for God that you do not have time to commune with Him daily.

Another thing that will activate the Power of God in your life is fasting. Fasting helps you put the body under subjection to your spirit so that you can obey God and do His Will better.

You know that the spirit-man desires to do the Will of God, while the flesh (because it is weak) will want its desires to be met. Some of those desires are not sinful and some are.

For instance, the desires for food and sleep are not sinful, but you can eat too much or at the improper times that the fulfilled desire can hinder the Free-flow of the Spirit of God through you.

Also, if you love sleep, it will affect your prayer-life adversely, because you will sleep more than is necessary. Too much sleep will bring weakness and laziness into your life, and these will make you ineffective in your walk with God.

Therefore, you must learn to limit those desires that are not necessarily sinful; and do not yield to the sinful desires of the body at all. There are: absolute fasting, total fasting, partial fasting, fruit or juice fasting, etc. You can even fast from newspapers and televisions, and use the extra time to pray and study the Word.

Then you must walk in love towards God, your brethren, and the rest of the people. Faith works by love, and without love, you are nothing.

Even if you have all faith so that you can remove mountains, if you have the gift of prophecy, and you receive the Revelations and Visions of God, without love, you amount to nothing and God will not allow you into His Kingdom.

Love will enable you to obey God and do the right things to your neighbours. You will need to have compassion for the people you are ministering to; be patient with them and forbear their weaknesses and immature behaviours.

Many of the miracles Jesus Christ performed were done because He had compassion on the people. Compassion will activate the Power and the Gift of God in you. The Spirit of God works with the meek in spirit. You must be gentle and not be ruled by harshness.

Humility is very necessary also. God resists the proud but gives grace to the humble (Jas 4:6). God will not share His Glory with anyone (Isa. 48:11).

Whatever God uses you to do, give all the glory and praise to Him. It is not because you ran or because you willed. No, it is because God showed you mercy. The power that wrought the miracle is His, and you are only a vessel and an instrument.

He that plants and he that waters are nothing; it is God that makes the seed grow and produce that worths all; and we must recognize that God is a Good God.

To walk in signs, wonders, and miracles require total and unreserved obedience. Obedience is better than sacrifice. Don't go by feelings: if God leads you to go and preach when you don't feel high spiritually, obey Him and go. That may be the day you will see the greatest miracle in your life.

We walk by faith and not by sight. You will be able to punish every act of disobedience when your obedience is complete (2 Cor. 10:6). Don't be a hearer of the Word, deceiving yourself; but be a doer of the Word.

God is of Purer Eyes than to behold iniquity (Habk. 1:13). If you hide iniquity in your heart, the Lord will not hear you. Therefore, you must live the life of holiness if you want to see mighty miracles through you. Let no sin or weight remain in your life: sin entangles, and weight hinders.

Get rid of them; let righteousness rule in your life. Above all, know that whatever you may accomplish for God, if you miss Heaven, if you go to Hell, you achieved nothing. Without holiness, no man can see the Lord.

Then you must be perfect as your Heavenly Father is perfect (Matt. 5:48). God cannot tell us to do what we cannot do: God is just. In every area of your life, be perfect.

In words, be perfect; in actions, be perfect; in character, be perfect; in spirit, faith, love, and purity, be perfect; whatever you do, be perfect. Even your thoughts are to be perfect. Perfection has to do with maturity. Even holiness should be perfected (2 Cor. 7:1).

You must not allow any idle word out of your mouth. Let no corrupt word proceed out of your mouth. Fresh water and bitter water do not flow from the same source. Curses and blessings ought not to flow from the same mouth of the child of God.

Be careful how you think because your thoughts will affect your words. Let your words be seasoned with grace, so that your hearers will benefit. In preaching, do not preach wrong things. Teach the Right Doctrines.

If you are going to walk in God's Supernatural Power, you will have to expect persecutions, tests, and trials. Jesus Christ passed through them, and you cannot expect the opposite.

Satan will entice people to persecute you as he did towards Apostle Paul. But don't be discouraged; neither be dismayed. Allow no fear into your heart. Do not fear him who can touch the body but has no power over the soul in Hell. Fear Him who can destroy both the body and the soul in Hell.

Remember to deal with any wrong foundation in your life, for if the foundation is destroyed, what can even the righteous do? For instance, if you live in sin, you have a wrong foundation. Don't think that, by exaggeration, you will glorify God.

No, God hates lies, and you don't help God by lying. If you supplanted your friend, by deceit, to marry her fiancé, go and ask for her forgiveness. Don't waste your life working for God, when you are heading to Hell. Give no place to the devil.

When the apostles and Disciples went out and preached everywhere, the Lord worked with them confirming their Gospel with signs and wonders. If you want to see mighty healings and miracles in your life, you must go out and preach the Gospel.

Preach in buses, preach in markets, preach in streets, preach in houses; go out for early-morning cries, preach in season and out of season, preach everywhere.

If you preach the Gospel of the Kingdom, then God will confirm the Gospel you preach, because God confirms His Word. Don't sit back and wait to preach in your church's pulpit.

There are so many things you can learn from the Bible that will help you manifest God's Power. Among them are: self-discipline, self-denial, wisdom, watchfulness, diligence, honesty, and perseverance.

Don't worry yourself if it seems as though you failed or did not accomplish much at your first outing. Worrying, instead of adding, will remove from you. Be confident in your God and His Word, and soon, everybody will be looking for you to be prayed for. Elisha persisted and received the double-portion of Elijah's anointing!

Forget the past and mind the future. Beware of bad and evil company; evil association corrupts good manners. Get rid of ignorance, mistakes, and foolishness. Preach and teach the Word of God, in season and out of season. Never walk against God and His Plans, Purposes, and Will.

Godliness with contentment is of great gain, for we brought nothing into the world and it is certain that we can carry nothing with us at our death. Greed and covetousness will hamper the manifestation of the Power of God through you.

David was described by God as a man after His Heart, and Abraham was described as a Friend of God. What will you be described as? You must have the fear of God in your heart; without the fear of God, you can't please God.

Touch not, taste not, and handle not anything that offends God and that is contrary to Godliness and our faith. Give diligence to pressing toward the mark, the prize of the High Call of God in Christ Jesus.

THE PLACE OF FAITH

A Believer who lives in unbelief cannot do well in his Christian life: it is impossible. But, many Believers live in faithlessness in different areas of their lives. God does not take delight in faithlessness, because the righteous shall live by faith.

Faith makes it possible for someone to please God. Why? Because whoever comes to God must believe that He is and that He rewards those who diligently seek Him (Heb. 11:6). Faith comes by hearing, and hearing by the Word of God (Rom. 10:17).

Faith is: believing that God can neither lie nor disappoint you. God cannot fail to fulfill His Word. Instead of His Word not to come to pass, heaven and earth shall pass away (Matt. 24:35).

Faith is: "I will do this because God said I should do it." It is: "I will not do this because God said that I should avoid it." As a matter of fact, faith is comprehensive and embraces many things.

The study of the eleventh chapter of the Book of the Hebrews will confirm this to you. Faith is not just about receiving healings, prosperity, breakthroughs, miracles, and such things. In fact, faith is obedience to the Word of God.

Faith will make you offer a more excellent sacrifice. Your work of faith gives you certified righteousness. Faith will make you please God against all odds. Pleasing God will make you rapturable.

Believing that God exists and that He rewards diligence and faithfulness will make you please Him. Faith will make you give heed to Godly fear and Godly fear leads to righteous living.

Faith will make you obey God no matter how difficult. God can tell you to do a difficult thing, but not an impossible thing. Faith will make you not to hold on to the things of this world.

Faith will make you have confidence in God, and you will wait patiently for the fulfillment of God's Promises. Faith will make you ride above natural laws; faith will give you a tangible miracle. Faith is judging God faithful; it is to believe that God cannot lie and He is able to fulfil His Word without fail.

Believing God's Word will expand and multiply you beyond your imagination and expectation. Faith is being sure of God's Promises, even though you see it afar off. It is better to die believing God than to die a sinner and an unbeliever.

Faith is comprehensive and touches all aspects of the Word of God. No part of the Word of God can be separated from faith, for faith comes by the Word of God.

Faith involves believing the Word of God, embracing it, and confessing the Word of God. When you go for the Word of God and give enough time to it, your faith will grow exceedingly. Now faith is the substance of things hoped for, the evidence of things not seen.

Having faith in God makes you see yourself as a pilgrim and a stranger in this world. Faith seeks a Homeland for it is not foolish. The end of faith (real faith) is Heaven. You cannot separate faith from repentance and holiness.

Being mindful of your past and the things of this world can make you go back (withdraw from the faith-life). The things you may be proud of may be the devil offering you an opportunity to go back from God.

Heavenly Country is a better country and cannot be comparable to anything in this life, anything in this world. God is not ashamed to be called your God as you live by faith. He has prepared very good things for you.

Faith will make you offer up your most treasured asset, even your life, for God's Sake. Whatever you may give up for God, God will give it back to you many folds and in better ways.

Faith will make you bless yourself and declare good things ahead of time. Faith will make you declare to others the things that God has said, and you will plan and work towards them.

Faith will make you not to fear men. You will fear and honour God, risking even your life for Him instead of following men. Faith will make you refuse to be regarded higher, against God's Plan for your life.

You will give up fame for the Cause of Jesus Christ. Faith will make you choose to suffer affliction with God's people and for God's Sake.

Faith will open your eyes to the temporal and temporary nature of the things of this world. Unbelief and faithlessness will blind your eyes to everlasting and eternal realities.

Faith will open and sharpen your understanding and make you put first things first. Walking by faith will remove the authority of men from you, and no matter what, you will do the Bidding of God, for your faith will give you protection; and protection is in obedience.

You will do what men cannot do and you will live supernaturally. Faith will give you victory over your enemies, and you will see breakthroughs in tough matters. Your work of faith will save you, even when you don't deserve it.

There is so much to faith that time and space will not permit to expose all about it and to declare what the heroes of faith have done. For by faith the elders obtained a good testimony.

By faith we understand that the worlds were framed by the Word of God, so that the things which are seen were not made of things which are visible. The spirit-realm controls the physical realm; the things which happen in the physical realm have been settled in the spirit-realm, directly or indirectly.

Instead of quarreling with or fighting someone, you may just have to deal with the spirit behind him or her, which uses him or her to carry out its wishes. The enemy is behind the scene.

Faith subdues kingdoms. Faith works righteousness; it obtains God's Promises. Faith stops the mouth of lions and the devourers. Faith quenches the violence of fire, trials, and persecutions.

It will cause you to escape the edge of the sword and other weapons, even atomic, hydrogen, and cobalt bombs. Faith will make you valiant in battle and turn to flight the armies of the enemies. Faith will cause the dead to come back to life.

Faith will make you pass through persecutions, even death because you have hope for the Resurrection and the reward. Faith will make you live a separated and an abnormal life for the Sake of Jesus Christ.

Faith will make you not to regard this world and its pleasures. You can receive a good report or testimony and still not obtain a particular promise, even your desire. Faith leads to perfection.

There are great faith and small faith (Matt. 8:10); feigned faith and unfeigned faith (1 Tim. 1:5, 2 Tim. 1:5); weak faith and strong faith (Rom. 4:17-20; Rom. 14:1); Abrahamic faith and Thomas' faith (Jn 20:19-29); wrecked faith and unwrecked faith (1 Tim. 1:19).

But, however small your faith may be, if there is no doubt in your heart, you can remove mountains (Matt. 17:20). Feigned faith is a pretending faith, while unfeigned faith is a sincere faith.

Abraham was not weak in faith but strong in faith, and did not consider his own body, already dead by human standards. He did not waver at the Promise of God through unbelief, but was strengthened in faith, giving glory to God, being fully convinced that what He had promised He was also able to perform.

He believed in hope contrary to hope, in the Presence of Him Whom he believed – God, Who gives life to the dead and calls those things which do not exist as though they did.

Abrahamic faith does not see and yet believes, while the Thomas' type sees before believing. Believe that the Lord shall supply all your needs, according to His Riches in Glory in Christ Jesus, our Lord.

And no matter how the surrounding circumstances may look like, believe that the Lord will supply whatever you need: spiritually, mentally, physically, financially, materially, ministerially, maritally, etc. The One that fed about three million people in the wilderness with manna, for forty years, will not fail you.

Wrecked faith is as a result of backsliding. Faith works by love, and without love, your great and strong faith is nothing (1 Cor. 13:2). Also, faith must be accompanied by works, for without works, faith is dead, as the body without the spirit is dead (Jas. 2:26).

Have faith in God, or rather, have the Faith of God; have the God-kind of faith: the God-kind of faith works by speaking forth into existence those things that do not exist. God calls invisible things by names as though they did exist.

Faith works by speaking and believing; you can speak with your spirit, and you can speak with your mouth. Therefore, be very careful how you speak, and what you speak. Ask, seek, and knock. He who asks receives; he who seeks finds; and to him who knocks the door will be opened to.

Jesus Christ is the Solid Rock. All other grounds are sinking sand. If you have Jesus Christ, your faith should be very strong, because He can neither lie, fail, nor disappoint you. He is the same yesterday, today, and forever.

Faith comes by hearing, and hearing by the Word of God (Rom. 10:17). If you think you don't have faith, just take time to fill yourself with the Word of God, and you will see yourself operate in a level of faith that will baffle you.

Never Say That God Said What He Did Not Say!

BE A PRAYER-WARRIOR

Who is a prayer-warrior? Literally, a prayer-warrior is someone who wages spiritual warfare effectively by means of prayer. Technically, the prayer-warrior is someone who knows how to obtain his requests from God, both for himself and for others; and he knows how to stop and destroy the works and plans of the devil.

Remember that I am not just talking about the knowledge: I included the application of what is known, when I spoke of knowing how to pray. The prayer-warrior spends enough time in prayer.

Jesus Christ told us a parable to the intent that we know that men ought always to pray and not faint (Lk. 18:1). The Word of God says that we should pray without ceasing, we should pray always (1 Thes. 5:17).

We are commanded to watch to prayer (1 Pet. 4:7), and to watch and pray (Matt. 26:41). Why should we pray? Because the Word of God says that we receive when we ask, we find when we seek, and we have an open door when we knock (Matt. 7:7).

If your son asks you of bread, you do not give him a stone; if he asks of a fish, you don't give him a snake. In the same vein, if he asks for an egg, you do not think of giving him a scorpion.

If we know to give good things to our children, how much more will our Father in Heaven give good things to us? (Matt. 7:9-11; Lk. 11:11-13). Do you trust man more than God? Cursed is he that puts his trust in man instead of in God (Jer. 17:5).

God, the Maker of all things, is able to do all things. He can neither lie nor fail to perform His Word (Heb. 6:18). Instead of one thing that has gone out of the Mouth of God not to come to pass, heaven and earth shall pass away (Matt. 24:35).

Has He said it? He will do it also. This is one reason we should obey the Instruction of the Lord that we should study the Word of God (2 Tim. 2:15) and be full of it (Col. 3:16).

If you know the Word of God, you will know His Provisions for you. If you are full of God's Word, you will know your rights, privileges, and inheritances in the Kingdom.

This will make you receive from God the things that you need, and to stop the works of the devil from coming to pass in your life. You will also be able to overcome tests, trials, and temptations.

The problem is that many Believers don't pray. Many don't maintain a consistent prayer-life. Many have made many decisions and resolutions which they failed to keep.

They decided that they will pray this long or that long every day, but they went back to prayerlessness after a short while. A prayerful Christian is a powerful Christian whereas a prayerless Christian is a powerless Christian.

Of course, everybody prays; even powerless Christians pray. But God has declared that the prayer of the sinner is an abomination to Him (Prov. 15:8). If you are a sinner, if you are not born again, the prayer that God wants from you right now is the prayer of repentance and acceptance of the Lord Jesus Christ into your life as your Lord and Saviour.

He came down from Heaven, suffered, died, and resurrected again for your sins, so that you may be justified and made righteous before God (Jn 1:12; Rom. 3:24).

Why don't people pray? Many don't pray because of laziness. They sleep too much and find it easier to do many other things than to pray.

Many don't pray because they feel, on the inside of them, that it really makes no difference whether or not they pray. They say that whatever will be, will be, and whatever will not be, will not be. But that is not true; the devil has subtly told people that.

Some don't pray because of business. My own definition of business is whatever makes you busy. Your job can keep you busy; your relationship can keep you busy; even preaching can keep you so busy that you won't pray as you are supposed to.

Ignorance of God and His Ways makes people not to pray as they are supposed to. Some don't know what the Bible teaches about prayer. Some teach about prayer very well and yet don't pray.

Satanic or demonic strongholds and obsession are other factors that make people not to pray. Have you ever wondered why you start feeling sleepy and weak when you want to pray or when you are praying?

You may see someone that will start sleeping when he starts praying, but when the same person wants to watch a football match in the television, the sleep leaves him. That is demonic remote-control.

This is one reason you don't need to eat too much (or even at all) in the night. When your body feels fasted in the night, it will be easier for you to overcome sleep in the night.

Also, eat at least three hours before going to bed. This will minimize or remove the ability of demons and their human agents to make you sleep and sleep and sleep. It will also make it hard for demons to force you have the experiences that you don't like in dreams.

Some people wake up early in the morning, and instead of rising up to pray, they decide to sleep a little more and they find out that they never wake up until it is late.

Some people decide to lie down on their beds and pray, and before long, they start sleeping and end up not praying effectively. To pray effectively, you must discipline yourself. You will need to plan and implement your prayer-time.

It is one thing to pray, and it is another thing to maintain a steady prayer-life. Some people, after listening to good messages or reading books on prayer, decide that they are going to pray two, three, or more hours every day.

Some may do it for one, two, three, or more days, and before you know it, they get back to inconsistent prayer-life. Praying long is good, but if it is one or two hours you are able to pray every day, maintain it and make it consistent: but increase the time, as you are able.

I recommend that every Believer should pray for at least two hours everyday, but it is not specifically written in the Bible. Take a day or more to do some personal fasting. Regular fasting with prayer will make you a spiritual giant.

Prayer should be very important to you as a Christian. Jesus Christ prayed effectively and always. Apostle Paul told us to pray always and without ceasing.

There are many conditions to receiving answers to your prayers. One condition is to pray in faith (Jas 1:6-8); another is to pray without doubting and wavering; another is to pray in the Name of Jesus Christ (Jn 16:24); another is to bear fruit that will remain (Jn 15:16); still, another is to do those things that please God (1 Jn 3:22).

Of course, prayer will not work in an unforgiving heart, because if you don't forgive, God will not forgive you also, and you will be sinful when screened spiritually (Mk 11:25-26). Pray according to the Will of God (1 Jn 5:14-15).

There are other conditions, but one thing you must realize is that the bottom-line lies in the fact that what we receive from God is as a result of the Sacrifice that Jesus Christ performed for us.

It is not of him that wills nor of him that runs, but of God that shows mercy (Rom. 9:15-16). Time and chance happen to everything on earth (Eccl. 9:11). Therefore, you should wait patiently for your answer if it delays. Delay is not denial, and God knows the best for you.

This is why it is necessary you pray according to the Will of God. Prayer is not "Give me this or that" only. Prayer is talking to God and waiting for Him to speak to you also.

Don't rush out of the Presence of God. Also, learn to pray in the Holy Ghost. Pray in tongues always and everyday. The Holy Spirit helps us to pray for the right things in the right way (Rom. 8:26-27).

We are a triumphant people, a triumphant Church, and we enforce the victory that the Lord has won for us by prayer and speaking forth of words of faith.

Learn to stay alone with God, praying to Him. Wait on God patiently. Speak to God and allow Him speak to you by listening and being quiet before the Lord.

Satan is afraid of the Gifts of the Holy Spirit; satan is afraid of good preaching and right teaching; yet, satan fears prayer more than all of them. It is prayer that holds all these things together and make them effective.

Without prayer, even your spiritual activities will fail, be unproductive, or be less productive. Yet, remember that fasting increases the power and effectiveness of prayer many folds.

Prayer is very powerful, and we have to pray always with all kinds of prayer. The effectual fervent prayer of the righteous avails much and is powerful. Prayer is a force that many have refused to use, even though it is within their reach. Men of all ages and nations have been praying.

In fact, man has that instinct within him; man has the desire to communicate with His Creator; hence, even unbelievers pray. But the prayer of the wicked is an abomination to God (Prov. 15:8).

However, God (being a Good God) gives His rain, sun, children, air, etc to all men; and if they were to buy them, with what will they buy them? He will also hear the cry of the needy!

God gave man authority over the earth, though man lost that authority to the devil when he sinned against God by disobeying Him; hence, the Bible calls the devil the god of this world (2 Cor. 4:4).

This is why the devil can cause pains, sufferings, sicknesses, earthquakes, and such things. But when the Lord Jesus Christ rose up from the dead, He said that all authority in Heaven and on earth has been given to Him and He gave that authority to the Church, His Body, who represent Him on earth (Matt. 28:18-20).

We, the Church, individually and as a group, have authority over the earth and we exercise that authority by prayer. There are different kinds of prayer, and we will take them up later.

We are commanded to watch and pray that we do not fall into temptation (Matt. 26:41). To watch is to be alert, sober, and vigilant. We have to open our eyes and ears (physically and spiritually) to know what is happening around us so that we can pray intelligently and effectively.

It is not enough to just pray; you've got to pray to receive results. Hence, Apostle Paul said that he doesn't fight aimlessly like the one beating the air (1 Cor. 9:26).

When you know the strongholds and plans of the enemy, you will fight against him more effectively. And the devil, many times, does not want to be recognized so that his plans and purposes will neither be thwarted nor destroyed.

Ask, and you shall receive; seek, and you shall find; knock, and the door shall be opened to you. For he who asks, receives; he who seeks, finds; and to him that knocks, the door will be opened (Matt: 7:7-8).

You do not have, because you do not ask. When you ask, you do not receive because you ask amiss that you may spend them on your own pleasures (Jas 4:2-3). Asking or praying in doubt and with double-mind will also hinder your answers.

Another thing that can hinder your prayer is sin and disobedience. God's people suffer because of ignorance (Hos. 4:6); and ignorance leads to unbelief which is a great obstacle to receiving your answers.

This is why you have to study the Word of God for yourself, so that you may know what the Lord Jesus Christ purchased for you, and you will pray more effectively.

The Bible says that we are to pray always or without ceasing (1 Thes. 5:17). We are to be instant in prayer (Rom. 12:12). No one should be forcing you to pray, but you have to make prayer a habit and a duty; and you will have to discipline yourself to pray as supposed.

If you show a careless attitude to prayer, that is how your prayer-life will be: inconsistent. Therefore, just as athletes train to perform well, you have to discipline yourself and pray till you make it your lifestyle.

One condition to receiving answers to your prayer is faith, believing that God has answered your prayer. Whatever you ask of when you pray, believe that you receive it and you shall have it (Mk 11:24).

Another condition is to pray according to the Will of God (1 Jn 5:14). Another is to do those things that please Him. And you have to bear fruit, that whatever you ask the Father, He will give it to you (Jn 15:16). And don't live in sin, for the prayer of the sinner is abominable to God.

Throughout the Bible, we see the records of people who prayed. Abraham interceded for Sodom and Gomorrah, though at last, ten righteous people couldn't be found there (Gen. 18:32); Moses interceded for the children of Israel so that God did not wipe them out as He had intended (Exo. 32:7-14).

Elijah prayed, and it did not rain for three and half years, and when he prayed afterwards, it rained (1 Kgs 17 & 18). Jesus Christ prayed a lot. Apostle Paul prayed and showed us an example.

Now, we will consider the different kinds of prayer. There is praying in the Holy Ghost. Praying in the Holy Ghost includes praying in tongues, praying prophetically, and groaning in the Spirit (1 Cor. 14:14-15; Rom. 8:26). You build up your most holy faith by praying in the Holy Ghost (Jude 1:20).

And there is the prayer of intercession. In the prayer of intercession, you stand to intercede on behalf of others, especially in trying to keep them from being punished.

There is the prayer of supplication, which is to ask for God's Help, Supply, Provision, and Intervention on your behalf and on the behalf of others, especially Christians.

When you petition God, you are telling God to do this or that for yourself and others, according to His Word; hence, the Word says that you should plead your case (Mic. 6:1; Mic. 7:9; Isa. 41:21). Of course, many kinds of prayer are related, but they need to be separated for better understanding.

There is the prayer of faith. The prayer of faith is the prayer that you pray because God has specifically promised you or others something, and you stand on that provision and pray, believing that you receive; and you shall have it.

No matter how the situation may appear not to have changed, hold on to your belief and confession, and instead of praying again for it, keep on thanking God for the answer and you will see the manifestation in no distant time.

We now consider the prayer of consecration. This kind of prayer needs to be prayed always by every Christian, submitting himself/herself to the Will of God for his or her life as Jesus Christ did (Matt. 26:38-42).

Be willing and ready to do the Will of God, no matter how hard it may look like. I will consider the prayer of confession. First, confess your sins to God, for he that covers his sins shall not prosper, but he that confesses and renounces them shall find mercy (Prov. 28:13). This is very important for every Christian.

Of course, a Christian should not live in sin, but many don't repent of their sins and continue to pray. You are deceiving yourself. And you know that you have to forgive others for God to forgive you (Matt. 6:14-15).

Next is to confess or declare what you want to be, what you want to happen, without doubting. Whoever says to this mountain, "Be removed, and be cast into the sea," and does not doubt in his heart, but believes that those things he says will be done, he will have whatever he says (Mk 11:23).

There is the prayer of agreement, which involves two or more people praying together in agreement over this or that thing. The people involved will need to believe and not doubt, for maximum result; and the prayer can be made even if they are not together physically.

The prayer of binding and loosing involves destroying the works of devils by speaking directly to the devils responsible for them, and to their works, to pull down and to root out, to destroy and to throw down, to build and to plant (Jer. 1:10).

And the Lord says that whatever you bind on earth, will be bound in Heaven, and whatever you loose on earth, will be loosed in Heaven (Matt. 18:18). There is the prayer of commitment in which you cast your cares to the Lord (1 Pet. 5:7).

The prayer of worship involves showing respect and love for God. It is the prayer of adoration. Pray always with all kinds of prayer!

Never Say That God Said What He Did Not Say!

YOU MUST BE LED BY THE HOLY SPIRIT

These are evil days; you must be led by the Holy Spirit, so that you can do the Will of God, and escape the plans and strategies of the devil, who is your enemy and God's archenemy. God loves us very much, but the devil hates us passionately, and he has no mercy.

In these end times and last days, the need to be led by God cannot be overemphasized, if we must fulfil God's Task and Purpose for us, and avoid the devil's deception. Many times, Divine Plans are different from human plans. The sons of God are led by the Spirit of God (Rom. 8:14).

If you are not led by the Spirit of God, then you have some questions to ask yourself. Of course, the Spirit of God is always there to lead you if you allow Him. You have to follow the Leader to be led.

When the Spirit of God speaks to your heart, when He gives you a witness about something in your heart, it is your responsibility to sense that witness and to follow the witness.

Don't blame God when you refuse to be led. If the Spirit of God, for instance, sees danger ahead of you and gives you a warning, if you refuse to heed the warning and you are caught up in the danger, you are responsible for it.

God loves His children and He will not want them to fall into danger. God will do all He can to help you, but He cannot force His Will on you if you refuse.

Children of God should be sensitive to God's Leading always. Of course, the devil will want to speak to you, as if it is God. Satan parades himself as an angel of light just as his ministers pretend to be ministers of Christ (2 Cor. 11:13-15).

But the Bible tells us to prove all things and hold on to that which is good (1 Thes. 5:21). Believe not every spirit, but test the spirits whether they are of God; many false prophets have gone out into the world (1 Jn 4:1).

There are many voices in the world and none of them is without significance or meaning (1 Cor. 14:10). You need, therefore, to distinguish between the Voice of God and the voice of the devil. There are many ways God leads His people; the devil can fake some of them.

For instance, the devil may fake an audible voice. This is one reason you should be able to recognize the Inward Witness of the Holy Spirit in your spirit, for the devil does not live in your spirit, but the Spirit of God does.

The primary way or the number one way God leads all His children is by the inward witness or inward intuition. It is like a checking on the inside of you, whether your heart (not your mind) is at peace about something or whether you are uncomfortable with it.

If the more you think about or pray about the thing, you feel good about it, the Spirit of God is giving you a go-ahead signal. On the other hand, if you feel bad about it, it is a stop-signal. You know you are saved by an inward witness (Rom. 8:16).

Another way God leads His children is by the still-small voice or inward voice. Your spirit has a voice, just like your physical body. The voice of your human spirit is your conscience, your inward voice.

There is the Authoritative Voice of the Holy Spirit also, and God leads His children that way. For instance, after Peter had the vision of the sheet from Heaven, as he thought about the vision, the Spirit of God told him that three men sought for him. He was directed by the Holy Spirit's Voice to follow them. The Voice may seem audible, but it comes to your spirit (Acts 10:19-20).

God talks by Audible Voice, as well: after Jesus Christ was baptized (and baptism is by immersion: if you were baptized by sprinkling, re-baptize by immersion.

Any baptized Believer can re-baptize you in the Name of the Father, and of the Son, and of the Holy Spirit; in the Name of the Lord), as He came up, God spoke audibly from Heaven (Matt. 3:17). Also, before the Lord went to the Cross, as He spoke to the people in Jerusalem, God spoke to Him from Heaven (Jn 12:23-33).

God can send an angel to direct and guide you; God sent an angel to speak to Mary (Lk 1:26-38). An angel spoke to the high-priest, Zechariah, before the birth of John the Baptist (Lk 1:11-22).

God spoke to Philip through an angel to go to where he would see the Ethiopian eunuch; when Philip obeyed and went there, God changed His Method by speaking to him again by His Holy Spirit (Acts 8:26-39). God has many methods; don't be too rigid.

Joseph, the husband of Mary, was spoken to by means of dreams many times. Through dream, he was told to take Mary as his wife, he was told to take Jesus Christ and Mary to Egypt, and he was told to come back to the land of Israel after the death of Herod (Matt. 1:20; Matt. 2:13; Matt. 2:19-20).

God spoke to King Solomon through dream (2 Chron. 7:12). Even, many of the prophets of the Old Testament received some of the things they said by means of dreams. However, dreams can come from your mind or from the devil.

Another way God speaks to His children is by vision. Of course, the Bible calls dreams 'visions of the night'; that is, the visions you see as you are asleep. There are three types of visions.

There is the inward vision in which your spirit sees things spiritually, while you are still conscious of your physical environment; this will happen even if your eyes are closed.

The vision that Peter had concerning the sheet from Heaven is by trance. Trance is a form of vision in which you see things when your physical senses are suspended (Acts 10:9-17). In a trance, you are not conscious of your physical environment while God speaks to you or shows you things supernaturally.

The last form of vision is the open vision. In the open vision, you are fully aware of your physical environment and yet you see supernaturally. In the open vision, you may see Jesus Christ, an angel, devils, and other beings or things. Many of the God's children are led by visions more often than angelic visitations and audible voices.

God leads by circumstances also. Check the circumstances surrounding you, because God can lead you by them. For instance, when you plan to travel, the circumstances may work out in such a way that the travel may not work out. The same may happen when you are pursuing a business endeavour.

There are angels who minister for the heirs of salvation (Heb. 1:14), and they can make circumstances favourable or unfavourable for you, to protect or guide you.

However, you must be careful to understand your circumstances aright, because the devil can also cause unfavourable circumstances for you. In that case, destroy the works of the devil in the Name of Jesus Christ, and at the Name of Jesus Christ every knee should bow (Phil. 2:10).

As I said, the devil may fake God's Method of leading His children. But don't be afraid, because you have the Word of God and the Spirit of God. You will not be led astray if you follow the Word and the Spirit.

God can also lead by prophecy, by tongues and interpretations, and by other means. He who prophesies speaks to men to exhortation, to edification, and to comfort (1 Cor. 14:3).

God even used a donkey to speak to Prophet Balaam (Num. 22:30). You can't limit God because He is not limited. Many times, the way God will speak to you will depend on you.

For instance, if you are not spiritually sensitive, He may use natural means to speak to you. But depending on natural means is risky, because the devil can easily imitate and fake it.

This is why you don't need to put out a fleece like Gideon did (Jdgs 6:11-40). If you tell God to open that door if He wants you to do something, the devil can open that door. Do you know that the devil can allow you to have good and legal things in order to deprive you of God's Best for you?

Always be sensitive. Don't seek voices, visions, or dreams, so that the devil will not mislead you. Ask God for direction and He will lead you the way He deems good and best.

The Word and the Spirit agree. The Bible, the Word of God, represents the Mind of God. Inasmuch as there are some things you may not find out from the Bible (for instance, which school to attend), nothing from God and His Spirit will contradict the Word of God, when properly interpreted in the right context.

The Word of God was written by the Inspiration of God (2 Tim. 3:16), and the holy men that spoke the Mind of God spoke as they were moved by the Holy Spirit of the Living God (2 Pet. 1:21).

The hardened heart cannot work out the Righteousness of God; the hardened heart will stand against God's Leading and Prompting. Learn to wait on God with open heart and mind. God wants to lead and guide you more than you want Him to lead and guide you.

God reveals secrets to us. The Holy Spirit tells us things to come; He tells us of past things also. The secret things belong to God, but the things that are revealed belong to us. God does nothing without revealing it to His Servants, the prophets.

However, God reveals what He wants us to know. He will reveal what He wants you to know to you; therefore, don't go around for prophecies so that you will not be deceived.

God is still in the business of revealing secrets and mysteries to His people. He still speaks to His children. My God is not a dumb God; He speaks even today.

You only have to tune in to the frequency that He speaks, and you will hear Him clearly. Even as God gives revelations and visions, the devil also has been working hard to give counterfeit revelations and visions to people.

The devil, sometimes, comes as an angel of light to deceive people. He can even speak to you to deceive you. All visions and voices are not God's.

This is why the Scripture instructs us to prove all things and hold on to that which is good, true, and Godly. We are told to test every spirit to see whether they are from God. Why? This is because many false prophets have gone out into the world (1 Jn. 4:1). God is Spirit; the devil is a spirit too.

1 Corinthians 14:22-33 reads thus, "Therefore, tongues are for a sign, not to those who believe, but to unbelievers; but prophesying is not for unbelievers, but for those who believe. Therefore, if the whole church comes together in one place, and all speak with tongues, and there come in those who are uniformed or unbelievers, will they not say that you are out of your mind?

"But if all prophesy, and an unbeliever or an uninformed person comes in, he is convinced by all, is convicted by all. And thus the secrets of his heart are revealed; and so, falling down on his face, he will worship God and report that God is truly among you.

"How is it then, brethren? Whenever you come together, each of you has a psalm, has a teaching, has a tongue, has a revelation, has an interpretation. Let all things be done for edification.

"If anyone speaks in a tongue, let there be two or at the most three, each in turn, and let one interpret. But if there is no interpreter, let him keep silent in the church, and let him speak to himself and to God.

"Let two or three prophets speak, and let the others judge. But if anything is revealed to another who sits by, let the first keep silent. For you can all prophesy one by one, that all may learn and all may be encouraged.

"And the spirits of the prophets are subject to the prophets. For God is not the author of confusion but of peace, as in all the churches of the Saints."

Earlier, Apostle Paul said, "There are, it may be, so many kinds of languages (or voices) in the world, and none of them is without significance. Let him who speaks in a tongue pray that he may interpret (1 Cor. 14:10,13).

"For if I pray in a tongue, my spirit prays, but my understanding is unfruitful. What is the conclusion then? I will pray with the spirit, and I will also pray with the understanding. I will sing with the spirit, and I will also sing with the understanding" (1 Cor. 14:14-15).

We see, from verse 10, that there are many voices in the world. There are also many languages in the world. There are: the Voice of God, the voice of an angel, the voice of the devil, the voices of demons, the voices of people, the voice of the mind, etc.

If you speak in tongues, pray that you may also interpret. However, if everybody in the church is praying individually (to be summarized by one person), you are free to speak in tongues or to pray with your understanding.

But the leader can tell you people to stop praying privately at any time; then, obey and be orderly, by stopping. If you must speak in tongues apart from when everyone is praying individually, then there should be an interpreter (which can be you yourself) or else speak silently or quietly.

But the Spirit has a lot to teach us that we might have not known. There are so many things in the Bible that we have not understood. We will understand many later, and we will understand others when the Lord comes.

Speaking in tongues plus interpretation equals prophecy. Interpretation will help others know what you spoke, so that the whole Church may be edified. He who prophesies speaks edification, exhortation, and comfort to men.

He who speaks in a tongue does not speak to men but to God, for no one understands him; however, in the Spirit he speaks mysteries. He who speaks in a tongue edifies himself, but he who prophesies edifies the Church (1 Cor. 14:2-4).

Therefore, brethren, desire earnestly to prophesy, and do not forbid to speak with tongues (verse 39). Let all things be done decently and in order.

Many are so much interested in prophecies, revelations, visions, and voices that they do not pay attention to the Inner Witness of the Holy Spirit Who indwells them and witnesses with their spirit to make them know what to do and what not to do, what to believe and what not to believe, and who to pay attention to and who not to pay attention to.

Many value prophecy, revelation, vision, and audible voice more than they value the Word of God. Ministries and churches established on prophecies, healings, and miracles without a strong base on the Word of God will sooner or later diminish, wane, or stop entirely.

Such ministries can easily be scattered by rumours. Even the deaths of the founders can bring them to stopping ends. To be on a safer side, put the Word of God (the Bible) first, and put the Spirit of God second.

Yes, the Spirit of God inspired the Word (2 Tim. 3:16); He moved the holy men who prophesied in the Old Testament, and the Early New Testament (and even now) (2 Pet. 1:20-21); and the Spirit, the water (the Word), and the Blood agree as one.

The Father, the Word, and the Holy Spirit are One (1 Jn 5:7-8). Man is born again of water (the Word) and of the Spirit (the Holy Spirit).

Apostle Peter said that the Prophetic Word of the Old Testament is surer, in confirming the Personality of Jesus Christ, than their Testimony of being with Jesus Christ on the mountain of transfiguration where Jesus Christ's Countenance changed and shone with light, and the Voice of God spoke to them (2 Pet. 1:16-21).

Brother, the Scripture was given to us so that we may know the Mind and Will of God. If you put the Bible you see behind you, if you don't stick to that Bible, how can you follow the Holy Spirit of the Living God?

Over the years, people have been deceived by visions, dreams, prophecies, revelations, and voices. Even though God still speaks, demons will try to deceive us, as if it is God that is speaking, and it is when we know the Word well and understand the Witness and Promptings of Holy Spirit well, that we can detect His Voice from their voices.

They sincerely believed that they came from God, even when a moderate knowledge of the Bible would have given them a better understanding. People go to camps and retreat grounds, and pray, pray, and pray to hear God's Voice, and they wouldn't even spend one hour a day to study the Bible during that retreat, when they can spend six hours praying daily during the retreat.

Believe me; many of them are deceived by visions and voices. Many can't distinguish God's Leading from devilish voices.

I am not encouraging you to be fearful, because God can always top the devil in everything. But please, pray and ask God to lead, direct, and guide you, and let Him do it the way He wants to do it.

You may be looking for a writing on the sky while the inner witness or the inward voice by the Holy Spirit has always been with you; but because you are not paying attention, you wouldn't get it; and if one devil speaks to you with a shout, you will value it more than that Voice or Leading of God that is in you.

I believe in prophecy, revelation, vision, and audible voice; I like them. But we are not ignorant of the devices of the devil (2 Cor. 2:11). Therefore, you have to know the truth, because it is better to be late than to be late: it is better to delay than to be found dead.

It is also better to follow God some distance behind, than to rush ahead of God and move towards the west, while He is moving towards the north. God loves us and does not want us to be deceived; but the responsibility lies with us.

People run around looking for those who will give them a Word from the Lord. Why not trust in God and get sensitive to the Holy Spirit Who lives inside you? But woe to the man who will say that the Lord said this or that, when the Lord has not spoken.

This is how people get preyed by deceivers, hypocrites, and demonic prophets who come as ministers of Christ. Do you not know that even satan comes as an angel of light? (2 Cor. 11: 14-15).

God leads His people by: the inner witness or prompting in their spirit by the Holy Spirit; the inner or inward voice of their spirit by the Spirit of God; the Authoritative Voice of the Holy Spirit; and by visions, dreams, prophecies, audible voices, angelic visitations, and tongues and interpretation.

However He chooses to lead you, be sensitive and submit. It is important to obey God promptly. Obedience is better than sacrifice; and to hearken than the fat of rams (1 Sam. 15:22).

It is one thing to know the Will of God, and it is another to follow it. Many live their lives without knowing the Will of God for their lives. Many people work for God without doing exactly what He wants them to be doing for Him.

There are general things God expects His people to do; and there are specific things He has purposed in His Heart that individuals or groups should do for Him. Unfortunately, many spend their whole lives doing the works of others.

Knowing the Will of God for your life requires seeking His Face in prayer (or in prayer and fasting), and waiting on God until He tells you. He who believes shall not be in haste (Isa. 28:16).

Don't rush in and rush out of God's Presence. Pray in the Spirit and with the understanding. Pray in tongues and in your known language. As you pray in the Spirit, you activate your spirit and he gets more sensitive to the Spirit of God.

Pray long enough and guidance will rise up from your spirit to your mind, and you will know exactly what to do.

The Spirit of God leads the sons of God. The primary way He leads them is by the inward witness or inward intuition. By this means, when He wants you to do something, He will impart a feeling, sense of peace or good feeling inside you concerning that very thing.

But when your spirit feels bad and insecure about something, the Spirit is telling you to avoid that thing or to be careful about it. But many times, people ignore this witness, and they land into trouble later, because they were expecting a voice, a vision, or a prophecy.

This inner witness or feeling is not mental, and it is not physical. Therefore, don't depend on your mental thoughts or your bodily feelings to judge whether God wants you to do something.

Some put a fleece as Gideon did to ascertain the Will of God; but in this dispensation, we don't walk by sight and God doesn't intend to be leading us by our physical senses. Of course, simple sense will help you know what you may have to do, based on what you see, hear, smell, feel, or taste.

But when you say, "Lord God, if you want me to do this, let this door open in the next ten minutes," you are treading on a dangerous ground, because you are operating in the physical realm. We know, from the Bible, that satan is the god of this world (2 Cor. 4:4).

Therefore, satan can open that door of yours, even before two minutes, and you may become happy and believe that God answered you faster than you expected. If you give that testimony in church, you will get ashamed of yourself when you fall into disaster.

Those that worship God, in this New Testament, worship Him in Spirit, and in truth (Jn 4:24). To worship in Spirit, is to worship according to the Spirit's Leading and Prompting. To worship in truth, is to worship according to the Word and Will of God.

Another way the Spirit of God can lead you is by the still-small voice. By that, your spirit won't just give you a witness but will speak to you. The human spirit has a voice, just like the human body.

The Holy Spirit actually lives inside your spirit, and because your spirit lives inside your body, the Holy Spirit also lives inside your body. This is why the Bible says that your body is the Temple of the Holy Spirit. Even your conscience is the voice of your spirit.

There is the more authoritative Voice of the Holy Spirit. By this method, the Spirit of God speaks to you, on your inside, by Himself. You actually hear it with your spiritual ears, even though it may seem to be physically audible.

In the Old Testament, God called Samuel when he was still young, and Samuel thought it was an audible voice from Eli, but it wasn't. Of course, God speaks to us audibly also.

But don't depend on audible voices because the devil can also speak to you audibly. His intention for doing this will be to deceive you or put fear into you.

After Apostle Peter had the trance in which he was told to kill and eat, as he pondered over the vision, the Holy Spirit spoke to him and said, "Three men seek for you." He has a Voice and He speaks internally and audibly too, depending on how He chooses.

But be careful of any external audible voice, because demons can speak to you audibly too. Know your Bible so that you won't be deceived; be sensitive to the Inward Witness of the Holy Spirit in your inside to see whether it agrees with the audible voice.

The Holy Spirit can speak to you by prophecy or tongues and interpretation, either from your own mouth or from the mouth of somebody else. However, be sure that the ones from others are actually from God.

As stated earlier, check your inner witness to see whether it agrees with it. If God has not spoken to you about that; if God does not speak to you about that later; and best of all, if your inner witness is against it, please, think twice.

Do you know that many people could bombard you with 'words' from the Lord, and yet none or only one of those words, actually, came from the Lord?

There are other ways through which God can speak to you. He can speak to you through visions and dreams. He can send an angel to give you a Message. But always remember that satan can also come, pretending to be an angel of light (2 Cor. 11:14).

One of the best things a Christian can do for himself is to know his Bible very well and be sensitive to the inner witness in his spirit by the Holy Spirit. This will make him not to be easily deceived.

But I am not encouraging you to live in fear of the supernatural. God can always top whatever the devil can do. The devil is only imitating and pretending.

Let us consider the issue of following the Will of God. Once you are convinced that God has said this or that, please follow it: do it or avoid it, as the case may be.

God may tell you to do a difficult thing, but He will never tell you to do an impossible thing. Know that the Thoughts of God are higher than your thoughts. God is wiser than all men put together.

Commit your way to the Lord, and do not lean on your own understanding; in all your ways acknowledge Him, and He will bring it to pass (Psa. 37:5; Prov. 3:5-6).

Love the Lord, even to death. If you value your life more than God, you are not worthy of Him. The people that overcame by the Blood of the Lamb and the Word of their Testimony did not love their lives to death (Rev. 12:11).

You may have to pass through a very great opposition and persecution as you follow God's Will for your life. Consider what Apostle Paul suffered in 2 Cor. 11:23-33.

People will criticize you and call you all kinds of names. The opposition may even come from your brothers and sisters in the same church. But never get discouraged; don't give up.

Somebody said, "You can call me crazy, but I am hearing God." Don't expect everybody to understand you. Even your wife may misunderstand you and work against you. But at the end, they will know that you were right and they were wrong.

The Pharisees and the Sadducees opposed and persecuted Jesus Christ. When Jesus Christ left, they faced His apostles and Disciples. The devil will always incite people against you. Also, he will try to frustrate you by attacking your finances and your progress.

Another thing to following the Will of God for your life is that you have to contend and fight with the forces of darkness to make sure that the Plan of God for your life comes to pass.

God may have a good plan and destiny for you, but if you are not prayerful, it may not come to pass. In case you doubt this, Prophet Daniel prayed, and the answer to his prayer was released the first day.

When God sent an angel to deliver the answer, the angel was withstood for twenty-one days by the prince of Persia, and until a stronger warring angel was sent, Daniel did not have his answer.

Therefore, you must be prayerful and know your rights, privileges, and inheritances in Christ Jesus so that the Will of God for your life will come to pass.

We do not wrestle against flesh and blood, but against principalities, against powers, against the rulers of darkness of this world, and against spiritual forces of wickedness in high places (Eph. 6:12-18).

Therefore, put on the whole Armour of God so that you will succeed and prosper spiritually, mentally, physically, financially, materially, and in any other area you may be involved in.

Beware of the devil's alternatives; don't listen to the devil, but insist on God's Will for you. Pharaoh gave Moses and the children of Israel alternatives of how to worship God, contrary to how God Himself wanted it (Exo. 8:28;10:8-11,24-26;12:31).

The enemy gave harsh conditions as terms for peace to the children of Israel, but King Saul was moved and empowered by the Spirit of God so that the enemy was conquered (1 Sam. 11).

Jesus Christ followed the Will of God for His Life, even to death. Abraham left his place at the Command of the Lord. Moses went back to Egypt to face Pharaoh so that he might deliver the children of Israel.

Caleb had to fight with strong armies in order to inherit what God promised him. David had to fight Goliath to be revealed to Israel and be approved by them, even though God had already anointed him king.

Daniel and his friends made up their minds never to offend God, and they followed His Plan for them. Finally, Apostle Paul was greatly opposed as he carried out the Will of God. Know and follow the Will of God!

Never Say That God Said What He Did Not Say!

THE PLACE OF OBEDIENCE, HOLINESS, AND RIGHTEOUSNESS

God deserves our total obedience and reverence. If you accept Jesus Christ as the Saviour of your soul, you must also receive Him as your Lord and Master. However, many Believers don't give their lives totally and completely to Him: they want to answer Christians while still doing what they want to do, even when the Word of God has directed them to avoid them.

God created the universe and everything in it. God created all men for His Good Pleasure. When the Lord God made man, He gave him all good things that he needed.

God gave Commandments to Adam on how he should live. However, when the devil tempted Eve, she ate of the forbidden fruit and gave to her husband, Adam, and Adam did eat. Due to that disobedience to God, man was separated from God and became God's enemy, even though God still loved him.

God demands our obedience to His Commandments. To disobey God's Commandments is to displease God. Disobedience is sin. Sin is the transgression of the Law; sin is lawlessness (1 Jn 3:4).

Sin is: knowing what to do and refusing to do it (Jas 4:7). Sin is anything done out of faith (Rom. 14:23). Faith comes by hearing and hearing by the Word of God (Rom. 10:17). Therefore, to do something out of faith is to do something contrary to the Word of God.

If God tells you to do something, do it. If He tells you to avoid something, avoid it: that is what obedience is. If you go to many Christian families, you will come to know that many don't understand what obedience is.

Will it surprise you to see a born-again wife whose husband tells to do something (something that is not contrary to God's Word) and she will not do it? Some will not only disobey their husbands that God has told them to submit to, but they will even abuse their husbands.

Now, those same women, if they are working in offices, will neither disobey nor abuse their bosses in the offices. Apart from the fact that the devil is using them to fight their husbands, that is demonic obsession.

Demonic obsession is a situation where, though someone is not demon-possessed, yet the person's mind is influenced by demons to dance to their tone. Even ministers' wives are not left out.

Do you know that many ministries and ministers are suffering and pressed down spiritually, because the devil is using the ministers' wives to torment, irritate, and discourage the ministers?

The same thing is seen in churches. Many people don't obey their pastors whom the Lord has set over them. Many talk to their pastors as if they are talking to church-members. However rich you may be in the church, the Lord has set the pastor over you and commanded you to obey your pastor.

Of course, I am not telling you to obey your pastor if your pastor tells you to do evil. If you make your pastor's work burdensome for him, you will give account of it to God on the Judgment Day (Rom. 14:12; Heb. 13:17).

Think of how a student will go out immediately to run an errand for his teacher or lecturer, even when the time is contrary to his schedule. Learn to respect and honour your pastor more than your boss at office or your lecturer at school.

You may have money more than them, but they represent God; and I tell you, they are higher than you spiritually. Even if you pray more than your pastor, there is a place of authority he has over you that you don't have.

In the military, people understand obedience and ranks. However, the devil fights in homes, churches and ministries to frustrate the leaders so that the leaders will not fulfill the God-given Assignments for them, and possibly offend God and perish in Hell.

But woe to him that will put a stumbling block to a Christian or to a minister of the Gospel (Matt. 18:6-7). If you can't obey your husband or your pastor, how will you obey God? Stop deceiving yourself before it will be too late for you. Of course, the husband must love his wife, and the pastor must take care of his members in love.

The Bible says that the Whole Duty of man is to fear God and keep His Commandments (Eccl. 12:13-14). You can't keep God's Commandments if you don't fear Him. If you don't have fear for your husband or your pastor, you can't obey him, and you wouldn't even know when you start insulting and abusing him.

The Lord Jesus Christ tells us that the proof that we love Him is our obeying Him and keeping His Commandments (Jn 14:21). Abide in the Lord Jesus Christ, by obeying His Word and His Spirit.

The Word of God says that without holiness, no man can see the Lord (Heb. 12:14). Only the pure in heart will see God (Matt. 5:8). The Church that the Lord is coming for is the Church that is without spot, wrinkle, or blemish (Eph. 5:27).

If you, as an individual, have spot, wrinkle, or blemish, you will not be raptured. May your whole spirit, soul, and body be kept blameless until the Coming of the Lord, because it is only those that endure to the end that will be saved (1 Thes. 5:23; Matt. 24:13).

What is holiness? Holiness is being without sin. It is sinlessness. Holiness is to be separated to God, to be consecrated or set apart for Him. Holiness is to be without spot, wrinkle, blemish, or any other thing that offends.

Holiness is complete and absolute obedience to God. The Bible talks of perfecting holiness (2 Cor. 7:1). To perfect holiness is to be complete in holiness; it is to mature in holiness. Some people live their lives confessing the same sins always. They confess, God forgives them, and they go back to it again and again.

Holiness and obedience involve making up your mind to be holy always and to obey God, no matter the cost. Some have chosen the ones they will obey and the ones they won't.

That type of attitude displeases God. Jesus Christ did not come to wash away your sins only: He also came to deliver you from the power of sins. As many as receive Him, to them He gives the power to become children of God (Jn 1:12). The power to become a child of God is the power to overcome sin and live above it.

Do you know that you are not bound to sin again? Don't let yourself to be overcome and enslaved again by the power of sin. If you do, the last state will be worse than the first (2 Pet. 2:20-21). There is nothing to envy in this world. If you gain the whole world and lose your soul, you gained nothing (Mk 8:36).

If you live to please your flesh, if you live according to the lust of the eyes and flesh, you will end in Hell Fire. Beware of the pride of life (1 Jn 2:15-17). God gave you life, but the life you are living is not your own.

We have heard it said that righteousness is right-standing with God. It is standing before God without a sense of guilt. When we are born again, we receive the Righteousness of Jesus Christ that makes us know that we are God's children.

Many have depended on this definition of righteousness alone and they live their lives anyhow, claiming that they have right-standing with God because of Jesus Christ. There are many unrighteous people who claim they are righteous.

When the Lord saves you and washes away your sins, He expects you to live a righteous life. The righteous life is the life that lives right. It is the life that does what it is supposed to do, and avoids what it should avoid. The Bible says that you should neither be deceived nor deceive others (Matt. 24:4; 1 Cor. 3:18; Eph. 5:6; 1 Jn 3:7).

He who does what is right is righteous just as Jesus Christ is righteous (1 Jn 3:7). He that lives in sin, he who sins is of the devil, for the devil has been sinning from the beginning (1 Jn 3:8).

Some believe that once you are saved, you are forever saved. But the Word says that some who are first will be last (Matt. 19:30), and that only those that endure to the end will be saved (Mk 13:13).

All the Israelites were delivered from the Egyptian bondage, all were baptized into Moses; they ate spiritual food and drank from the Rock (Christ) that followed them. Yet God was displeased with many of them and their bodies were scattered in the desert because God killed them.

It pays to serve God. It pays to be holy, righteous, and obedient. Remember that disobedience is like the sin of witchcraft (1 Sam. 15:23). It is better to obey than to sacrifice. God is bigger and greater than all, and He requires our absolute obedience.

Cry out to God concerning any area you find yourself weak in, and He will deliver you. Call to Him and He will answer you (Jer. 29:12-13; Jer. 33:3). If you have any habit you find difficult to break, take some time to fast as the Spirit leads you, and that bad habit will break and crumble.

In your relationship with others, don't repay evil with evil, but rather, reward evil with good. You should also be able to know the Good, the Acceptable, and the Perfect Will of God.

There is a difference between the Permissive and the Perfect Will of God; the Perfect Will of God is the best for anyone. If you diligently obey the Voice of God, you will be the head and not the tail; all people (and even devils) shall be afraid of you.

We operate by the law of liberty; we have been called to liberty, but we must not use our liberty as an occasion for the flesh. We are no more in bondage, but we must not live our lives anyhow, but offer the members of our body as instruments of righteousness to holiness.

God hates complaining, murmuring, and bearing of grudges. God has promised to meet all your needs, and not all your wants. Of course, He gives you your wants as well, but He knows the best for you. If you give a ten-year old boy your car to drive in the highway because he is your child and you love him, do you really love him? Also, God's Time is the best.

The Israelites asked for a king, because they wanted to be like the other nations and God gave them kings, but were they better under those kings? They complained of meat in the wilderness and God gave them quail, but while they ate it, the Anger of the Lord burned against them; this happened because, instead of asking in faith, they murmured and complained.

God corrects, rebukes, and reproves His children using different means, and for different reasons. He does these to make them better in different areas of their lives. There is nothing that is hidden from God; all the secrets of men are open to Him and they will be exposed at the appointed times.

God hates sensuality. By sensuality, I mean living according to your senses, and not according to the Spirit of God and His Word. Humans have five sense organs of eye, ear, nose, tongue, and skin, which are for sight, hearing, taste, smelling, and feeling respectively. In sensuality, we are concerned with walking by sight, hearing, and feeling.

Learn or study to be quiet. In the multitude of words, sin is not absent. He who can bridle his tongue can bridle his whole body; he who is faithful in money will be faithful in many other areas; and he who can avoid sexual immorality can avoid many other sins. Control your passions and motives, and bring them under subjection to the Word of God.

Sincerity is not enough. That you are sincere (which is very good) does not mean that you cannot make mistakes, that you cannot lose God's Blessings, and that the devil will not have a place in your life. God's people perish and suffer loss due to ignorance. You must, therefore, add knowledge and other Christian virtues to your sincerity.

The Word of God says, "For God so loved the world that He gave His Only Begotten Son that whoever believes in Him should not perish but have Eternal Life (Jn 3:16)." This is a verse many of us have quoted often, but have failed to understand a truth in it.

I want you to notice, particularly, that the verse declares that the Believer should not perish and not that the Believer shall not perish. The one that believes on the Lord Jesus Christ should not perish.

If you believe on the Lord Jesus Christ, if you are born again, you are not supposed to perish. When someone or something should not perish, it means that the person or thing ought not to (is not supposed) to perish. It also means that the person or thing may perish.

If you are hanging on a strong and stable crane, high above the ground level, you should not fall down and crash by the influence of the force of gravity. However, if you separate yourself from the crane, you will crash on the ground.

People of God perish because of lack of knowledge (Hos. 4:6). Ignorance of God and His Ways will make you perish; though, in this case, the perishing is not applicable to perishing in Hell Fire alone; in fact, this place is talking about losing God's Provisions for you, among other applications.

The devil is no good entity; if you don't know your rights and privileges in Christ Jesus, he will steal from you, kill you, and even destroy you (Jn 10:10). Don't allow the enemy to succeed in prevailing over you. Let none of his works come to pass in your life. Give no place to the devil (Eph. 4:27).

This is why you have to study the Bible, because, in reading and studying it, in meditating on and speaking forth its contents (the things applicable to you), you overcome the devil and his devils. You are sitting with Christ at the Right Hand of God (Eph. 2:6).

Well, my topic is that the Believer should not perish in Hell Fire. However, many Believers will perish in Hell Fire. Casual reading of the New Testament will reveal this truth to you. God does not intend that it should be so, but it will be so to many.

The Bible says that it is not the Will of God that any soul should perish, but those that refuse Jesus Christ will perish in Hell Fire. Those that live in sin and disobedience will perish in Hell Fire.

As a matter of fact, God is not the one that sends people to Heaven or Hell; actually, people choose where they will go, even without their knowledge. Where you go is dependent on what you do with Jesus Christ, His Holy Spirit, and God's Word.

God sets before you life and death, blessing and curse (good and bad), and you choose the one you want (Deut. 30:19). God does not force anyone. Of course, He can change circumstances and conditions around you to help you take the decision to obey; however, He still, will not force you.

Hell Fire was not made for man. Hell was made for satan and his fallen angels, his demons. Why? It is because they rebelled against God.

However, the man that rebels against God is putting himself in the same position as the devil, and the Bible says that he will suffer the same condemnation and punishment in Hell Fire. The punishment of Hell Fire is everlasting and eternal.

The fire of Hell does not quench and its worms do not die. If all the sufferings in this world are put together, and one person is made to carry them and bear them, yet it will not equal what someone will suffer in Hell for 24 hours.

My brother, run from the damnation of Hell Fire while there is time. After death, there is no room for repentance; neither is there room for forgiveness.

The Lord Jesus Christ asks, "Why do you call Me, Lord, Lord, and do not do what I say?" (Lk. 6:46). Many will say to Him on that Day, "Lord, Lord, have we not done this or that in Your Name?" But He will tell them that He never knew them (Matt. 7:21-23).

Notice that many of them even prophesied. It is only those that do the Will of the Father that will enter the Kingdom of Heaven (verse 21). You may be baptized and confirmed in your church, but that is not the answer.

If you want to enter the Kingdom of Heaven, you must be born of water and of the Spirit (Jn 3:5). That is a higher level of "I am born again" (Jn 3:3). The water is the Word of God (Eph. 5:26), and the Spirit is the Holy Ghost.

You must obey the Word of God, and you must listen to the Spirit of God. Many who are first will be the last, and the last first (Matt. 19:30). Let this not be your portion.

Some people argue and say that God knows those who will go to Heaven and those who will go to Hell. In other words, they say that some are meant for Heaven and some are meant for Hell. This is no truth.

Of course, the Bible says that God will have mercy on whom He would have mercy (Rom. 9:14-20). The Bible says that God loved Jacob and hated Esau (Rom. 9:9-14). But you've got to interpret that Scripture well, in order not to misdirect yourself.

The Bible says that it is those that endure to the end that will be saved (Matt. 24:13). In other words, if you fall by the wayside, you will not be saved. He who despises God, He will despise (1 Sam. 2:30).

The end of a matter is better than the beginning (Eccl. 7:8). It is one thing to start well, but it is another to end well. Don't fall by the roadside. Many are called but few are chosen (Matt. 20:16).

Why were they chosen? It is because they were faithful. Count yourself to be death with Christ and alive for Him. The life that you live now, should be for Him.

The Word of God talks of the children of the Kingdom being cast away into the Outer Darkness wherein is gnashing of teeth (Matt. 8:12). Those children were meant for the Kingdom of Heaven, but due to sin, disobedience, and unrighteousness, they lost their place in it.

God, after saving the children of Israel from the Egyptian bondage and allowing them to have many spiritual and mighty experiences, destroyed those that sinned and did not believe (1 Cor. 10:1-13).

The Word of God says that because iniquity shall abound in the last days, the love of many shall wax cold; however, some people's love will not wax cold and they will endure to the end (Matt. 24:12-13).

It is those that endure to the end that will be saved. Without holiness, no man can see the Lord (Heb. 12:14). Blessed are the pure in heart, for they shall see God (Matt. 5:8). If you are not holy and pure, forget Heaven.

However, whatever you might have done, repent now; confess your sins to God and make the necessary restitutions; and God will wipe away your sins and unrighteousness.

If you confess your sins, He is faithful and just to forgive your sins and cleanse you from all unrighteousness (1 Jn 1:9). There is no hard-man with God.

All your pride and boasting is because your time is not up. When your time expires, God will judge you and He is no respecter of persons (Rev. 2:20-23). God says, "Return to me, you backslider!" Obey Him now so that you will not say, "Had I known...."

This is not a question of whether you are an apostle, a prophet, an evangelist, a pastor, a teacher, a bishop, or an archbishop, a president and founder, a general overseer, an elder, a deacon or a deaconess, a men's or women's leader, a Sunday School teacher, a singer, an intercessor or whatever you may be; if you don't obey God and His Word, forget Heaven and prepare to live with the devil eternally.

Abstain from the lust of the flesh which war against your soul. Flee youthful lusts. God will not allow any temptation that is greater than you to come to you, but don't go where angels fear to tread on. Man can never be wiser than God; when God says, 'Flee,' do just that.

When you are enticed, do not give in to the enticement or temptation. Don't get entangled with sin and disobedience. There are many errors among Believers today; avoid those errors so that it will be well with your soul.

Examine yourself to see whether you are still standing in the faith. If you judge yourself, you will not be judged. Beware of hypocrisy and compromise. All hypocrites will end in eternal separation from God.

Unfaithful servants will be cast into the Outer Darkness. Those who compromise the Word and Standard of God will find themselves in the Lake of Fire which burns with fire and brimstone.

Wives, submit to your husbands in the Lord; husbands, love your wives as your own bodies. If you put a stumbling block to your spouse, so that your words and actions cause him or her to live contrary to the Word and Will of God, God will require it from you: you will give account of your relationship with your spouse to God.

Abhor what is evil; cling to that which is good and true. You must forgive others so that God will forgive you your own sin. Awake to righteousness and shun sin and immorality.

Many have already been corrupted by the lust of the flesh, the lust of the eyes, and the pride of life. The minds of many have already been polluted by demonic suggestions.

He who overcomes will inherit all things. The overcomer will be blessed forever. Let your inward man direct and control your outward man, and not vice versa.

If you live according to your flesh, you shall die; but if through the Spirit, you put to death the deeds of the flesh, you shall live. God did not call us to serve Him for nothing. He will reward our obedience and punish the disobedient. Cease to do evil, learn to do well.

If you live your life anyhow, you will be devoured by the sword of God's Judgment. If you judge yourself, you will not be judged. Walk in the highway of righteousness, the way that pleases God and does His Good Will.

When Moses was instructed by God to build the tabernacle, God told him to make it according to all that He showed him, after the pattern of the tabernacle, and the pattern of all the instruments thereof.

God emphasized this when He said, "See to it that you make them after their pattern, which was shown you on the mountain" (Exo. 25:9,40).

Apostle Paul stressed the importance of this when he referred to this interaction between God and Moses in the Book of Hebrews and used it to compare to Jesus Christ's Ministry (Heb. 8:4-6).

God has a pattern for whatever He tells us to do. The Bible speaks of a pattern of good works (Tit. 2:7). We are not to seek the praise of men but that of God. We are ambassadors of Christ, and we should represent Him well.

Even, when we say that this or that person is a man of God, we are saying that the person is sent by God and represents God. Apostle Paul emphasized the importance of doing things the right way when he said that if anyone competes in athletics, he is not crowned unless he competes according to the rules (2 Tim. 2:5).

No wonder he instructed us to run in such a way that we may obtain the prize. Everyone who competes for the prize is temperate in all things. Now they do it to obtain a perishable crown, but we an imperishable crown.

This made him to run thus: not with uncertainty. Thus he fought: not as one who beats the air: but he disciplined his body, and brought it into subjection, lest, when he had preached to others, he himself should become disqualified (1 Cor. 9:24-27).

Paul says, "But what things were gain to me, these I have counted loss for Christ. Yet indeed I also count all things loss for the excellence of the knowledge of Christ Jesus my Lord, for Whom I have suffered the loss of all things, and count them as rubbish, that I may gain Christ,

"And be found in Him, not having my own righteousness which is from the Law, but that which is through faith in Christ, the righteousness which is from God by faith;

"That I may know Him and the power of His Resurrection and the fellowship of His Sufferings, being conformed to His Death, if by any means, I may attain to the Resurrection from the dead.

"Not that I have already attained, or am already perfected; but I press on, that I may lay hold of that for which Christ Jesus has also laid hold on me. Brethren, I do not count myself to have apprehended;

"But one thing I do, forgetting those things which are behind and reaching forward to those things which are ahead, I press towards the goal for the prize of the Upward Call of God in Christ Jesus.

"Therefore, let us as many as are mature, have this in mind, and if in anything you think otherwise, God will reveal even this to you" (Phil. 3:7-15).

God wants faithfulness in whatever He calls you to do. We are pilgrims, sojourners, and strangers in this world, and we must live our lives with that consciousness.

The questions are, "Do you know what He has called you to do? Are you doing it? If so, are you doing it God's Way or Pattern?" God called us to become His children by the acceptance of the Gospel. Have you become born again? If so, are you living the Christian life?

Then how is your Christian life? Also, God calls each of us to do specific thing(s) for Him. Do you know that (those) thing(s)? Are you doing it (them)? How are you doing it (them)?

It is possible to live your whole life on earth without knowing what God has called you to do. This is why many have lived and died without even hearing that there is a Jesus Christ.

Many have heard about Him, but have hardened their hearts to the Gospel; but many have not heard about Him, even now.

We have the responsibility to preach the Gospel and teach the Word of God to the ends of the world. This is what we call 'the Great Commission.' How are you committed to the Great Commission, individually and collectively?

You must preach the Gospel (the Good News of the Kingdom of God). You must preach by yourself because, in a sense, everybody is a preacher and an evangelist. No wonder Apostle Paul told Pastor Timothy, "Do the work of an evangelist" (2 Tim. 4:5).

The Bible tells us that some are called, specifically, as evangelists. But you must preach, starting from your home, office, or school. You can sponsor others financially to help them preach where you may not go.

Then many who have been born again live their Christian lives the way they want to. Many have chosen (consciously or unconsciously) what they will obey and what they will not obey.

People do many different things which are ungodly, unbiblical, and satanic in churches and say, "It does not matter." But what will they do on the Day of Judgment when they find out that they actually matter? But then, it will be too late, and there will be no second chance. God is no respecter of persons, for He created all.

Then they will cry and say, "Had I known, I…" and their cries will not be heard. These will go into everlasting punishment in Hell Fire. They will have their appointment with the hypocrites and compromisers.

The angels told Lot, saying, "Escape for your life, do not look behind you nor stay anywhere in the plain. Escape to the mountains, lest you be destroyed" (Gen. 19:17). My brethren, let us amend our ways while there is still time.

God did not call us to destroy us along the way; but if anyone destroys himself, let him not blame God. Work out your own salvation with fear and trembling. If you live in pleasure, living to gratify your flesh, you are heading to Hell Fire. Live a holy life, and get perfected in holiness.

There is no agreement between light and darkness; do not do evil or exaggerate, thinking you want to help God. Live in righteousness and it will be well with your soul. God's Grace is available to us always.

It is the Will of God that you are sanctified. God wants you to be consecrated to doing His Word and Will, no matter the cost. There are things you must sacrifice for the Cause of Jesus Christ.

You must carry your cross daily and follow Him. We must obey the Commandments of our Lord and Master. We must serve God, our Maker; He is worthy of our service.

Make every effort to make your calling and election sure, because if you do this, you will be with God and the Lord Jesus Christ forever. Take heed to yourself and the doctrine that you preach, teach, and enforce. In doing this, you will save both yourself and the people that hear and follow you.

We are to walk in the light and truth. To walk in the light is to act and do according to the Word of God, which is a lamp to our feet, and a light to our path.

To walk in the truth is to live, act, and speak according to the Word of God, which is truth. Also, to walk in truth is also to be honest, transparent, and truthful.

We are the light and the salt of the world. We are a source of direction to the people of the world; God uses us to show them the right way, and to lead them out of darkness.

As the salt of the world, we are to add flavour and taste to people's lives, and we should cause them to be preserved by the Power of God.

Jesus Christ is our Focus, and the Word of God (the Bible) our standard. Apostle Paul's life and ministry is worthy of emulation, even though he did make some mistakes.

Moreover, brethren, I do not want you to be unaware that all the fathers of Israel were under the cloud, all passed through the sea, all were baptized into Moses in the cloud and in the sea, all ate the same spiritual food, and drank of that spiritual rock that followed them, and that Rock was Christ.

But with most of them God was not well pleased, for their bodies were scattered in the wilderness. Now these things became our examples, to the intent that we should not lust after evil things as they also lusted.

And do not become idolaters as were some of them. As it is written, "The people sat down to eat and drink, and rose up to play." Nor let us commit sexual immorality, as some of them did, and in one day twenty-three thousand fell.

Don't say, "That was in the Old Testament," because God struck Ananias and Sapphira in the New Testament. Let us not tempt Christ, as some of them also tempted, and were destroyed by serpents; nor complain, as some of them also complained, and were destroyed by the destroyer.

Now all these things happened to them as examples, and they were written for our admonition, upon whom the ends of the ages have come. Therefore, let him who thinks he stands take heed lest he fall.

No temptation has overtaken you except such as is common to man, but God is faithful, Who will not allow you to be tempted beyond what you are able, but with the temptation will also make the way of escape, that you may be able to bear it (1 Cor. 10:1-13).

People backslide and fall away from the faith, from Jesus Christ and His Word. Even people who had been used mightily by God have gone away from God and became separated from the Life of God. My brethren, this ought not to be so.

He that has entered God's Rest has himself also ceased from his work as God did from His. Let us, therefore, be diligent to enter that rest, lest anyone fall according to the same example of disobedience.

For the Word of God is living and powerful, and sharper than any two-edged sword, piercing even to the division of soul and spirit, and of joints and marrow, and is a discerner of the thoughts and intents of the heart.

And there is no creature hidden from His Sight, but all things are naked and open to the Eyes of Him to Whom we must give account (Heb. 4:10-13).

The covenant we have in Jesus Christ is a better covenant than the one the Israelites had with God, and it is based on better promises. The punishment for rejecting Jesus Christ and His Word is worse than the punishment the Israelites received for disobeying the Law, though we may not see it now.

Beware of the little leaven that leavens the whole lump; beware of the little foxes that destroy the vine. Beware of the little 'it-doesn't-matter' that spoils things in the House of God. Beware of the false prophets and the false teachers.

Concerning the specific assignment(s) God has for each one of us, let us take time, in prayer, fasting, and waiting on Him, to know what He wants us to do. And whatever the cost and sacrifice, let us not love our lives even to death.

Let us not do what we want to do. Remember that it is to God that you will render account to. Don't love the praise of men.

If God called you to be an evangelist, don't remain a pastor; if He called you to be a pastor, don't remain an evangelist. If God doesn't want you to open a church, don't open one.

Do you know that you can have one of the largest churches in the world, and organize one of the largest crusades in the world, and still not follow God's Plan for your life? God will help you fulfil His Task for you.

God has a pattern for success; follow that pattern to be successful in life. Learn to call what God calls 'success,' 'success,' and what He calls 'failure,' 'failure.' If you follow the pattern of the world, you can't be successful in God's Sight. Remember that life is not in the abundance of what you possess.

Strike the shepherd, and the sheep will be scattered. As a minister, you have to know that if you don't follow the pattern of Godliness, others will follow you do the same things.

Sin can hinder your ability, as a Believer, to exercise the power and authority which the Lord has made available to the Believers. Therefore, it is up to you to decide to live your life in holiness, and free of sin and disobedience.

Sin is going contrary to the Word of God. Sin is disobedience, and disobedience is sin. When God tells you to do something, if you don't do it, it is sin. If He tells you to avoid something, if you don't avoid it, if you do it, it is sin.

Sin entered the world by one man (Adam), and one Man (Jesus Christ) came to take away sin. Sin came from the devil but righteousness, peace, and joy came from the Lord.

There are three basic definitions of sin, as found in the Bible. Sin is lawlessness, the transgression of the Law (1 Jn 3:4). Sin is anything not done in faith (Rom. 14:23). Sin is: knowing what you should do and not doing it (Jas 4:17).

These three definitions of sin are comprehensive and they touch many different things. God hates sin, though He loves the sinner. God is of Purer Eyes than to behold sin (Habk. 1:13).

Sin will keep you far from God. God will do everything to save the sinner, but if he refuses, he bears the consequences.

Sin is the transgression of the Law. To transgress the Law is to go against the Law. When the Law is mentioned, some think that the Law has been done away with. This needs proper interpretation. Jesus Christ came to fulfil the Law and the Prophets, and not to destroy them (Matt. 5:17).

The ritual Laws of the Old Testament have been done away with, but not the moral Laws. Today, instead of resting and worshipping God on the Sabbath (Saturday), we rest and worship on the first day of the week (Sunday) (1 Cor. 16:2; Acts 20:7).

The important thing there is that God loves us and wants us to rest. He gives His beloved rest. It is not because we work every time that we succeed. God is able to supply all our needs.

Actually, we are supposed to worship God everyday. So, everyday is our day of worship. But unlike in the Old Testament where they couldn't even cook on the Sabbath, we know now that the Law was made for man and not man for the Law (Mk 2:27).

But we know that "You shall have no other god before Me" still exists. "You shall honour your father and your mother," "You shall not commit adultery," etc still exist today. But even when we do these things, we do them out of love for God and for man.

All the Law is summed up in love: you shall love the Lord God with all your heart, with all your mind, and with all your strength, and you shall love your neighbour as yourself (Deut. 6:5; Matt. 22:37).

We live by the Law of Liberty (Jas 1:25; Jas 2:12), and we do not use our liberty as an opportunity for the flesh (Gal. 5:13).

Sin is anything not done in faith. The Bible says that if you do something in doubt, it is sin, and sin leads to condemnation (Rom. 14:23). Think of the many it-doesn't-matters among Christians today.

I have snapped pictures in a university and you see a lot of things with respect to dressing in the environment. In fact, a time came that I stopped snapping normal pictures except passports, apart from special cases, there. In the university environment, you see a lot of indecent dressings, both among ladies and among young men.

Even among people who call themselves Believers, you see a lot of indecent dressings. People dress indecently to many campus fellowships and churches.

People paint themselves and look like unbelievers, and yet these are people who had been born again and washed with Christ's Precious Blood. Later, they despised the Blood, and live however they want in the name of it-doesn't-matter.

They wear body-hugs and transparent dresses. The worst is that when many of them came in newly in their first year, they used to dress decently, but as time went on, they disappointed both God Who gave them the admission and their parents who sponsor them.

There are many other areas where people live in doubt and say that it makes no difference. Right in their heart, they are not confident of what they are doing, even though many people tell them that it is sinful.

Students live the life of examination malpractice, and yet they are Believers. Do you know why, after Jesus Christ had talked about regeneration in John 3:3, He talked of living by the Word and the Spirit in John 3:5?

The last definition of sin is not doing the good that you know that you should do. In the Epistle of James, James speaks of a case in which a brother comes to you for help and you know that you can and should help him, but instead of helping him, you tell him to go in peace (Jas 2:14-17).

This definition of sin holds many Christians. For instance, if the Spirit of God speaks to your heart to go out for evangelism or to preach to a particular person, if you don't do it, it is sin and disobedience.

No wonder the Word of God says that if the Christian refuses to preach to and warn the sinner, and that sinner dies in his sin, the sinner will go to Hell Fire for his sins, but his blood will be required from the Christian (Ezek. 33:6-9).

If the Spirit witnesses to your heart to pray, then pray; if He tells you to study the Bible, do just that. Preach the Word of God. Be prepared in season and out of season (2 Tim. 4:2). If you know you should love your wife and refuse to love her, it is sin to you.

Of course, I had said that sin is disobedience and disobedience is sin. When God gives us His Commandments, He expects us to obey them. Our obedience to God's Word is for our own good. If we obey Him, He will bless us.

Also, our obedience to the Word of God will keep us from harms. For instance, when God tells you not to commit fornication, He expects you to obey Him, and He will bless you for obeying Him. However, apart from that, it will save you from many venereal diseases.

Disobedience to the Word of God will receive punishment, both in this life and after death. It is true that because of Jesus Christ's Intercession for us at the Right Hand of the Father, God's Judgment does not fall on us immediately like in the Old Testament.

However, when the time of grace God gives you expires, you will be judged (Rev. 2:21). Furthermore, Hell Fire is reserved for sinners and the disobedient.

Has the Lord as great delight in burnt offerings and sacrifices, as in obeying the Voice of the Lord? Behold, to obey is better than sacrifice, and to hearken than fat of rams. Rebellion is as the sin of witchcraft; and stubbornness is as iniquity and idolatry (1 Sam. 15:22-23).

Those were the Words Prophet Samuel spoke to King Saul, after the king disobeyed God's Commandment to him. What is worthy of note in this place is that the king obeyed God but his obedience was partial.

We can then deduce, from God's Reaction, that partial obedience is disobedience. His disobedience cost him the kingdom of Israel, for he was dethroned as a king without an offspring to succeed him. Apart from that, he died in the battle field.

The devil wants to destroy you, he wants to kill you and steal from you. Don't give him a place through disobedience (Eph. 4:27). He that breaks the hedge shall be bitten by the serpent (Eccl. 10:8).

The problem is that many don't value our inheritance in Christ Jesus. Many Christians have despised Esau and spoken badly of him. But do you know that many have behaved and acted worse than Esau?

Some have sacrificed their souls and inheritance for an employment. Some have lost their destinies for a ten-minute sex. Can you lose your life for the Cause of Christ? (Heb. 12:16-17; Matt. 10:39).

Shadrach, Meshach and Abed-Nego told King Nebuchadnezzar that their God was able to deliver them, and He will deliver them. However, they went on to tell the king that they will not bow to his golden image, they will not disobey their God, even though their God refuses to deliver them (Dan. 3:16-30).

You have not yet resisted to bloodshed, striving against sin (Heb. 12:4). Jesus Christ was tempted at all points, and yet He did not sin. You are a Christian; therefore, be like Christ!

True freedom is freedom from sin and disobedience. True gain is making Heaven at last and receiving abundant reward from God in His Eternal Kingdom. If you say you are free, when you are still bound by sin and disobedience, you are in bondage.

If you gain the whole world and lose your soul at last, you gained nothing. Make up your mind to obey God at all time, no matter the cost and sacrifice.

Do you have confidence in God? Do you believe that you have His Approval? Are you doing what He wants you to be doing the way He wants you to be doing them? Each of us must seek to receive God's Approval in every area of our lives.

The Bible says that it is not he that approves himself that is approved but whom the Lord approves (2 Cor. 10:18). It is not him that men approve that is approved, but whom the Lord approves. Do you know that a group of Christians may approve you, and yet God will not approve you?

This is why you should not seek the praise of men, but the Praise of God. To seek the approval of men is death, but to seek the Approval of God is life. Of course, if you do the right thing, good people will approve you and that is good.

When you please God, He will approve you. Enoch walked with God and pleased Him, and God approved him and took him away that he did not see death (Gen. 5:24; Heb. 11:5). Moses pleased God and received the testimony that he was faithful in all his house (Heb. 3:2).

Joshua and Caleb pleased God, and while the other adults that left Egypt with them died, two of them entered the land of Canaan. Daniel, Shadrach, Meshach and Abed-Nego pleased God when they refused to defile themselves, and God blessed them exceedingly in the land of Babylon.

The Word of God says that we should be diligent (King James Bible says, 'study') to show ourselves approved to God, workmen that need not be ashamed, rightly dividing (that is, correctly handling) the Word of God, the Word of Truth (2 Tim. 2:15).

This means that to be approved, you must be diligent, having made the decision. Approval by God requires sacrifice and self-discipline.

Ask yourself if you know what God wants you to be doing or to do. If you know, are you doing it? Have you done it? If you are doing it, are you doing it (did you do it) the Lord's Way?

Doing what God wants you to do the Lord's Way is what gets you His Total Approval. Don't settle for God's Permissive Will; go for His Perfect Will.

The minister that God will approve must be prayerful. It is said that prayer is the master-key. Jesus Christ prayed well during His Earthly Ministry and that was why He could fulfil God's Assignment for Him. Through prayer, He was able to know God's Will for His Life and was able to do it.

Jesus Christ prayed daily and His ministers must pray daily too. Don't pray well some days, and be prayerless the others. Maintain a consistent prayer-life. I think every minister should spend a minimum of two hours in prayer everyday.

The minister that God will approve should be full of the Word of God. No wonder the Word of God tells us to study to show ourselves approved to God, a workman that needs not be ashamed, rightly dividing the Word of Truth (2 Tim. 2:15).

Let the Word of Christ dwell in you richly in all wisdom (Col. 3:16). It has to dwell in you richly, and not just by manageable measure. Also, it must be in all wisdom: the Word of God says that we should rightly divide the Word of God and compare Scripture with Scripture (1 Cor. 2:13).

Apostle Paul told Timothy to preach the Word, to be instant in season and out of season. Timothy was to reprove, rebuke, exhort with all longsuffering and Doctrine (2 Tim. 4:2).

Timothy was to put the brethren in remembrance of good teaching to be a good minister of Jesus Christ, nourished up in the Words of Faith and of Good Doctrine, which he had attained (1 Tim. 4:6). He was to give attention to reading, to exhortation, to Doctrine (1 Tim. 4:13).

It is the Word that saves, sanctifies, and builds up. To be approved by God, you are to preach the message that works: you are to preach Jesus Christ, and not yourself. The message that works is the preaching and teaching of the Word of God, and not philosophy, psychology, and things of unbelief, doubt, and human wisdom.

If the Lord is going to approve you, you must do what you preach and teach. Don't be like the Pharisees who would say one thing and do the contradictory thing. God hates hypocrisy. Whatever may be hidden now will be brought to light at the Coming of the Lord Jesus Christ.

Ask God to give you the grace to practice what you preach. You have to be an example to the Believers and to your followers (1 Tim. 4:12). Let not God's Name be blasphemed for your sake (Rom. 2:24).

The Lord Jesus Christ tells us that we are to be doing the works that He did, even greater works (Jn 14:12). The Works of Jesus Christ include: preaching, teaching, healing, casting out devils, miracles, signs, and wonders.

Don't be afraid of the devil and his works because you are sitting with Christ at the Right Hand of God (Eph. 2:6). You have the power and authority to trample on serpents, scorpions, and all the power of the enemy, and nothing shall by any means hurt you (Lk. 10:19).

You must be holy, for the Lord is holy (1 Pet. 1:15). Be perfect as your Father in Heaven is perfect (Matt. 5:48). Be dedicated to God in absolute obedience and consecration. Jesus Christ came to save us from the power of sin and the effects of sin.

God may tell you to do a difficult thing, but never an impossible thing. His Commands are not grievous and burdensome (1 Jn 5:3). God's Yoke is easy and His Burden is light (Matt. 11:30). God will bless you abundantly if you are obedient to Him.

The minister that God is going to approve must be led by the Spirit of God. As many as are led by the Spirit of God, these are the sons of God (Rom. 8:14). Don't be like the horse that will run faster than is necessary; and don't be like the mule that will need to be pulled to move as needed (Psa. 32:9).

Be sensitive to the Holy Spirit's Promptings and Witness. He will teach you all things and show you things to come (Jn 14:26; Jn 16:13). He will remind you of what you had learned and known (Jn 14:26). It is not by power nor by might, but by the Spirit of God (Zech. 4:6).

The Word of God says that we are to prove all things, and hold on to the good (1 Thes. 5:21). Believe not all spirits, but test the spirits whether they are God's, for many false prophets have gone into the world (1 Jn 4:1).

Beware of the ministers you relate with, because evil company corrupts good manners (1 Cor. 15:33). Don't try to help God, and never try to get a substitute to God's Power and Blessings.

Patiently, wait on God for His Appointed Time. Don't be associated with demons, for whatever they offer is worthless.

If you want God to approve you, then you must be blameless, a husband of one wife, temperate, sober-minded, of good behaviour, hospitable, apt to preach and teach, not given to wine, not violent, not greedy for money, but gentle, not quarrelsome, not covetous.

You should rule your own house well, having your children in submission with all reverence. You must not be a novice, and you should have a good testimony among those who are outside (1 Tim. 3:2-7).

For God to approve you, you must be reverent, not double-tongued. You must hold the mystery of the faith with a pure conscience. Even, your wife ought to be reverent, not slanderer, temperate, faithful in all things (1 Tim. 3:8).

I used 'ought to' instead of 'must' for the minister's wife because the devil is fighting many ministers through their wives and trying to suppress their Christian lives and ministries through them. The wives of many of them are the ways they are, because many of them don't know how to handle them.

Of course, many ministers married before they were born again and their wives have refused to be born again also. But even believing wives are not exempted.

Of course, the King James Version italicized the word 'must,' showing that it is not in the original text, but was added for a better understanding. Take authority over your wife and break the power of the enemy over her life in the Name of Jesus Christ and you will see a change.

This is why a minister should not depend on physical appearance to marry someone. Pray well and depend on the Holy Spirit. That is not to say that your God-given wife may not give you headache.

As a matter of fact, God can allow your wife to trouble you (though the trouble was induced by the devil) to train you the way He wants to. But He will be there always to help you overcome.

The Christians and the ministers are responsible for many of the things we accuse satan and the unbelievers of. The work of the devil is to kill, steal, and destroy, while our work is to stop and destroy the works of the devil; if we don't do our part, the devil will succeed, and God will hold us responsible.

An unbeliever who dies in sin will be punished, but the Christian who refused to preach to him will be held responsible.

There is nothing like being approved by God. When God approves you, you can be sure of Heaven; and you will inherit the Kingdom of Heaven with great rewards.

Don't seek the praise of men, but do everything you can to please God. If you are sure that God is moving you this way, then go the very way and it will be well with your soul.

From the Life of Jesus Christ, we learn that we should make prayer our priority; we also learn that we should submit ourselves to the Will of God, no matter the cost. From the life of Apostle Paul, we learn that if you sell yourself out to God to do His Will, you will go through severe trials and persecutions.

From the life of Moses, we learn that how you end is more important than how you started. The Old Testament heroes and heroines of faith, and the early New Testament Disciples and ministers left us a rich inheritance of examples to emulate.

Being approved by God is not in titles or names. You can be famous among Believers and yet not be approved by God. You can go by such titles as, 'pope,' 'archbishop,' 'bishop,' 'reverend,' 'apostle,' 'prophet,' 'evangelist,' 'pastor,' 'senior apostle,' 'prophetic evangelist,' 'reverend (doctor),' and the rest, and still not be approved by God.

Actually, some people assume someone took a particular title because of pride, but it is not always like that. By the way, ministry is not in names, but titles can help define your ministry and keep you focused.

Someone may use a big title and not be proud, while someone with a seemingly lesser title may be proud. Do you know that someone can even be proud to be humble without people's knowledge?

God is interested in our continuance with what He has called us to do. Many times, we obey God, but we don't continue with it. Sometimes, we may stop doing the right thing because we do not see the results we expect immediately. But be courageous because God's Word can never fail, though it may tarry.

Never leave your first love, and never stop doing your first works. Continue in them because, it is by forbearance that you inherit the promise.

It is him that endures to the end that will be saved. God is not a man and does not judge as men judge. You may be rich and holy in people's eyes, while before God, you are poor and corrupt.

If a sinner forsakes his sins and does righteousness, none of his sins will be remembered; rather, he will be remembered for his present righteousness.

Likewise, if a righteous man forsakes his righteousness and does evil and wickedness, none of his righteousness will be remembered; rather, he will die and suffer for his present sins and wickedness.

Whenever God calls you, follow Him. Whatever He tells you to do, do it. However the Lord tells you to do what He wants you to do, do it that way.

God knows better than any man, and He is more dependable than any other. Do not be wise in your own eyes, but trust in the Lord and do the right things.

As a leader, there are steps you must take. Remember that many are looking up to you, and if you fall and fail, they may fall and fail too. Follow the pathway to leadership to lead effectively. When you lead effectively, God will approve you and reward you abundantly.

Speak whatever the Lord has commanded you to speak, and don't be afraid. You have been called for rooting out and planting, pulling down and building up. None shall prevail against you. Neither the devil nor man can stop you from doing what the Lord has commissioned you to do for Him, if you keep in pace with God.

Remember Lot's wife. She turned to a pillar of salt because she disobeyed the Commandment given to them. Who knows whether she looked back because she called to remembrance the much wealth they left behind! But life is more important than riches.

No one who puts his hand to the plough and looks back is fit for service in the Kingdom of God. Sit down and count the cost of being a Christian; consider the reward for obedience and the punishment for disobedience.

Over the thousands of years gone by, God has dealt with people, or rather, people have related with God in such a way that we can call them God's generals.

The term 'general' is a military rank of top value, second only to the field-marshal. There are also lower ranks in it: major-general, brigadier-general, and lieutenant-general. The Christian life or the ministry is a life of spiritual warfare, and so we can use that term in Christianity, though you will not find it in the Bible.

In the army, all are not generals, but some are corporals, sergeants, captains, and others. Without the recruits, corporals, and sergeants, the general will not be effective in his work.

Now, the Lord Jesus Christ is our General and Field-marshal, but we will use that term, in a relative sense, to show that God has major works for many people and people have done major works for God.

No matter what you might have done for the Lord or what you can do for Him, do not take the glory, but all the glory should go to God the Father, and His Son Jesus Christ. The Holy Spirit works to bring glory to Jesus Christ (Jn 16:14).

Man is nothing without God. It is God Who works in you both to will and to do His Will (Phil. 2:13). It is not of him that wills nor of him that runs, but of the Lord that shows mercy (Rom. 9:16).

The race is not to the swift, nor the battle to the strong (Eccl. 9:11). Don't think of yourself above measure, but think soberly (Rom. 12:3).

Also, nothing you do for God, according to His Will, is too small to Him. God rewards faithfulness, and not just position or responsibility. Remember that God does not judge as men judge. In the Bible, people who came at different times within a specified period received the same reward.

Somebody that started work at about 8:00 a.m. received the same reward with another that started work at about 5:00 p.m. even though the workers that started earlier did not like it; the master justified himself (Matt. 20:1-16).

There are the office ministries of the apostles, prophets, evangelists, pastors, and teachers. There are ministers that help both the ministers and the Church, as a whole. They include, among others: the music ministry, the intercessory ministry, and the financial support ministry.

There are Gifts of the Holy Spirit which the Holy Spirit gives to Spirit-filled Believers. They include: the word of wisdom, the word of knowledge, the discerning of spirit, the gift of faith, the gifts of healings, the working of miracles, the gift of prophecy, the gift of diverse kinds of tongues, and the interpretation of tongues.

There are also such ministries and gifts as: leading, exhortation, showing mercy, giving, speaking, administrations, helps, etc (Eph. 4:11-12, 1 Pet. 4:10-11; 1 Cor. 12; Rom. 12:8).

There are the generals of God that people have not recognized. Do you know that even though all Christians are intercessors and are supposed to intercede, there are people who have specific ministries (or higher levels of ministry) in intercession, and they can do more for God praying, than many preachers can do? But they need to preach also.

People may not see you, but never mind. Occupy the position that God gave you and be faithful in it. Some have done things for God, by sponsoring ministers and ministries, more than many of the ministers that we celebrate.

If God called you to preach by yourself, don't think of sponsoring others without doing the actual preaching; preach by yourself, and then sponsor those you have money to sponsor (those you are led to sponsor).

Even in the kingdom of darkness, there are different levels of commitments, assignments, and positions: they dedicate their energy to serving the devil at the level they find themselves.

Likewise, don't wait for the pulpit before you can preach; preach in schools, preach in buses, preach in streets and markets, preach everywhere, in season and out of season. Win souls for the Lord Jesus Christ.

In the Bible, there are many people we can describe as generals of God in their dispensations. They include: Enoch, Abraham, Joseph, Moses, Joshua, Samuel, David, Elijah, Elisha, Isaiah, Ezekiel, Daniel, John the Baptist, Peter, Paul, and others.

In the recent past, we can include John G. Lake, Smith Wigglesworth, A.A. Allen, etc. Even in the current times, there are people we can describe as God's generals, but I wouldn't mention anyone for now.

For the apostle who may be doing a great work for the Lord, he must work with people to be as effective as he should be. The same applies to other ministers. When a 'powerful' evangelist visits a town, many pastors will work with him, and people will do different things to make the crusade effective.

Even, the pastor who may be doing a great work for the Lord has departmental leaders and workers that make his work effective. We need each other to succeed.

That someone is taken as a general of God does not necessarily mean that he never made mistakes. The Gifts and the Calling of God are irrevocable. God does not want His children to sin, not to talk of people with High Callings of God.

However, if you sin or make a mistake, repent and confess, and God will forgive you. Remember that God is no respecter of persons. He respects His Word, and judges according to His Word.

God hates pride. If you don't turn away from your sin, you have lost your position as a general of God, because if you die in your sin, you will go to Hell and not Heaven.

If you are following somebody, don't follow too close. Jesus Christ is the Author and Finisher of our faith, and He is our Ultimate Model. Apostle Paul spoke of imitating him as he imitates Jesus Christ; but what happens when he is no more imitating our Lord? You can't imitate him then.

If you like somebody's faith, you may imitate him, but don't take anything in his life that is not good. Don't follow me to do any wrong thing: God owns you, not me. This is why you should know the Word of God and the Voice of the Holy Spirit.

No matter what your responsibility is, make sure you are prayerful. Jesus Christ started with prayer and ended with prayer. The devil is not through with you yet, as you are still alive.

Some were prayerful in their early years of ministry, but as their ministries expanded, they became too busy to pray as supposed. You must watch and pray. Put on the whole Armour of God so that you can be able to withstand the devices of the wicked one. Don't joke with prayer.

Also, don't live in sin. Many were humble at first, but they are now full of pride. God hates pride very much; you couldn't amount to anything without God.

Apostle Paul planted while Apostle Barnabas watered, but God gave the increase. The one that planted and the one that watered are nothing; it is God that gave the increase Who is Something.

Also, beware of money; many have got so much interested in money that they have lost the anointing. This is why some ministers have gone after strange powers.

Another area of great importance is the area of adultery, fornication, and other forms of sexual immorality. Fornication is not only a sin against God, but also a sin against yourself. If you join yourself with a harlot, you are one with her, and the spirits and curses following her can get at you, whether or not you know it.

Sin is deceitful; the devil will not show you what you will suffer, but he will show you what you will enjoy for few minutes, days, months, or years. If you have thrown out your wife, and married another, repent and correct your ways before it is too late.

It is not because you are too handsome that the lady is pursuing (coming after) you; they sent her to drain your anointing and reduce you to nothing.

But thanks to God that He is able to keep us till the end. They that are with us are more than they that are with them. Greater is He that is in you than he that is in the world.

The host of Heaven is behind us, who shall we be afraid of? He that started the good work in us is able to accomplish it to the end. Amen.

Never Say That God Said What He Did Not Say!

HAVING A STRONG RELATIONSHIP WITH GOD

As a Believer, you have the authority that God gives to His children, and you have access to the great power that is obtainable in God. However, how you operate in the authority that God gave you, is dependent on your place in God. The amount of power resident in you, is dependent on your relationship with God.

There are different levels of relationships. Some relationships are loose, while others are strong. Some are casual, while others are intimate.

In our relationship with God, we should develop a strong and an intimate relationship with Him. This is evident because the first Commandment in the Ten Commandments is that we shall have no other gods before the Living God (Exo. 20:3).

Also, when Jesus Christ was asked about the greatest Commandment, He said that the first and Great Commandment is to love the Lord your God with all your heart, with all your soul, and with all your mind (Matt. 22:36-38).

Hear, O people of God, the Lord our God, the Lord is One. And you shall love the Lord your God with all your heart, with all your soul, with all your mind, and with all your strength. This is the first Commandment (Mk 12:29-30).

Man is tripartite in nature, comprising spirit (or heart), soul (or mind), and body. All these components or natures of man must be fully dedicated to God. No wonder Apostle Paul prayed that the whole spirit, soul, and body be preserved blameless at the Coming of our Lord Jesus Christ (1 Thes. 5:23).

You dedicate your spirit to God by first being born again, so that your spirit is regenerated and made a new creature in Christ Jesus. You then desire the sincere milk of the Word of God so that you can grow thereby.

Also, your spirit should be filled with the Holy Spirit, the Spirit of Power, and you get edified by praying in the Holy Spirit. You build up your most holy faith by praying in the Holy Ghost (Jude 1:20).

Many in the Church need revival. By prayer (sometimes, added with fasting), you get more sensitive to the Holy Spirit, and it will be easier for Him to lead you.

You also renew your mind with the Word of God so that you think as God thinks and make decisions according to His Will and Mind (Rom. 12:1-2).

You are to present your body, which is the Temple of God, a living sacrifice, holy, acceptable to God, which is your reasonable service.

Shall we continue in sin that grace may abound? Certainly not! How shall we who died to sin live any longer in it? Just as Christ was raised from the dead by the Glory of the Father, even so we also should walk in newness of life.

Our old man was crucified with Him, that the body of sin might be done away with, that we should no longer be slaves of sin. Reckon yourselves to be dead, indeed, to sin, but alive to God in Christ Jesus our Lord. Therefore, do not let sin reign in your mortal body, that you should obey it in its lusts.

And do not present your members as instruments of unrighteousness to sin; but present yourselves to God as being alive from the dead, and your members as instruments of righteousness to God.

Sin shall not have dominion over you, for you are not under Law but under grace. Do you not know that to whom you present yourselves slaves to obey, you are the one's slaves whom you obey, whether of sin leading to death, or of obedience leading to righteousness?

But God be thanked that though you were slaves of sin, yet you obeyed from the heart that form of Doctrine to which you were delivered. And having been set free from sin, you became slaves of righteousness.

Just as you presented your members as slaves of uncleanness, and of lawlessness leading to more lawlessness, so now present your members as slaves of righteousness for holiness.

Having been set free from sin, and having become the Slaves of God, you have your fruit to holiness, and the end, Everlasting Life. For the wages of sin is death, but the Gift of God is Eternal Life through Christ Jesus our Lord (Rom. 6).

Without prayer, your relationship with God cannot be strong. Every Christian should pray for at least two hours everyday. Take enough time to worship God. Pray in tongues, so that you can speak mysteries to God and pray for things you may not know about.

Be consistent in your prayer-life. Watch and pray so that you do not fall into temptation. Watchfulness and vigilance should be part of you so that you can know the enemy's plans and stop them.

Having a strong relationship with God requires that you live the life of faith. The righteous is to walk by faith, and not by sight. Without faith, you cannot please God, because he who comes to God must believe that He is and that He rewards those who diligently seek Him. By faith, God called forth the whole creation into existence.

Faith is the substance of things hoped for, the evidence of things not yet seen. Whatever God has promised you, He will give it to you, even though you may not be seeing it physically now. In no distant time, it will be yours. Pray and believe.

The Word of God contains the Mind and Will of God. This is one reason you have to study the Word of God with commitment. Let the Word of Christ dwell in you richly in all wisdom. Faith comes by hearing, and hearing by the Word of God.

It is by the Word of God that you can prove all things so that you can hold on to that which is good. The Word of God is the source of the Blessings of God. One Word from God can change your life forever. The Spirit of God inspired the Word, and two of Them agree.

All Scripture is given by the Inspiration of God, and is profitable for Doctrine, for reproof, for correction, for instruction in righteousness; that the man of God may be complete, thoroughly equipped for every good work (2 Tim. 3:16-17).

No prophecy of the Scripture is of any private interpretation, for prophecy never came by the will of man, but holy men of God spoke as they were moved by the Holy Spirit (2 Pet. 1:20-21). Desire the sincere Word of God so that you may grow and mature.

But be a doer of the Word, and not just a hearer. If you hear the Word without doing it, you deceive yourself. It is not the hearer that is commended, but the doer.

If anything, the more you hear the Word, without doing it, the more your punishment will be, also. Obedience is better than sacrifice. Rebellion is like the sin of witchcraft. If you don't mix the Word with faith, it will not avail anything to you, because you will not do it.

As obedient people of God, don't fashion yourselves after the former lust, but as He Who called you is holy, so be holy in all manner of conduct.

If you desire a strong relationship with God, then you must win souls for the Lord Jesus Christ. Jesus Christ came to save sinners. You must preach the Gospel always, even against your time table or schedule.

If you are ashamed of Christ Jesus before men, He also will be ashamed of you before God and the holy angels. He that wins souls is wise.

The wise shall shine like the brightness of firmament, and those who turn many to righteousness like the stars forever and ever (Dan. 12:3). Let God be proud of you.

Giving to God and to men will help you maintain a strong relationship with God. The Bible says that where your treasure is, is where your heart will be also.

As you give to God, you have the confidence that when you get to Heaven, the Lord will reward you abundantly; and it will help you prepare for Heaven. Of course, God will reward you in this world also.

When you give to the people of God in the Name of Jesus Christ, you give to God. When you give to God's Servants, you will be blessed. As you give to the poor, you lend to God and He will repay you abundantly.

Having a strong relationship with God will require self-discipline and self-denial. You don't get taken up by the things of this world; rather, you set your mind on things Above, where Jesus Christ is.

Limit the time you spend on television and films, even for Christian programmes and films. Don't be gluttonous in your feeding. Also, do not sleep too much; sleep to get rest, and when sleep has cleared your eyes, give yourself to profitable and Godly things. The lazy man shall not excel in his endeavour.

To maintain a strong relationship with God, you must be led by the Spirit of God. The Spirit of God is the Spirit of Truth, and He will lead you into all truth. The Holy Spirit will reveal secrets to you, and tell you God's Plan and Purpose for your life.

No man can excel by the strength of the flesh. It is not by might, nor by power, but by the Holy Spirit of the Living God (Zech. 4:6). He is your Comforter, Helper, Advocate, Strengthener, Counselor, Intercessor, and Standby.

He will help you accomplish God's Assignment for your life. But He is a Gentle Spirit; therefore, you must give Him room to lead you.

Make every effort to be more like Jesus Christ our Lord. Jesus Christ had a strong relationship with God, the best any can have; therefore, put God first and every other thing second.

You can't expect to drink from the Lord's Cup and the devil's cup at the same time. You can't eat at the Lord's Table and the devil's table at the same time.

God does not do anything without revealing it to His Servants, the prophets. God seeks for a man who will stand in the gap between God and others, so that the people can receive God's Blessings and Provisions, and also escape God's Judgment.

God is a Jealous God; He will not share His Glory with another. The Spirit of God that dwells in us lusts to envy. God does not want us to be worldly as the people of the world.

He expects that your whole spirit, soul, and body be kept for Him. Your body is the Temple of the Holy Spirit. You can't serve God and satan at the same time.

You need to have a strong hunger and thirst for God and the Things of God. He who thirsts shall be filled, and his thirst shall be quenched. If you hunger and thirst for righteousness, God will satisfy that hunger and thirst. As you hunger and thirst for God, your relationship with Him will be more intimate.

Draw close to God, and the devil will not be your problem. Satan couldn't touch Job of Old Testament or anything that belonged to him without God's Permission. But the problem is that many spend so much time thinking about the devil and fearing him.

People spend a lot of time praying against the devil, his demons, and their works, while they spend smaller time praising, worshipping, seeking, and asking God. Many fear the created being – satan – more than they fear God, the Creator. These are very improper.

Depend on God for whatever thing you may be doing. This is why it is necessary to find out what the Will of God is for your life, because God is committed to whatever He starts.

Except the Lord builds the house, the builders build in vain; except the Lord watches over the city, the watchman stays awake in vain. Commit your ways to the Lord; trust also in Him, and He will bring it to pass.

All the things of this world are vanity. They worth something, when used for the Glory and Will of God, and for the furtherance of His Kingdom.

Don't spend your time pursuing the things of this world, while you have no time for what God wants you to do. It shall profit you nothing to gain the whole world and lose your own soul.

The Whole Duty of man is to fear God and keep His Commandments; and His Commandments are not burdensome. It is when you fear God and keep His Commandments that you can say, with certainty, that you have a close relationship with God. Dare to be a Godly man, woman, youth, boy, or girl!

BECOMING AN EXAMPLE TO THE BELIEVERS

Believers believe in the Lord Jesus Christ. The Disciples were first called Christians in Antioch (Acts 11: 26). To be a Christian is to be like Christ.

However, it is a well-known fact that many Believers fall short of the Likeness of Christ, even to a great gap. But God wants His people, the Believers, to be like His Son, Jesus Christ, because Jesus Christ came to bring many sons to glory.

Due to this, God, through Apostle Paul, commands us to be examples to the Believers. Do you know that many believe that no one can be like Christ in this present world? But the Lord tells us to be perfect just as our Heavenly Father is perfect (Matt. 5:48).

Be holy for the Lord God is holy (1 Pet. 1:15). Be holy, be perfect in your life; whatever you do, in word or in actions, be perfect and holy.

The Bible says that without holiness, no man can see the Lord (Heb. 12:14). If you are not pure in heart, you cannot see God (Matt. 5:8); and out of the abundance of the heart, the mouth speaks (Matt. 12:34).

Where your treasure is, is where your heart will be (Lk. 12:34). Out of the heart, proceeds the issues of life (Prov. 4:23).

Even, life and death are in the power of the tongue, the mouth (Prov. 18:21). Your words and actions are a reflection of what is in your heart.

You must love God with all your being, and more than all beings and things. If you love anything or anyone more than the Lord Jesus Christ, you are not worthy of Him.

Be an example to the Believers in word, in conduct, in love, in spirit, in faith, in purity (1 Tim. 4:12). In your school, be an example; in home, be an example; in market, be an example; in church, be an example; wherever you may be and whatever you may do, be an example.

Let not the Name of the Lord be blasphemed among the heathen for your sake (Rom. 2:24). Let God be proud of you; let Him have confidence in you as He had in Job.

In word, be an example to the Believers: let no corrupt word come out of your mouth but that which is good (Eph. 4:29). Some people can destroy others with their words. Don't tell your brother that he is a fool (Matt. 5:22).

Refrain from gossip, slander, back-biting, and jesting. Learn to encourage people with your words, instead of destroying them with the same. Remember that men shall give account of every idle or careless word they speak on the Last Day (Matt. 12:36).

Don't judge your brother, because there is only one Judge: Jesus Christ. By the way, why do you pay attention to the speck in your brother's eye, while you do nothing about the plank in your own?

Be an example to the Believers in conduct also. Be careful how you behave yourself. Conduct yourself in a Godly manner.

As a minister, be trustworthy in your conduct. If you are a civil servant, don't expect a bribe before you do your work. As a student, you must not get involved in an examination malpractice, either by helping somebody or by receiving help from another during examinations.

Your behaviour should be worthy of emulation. People should speak well of you, though they may persecute or be against you. But this does not mean that all men will speak well of you.

Another area that the Bible commands us to be examples in is in love. All the Law is summed up in your loving God with all your heart, with all your soul, and with all your strength. The extension of it is in loving your neighbour as yourself (Matt. 22:35-40).

If you love Jesus Christ, then keep His Commandments (Jn 14:15), and His Commandments are not burdensome (1 Jn 5:3). God can tell you to do a hard thing, but not an impossible thing.

If God tells you to pray, pray; if He tells you to study His Word, do just that. If the Lord tells you to evangelize, evangelize; follow the Leading of the Holy Spirit, because the Holy Spirit speaks the Mind of God.

If you follow God's Spirit, He will lead you out of trouble and take you to a good place. God's Commandments are to make us; they are for our good, and they are not meant to destroy us.

There is so much more to love than we have realized. Have you ever wondered why the Lord Jesus Christ stated that He left us with a New Commandment, which is to love one another? (Jn 13:34).

Though you speak with the tongues of men and of angels, though you have the gift of prophecy and receive revelations, though you have all faith so that you could remove mountains, you are nothing if you don't have love.

What then is love since the Bible says that you can bestow all your goods to feed the poor, give your body to be burned, and still not have love? Well, the Bible tells us what love is.

Love suffers long and is kind; love does not envy; love does not parade itself, is not puffed up; love does not behave rudely, does not seek its own, is not provoked, thinks no evil; love does not rejoice in iniquity, but rejoices in the truth (1 Cor. 13:1-8).

Love bears all things, believes all things, hopes all things, and endures all things. Love never fails. You see that if you live your life in love, you are a super-human. Of course, the life of love will get you to Heaven.

God is Love and we are children of God. Therefore, we are a people of love. No wonder the Love of God is shed abroad in our hearts by His Holy Spirit (Rom. 5:5). Use the love that God has given you; increase and multiply it, and it will be well with your soul.

You must be an example to the Believers in spirit. We are sprit-beings who have souls and live in physical bodies. The Life of God, the Eternal Life that we received when we were born again is a life in the Spirit of God.

Even, the Word of God that gets us born again, that makes us grow and mature, is life and spirit. The spiritual controls the physical. God spoke the physical world into existence using His Spiritual Power. Be filled and be being filled with the Spirit of God; don't stop at the Holy Ghost baptism; go on.

Life in the Spirit is wonderful. Smith Wigglesworth said that he would rather have the Spirit of God upon him for five minutes than to have a million dollars. What a great statement!

The Anointing and Power of the Holy Spirit is what we must thirst and hunger after. We must live our lives, and we must minister, in the Holy Ghost.

Allow yourself to be led by the Holy Spirit; soak yourself in the Word of God, because the Word of God is power. Let the Fruit of the Spirit be abundant in your life.

Be an example to the Believers in faith. The fathers received good report by faith (Heb. 11:2). Without faith, it is impossible to please God. You must believe that God exists and that He will reward you, to be able to please Him.

Faith is the substance of things hoped for, the evidence of things not seen. Faith comes by hearing the Word of God (Rom. 10:17). Abel offered to God a more excellent sacrifice by faith. Enoch walked with God by faith. Noah obeyed God by faith; Abraham obeyed God by faith.

Moses chose to suffer with the people of God by faith. The prophets of the Old Testament and the early Disciples and ministers of the New Testament pleased God by faith. You must be a man of faith.

Nothing is impossible to him that is with God. God can neither lie nor fail to perform His Word. Has He said it? He will perform it. All power belongs to our God (Psa. 62:11). Neither the devil, his cohorts, nor his works can stand before God.

Lastly, we are commanded to be examples in purity. As a man, be pure; as a lady, be chaste. Don't be immoral in your life. Avoid sexual immorality. Your body is the Temple of God. Don't sell your birthright for a five-minute sex like Esau (Gen. 25:29-34; Heb.12:16-17).

Flee youthful lust and avoid being in a closed dark room alone with the opposite sex. Don't help the devil get you into sin, and don't be wiser than God.

Of course, there are many other ways we have to be exemplary. Run your Heavenly and Christian race in such a way as to obtain the reward and prize. Learn to be orderly, for God loves orderliness.

Whatever you do, in word or in deed, do all in the Name of the Lord, giving glory to the Father. Always put God first in everything you do. Amen.

We are Bondservants of the Lord, and we must sacrifice all for the Lord, even our lives as the Lord needs them. Others should see self-sacrifice and self-denial in us so that they too can lay down their substances, treasures, and lives for the Lord.

The Bible is the Book of books, and it contains the best examples of both faithfulness and unfaithfulness. Study it to know what the people that went before you did.

Learn from their victories, obedience, faith, and exploits. Avoid their mistakes. The things of the past were written for our admonition, so that we can learn from them.

GO FROM GLORY TO GLORY

We have been called to manifest the Glory and Power of God, both in our lives and in the lives of others. We are to demonstrate the Glory and Power of God, both before the Believers and the unbelievers.

The Glory of God is the Presence and Power of God being manifested or demonstrated. God's people have been called to manifest the Glory of God. This is one reason that God puts His Spirit in and upon His people.

The Holy Spirit manifests the Glory of God, and God wants the earth to be filled with the Glory of God as the waters cover the sea (Psa. 72:19). The Manifestation of the Holy Spirit by the Gifts of the Holy Spirit in the lives of Believers is a way that God manifests His Glory. There are many other ways.

After Moses had been in the mountain for forty days and forty nights, his face radiated physically, so that people could see it. That was the Glory of God. Even now, though you may not see the light or radiation physically, yet in the spirit-realm, devils and their agents see it.

On the mountain of transfiguration, the Face of Jesus Christ was changed so that the three apostles that were with Him saw His Face radiating light. That was the Glory of God. Even in this dispensation, whenever God chooses, the radiation can be seen physically.

When you preach the Gospel, when you teach the Word of God, the Spirit of God backs the Gospel and Word you speak, and you will see signs, wonders, and miracles. The signs, wonders, and miracles are the manifestations of the Glory of God.

The Lord Jesus Christ, in His Earthly Ministry, manifested the Glory and Power of God in His Life and Ministry in signs, wonders, and miracles. He tells us in the Word that we who believe in Him will do the same works that He did, even greater works (Jn 14:12).

Moses demonstrated the Power and Glory of God to the Egyptians. Even in the wilderness, God demonstrated His Glory in bringing water out of a rock, in sending manna and quail to them, and in protecting them. The fall of Jericho was a demonstration of the Power and Glory of God.

Elijah brought fire down from Heaven, and he also withheld rainfall for three and half years. Elisha prayed to God and the army that came to arrest him could not see again; even at death, his bone raised the dead.

The children of Israel observed the Glory of God as a devouring fire on the top of the mountain. While they saw it as a devouring fire, Moses saw it as a glory-cloud and walked into the cloud.

Before the time, the people had seen the Glory of the Lord in the cloud at the time they complained about bread. When Moses finished building the tabernacle as the Lord commanded him, the cloud covered the tabernacle of meeting, and the Glory of the Lord filled the tabernacle.

And Moses was not able to enter the tabernacle of meeting, because the cloud rested above it, and the Glory of the Lord filled the tabernacle (Exo. 16:7,10; Exo. 24:16-17; Exo. 40:34-35).

The Word of God says that all the earth shall be filled with the Glory of the Lord (Num. 14:21). Often, the Glory of the Lord appeared to the children of Israel in the form of the cloud (the glory-cloud).

When King Solomon finished building the Temple, it came to pass, when the priests came out of the holy place, that the cloud filled the House of the Lord, so that the Glory of the Lord filled the House of the Lord (1 Kgs 8:10-11).

According to the record in 2 Chronicles 5:11-14, it came to pass when the priests came out of the most holy place (for all the priests who were present had sanctified themselves, without keeping to their divisions),

And the Levites who were singers…clothed in white linen, having cymbals, stringed instruments and harps, and…priests sounding with trumpets – indeed it came to pass when the trumpeters and singers were as one, to make one sound to be heard in praising and thanking the Lord,

And when they lifted up their voice with the trumpets and cymbals and instruments of music, and praised the Lord, saying, "For He is good, for His Mercy endures forever" that the House, the House of the Lord, was filled with a cloud.

When the House was filled with the cloud, the priests could not continue ministering because of the cloud, for the Glory of the Lord filled the House of God.

Whenever you want the Glory of the Lord to manifest in your midst, let the people there sanctify themselves; let them confess any sins to God and be washed in the Blood of Jesus Christ.

Then, as you pray, praise, and worship God in one accord, the Glory of God will fall in your midst; and it can even be noticed physically. When the glory falls, people will get saved, healed, and filled with the Spirit, even when no one has prayed for them.

In the Book of Acts of the Apostles, as the Disciples were all with one accord in one place, suddenly, there came a sound from Heaven, as of a rushing mighty wind, and it filled the whole house where they were sitting.

Then there appeared to them divided tongues, as of fire, and one sat upon each of them. And they were all filled with the Holy Spirit and began to speak with other tongues, as the Spirit gave them utterance (Acts 2:1-4). That was the Glory of God in manifestation.

The reason many meetings, gatherings, or fellowships don't see this (or see it more often) is because many gather together but their hearts and minds are not together. In fact, some harbour bitterness, wrath, unforgiveness, and hatred in their hearts.

After Peter and John had been persecuted for preaching to the people in the Name of Jesus Christ, they were allowed to go. When they met the other apostles and Disciples, and reported to them all that the chief priests and elders had said to them, when they heard that, they raised their voice to God with one accord and said, "Lord, you are God…."

And when they had prayed, the place where they were assembled together was shaken, and they were all filled with the Holy Spirit, and they Spoke the Word of God with boldness (Acts 4:18-31).

Another place where the Power and Glory of God fell was in the prison where Paul and Silas had been imprisoned. When they had laid many stripes on them, they threw them into prison, commanding the jailer to keep them securely.

Having received such a charge, he put them into the inner prison and fastened their feet in the stocks. But at midnight Paul and Silas were praying and singing hymns to God, and the prisoners were listening to them.

Suddenly, there was a great earthquake, so that the foundations of the prison were shaken, and immediately all the doors were opened and everyone's chains were loosed (Acts 16:22-32).

There are many places where the Glory, Power, and Presence of God were revealed in the Bible. Ezekiel saw the Glory of God in a vision and fell on his face. Like the appearance of rainbow in a cloud on a rainy day, so was the appearance of the likeness of the Glory of the Lord (Ezek. 1:28).

The Glory of the Lord was revealed to Prophet Ezekiel again and again. When you see the Glory of the Lord, you will fall down as Ezekiel did.

The Lord will not share or give His Glory with/to another (Isa. 48:11). God was not happy when He said, concerning His people, "Has a nation changed its gods, which are not gods? But My people have changed their glory for what does not profit.

"Be astonished, O heavens, at this, and be horribly afraid; be much desolated. For My people have committed two evils: they have forsaken Me, the Fountain of Living Waters, and hewn themselves cisterns – broken cisterns that can hold no water (Jer. 2:11-13).

People of God leave the real things for the shadows; people can go to churches for years and not have one single deep experience with God.

When people worship idols, they change the Glory of the Incorruptible God into an image made like creeping things (Rom. 1:23). Covetousness and greed are forms of idolatry, according to the Word of God.

When you sin, you fall short of the Glory of God. (Rom. 3:23). You can be restored to the Glory of God by repentance and confession. Whether you eat or drink or whatever you do, do all to the Glory of God.

Give no offence to anyone or the Church of God. Please all men in all things, not seeking your own profit, but the profit of many, that they may be saved (1 Cor. 10:31-33).

Christ in us is our Hope of Glory (Col. 1:27). We have been blessed with all spiritual blessings through Christ, because we are in Him and He is in us.

If we abide in Jesus Christ and His Word abides in us, we shall bear much fruit, and when we ask God anything, we will receive it. When Christ Jesus died and rose again, He defeated the devil for us and gave us the victory.

Believers receive power and authority from Him to tread on serpents, scorpions, devils, and their works; nothing shall hurt them.

Even at His Coming, we shall be glorified with Him forever. We all, with unveiled face, beholding as in a mirror the Glory of the Lord, are being transformed into the same image from glory to glory, just as by the Spirit of the Lord (2 Cor. 3:18).

The Work of the Holy Spirit is to glorify the Lord Jesus Christ, and He does it as we allow ourselves to be used by Him!

Manifesting the Glory of God is also in destroying the works of the devil. The reason the Son of God was made manifest was to destroy all the works of the devil.

We have been empowered to carry on with the Work of the Lord and we must destroy the works of the devil. God wants to use us to prove to the devil that He is all-powerful and above all.

God instructed His Adam and Eve to have dominion. God intends that we, as born-again Spirit-filled children of His, have dominion over the created things in this world. We also have dominion over the works of the devil.

We have been called and set over the nations and over the kingdoms, to root out and to pull down, to destroy and to throw down, to build and to plant. These are how we manifest God's Glory.

It is the Will of God that you excel both in life and in Godliness. As you excel in life and in Godliness, you manifest the Glory of God. He that is anointed demonstrates the Power and Glory of God. The anointing breaks every yoke of the devil, and lifts every burden of the enemy.

Arise and shine for your light has come and the Glory of God is risen upon you. For behold, the darkness shall cover the earth, and deep darkness the people; but the Lord will rise over you, and His Glory will be seen upon you.

Manifesting the Glory of God requires you pay some price. Of course, the Lord has already paid the Ultimate Price for all of us. But whoever will come after Jesus Christ must deny himself, take up his own cross, and follow Him.

The price is the price of obedience: doing what God wants you to do. If the Lord tells you to preach to that your neighbour, do it; if He tells you to sacrifice that your job, do it; if He tells you to fast for seven days, do it. He is our Lord and Master, and He deserves our obedience and reverence.

As a Believer, you need a fresh anointing. Don't depend on the glory of yesterday; don't relax to celebrate the manifestations of yesterday. God has so much provision for you today that you will be marveled, if you keep in pace with God. Live a power-filled life always. Be on fire for the Lord always.

Put your angels to work by being prayerful, holy, and by maintaining a heart full of faith, praise, and thanksgiving. When you praise and worship God, God Himself comes to fight for you, and you will be delivered from all the works of the devil.

Trouble whatever troubles you. Use the Name of Jesus Christ against anything that works against you; at the Name of Jesus Christ, every knee should bow. Don't lie low for the devil to have his way in your life. Resist the devil, his demons, and his agents, and they will flee from you.

The Lord is my Strength and my Salvation, of whom shall I be afraid? The Lord shall keep us from all the plans of the wicked one; therefore, our victory is assured. What can man do to us? Live your life with the consciousness of the fact that God and His angels are with you.

You've got to draw water out of the wells of salvation. The wells are there; there is enough provision and room for us in Christ Jesus our Lord. But we must draw out and take those inheritances of ours by prayer, faith, and praise. If we are faithless, God will remain faithful, for He cannot deny Himself.

Declare the Lord's Doings among the people, both by testimony and by action (present reality). The signs, wonders, and miracles that God does are to bless people and draw their attention to God, so that they will obey and reverence God.

We are the mighty ones of God, who have been called to show forth His Praise. The prophet said, "Lord, who has believed our report? And to whom has the Arm of the Lord been revealed?" When the Power, Glory, and Word of God are revealed to people, they believe our report about God and His Son Jesus Christ.

There are different levels of the anointing; therefore whatever level you may be operating from, aspire and go for the next level. The more the level of your anointing and faith, the more will be the manifestation of the Glory and Power of God through you.

Elisha struck the river and asked, "Where is the Lord God of Elijah?" The river divided because the Lord God Almighty answered. The Lord God is there with you. Believe His Word, and speak according to His Word in faith, and you will see the result that you need.

Do not doubt the Word of God because of what you may be seeing. John the Baptist asked whether or not Jesus Christ was the Expected One, possibly because the Lord did not deliver him, contrary to his expectation. We must be moved by what the Word says, instead of what we see or hear.

We are to move from glory to glory. Don't be satisfied with the level of glory you have found yourself in: go for the next level of glory! The Lord is with you, and He has given you all the things you need to move to the next level, if you will cooperate with Him.

We are changed from glory to glory by the Spirit of the Lord (2 Cor. 3:18). Now the Lord is the Spirit and where the Spirit of the Lord is, there is liberty.

After Moses had been in the mountain for forty days and forty nights, the children of Israel noticed that his face shown with the Glory of God. They could see visible radiation of God's Glory in his face.

But Moses had seen God's Glory before, and he had moved in God's Glory before (remember that God had appeared to him, and he had demonstrated signs and wonders); however, in this place, he moved to another level of God's Glory.

That was Old Testament, and we are in the New Testament which is established upon better promises (Heb. 8:6). If the ministry of death was glorious, which glory was to be done away, how will the Ministry of the Spirit not be more glorious?

For if the ministry of condemnation had glory, the ministry of righteousness excels much more in glory. For even what was made glorious had no glory in this aspect, because of the glory that excels.

For if what is passing away was glorious, what remains is much more glorious. This means that all those mighty things that we read about in the Old Testament are not comparable to the things that are available to us in the New Testament.

The Glory of God is the Presence and Power of God. It is the Manifestation of the Spirit of God to people and through people. The Spirit of God manifests through God's people and can manifest even to unbelievers. You need the Glory of God in your life.

No wonder Moses told God not to send them forward without His Presence. It is the manifestation of the Glory of God through you that distinguishes you from the others. When you see His Glory, you will not remain the same!

We change from glory to glory; we are moved from one level of glory to another level of glory. Don't settle down at the level of glory you have; go for the next.

After the glory of being born again, go for the glory of being baptized and filled with the Holy Spirit. After speaking in tongues, move to the next level of the demonstration of the Power of God through healings and miracles. Progress to other levels!

I will use the account or story in Exodus to describe the Glory of God to you. Moses went up with Aaron, Nadab, and Abihu, and seventy of the elders of Israel, and they saw the God of Israel.

And there was under His Feet as it were a paved work of sapphire stone and it was like the very heavens in its clarity. But on the nobles of the children of Israel He did not lay His Hand. So they saw God and they ate and drank.

Then the Lord said to Moses, "Come up to Me on the mountain and be there, and I will give you tablets of stone and the Law and the Commandments which I have written, that you may teach them."

So Moses arose with his assistant Joshua, and Moses went up to the Mountain of God. And he said to the elders, "Wait here for us until we come back to you. Indeed, Aaron and Hur are with you. If any man has a difficulty, let him go to them."

Then Moses went up into the mountain and a cloud covered the mountain. Now the Glory of the Lord rested on Mount Sinai, and the cloud covered it six days. And on the seventh day He called to Moses out of the midst of the cloud.

The sight of the Glory of the Lord was like a consuming fire on the top of the mountain in the eyes of the children of Israel. So Moses went into the midst of the cloud and went up into the mountain. And Moses was on the mountain forty days and forty nights (Exo. 24:9-18).

You can notice varying levels of glory and relationship with God here. The other people couldn't go up except Moses, Joshua, Aaron, Nadab, Abihu, Hur, and seventy of the elders of Israel.

After going for an extent up the mountain, they saw the Glory of God. Then Moses and Joshua left them up the mountain for another level of glory. Finally, Moses left Joshua after some extent and moved up into the mountain for a higher level of glory and relationship with God.

It is interesting to note that the level of glory you witness and the relationship you have with God will determine your position or the responsibility God will give you, for Joshua replaced Moses at his death.

The same varying levels of glory and relationship with God are seen in the Ministry of Jesus Christ. Many people followed Jesus Christ, and they were so many that, sometimes, they trod on one another.

Out of the multitude that followed Him, Jesus Christ selected a seventy that He sent out for missionary work. He also had His twelve special people. Out of the twelve, He had a special three of Peter, John, and James.

Then out of the three came the closest to Jesus Christ – John. Also, out of the three came the leader of the apostles – Peter. Where do you belong? Your dedication to God and level of obedience to Him will determine your position with Him.

We will yet look at another story in Exodus. Moses experienced and demonstrated the Glory of God so much. And it came to pass, when Moses entered the tabernacle, the pillar of cloud descended and stood at the door of the tabernacle, and the Lord talked with Moses.

All the people saw the pillar of cloud standing at the tabernacle door, and all the people rose and worshiped, each man in his tent door. So the Lord spoke to Moses Face to face, as a man speaks to his friend.

And he would return to the camp, but his servant Joshua the son of Nun, a young man, did not depart from the tabernacle.

Then Moses said to the Lord, "See, You say to me, 'Bring up this people.' But You have not let me know whom you will send with me. Yet You have said, 'I know you by name, and you have also found grace in My Sight.'

"Now therefore, I pray, if I have found grace in Your Sight, show me now Your Way, that I may know You and that I may find grace in Your Sight. And consider that this nation is Your people."

And He said, "My Presence will go with you, and I will give you rest." Then he said to Him, "If Your Presence does not go with us, do not bring us up from here. For how then will it be known that Your people and I have found Grace in Your Sight, except You go with us?

"So we shall be separate, Your people and I, from all the people who are upon the face of the earth." So the Lord said to Moses, "I will also do this thing that you have spoken; for you have found grace in My Sight, and I know you by name."

And he said, "Please, show me Your Glory," and He said, "I will make all My Goodness pass before you, and will proclaim the Name of the Lord before you. I will be gracious to whom I will be gracious, and I will have compassion on whom I will have compassion."

But He said, "You cannot see My Face; for no man shall see Me, and live." And the Lord said, "Here is a place by Me, and you shall stand on a rock. So it shall be, while My Glory passes by,

"That I will put you in the cleft of the rock, and will cover you with My Hand while I pass by. Then I will take away My Hand, and you shall see My Back; but My Face shall not be seen (Exo. 33:9-23).

Can you imagine what happened here? God had been appearing and speaking to Moses, and Moses had done so many miracles and wonders; yet, here, he said, "Show me Your Way, that I may know You."

Moses was still humble enough to desire to know God's Way. Some have not even seen one-tenth of what Moses saw, and they boast of so many things.

They wouldn't even take enough time to read or study their Bible again, and they listen to wrong spirits and teach wrong doctrines and messages.

Also, Moses told God that it is His Presence that will make them separate or distinguished from the other people. Brother, the Power and Glory of God will distinguish you.

The problem is that many have settled for lower levels of glory, and many are bound by the traditions of men and conventional ways that they have chosen not to give up. But the Glory of the Lord makes the difference: the Spirit makes the difference.

God is glorious in power (Exo. 15: 6), and He is glorious in holiness (Exo. 15:11). He is glorious in name also. Glorious things are spoken of God (Psa. 87:3). The Church, which is the Body of Christ, is a glorious Church of a Glorious Jesus Christ.

Jesus Christ moved from glory to glory while He was on earth; and we are to move from glory to glory also, for what He did, we shall do also. We shall do even greater works than He did (Jn 14:12).

In Christ Jesus, we have available to us an exceeding abundant life. There is an exceeding abundant grace available to us through Christ our Lord.

We are to receive this grace actively; we must not lie low and suffer unnecessarily when the grace and power to overcome and be victorious is there. Fight the good fight of faith and lay hold on Eternal Life.

There are many things we can learn from the eagle. The Bible says that those that wait on the Lord shall renew their strength; they shall mount up with wings like eagles, they shall run and not be weary, they shall walk and not faint.

Eagles eat fresh meat; they soar on the wind, and don't fly; and if they notice something wrong with them, they separate themselves to correct it. This separation, normally, takes a long time of about a month, until their strength is renewed.

The Lord gives strength to the weak, and to those who have no might He increases strength. We are to renew the Glory of God in us as we move from one level of glory to another level.

Get involved in retreats, camps, and other special programmes and meetings, both personal and in group. This will help increase the Power and Glory of God upon you, and you will move from glory to glory, from one level of power and authority to another level.

The faithful will be rewarded with Eternal Glory and unconceivable bliss. Spending eternity with God is another level of glory, which, no matter the anointing you may carry now, if you miss it you are a great loser.

There is the Spirit upon you, Who came upon you to anoint you with different levels of the anointing, as you obey and follow Him. As you pay the right sacrifice in obedience, discipline, and self-control, the anointing in your life will increase.

The earth shall be filled with the Knowledge of the Lord as the waters cover the sea. This is the day that we have to manifest and show the Power, Might, and Glory of our Lord and Christ in order to bring glory to the Father.

PSALMS CONCERNING GOD'S PROVISIONS

"I will bless the Lord at all times; His Praise shall continually be in my mouth. My soul shall make its boast in the Lord; the humble shall hear of it and be glad. Oh, magnify the Lord with me, and let us exalt His Name together.

"I sought the Lord, and He heard me, and delivered me from all my fears. They looked to Him and were radiant, and their faces were not ashamed. This poor man cried out, and the Lord heard him, and saved him out of all his troubles.

"The angel of the Lord encamps all around those who fear Him, and delivers them. Oh, taste and see that the Lord is good; blessed is the man who trusts in Him! Oh, fear the Lord, you His Saints! There is no want to those who fear Him.

"The young lions lack and suffer hunger; but those who seek the Lord shall not lack any good thing. Come, you children, listen to me; I will teach you the Fear of the Lord. Who is the man who desires life, and loves many days, that he may see good?

"Keep your tongue from evil, and your lips from speaking deceit. Depart from evil and do good; seek peace and pursue it. The Eyes of the Lord are on the righteous, and His Ears are open to their cry. The Face of the Lord is against those who do evil, to cut off the remembrance of them from the earth.

"The righteous cry out, and the Lord hears, and delivers them out of all their troubles. The Lord is near to those who have a broken heart, and saves such as have a contrite spirit. Many are the afflictions of the righteous, but the Lord delivers him out of them all.

"He guards all his bones; not one of them is broken. Evil shall slay the wicked, and those who hate the righteous shall be condemned. The Lord redeems the soul of His Servants, and none of those who trust in Him shall be condemned (Psa. 34).

"God stands in the congregation of the mighty; He judges among the gods. How long will you judge unjustly, and show partiality to the wicked? Selah Defend the poor and fatherless; do justice to the afflicted and needy.

"Deliver the poor and needy; free them from the hand of the wicked. They do not know, nor do they understand; they walk about in darkness; all the foundations of the earth are unstable.

"I said, 'You are gods, and all of you are children of the Most High. But you shall die like men, and fall like one of the princes.' Arise, O God, judge the earth; for You shall inherit all nations (Psa. 82).

"His foundation is in the holy mountains. The Lord loves the gates of Zion more than all the dwellings of Jacob. Glorious things are spoken of you, O City of God! Selah I will make mention of Rahab and Babylon to those who know Me; behold, O Philistia and Tyre, with Ethiopia: 'This one was born there.'

"And of Zion it will be said, 'This one and that one were born in her; and the Most High Himself shall establish her.' The Lord will record, when He registers the peoples: 'This one was born there.' Selah Both the singers and the players on instruments say, 'All my springs are in you' (Psa. 87).

"Bless the Lord, O my soul; and all that is within me, bless His Holy Name! Bless the Lord, O my soul, and forget not all His Benefits: Who forgives all your iniquities, Who heals all your diseases,

"Who redeems your life from destruction, Who crowns you with lovingkindness and tender mercies, Who satisfies your mouth with good things, so that your youth is renewed like the eagle's.

"The Lord executes righteousness and justice for all who are oppressed. He made known His Ways to Moses, His Acts to the children of Israel. The Lord is merciful and gracious, slow to anger, and abounding in mercy.

"He will not always strive with us, nor will He keep His Anger forever. He has not dealt with us according to our sins, nor punished us according to our iniquities. For as the heavens are high above the earth, so great is His Mercy towards those who fear Him; as far as the east is from the west, so far has He removed our transgressions from us.

"As a father pities his children, so the Lord pities those who fear Him. For He knows our frame; He remembers that we are dust. As for man, his days are like grass; as a flower of the field, so he flourishes. For the wind passes over it, and it is gone, and its place remembers it no more.

"But the Mercy of the Lord is from everlasting to everlasting on those who fear Him, and His Righteousness to children's children, to such as keep His Covenant, and to those who remember His Commandments to do them. The Lord has established His Throne in Heaven, and His Kingdom rules over all.

"Bless the Lord, you His angels, who excel in strength, who do His Word, heeding the voice of His Word. Bless the Lord, all you His hosts, you ministers of His, who do His Pleasure. Bless the Lord, all His Works, in all places of His Dominion. Bless the Lord, O my soul! (Psa. 103).

"Blessed is the man who walks not in the counsel of the ungodly, nor stands in the path of sinners, nor sits in the seat of the scornful; but his delight is in the Law of the Lord, and in His Law he meditates day and night. He shall be like a tree planted by the rivers of water, that brings forth its fruit in its season, whose leaf also shall not wither; and whatever he does shall prosper.

"The ungodly are not so, but are like the chaff which the wind drives away. Therefore the ungodly shall not stand in the judgment, nor sinners in the congregation of the righteous. For the Lord knows the way of the righteous, but the way of the ungodly shall perish (Psa. 1).

"Praise the Lord! Blessed is the man who fears the Lord, who delights greatly in His Commandments. His descendants will be mighty on earth; the generation of the upright will be blessed.

"Wealth and riches will be in his house, and his righteousness endures forever. Unto the upright there arises light in the darkness; he is gracious, and full of compassion, and righteous. A good man deals graciously and lends; he will guide his affairs with discretion.

"Surely he will never be shaken; the righteous will be in everlasting remembrance. He will not be afraid of evil tidings; his heart is steadfast, trusting in the Lord. His heart is established; he will not be afraid, until he sees his desire upon his enemies.

"He has dispersed abroad, he has given to the poor; his righteousness endures forever; his horn will be exalted with honour. The wicked will see it and be grieved; he will gnash his teeth and melt away; the desire of the wicked shall perish (Psa. 112).

"Blessed are the undefiled in the way, who walk in the Law of the Lord! Blessed are those who keep His Testimonies, who seek Him with the whole heart! They also do no iniquity; they walk in His Ways.

"You have commanded us to keep Your Precepts diligently. Oh, that my ways were directed to keep Your Statutes! Then I would not be ashamed, when I look into all Your Commandments.

"I will praise You with uprightness of heart, when I learn Your Righteous Judgments. I will keep Your Statutes; Oh, do not forsake me utterly! (Psa. 119:1-8).

"Be merciful to me, O God, be merciful to me! For my soul trusts in You; and in the shadow of Your Wings I will make my refuge, until these calamities have passed by. I will cry out to God Most High, to God Who performs all things for me.

"He shall send from Heaven and save me; He reproaches the one who would swallow me up. Selah God shall send forth His Mercy and His Truth. My soul is among lions; I lie among the sons of men who are set on fire, whose teeth are spears and arrows, and their tongue a sharp sword.

"Be exalted, O God, above the heavens; let Your Glory be above all the earth. They have prepared a net for my steps; my soul is bowed down; they have dug a pit before me; into the midst of it they themselves have fallen. Selah

"My heart is steadfast, O God, my heart is steadfast; I will sing and give praise. Awake, my glory! Awake, lute and harp! I will awaken the dawn. I will praise You, O Lord, among the peoples; I will sing to You among the nations. For Your Mercy reaches unto the heavens, and Your Truth unto the clouds. Be exalted, O God, above the heavens; let Your Glory be above all the earth (Psa. 57).

As a general rule, you should be able to know the difference between the Old Testament and the New Testament. There are some things that were allowed in the Old Testament dispensation, which are not allowed in the New Testament dispensation.

For instance, whereas people were rewarded according to their works in the Old Testament, we are not to reward evil with evil in the New Testament. The Bible says, "You have heard that it was said, 'An eye for an eye and a tooth for a tooth.' But I tell you not to resist an evil person. But whoever slaps you on your right cheek, turn the other to him also.

"If anyone wants to sue you and take away your tunic, let him have your cloak also. And whoever compels you to go one mile, go with him two. Give to him who asks you, and from him who wants to borrow from you do not turn away.

"You have heard that it was said, 'You shall love your neighbour and hate your enemy.' But I say to you, love your enemies, bless those who curse you, do good to those who hate you, and pray for those who spitefully use you and persecute you,

"That you may be sons of your Father in Heaven; for He makes His sun rise on the evil and on the good, and sends rain on the just and on the unjust. For if you love those who love you, what reward have you? Do not even the tax collectors do the same?

"And if you greet your brethren only, what do you do more than others? Do not even the tax collectors do so? Therefore you shall be perfect, just as your Father in Heaven is perfect" (Matt. 5:38-48).

Also, in the Old Testament, they lived by their righteousness; but in the New Testament, even though we are to live in holiness and obey God, as a prove that we truly love Him, yet we live by the Righteousness and Sacrifice of Jesus Christ. To this end, the Bible says, "For Christ is the End of the Law for righteousness to everyone who believes.

"For Moses writes about the righteousness which is of the Law, 'The man who does those things shall live by them.' But the righteousness of faith speaks in this way, 'Do not say in your heart, "Who will ascend into Heaven?"' (that is, to bring Christ down from Above) or, '"Who will descend into the abyss?"' (that is, to bring Christ up from the dead).

"But what does it say? 'The Word is near you, in your mouth and in your heart' (that is, the Word of Faith which we preach): that if you confess with your mouth the Lord Jesus and believe in your heart that God has raised Him from the dead, you will be saved.

"For with the heart one believes unto righteousness, and with the mouth confession is made unto salvation. For the Scripture says, 'Whoever believes on Him will not be put to shame.' For there is no distinction between Jew and Greek, for the Same Lord over all is rich to all who call upon Him. For 'whoever calls on the Name of the Lord shall be saved'" (Rom. 10:4-13).

In this New Testament, we operate with the spirit of love, mercy, forgiveness, and love, unlike in the Old Testament, where they operated with the spirit of judgment. This why the Bible says, "Now it came to pass, when the time had come for Him to be received Up, that He steadfastly set His Face to go to Jerusalem, and sent messengers before His Face.

"And as they went, they entered a village of the Samaritans, to prepare for Him. But they did not receive Him, because His Face was set for the journey to Jerusalem. And when His Disciples James and John saw this, they said, 'Lord, do You want us to command fire to come down from Heaven and consume them, just as Elijah did?'

"But He turned and rebuked them, and said, 'You do not know what manner of spirit you are of. For the Son of Man did not come to destroy men's lives but to save them.' And they went to another village (Lk. 9:51-56).

"If it is possible, as much as depends on you, live peaceably with all men. Beloved, do not avenge yourselves, but rather give place to wrath; for it is written, 'Vengeance is Mine, I will repay,' says the Lord.

"Therefore 'if your enemy is hungry, feed him; if he is thirsty, give him a drink; for in so doing you will heap coals of fire on his head.' Do not be overcome by evil, but overcome evil with good" (Rom. 12:18-21).

DEMONIC AND SATANIC ACTIVITIES TODAY

The Bible says that the works of satan and his hosts are stealing, killing, and destroying (Jn 10:10). And the reason Jesus Christ came was that He might destroy the works of the devil (1 Jn 3:8). Therefore, our work, as Christians, is to destroy the works of the devil.

In these days of concentrated satanic and demonic activities, we have to be wise and operate according to the Word of God in order to be free from the plans, purposes, and works of the devil and his hosts. Yes, Jesus Christ has freed us from the power of the devil; but the Bible tells us what to do in order to maintain and enjoy that freedom and victory that our Lord got for us.

This is why the Bible says, "Nor give place to the devil" (Eph. 4:27), and "Resist the devil and he will flee from you" (Jas 4:7). This is talking of the responsibility that God gave you as a Christian: it is not God that will resist the devil for you, but you yourself. And He has given you the resources you need to resist the devil. If you give the devil a place in your life, then the devil will gladly have that place.

Yet, "Behold, I give you the authority to trample on serpents and scorpions, and over all the power of the enemy, and nothing shall by any means hurt you" (Lk. 10:19). And, "No weapon formed against you shall prosper, and every tongue which rises against you in judgment, you shall condemn. This is the heritage of the Servants of the LORD, and their righteousness is from Me," says the LORD (Isa. 54:17).

Also, "And these signs will follow those who believe: in My Name they will cast out demons; they will speak with new tongues; they will take up serpents; and if they drink anything deadly, it will by no means hurt them; they will lay hands on the sick, and they will recover" (Mk 16:17-18). These and many others are God's Provisions for us as His children; but we must also take up our responsibilities, so that we will enjoy the things that Jesus Christ has provided for us to the fullest.

In these end-times, learn and get used to studying the Word of God (in order to know your rights, privileges, power, and authority as a Believer in Christ Jesus); and apply what you know, because it is applied knowledge that brings the desired results. Learn to fast and pray in these days of concentrated demonic activities. But don't be afraid, for God is with you and for you! Flies do not perch on boiling oil, even as serpents do not coil around red-hot iron. Therefore, maintain a red-hot spiritual life always.

Learn to pray over and bless your food and water. The Bible says, "For it is sanctified by the Word of God and prayer" (1 Tim. 4:1-2). Many products in the market are polluted by witches and demons. Pray and bless the things you buy in the market, especially edible things and pre-packed and canned foods. Pray over yourself when you go for such services as barbing and hair-keeping. Be sensitive to know who you should not patronize, even for things like dry-cleaning.

Please, no matter how I may sound, before you take any drug or medicine (for those who like taking drugs/medicine), pray over them. There are satanic and demonic products in the form of drugs and medicine; and there are also satanic, demonic, and occult doctors, pharmacists, and nurses in many hospitals, whether public or private, local or foreign. If you want to go to hospital, pray over yourself and cover yourself with the Blood of Jesus Christ before you go. You may also tell a trusted person to pray for you; but never forget to pray by yourself.

No matter how urgent the case may be, if you can't pray, then don't go! Many people have lost their lives in hospitals, not because of the sickness or disease that attacked them, but because of satanic medicine and medical practitioners. It will even be difficult for police to detect these practices, because they are spiritually remoted and performed. And you know that many policemen are not spiritually sensitive; therefore, even if a policeman is there, the doctor can do what he wants to do, and the security agent can't even notice it.

Please, pray over the clothes and wears you buy, especially the second-hand ones, because many of them actually come from the underworld. Someone may doubt the possibility; but do you know that the Bible says that God created the physical world from the spiritual world (things that exist from things that do not exist)? (Heb. 11:3). The spiritual controls the physical, whether the good realm or the bad realm. Even unbelievers believe that after performing some demonic rituals, they can disappear and reappear at will.

In geography, we are told that the 70% of the earth's surface is covered with water. Do you know the vastness of the expanse of water in the Atlantic Ocean, for example? If a ship appears from the mermaid kingdom in that great expanse of sea and sails to the seaport, how do you know where it came from? Yes, it can carry any national flag they want it to carry.

And you know that there are submarines which go under water and come up when they want; so if the one from the underworld appears as a submarine, how do you know where it came from? They will come with whatever paper for the goods that you may want at the seaport, and they can interfere with whatever signal you may send or receive. Yes, they can operate physical shipping industries that will carry their goods at whatever point in the sea. Even if you may argue that the signal or information says that the ship came from another physical seaport, it makes no difference, because they can always outsmart you.

Don't be deceived: they will still have physical clearing agents for the goods, and distributing or marketing companies and agents for their materials. You may even work in a physical satanic company without your knowledge; and you will say, "I know how these things are produced." Do you also know how they got many of the 'imported' chemicals and materials they use in the factory?

Pray over your meat and fish. Please, pastor, when people bring life-animals for thanksgiving and gifts, pray over them and sanctify them. As odd as I may sound, some of those animals are more than animals. And even many of those ones which are normal animals might have been dedicated to devils (with different proclamations and curses) before they bring them to you. This is also applicable to the ones you buy in the market by yourself, even the ones you use for general cooking in camps, ceremonies, and retreats.

Before you travel, pray. Many of the accidents you hear of are not mechanical, but spiritually remote-controlled. Many plane-crashes, motor-accidents, and shipwrecks, which are blamed on mechanics, vehicle producers, and transport companies are actually caused by witches and devils. This is not for you to be afraid, because angels are guarding you; in fact, fear can open a way for the devil. Entertain no fear, because satan is nobody before your Almighty God!

Pray for your children and family, because witches want to enslave and initiate them if they have the opportunity. There are many conscious agents of satan in nursery schools, primary schools, secondary schools, universities, work-places, streets, and markets. Train your children to refuse edible things from strangers, and to pray over what they eat and drink. Pray over gifts you receive and the things you buy in the market. During/after your ceremonies and weddings, pray over the gifts you receive.

The devil and his devils are desperate these days more than before, because he knows that his time is short. If he can't destroy you, he will want to kill you; and if he can't kill you, he will want to steal from you. Therefore, watch and pray, lest you enter into temptation (Matt. 26:41).

The Bible says, "Owe no man anything…" (Rom. 13:8) and, "…the borrower is servant to the lender" (Prov. 22:7). It is not that it is sinful to borrow, because the Word also says, "…and from him who wants to borrow from you do not turn away" Matt. 5:42). But to borrow and refuse to pay is evil. It is also not good to postpone paying your debts when you are in the position to pay the debt.

Also, debt has spiritual significance; therefore, if you are not prayerful, somebody can use the credit-contact to drain your money or influence your life financially. He who goes on borrowing, goes on sorrowing. Learn to trust in God, instead of trusting in men and creditors. Also, the time, energy, and effort you put in to borrow and think on how to pay can bring stress and shame on you.

Pray for your newborn child and children; cover them with Blood of Jesus Christ. Pray over what you give out to strangers like beggars: cover it with the Blood of Jesus Christ.

Pray and cover yourself, your family, business, occupation, and property with the Blood of Jesus Christ. Believers need to pray a lot these days (and also fast), especially in group prayers.

Pray before you embark on journeys by land, air, or water. And if you have an uneasy feeling as you want to travel, then pray through before traveling. But this is not to tell you to live in fear, because angels are already guarding you. However, be prayerful generally.

DIVINE REVELATIONS AND NEAR-DEATH EXPERIENCES (NDE'S)

If it is contrary to the Word of God, then it is from satan – the devil and God's archenemy – who deceived Eve (from the beginning) with: "Did God really say…." That which is against God and His Word cannot be from God, the Maker of all things, Who holds the whole world in His Hand, because God's Word and His Spirit agree. The Lord Jesus Christ, Who defeated satan on the Cross of Calvary about two thousand years ago, is the Same – yesterday, today, and forever. He is coming very soon; get ready to meet Him: Heaven and Hell are real; let no one deceive you.

And the Word says, "Beware of false prophets, who come to you in sheep's clothing, but inwardly they are ravenous wolves. You will know them by their fruits. Do men gather grapes from thornbushes or figs from thistles? Even so, every good tree bears good fruit, but a bad tree bears bad fruit. A good tree cannot bear bad fruit, nor can a bad tree bear good fruit. Every tree that does not bear good fruit is cut down and thrown into the Fire. Therefore by their fruits you will know them.

"Not everyone who says to Me, 'Lord, Lord,' shall enter the Kingdom of Heaven, but he who does the Will of My Father in Heaven. Many will say to Me in that Day, 'Lord, Lord, have we not prophesied in Your Name, cast out demons in Your Name, and done many wonders in Your Name?' And then I will declare to them, 'I never knew you; depart from Me, you who practice lawlessness!'" (Matt. 7:15-23).

To tell you the truth, a lot of the noise made by many Believers means little or nothing to God. Many Believers and ministers cause God more pain and heartbreak than unbelievers. Many ministers preach and teach what God never thought of, not to talk of saying it: Many of them preach, teach, and practice the mind of the devil. Many Believers live however they want, while shouting, "Praise the Lord!" and "The Lord is good!" Well, let all of us amend our ways while there is still time, because God cannot change His Word for any person.

One time, I went to an open-air crusade which was titled: Mega Fire Crusade with one celebrated evangelist. It was a two-day crusade. I went the last day; and I stayed from the beginning of the preaching till the closing of the crusade. Brethren, the man didn't even mention or pray about either receiving Jesus Christ or avoiding sin. But he mentioned and prayed about car, building, marriage, factory, business, healing, and giving.

And he took two sets of offerings/donations, and invited people to the church that organized the crusade, telling them that he would anoint them during the church service. I was so unhappy that I met him after he came down, while they were about carrying him to his hotel room. He asked what my problem was, thinking that I came for prayer. I told him what I observed in his ministration, telling him that I am an evangelist and the primary aim of crusades should be to draw souls to Jesus Christ.

Guess what? He never even regretted or apologized, but defended himself, saying that sometimes it is like that. But, brethren, the crusade was only for two days. This is not a story that somebody told me, but what I experienced myself.

When I walk along the street and see how many ladies and women dress, I weep. And when you pass through beer parlours and joints, and see our young men, you will wail. What about the things happening among Believers, ministries, and churches?

Jesus Christ is coming very soon: Heaven and Hell are real. Let us get ready for His Return, knowing that the Christian race and God's Judgment are individual, and not collective. There is Only One Jesus Christ; and there is only one Bible. If you love the Kingdom of Heaven, then start reading and studying your own Bible for yourself, so that when those who teach you lies are condemned by God, you will not be condemned alongside with them.

It is not every place that is called by the name of church, ministry, fellowship, or mission that is preparing people for Heaven. Many of them are preparing people for Hell Fire. You will come to terms with the reality in the end. And the great regret is that by then, there will not be a second chance.

It is not just a matter of, "Thank You Jesus!" It is a matter of obeying His Word and Commandments, not being hypocrites who claim to be Believers, but live and act however we want, not regarding the things contained in the Bible, which He gave us. God is no respecter of any person; He will judge all men using His Word as His Standard. Remember that the righteous Lucifer became His archenemy by sin, and the holy Adam became separated from Him by disobedience.

Someone can accuse others of spreading the 'gospel of sin', and of making people sin-conscious. Read 1 Cor. 10:1-14, and see who the 'gospel' of sin is meant for (even though there is no such thing as 'the gospel of sin'). But beware, that you do not run and labour in vain! Also, know that idolatry does not only mean the worship of carved and molten images (Jas 4:4-5). Refer to Rom. 6:1 and 2 Cor. 6:1. May God open the eyes of your understanding, so that those who follow you may enter the Kingdom of Heaven!

NOW, I AM NOT JUDGING ANYONE, NOR AM I ENCOURAGING JUDGING ANYONE; but we must speak to warn those who are derailing, not to judge them; because they can still repent, as long as they are still alive, if they open themselves to the Holy Spirit's Promptings. And this applies to both the leaders and the led!

Read: Matthew 7:15-27; 2 Corinthians 11:13-15; 2 Peter 2:1-22; 1 John 4:1; Jude 1:3-13; and see that Jesus Christ, Paul, Peter, John, and Jude spoke against false preachers, teachers, prophets, and ministers. Did they do it to condemn them? No; rather, they did it to warn their followers and those who may be deceived by them.

Many people speak against Divine Revelations from God (including the testimonies of those who had Near-death Experiences) about Heaven and Hell. God has chosen to do it His Own Way, as He had been doing before. Why not believe God? Revelations like these are meant to encourage the faithful and warn the faithless (unfaithful). "The Bible is our standard and guide"; but, many people use this statement to trample on and work against the Will and Purpose of God.

The true testimony-bearers did not say that dressing a particular way alone will take you to Heaven; they emphasized on salvation, holiness, and total obedience to the Word of God. And be mindful that holiness and righteousness is both inward (of the heart and the mind) and outward (of the body). Refer to 2 Corinthians 7:1 and Romans 12:1-2.

And as for whether they should sell the testimonies, they are to allow God lead them in that area. By the way, if a true man of God is invited to preach to people (or teach them), inasmuch as he has his transport fare (or can get there) or is transported to the place of the ministration, he goes there and preaches free of charge to all who are there to listen; and he does so joyfully to win and establish souls for the Lord. If you give him some money after the ministration, and he collects it, is it evil?

Even if you don't give him, God will take good care of him; but if he comes with compact discs (CDs), DVDs, books, or tapes, must he give them to you free of charge? Your buying (willingly) any material, is it not for your own good and future use/revision? Can you mention one man of God that gives all his materials free of charge to people, except where (in some instances) the minister himself, someone else, a group of people, or the ministry/church pays for them (or for some of them)? Or, are they selling them at exorbitant prices?

And if the compact discs, tapes, and books are not produced, how will those within the vicinity of the programme who didn't attend the programme hear from the man of God directly? Or, is it better for them to hear misinterpreted and misinformed reports from those who attended the programme? And what about the areas the man of God may not speak on for that time; is it not from the materials he came with (or his materials that are sold by traders) that people will learn? By the way, the Bible you have and read, did you get it free of charge?

Unbelievers and businessmen spend money to buy or get what they want; should Christians complain, because they paid small money to get books, CDs, and tapes? Many Believers/Christians will spend a lot of money on food, clothes, schools and certificates, and other physical and mental things; but when it comes to spending money for spiritual things, they will hypocritically complain. Don't they know that "man shall not live by bread alone, but by every Word that comes out of the Mouth of God"?

And on the case of knowing who is in Heaven or in Hell (after having died), even the person you think you know may have a hidden (inward) sin or a grave 'mistake' which you will not know. By the way, the finally dead person has died, and cannot change his or her situation of everlasting friendship or separation from God.

When Apostle John heard something(s) in the Book of Revelation and wanted to write it (them) down, he was commanded not to write it (them) (Rev. 10:4). When Apostle Paul went to Heaven (Paradise), there were things he heard and saw, which he was not allowed to say or write (2 Cor. 12:4). Prophet Daniel was told to seal up part of the revelations he got (Dan. 12:4). Even Jesus Christ Himself knew many things which He didn't tell His apostles, as at the time He was with them (Jn 16:12).

However, they all revealed and said many of the things that they heard, saw, and knew! And read what was told Prophet Daniel in that place: he was told to seal it up until the time of the end. This means that at the appointed time, maybe in the time of the end (the last days), they will no longer be sealed up, but be revealed. Also, remember that it also says that knowledge will increase in the last days.

Apostle John, in the Book of Revelation, chapters 2 & 3, mentioned the names of specific churches. Except you want to deceive yourself, Apostle John, mentioning: the church of Ephesus, the church in Smyrna, the church in Pergamos, the church in Thyatira, the church in Sadis, the church in Philadelphia, and the church of the Laodiceans, is the same as mentioning names of specific churches. Therefore, God can mention names of specific churches – it is Scriptural! And that your church's name was not mentioned does not guarantee that it is better than those that might have been mentioned: so, check yourself, and correct anything that is to be corrected.

Now that one person is controlling all the branches of the churches, ministries, or fellowships in a particular country (or even in the whole world), why wouldn't his name be mentioned by God? Apostle Paul rebuked Apostle Peter publicly (Gal. 2:11-14); did he judge or condemn him by that? Was he not trying to put him in the right order out of brotherly love?

If you hadn't known it, Apostle Peter had greater authority than Apostle Paul in the Church. "Do not rebuke an older man (an elder, the KJV), but exhort him as a father (1 Tim. 5:1)," must be interpreted well. Advising Timothy on the administration of the church, Paul said, "Those who are sinning rebuke in the presence of all, that the rest may also fear (1 Tim. 5:20)".

What of where an elder is sinning and committing sin that is open to everybody and leading them astray?

Remember that the purpose of rebuking before all, according to the Bible, is for others to fear and avoid doing the same (or similar) things. And Jesus Christ, after saying, "Do not judge (Matt. 7:1)," also said, "Judge with righteous judgment (Jn 7:24)." So, learn to interpret the Word of God well in every situation.

That Apostle Paul wrote more books, and did extended Gospel work among the Gentiles, didn't make him rise above Peter. Think of it, even though Elisha got the double portion of Elijah's anointing (or the Holy Spirit upon him), he didn't rise above Elijah. And you know that Elijah was carried alive to Heaven, while Elisha died from sickness, and had his body decayed. Though John the Baptist didn't perform any recorded healing miracle, yet the miracle-working Moses didn't rise above him. And John the Baptist came in the spirit of Elijah, and not of Elisha!

For those who may say, "Never listen to any of those revelations," if revelations and visions (or listening to them) will be discouraged, because false revelations and visions exist, then reading Christian books and literatures, or listening to preachings and teachings must also be discouraged, since false preachings, teachings, and 'Christian' books and literatures also abound.

And you know that God Himself put preachers and teachers in His Church (even after having given us the Bible and Scriptures), just as He also put prophets too. No one man has all the inspirations, preachings, teachings, and ministries that God wants to pass across to His people. Yes, the devil and his demons can also give dreams, visions, revelations, audible voices, prophecies, and miracles; therefore, always study your Bible to know the Mind of God.

But do not let any person – preacher or what – stop you from hearing what God wants to tell you! And you can be sure that the devil doesn't promote the Cause of God and His Word, when analyzed, summarized, and weighed very well. And those from God don't and can't contradict the Word of God, when well interpreted and understood. In the last days, visions and revelations will abound – both good and bad, God-Sent and devil-sent.

And one of the signs of the last days is that people (even Believers) will harden their hearts from God's Voice and Messages, and try to disprove them with such misleading questions and comments as: (1) "In the Bible when the rich man asked Abraham to send Lazarus to his living brothers, Abraham said, 'If they don't hear Moses and the prophets, neither will they be persuaded though one rise from the dead' (Lk. 16:31)." Was it Abraham or Jesus Christ that made the statement? Certainly, it was Abraham, and not Jesus Christ.

Read the story very well, as told by Jesus Christ. Abraham didn't even have the ability to make Lazarus pass the gulf that was between the Paradise (where they were) and Hades (where the rich man was) to give the rich man a drop of water if Abraham had wanted to send Lazarus to the rich man. How then could that level of decision of sending Lazarus to the rich man's brothers be taken by an ordinary 'dead' (though living) Abraham? Abraham neither had the authority to send Lazarus to them, nor the power to raise Lazarus from the dead.

This was before Jesus Christ's Death and Resurrection, when both Paradise (for righteous men) and Hades (for sinners) were still beneath the earth and 'near' each other; now, only Hades is beneath the earth: Paradise is now Above. Jesus Christ took the righteous people who were in the underneath Paradise up to Above after His Resurrection.

The Bible says, "And Jesus said to him, 'Assuredly, I say to you, today, you will be with Me in Paradise'" (Lk. 23:43). The forgiven criminal was going to the underneath Paradise, from where he was taken to an Above Paradise – Heaven – after the Resurrection of Jesus Christ. And the Word says, "And Jesus cried out again with a loud Voice, and yielded up His Spirit.

"Then, behold, the veil of the temple was torn in two from top to bottom; and the earth quaked, and the rocks were split, and the graves were opened; and many bodies of the Saints who had fallen asleep were raised; and coming out of the graves after His Resurrection, they went into the holy city and appeared to many" (Matt. 27:50-53). Notice that they could only come out of their graves after Jesus Christ's Resurrection. And they were taken to an Above Paradise!

Of course, you can see the level of the rich man's torment in Hell. But I want you to notice that Abraham, based on the rich man's request, told him that his brothers have Moses and the Prophets, that they should hear them. Abraham was saying that the living should obey the Word of God, to avoid going to Hell. Therefore, those who do not obey the Word of God, but live to please the desires of their hearts and minds, will end in Hell.

Then again, when the rich man told Abraham that his brothers would hear if someone rises from the dead to preach to them, Abraham told him that if they did not hear Moses and the Prophets (the Word of God being preached and taught), neither would they be persuaded though someone rose from the dead. First, it was Abraham, and not God or Jesus Christ, who told the rich man that. God knows better than Abraham; and if He knows that people will listen to someone that rises from the dead, He can send the person.

Abraham couldn't even cross the gulf between Paradise and Hell; how then could he send Lazarus back to the earth? He did not have that level of authority or power to send a dead person to the living; but God has the power, ability, and authority to do that. Also, notice that Abraham did not say that nobody (none) could/would hear the dead that rises from the dead, but that the rich man's brothers would not hear. Why would they not hear? Because they had made up their minds on what they wanted; and they might have even scorned the fellow, saying that he did not actually die. (And, being hardened, they could have even said that it was a spirit posing as a human, who was dead, if Lazarus had appeared to them physically).

But many people will believe the story that would be told them by someone who rises from the dead; and many people will still not believe the story told them by someone who rises from the dead, no matter what, because the devil has hardened their hearts and they have made up their minds on what they want. The Bible says, "And behold, there was a great earthquake; for an angel of the Lord descended from Heaven, and came and rolled back the stone from the door, and sat on it.

"His countenance was like lightning, and his clothing as white as snow. And the guards shook for fear of him, and became like dead men. …Now while they were going, behold, some of the guards came into the city and reported to the chief priests all the things that had happened. When they had assembled with the elders and consulted together, they gave a large sum of money to the soldiers,

"Saying, 'Tell them, "His Disciples came at night and stole Him away while we slept." And if this comes to the governor's ears, we will appease him and make you secure.' So they took the money and did as they were instructed; and this saying is commonly reported among the Jews until this day" (Matt. 28:2-15). Can you imagine the hardness of men's (some men's) hearts and minds?

Instead of being grateful to God for saving them from death, and also giving them the opportunity to witness such a great sight, they decided to accept money and spread false story.

Who will blame God when He judges and punishes sinners with Eternal Death in His Great Wrath? But His Hands are still open now for whoever will submit to His Word and Grace!

Notice also that it was some of the guards (not all of them) that went to report; some of them might have repented from that incident. Yet the religious chief priests and elders hardened their hearts. Abraham was right when he told the rich man that his brothers would not hear though someone rises from the dead, because whereas some people will accept the testimony of the person who rises from the dead, many will still never believe his testimony, because their minds are made up.

(2) "That person said that she didn't know of this particular church, how then did she say that she heard the church is a holiness church?" Even with common sense, when the person was called by a woman on Monday to enquire about the very church, having given the woman answers, what stops her from asking about the church between Monday and Wednesday before the Lord spoke to her (as she said) on that Wednesday when the statement she made applied?

(3) "This is not the Bible (or even Koran) Jesus." The person was saying that Jesus Christ can't be too harsh with people to punish them the way described by the testifier(s) {or, maybe, the person was speaking of the way one of the testifiers was punished by God}, without knowing that our God, Who is also a Consuming Fire, destroyed everybody with the Flood (except Noah and his family), rained down fire to destroy all the dwellers of Sodom and Gomorrah (except Lot and his family), and even judges Believers with death, because they eat at the Lord's Table unworthily.

(4) "That person said, 'I Am That I Am,' on coming out of the experience; therefore, it can't be from God." When the prophets prophesied in the Name of the Lord, didn't they speak on Behalf of God? (5) "That testifier said that the only woman in Heaven is Mary, the mother of Jesus." When on earth did the person say such a thing? The person actually said that only a small percentage of people that left the earth made Heaven; and out of the people that made Heaven, only a small percentage of them are women, partly due to their attachment to jewellery, indecent dressing, make-up, and weavons/attachments.

(6) "If God really wanted to speak to the world through that person, He would have made her death and coming back public." Do you see the sense of man, when he decides to allow the devil to deceive him? (7) "Those people just used that boy to organize previous testimonies (reports) from others." Man, why do you want to be lost in Eternal Damnation in Hell Fire? (8) "The (those) testimonies are (were) made to make money." Make money from you by lying to get you ready for Heaven, and ending in Hell themselves?

(9) "Who has gone to Heaven and come back?" They wilfully forget that Apostle Paul and Apostle John went to Heaven and came back. (10) "No one can see God and live." Forgetting that Moses, Isaiah, Ezekiel, and John saw the Similitude of God (and hence saw God), and lived. (11) And one 'preacher' said, "If God wants to tell Believers or people something, He wouldn't use a dead or/and 'risen' person, but He will use pastors (or preachers)." Is that pride or deception?

These are few questions (or related statements) which people asked (or made) to disprove those Divine Revelations. And somebody (or some people) called them DEVELATIONS, trying to indicate that they came from the devil. People, why do you want satan, the devil, to take you to Hell Fire? And somebody may say that the Bible is our final authority (which is a very true statement).

But why do very many different persons, Believers, preachers, teachers, and ministers all say that the Bible is our final authority and standard, and also declare that they are preaching and teaching the raw and undiluted Word of God; and yet, in practice, they preach, teach, and practice different things? This is the more reason why you should maintain a tender heart, and allow the Holy Spirit speak to you.

Yes, the Bible is the final say and standard for all of us. Yet the things in the Bible were got by visions, revelations, dreams, audible voices, and inward inspirations/revelations. Can the Bible tell you which school to attend, which supermarket to shop in, or which vehicle to board? The Bible goes alongside with the Leading of the Holy Spirit.

However, we must disregard whatever contradicts the Bible. But true reports do not contradict the Bible; rather, their reports promote the Bible, except when you had allowed yourself to be loaded/filled with whatever false and misapplied teachings and doctrines you desire, because they suit your flesh; and you don't want to change.

The Bible tells us about Heaven and Hell: what we should do to gain Heaven, and what we must avoid to avoid Hell. But many Believers don't even regard and obey the Bible as they should. This is why God, seeing that many people have entered (and are heading towards) Hell, is giving more revelations and visions to spur us into taking the Bible serious (or more serious).

Someone may say, "How do you know that they have actually gone to Heaven?" Does asking that question not confirm and guarantee that God did not tell you that they didn't go to Heaven? And if you say that you were told that they didn't go to Heaven or/and Hell, who told you that – God or satan?

Many of those testimonies have been shared (or posted) in the Internet. Things shared in the Internet are read by many people. If one person who reads the post(s) gets and receives the Message being passed across, he may run with it, by spreading it to others; by that, the knowledge is more widely spread. There are millions of people who are following some preachers and ministers, even those outside their ministries and churches; and many of them think that because they prophesy and perform miracles, then all the things that they preach, teach, and practice are right.

But this is not true, in the ultimate sense. Therefore, instead of keeping quiet, and allowing them to follow anyone to Hell Fire, while Jesus Christ is crying for the abundance of lost souls, we are to stand up for God and warn the people. Much of the corruption in the church-world today is because people say that they want to mind their own business, even when the Lord wants them to mind His Own Business.

We are labourers together with God; and we have divisions and inter-mingleness of labour in the Kingdom of God. One may receive a Message from God; another may run with the Message to spread it; while another may be involved with fighting the devil, who may want to stop or hinder the spreading of the Message; another may be involved with taking care of those who were wounded by the devil in the course of doing their duty in the Kingdom; yet, we are working for the Same God.

Brother, if you had not known it, it is not an impossible thing that any of those testifiers can still backslide, if we don't give them any helping hand and support (but our God will hold them strong in Him!). Some of those testifiers are spiritual babies, who don't know the Bible well; and they need those who would prove, by the Bible, that their revelations are Biblical. I remember what Jesus Christ told one converted Muslim when he was taken to Heaven (or beyond the earth) and shown/told some things.

The Muslim (who turned to a preacher) had been a very rich Muslim, who was also involved in many secret societies (his conversion and testimony were not hidden and secret; he is from Northern Nigeria, Sokoto, and had Saudi Arabian citizenship: And Muslims fought hard to kill him after his conversion, because of the many things he exposed about Islam).

Now, after showing/telling him some things, and giving him a commission, Jesus Christ asked him, saying, "Will you be faithful to do what I have told you to do?" He answered Him with a Yes. The Lord Jesus Christ told him that He was asking him, because He had taken many people, both from his country (Nigeria) and from other countries of the world, and shown them extra-terrestrial things (like Heaven and Hell); yet, after they had gone back to the world, after some times, some (or many) of them started thinking that it was just a dream that they had.

And we will not sit back and watch those, who don't want to hear the Spirit of God, destroy these Heavenly Messages. So, we will not fold our hands and leave the testifiers stranded; but we will (by the Help of the Holy Spirit) use the Bible and inward inspirations to support and help them.

The Church is marching on; and gates of Hades shall not prevail against the Church of Jesus Christ, the Son of the Living God! The issue is: whether you yourself, as a preacher, was mentioned or not, or the church you attend was mentioned or not, let each and every one of us correct himself/herself of whatever is Biblically wrong – of whatever is wrong in the Sight of God. And for those who might have been mentioned, what have they done to correct themselves? God is calling, because He loves us!

Also, know that the churches and ministers that might have been mentioned are just samples, because there are thousands of needing-revival, requiring-purging, backslidden, half-bred, falsely indoctrinated, fake, satanic, demonic, and false ministers, apostles, prophets, evangelists, pastors, teachers, deacons, elders, musicians, church workers, church members, churches, ministries, and fellowships in our different countries and the whole world at large.

Let me include some things the Lord Jesus Christ told the seven churches in the second and third chapters of the Book of Revelation. The seven churches were in Asia Minor. They included the churches in Ephesus, in Smyrna, in Pergamos, in Thyatira, in Sardis, in Philadelphia, and in Laodicea. The churches were in different states of spirituality and carnality, just as the churches of today. The Lord had to encourage them, and warn them, by the hand of Apostle John.

The Lord was happy with those who did well (or, their good deeds); and He was unhappy with those who did not do well (or, their evil deeds/conditions). Even some who did well still had areas they had to correct. Because He desired that all of them do well, He had to send Messages to them according to their works and needs. The Messages sent to these churches are of benefit to us in this present age, if we open our hearts and minds to the Holy Spirit, and allow Him to purge, sanctify, consecrate, and edify us, so that we may become what the Lord wants us to be.

He was not happy with some of them; and He rebuked them. Some of them had left their first love. Some held to the doctrine of Balaam, who taught Balak to put a stumbling block before the children of Israel, to eat things sacrificed to idols, and to commit sexual immorality. They had also those who held the doctrine of the Nicolaitans, which thing He hates (hated). They allowed one Jezebel, who called herself a prophetess, to teach and seduce His Servants to commit sexual immorality and eat things sacrificed to idols.

Some had name that they were alive, but they were dead. He did not find the works of many of them perfect before God. Many of them were neither cold nor hot. The Lord wished that they were either cold or hot. And because they were lukewarm, and neither cold nor hot, He was going to vomit them out of His Mouth.

Some said that they were rich and had become wealthy, and had need of nothing. They did not know that they were wretched, miserable, poor, blind, and naked. No wonder the Bible says that we should neither be wise in our own eyes nor lean on our own understanding (Prov. 3:5-7). There is a way that seems good to a man, but the end of that road is death and destruction (Prov. 14:12). If we judge ourselves, we would not be judged (1 Cor. 11:31).

He warned them to remember where they had fallen from. He told them to repent and do the first works, else He would come to them quickly and remove their lampstand from its place – unless they repented. He told (and tells) anyone that had (and has) ear to hear to hear what the Spirit said (and is saying) to the churches. He advised them to not fear any of those things which they were about to suffer.

Indeed, the devil was about to throw some of them into prison, that they might be tested; and they were to have tribulation ten days. He commanded them to be faithful until death. The Lord told many of them to repent, or else He would come to them quickly and would fight against them with the sword of His Mouth. If Jesus Christ rebuked those churches, for them to repent and become faithful Believers, who are you to get annoyed when God decides to rebuke you? He rebukes and chastens those that He loves.

By the way, neither me nor anyone needs to approve or recognize the testimonies before they become true; for none of us is God! This race needs God's Grace and Mercy. Even as I write, I myself needs God's Grace and Mercy to make it to the end, because these last days are perilous. As an apostle who has evangelistic and teaching ministries, I need the grace to do what I teach.

When you teach or preach the Word of God sincerely, you teach and preach under the Anointing of the Holy Spirit. But when you finish, you have become that 'small' and 'ordinary' Christian, who must also discipline himself and bring his body under subjection to his spirit, to be able to obey God like every other Believer. To this end, Apostle Paul said, "But I discipline my body and bring it into subjection, lest, when I have preached to others, I myself should become disqualified" (1 Cor. 9:27).

Now, I say these things for the wellbeing of Christianity: If all these people who troop to crusades, ministries, and churches live to please God with perfect hearts, I tell you that Jesus Christ may be coming sooner! I would want to have a church of one hundred members, where about ninety of them are ready for the Coming of Jesus Christ, than to pastor ten thousand members, of which God may not even find five people who are ready for the Coming of His Son.

And it is better to have a mini crusade, where people sincerely repent and are faithful to God, than to organize a mega crusade, where thousands come out for altar call and go back to live however they want. Therefore, we evangelists, if we are troubled by the decadence in Christianity, knowing that many people trust us, should also use the opportunity we have to, at least, point out these things to, at least, the ministers and church-workers.

Some ministers say that they have special revelations on particular areas. Well, I myself have the revelation to help people understand the Truth of the Word of God and to follow the Leading of God's Holy Spirit. It is like I used to think a certain man of God was a 'holiness preacher/teacher' until listened to some of his messages I collected from one of his pastors. Then I understood that he is not a 'holiness preacher/teacher,' but a man of God who teaches the Word of God (of which holiness, which he emphasizes on, is included) and also demonstrates the Spirit and power.

The man demonstrates (has demonstrated) great miracles, signs, and wonders that many of the people we celebrate haven't done. But the thing is that he doesn't like proclaiming himself but God, Who does (did) those things; and he found out early enough that without holiness, no eye shall see the Lord. He found out that if one has all the miracles, healings, breakthroughs, deliverances, and anointing, and loses Heaven, the fellow lost everything and gained nothing.

Therefore, no matter the area you may say that you are called to 'specialize' on, preach, teach, and practice the Whole Counsel of God. And whatever we may have or achieve, we are nothing before God; and we must know that without holiness no one can see the Lord. Let us and those who follow us be aware of this real Truth.

Some people 'want' revelations, visions, and prophecies to be tested by the Word of God. Those people know whether they are sincere or whether they want to deceive others, having been deceived. I am a strong believer in this approach, because it is Biblical. The Bible says, "Prove all things; hold on to that which is good (1 Thes. 5:21). Beloved, do not believe every spirit, but test the spirits, whether they are of God... (1 Jn 4:1). Let two or three prophets speak, and let the others judge (1 Cor. 14:29)."

To explain some things, Jude speaks of sinners being reserved for the blackness of darkness forever (Jude 1:13). Jesus Christ Himself speaks of the sons of the Kingdom being cast into the Outer Darkness; and there will be weeping and gnashing of teeth (Matt. 8:12). Of course, you are already familiar with the heat of the fire of Hell. The Word says that their worm does not die, and the fire is not quenched (Mk 9:44).

Hell is a combination of fire, worms, darkness, etc. This does not mean, however, that you cannot see/notice/recognize someone in Hell, because you are more sensitive in Hell than you are on earth. This is why your spirit and soul can know things you didn't really perceive with your physical senses. Some people say that since they will be many in Hell Fire, they will put off the fire of Hell; but they don't know that the God, Who can mix fire and darkness, knows the frequency and magnitude of the fire which can comfortably absorb even trillions of entities! I hope you know that human beings have neither filled up the earth's surface nor used up all the oxygen, in spite of thousands of years of occupying the earth!

You have got to know that the time of the demons has not come; hence they spoke to Jesus Christ, saying, "Have You come to torment us before the time?" (Matt. 8:29). It is not the devil that formed Hell; it is God that formed it. It is not the devil that sends people to Hell; but God is the One Who sends people to Hell, as a way of punishing sinners and the disobedient. Even though a demon may carry or take you to Hell; but it is just because God has sent you there by releasing you to them. But on the case of men, it is appointed unto men to die once, and after that the judgment (Heb. 9:27).

Yes, the fire of Hell may not touch the demons now, because their time has not come; but when their time comes, God will either change their bodies to feel the effect of the fire, remove/neutralize the power that makes them not to feel the heat, or change the power and mode of the fire to burn them. Or, don't you know that even now someone can enter into physical fire and not feel the effect, because of demonic and satanic powers, after having performed some satanic rituals?

Even on the positive side, the fire of Nebuchadnezzar refused the bodies of Shadrach, Meshach, Abed-Nego, because God was there with them. And remember that the Bible says that Death and Hell will be cast into the Lake of Fire (Rev. 20:14). Therefore, if the demons don't feel the fire of Hell, they will certainly burn, cry, wail, and weep in the fire of the Lake of Fire. Understood?

Know that Hell or Hades is a temporary place of suffering for the dead sinner. The Lake of Fire, which the devils and sinners will be put into later, is actually the permanent place of extreme suffering for both the devils and human sinners. And the devil and his demons, for now, may be tormenting those who are presently suffering in Hell. But at the fulness of time, the devil and his fallen angels and demons will be cast into the Lake of Fire. And any person whose name is not found written in the Book of Life will also be cast into the Lake of Fire.

It is true that the time of fallen angels and demons has not come; but when their time comes, they will know that God has the kind of fire, that is available in the Lake of Fire and Brimstone, which will burn and torment them to wail and cry. The Bible says, "The devil, who deceived them, was cast into the Lake of Fire and Brimstone where the beast and the false prophet are. And they will be tormented day and night forever and ever.

"Then I saw a Great White Throne and Him Who sat on it, from Whose Face the earth and the heaven fled away. And there was found no place for them. And I saw the dead, small and great, standing before God, and books were opened. And another Book was opened, which is the Book of Life. And the dead were judged according to their works, by things which were written in the books.

"The sea gave up the dead who were in it, and Death and Hades delivered up the dead who were in them. And they were judged, each one according to his works. Then Death and Hades were cast into the Lake of Fire. This is the Second Death. And anyone not found written in the Book of Life was cast into the Lake of Fire" (Rev. 20:10-15).

As for whether Jesus Christ can accompany someone to Hell to show the person something in Hell, as someone said: "How can Jesus, as holy as He is, enter Hell with the guy, as if they are going on excursion; and don't you know that people in Hell can't see God's Face, how come the woman had the opportunity to be asking Jesus for forgiveness while she was already in Hell?" Bible and spiritual knowledge will tell you that it is possible.

If satan could come to where the sons of God came to present themselves to God (Job 1:6), and even spoke to God, how can't someone in Hell see Jesus Christ when He goes there on a mission to show someone mysteries about Hell? Yes, sinners cannot see God's Face; but you have to know that even though Jesus Christ is God, yet He is the Son of God and Mediator between God and men; and many sinners who couldn't see God saw Jesus Christ while He was on earth.

God created Hell, and He can enter there if He wants to; and the fire and heat of Hell cannot touch Him, even as the Fourth Person (Who had the Form of the Son of God) (Dan. 3:25) entered the fire of Nebuchadnezzar. And remember that God is everywhere (though His Manifest Presence is not everywhere). The Word says, "Where can I go from Your Spirit? Or where can I flee from Your Presence? If I ascend into Heaven, You are there; if I make my bed in Hell, behold, You are there" (Psa. 139:7-8).

The magnitude of the pain, either from the heat of the fire of Hell or the torments of the demons of Hell, is irrelevant for now; because Hell is a place of great suffering and torment; and no one will want to suffer, either from the heat or from the torments.

No one church is the only bearer of the Truth of the Word of God. And it is not only the churches that might have been mentioned for disobedience or rebellion that are taking their members to Hell by their teachings and practices.

Evil people do not have Eternal Life but eternal death. Men's souls are eternal; and demons and devils are eternal beings also: Therefore, they will suffer forever in the Lake of Fire. We see that Jesus Christ states in the Book of Mark that their worm does not die and the fire is not quenched (Mk 9:44). Did (Does) our Lord lie when He said (says) that the fire is not quenched? Hell Fire is forever!

To clear doubts, the Bible itself says that Hell Fire is eternal (and not just forever). Let me say this, because of those who say that Hell Fire is forever but not eternal. Yes, everlasting or forever can stand for a period of time or for eternity. Everlasting or forever actually means till the stated time expires, and eternity means that there is no time limit.

But the Bible tells us specifically that the everlasting and forever of Hell Fire (the Lake of Fire) is eternity. The Word says, "...are set forth as an example, suffering the vengeance of eternal fire" (Jude 1:7). Therefore, Hell Fire is everlasting, forever, and eternal.

Yes, evil people go to Hell or Hades immediately after death, even though there is a corridor between death and either Heaven or Hell. And some people have actually come back from that corridor without either entering Heaven or Hell, but having seen them; though God actually takes some people (either in vision or in death) to Heaven or/and Hell to show them things they will report to the children of men when they come back.

He does these things, because He loves men and does not want any person to enter Hell. But many people are so hardened like the brothers of the rich man, of whom Abraham said, "If they do not hear Moses and the Prophets, neither will they be persuaded though one rise from the dead" (Lk. 16:31).

On the case of the possibility of increasing the heat or fire of Hell, God has different functions for His creatures, including angels. But have you ever seen it in the Bible where King Nebuchadnezzar told his men to increase his own fire seven times? (Dan. 3:19). Even in physics, though water boils at 100 degrees Celsius (which temperature human beings cannot withstand), yet it takes higher degrees of Celsius temperature to melt aluminum or iron into liquid form, not talk of vapourizing any of them.

For one particular testifier, at the point of her death, she was not born again, and so was left to the power of the demons; and demons torture people who are dead in Hell, which God formed for the torment of the disobedient. Yes, there are torture places in the kingdom of darkness for those who disobey their rules; but these are not (necessarily) the same place where those who are dead are tortured.

And after the devil and his fallen angels have tortured those that go contrary to their commands, when they actually die physically, they go to be punished and tortured in God's Own torture place, which is Hell (though devils increase people's torments there). The fact that there are prisons and death sentences and executions by men for criminals and murderers does not negate God's Own 'prison' and Hell.

Yes, the final Judgment has not come; but dying without Jesus Christ, or in sin, is as good as having been judged. God sees differently, and says, "...but he who does not believe is condemned already..." (Jn 3:16). Now and the final Judgment are the same, as long as the fellow is dead and appointed for judgment. Therefore, a sinner who dies now goes to Hell (and even if you hang for some time, you will still go to Hell after some time).

And even when you are still alive and have made up your mind that nothing can make you change your evil ways, then you are as good as having been judged, in a way, because the Bible says that it is the Word of God that will judge people on the Last Day; though with God, nothing shall be impossible.

Are there not many agents of the kingdom of darkness, who, though will experience what should show them that God's Power is superior to the power of devil, yet they do not change or embrace Jesus Christ, because their hearts (minds) have been hardened by satan? And satan can also harden the heart (mind) of someone, who may be carrying Bible in pretence (or, might have even known Christ).

When one particular testifier spoke of a force pulling her out of Hell, that was God's Power that pulled her out of that torment, because of His Mercy, so that she could come back to the earth, repent, accept Jesus Christ, and testify. Remember that God will have mercy on whom He chooses to have mercy on.

As for cleansing, you have got to know that our God is high and highly lifted up! He doesn't do everything by Himself: He has assigned different functions to different beings, including men and angels. When the devil rebelled against Him, He didn't fight the devil; that would have been giving much credit to satan. What God just did was to empower Michael the archangel and His warring angels; and they expelled the former Lucifer from Heaven.

God used one of the seraphim to touch Isaiah's tongue or mouth with the coal of fire (live coal) so that his iniquity was taken away and his sin purged (Isa. 6:6-7). When satan withstood Joshua, the high priest, because he was wearing filthy garments, the Angel of the Lord (God Himself) spoke and said to those who stood before Him, saying, "Take away the filthy garments from him" (Zech. 3).

I tell you that if she had not come back to life, she couldn't have been saved, because God cannot contradict His Word. However, God sees the end from the beginning. This is why, speaking to Abraham, He said, "I have made you father of many nations," when as yet he didn't have Isaac. He didn't say, "I will make you father of many nations." God had (has) a special mission for her, out His Love and Mercy, not because she is better than others.

This is why God can overshadow His chosen vessels with His Spirit, even before they actually submit to Jesus Christ; but if they refuse to submit, He will destroy them. Did God not call and speak to Adam even after he had sinned? God created and formed all things; therefore, He can relate with sinners (in some ways), just as He spoke to satan himself on the case of Job. Angels of God protect even the unbelievers to an extent; if not, the devil would have wiped them out.

Our 'headache' shouldn't be whether we will be in Heaven or in the New Earth. Our concern should be to please God and make His Kingdom at last. Angels come to earth from Heaven; and they also go to Heaven from the earth. And Jesus Christ says that we shall be like the angels, if we are counted worthy for the Resurrection from the dead (Lk. 20:35-36). Do you think that it is not possible for us to live both in Heaven and the New Earth?

In Hell Fire, worms, which do not die, eat (pass through) people's bodies. I have already stated that Hell Fire is eternal, as the Book of Jude tells us. God told Adam that he will die in the day that he eats of the forbidden fruit. Did Adam cease to exist on the day he ate the forbidden fruit? But he died spiritually, being separated from the Life of God. There are spiritual death (separation from God), physical death (ceasing to live physically), and the Second Death (Eternal Torment in Hell Fire or the Lake of Fire).

Sin separates you from God (spiritual death); and at death, spiritual death leads to eternal suffering of God's Punishment (Second Death) in Hell Fire. The Bible says, "…are set forth as an example, suffering the vengeance of Eternal Fire" (Jude 1:7). If you had been thinking that when people are cast into the Lake of Fire, then they are annihilated forever by way of being cut off from existence, then you had been making a great mistake.

And I tell you, if it all ends with the Judgment, then sinners somehow may assume they didn't 'lose.' If you 'enjoy' your life on earth, living in disobedience to God, and after the Judgment you cease to exist, do you think you 'really lost' anything, though losing Heaven is losing a very great thing? Then many more people can start living however they want; after all, when they are judged, they cease to exist! Then why didn't God wipe out the entire human race and create another set of good human beings?

The Bible says, "And they shall go forth and look upon the corpses of the men who have transgressed against Me. For their worm does not die, and their fire is not quenched. They shall be an abhorrence to all flesh" (Isaiah 66:24). So, God is going to leave a reminder for the good and faithful resurrected humans and the angels, in order to discourage any future disobedience or rebellion!

If you thought that when satan and his cohorts are cast into the Lake of Fire, then they will cease to exist, then what did they 'really lose'? And why did God allow them to continue to exist in the world, deceiving people and causing problems for human beings, and trying to destroy God's Plans? When then will they taste their torment? Don't misinterpret the Bible. The Bible didn't say that Hell and death have an end, but that they will be cast into the Lake of Fire; and the Lake of Fire is forever and eternal, according to the Book of Jude.

God does not tell us to follow man-made denomination; anyone whose preaching or teaching is not focused on the Kingdom of God, but on denomination, belongs to the group which will not make Heaven, but Hell. The fellow is not working for God, but for satan. However, be careful that you are not misinterpreting the preaching, teaching, action, or practice of some of those testifiers.

When you are lying down and sleeping, you don't know what is happening around you; yet you see yourself doing or saying things in your dream: God has used dreams to tell you that you are not all about that sleeping body, but you have got a soul and a spirit; why not be wise and learn from your dream experiences? Or you think your dreams are meaningless and non-existent?

When Adam lost the Life of God by disobedience, it was enough death; when somebody is tormented in the Lake of Fire, along with the devil and his fallen angels, that is great death in operation! When you die without Jesus Christ, or in sin, you are as good as having been judged (Jn 3:18). God, being the God of order, has given time to all humans (who die after some period of time), and when that time expires, He will call all of them (living and dead) for the Final Judgment.

You are actually judged at your death, and counted as holy, righteous, and justified, or sinful, evil, and condemned; the Final Judgment is actually for formality (Heb. 9:27; Jn 3:18).

The things that we need to know have been given and revealed to us. Even God taking people (through visions and death) to show them Heaven or/and Hell is just because we don't take His Word serious, because those things are found in the Bible, and can be known if we are open to the Spirit of God.

Concerning the resurrection from the dead at the Last Day, you need to ask yourself: "Is it resurrection from what/where to what/where?" Your soul does not die; so also is your spirit. Those people that they said they saw in Hell are not there with their physical bodies, but with their souls (which do not die). And just as you feel the effect of your enjoyment or suffering in your dreams, that is how you will feel the joy of Heaven (Paradise) or the suffering of Hell, when you die, as you wait for the resurrection.

Now, that resurrection is the resurrection of your soul putting on physical body again to be judged physically by God, because you existed as a physical being. But that is not now. Of course, before the Final Judgment and expiration of man's time, there would have been the Rapture of the Saints and the Millennium Reign of Jesus Christ with His faithful Saints.

But, whereas the Saints will resurrect with glorified bodies, the sinners will resurrect with the ordinary fallen bodies. Prophet Daniel said: "And many of those who sleep in the dust of the earth shall awake, some to Everlasting Life, some to shame and everlasting contempt" (Dan. 12:2). Here the Bible says that the state of both the righteous and the unrighteous (after resurrection) will be everlasting, but opposite to each other (just as light and darkness, or good and evil, are opposite to each other).

Jesus Christ Himself tells us that in Hell Fire, you do not cease to exist, but you will be going through on-going suffering, torment, and pain; and you will have your full sensitivity (even greater) there. Refer to the Book of Luke, chapter sixteen, and verses nineteen to thirty-one.

If you gain the whole world, and lose your soul in the end, you gained nothing. To tell you the truth, if you have all the miracles and prophecies you want from God, and in the end, hear, "Get behind Me, you worker of iniquity," you lost everything. If you live contrary to the Word of God, you better get ready for the Coming of Jesus Christ, because that your prophet or pastor, who tells you what the devil inspired him to say, will not save you from the Wrath of God.

God is no respecter of persons, whether you carry Bible or call Jesus. "But why do you call Me, 'Lord, Lord,' and do not do what I say?" (Lk. 6:46). And for those who put their trust of being saved on church attendance, baptism, communion, full membership, payment of big tithes and big donations to church projects, and friendship with the pastor, somebody should tell you that you are on your way to Hell Fire without a living relationship with Jesus Christ as your Lord and personal Saviour, and living to please Him.

Those of you who spread pornographic images in the internet, Hell Fire does not respect film actors, actresses, producers, and directors: get ready, because you will come to realize that worldly fame is satanic deception! God loves you and does not take delight in your perishing in Hell Fire; but if God turned His Face away from Jesus Christ Himself when He was carrying the sins of the world at the Cross of Calvary, who are you that God will allow you into His Kingdom with sin?

If you want to know the terror of Hell Fire, look at the Suffering of Jesus Christ (God Himself). And for those of you who don't believe in Hell Fire, no matter what you chose to believe, you will come to terms with the reality in the end. Let no one deceive you; and don't deceive anyone!

Many are called, but few are chosen; and it is not all those who are chosen that will be glorified, because the Bible says that it is the faithful that will be glorified. Therefore, among the few that are chosen, it is the fewer, who will be faithful and obedient, that will be glorified. The Word says, "Enter by the narrow gate, for wide is the gate and broad is the way that leads to destruction, and there are many who go in by it.

"Because narrow is the gate and difficult is the way which leads to life, and there are few who find it. Beware of false prophets, who come to you in sheep's clothing, but inwardly they are ravenous wolves. You will know them by their fruits…" (Matt. 7:13-16). It is not by their miracles or prophecies, because many false prophets will rise up and deceive many. False christs and false prophets will rise and show great signs and wonders to deceive, if possible, even the Elect (Matt. 24:11,24).

And because lawlessness (iniquity) will abound in the last days, the love of many will grow cold. But he who endures to the end shall be saved (verses 12 & 13). The Bible states: "For such are false apostles, deceitful workers, transforming themselves into apostles of Christ. And no wonder! For satan himself transforms himself into an angel of light. Therefore it is no great thing if his ministers transform themselves into ministers of righteousness, whose end will be according to their works (2 Cor. 11:13-15).

"Now the Spirit expressly says that in latter times some will depart from the Faith, giving heed to deceiving spirits and doctrines of demons, speaking lies in hypocrisy, having their own conscience seared with a hot iron (1 Tim. 4:1-2). For the time will come when they will not endure Sound Doctrine, but according to their own desires, because they have itching ears, they will heap up for themselves teachers; and they will turn their ears away from the Truth, and be turned aside to fables (2 Tim. 4:4).

"Take heed to yourself and to the Doctrine. Continue in them, for in doing this you will save both yourself and those who hear you (1 Tim. 4:16). But there were also false prophets among the people, even as there will be false teachers among you, who will secretly bring in destructive heresies, even denying the Lord Who bought them, and bring on themselves swift destruction. And many will follow their destructive ways, because of whom the way of Truth will be blasphemed" (2 Pet. 2:1-2).

I maintain that, by my understanding of the Scriptures and the inward conviction by the Holy Spirit of the Living God, that perming, jerry curling, or frying your hair (male or female) and the use of weavons and wigs are sinful, satanic, demonic, of mermaid, against God, anti-Christ, worldly, and Hell-attracting. Why? Because, when you perm your hair or use weavon, you are accusing God (consciously or unconsciously) that He is an imperfect Creator.

And it is inferiority complex, which says that the hair of the whites is superior to the hair of the blacks, that makes people insult our Awesome God. There is no difference between frying your hair and bleaching your skin (which some people do, to tell God that He is stupid for giving them the skin complexion that they have), whether or not you agree with the Truth.

Of course, you can still repent and correct your ways before death or the Coming of our Lord Jesus Christ; because, except you repent, you cannot enter Heaven but Hell, because no sin can enter Heaven. That is iniquity and living in sin. Many people say that they don't believe in Hell Fire: whatever you choose to believe, you will come to terms with the reality of Hell Fire in the end; then, you will have no second chance, but to suffer everlasting suffering in Hell Fire.

But if you will listen to the Voice of the Holy Spirit, you will escape the punishment of Hell Fire and eternal separation from the Almighty God. Many people like the thought that Hell Fire doesn't exist in order to comfort themselves in their sins. Who is satan, the devil? Was he not the Lucifer who was very close to God and well-honoured? Who was Adam? Was he not the one that was made in God's Image and represented God on earth? How come two of them became God's enemies?

Two of them, who were holy and perfect before God, made themselves sinners and God's enemies by pride and disobedience. Whoever makes himself a friend of the world makes himself an enemy of God (Jas 4:4). It doesn't matter how long you have been a Believer, how much of the Bible you know, how big your church or ministry is in people's eyes (because all those multitude of people may be going to Hell Fire with you), or how much anointing you have.

Perhaps you may need to be reminded that God made an ass to speak to Balaam in a human voice; and He used a heathen King Cyrus to build His Temple in Jerusalem. What is very different if God uses you to perform miracles? Maybe, you need to be told that Jesus Christ Himself said that, because of iniquity, He will reject many people who had prophesied, cast out demons, and done many wonders in His Name (Matt. 7:21-23).

And the Lord says, "STRIVE to enter through the NARROW GATE, for many, I say to you, will SEEK to ENTER and WILL NOT BE ABLE" (Lk. 13:24). Brothers and sisters, don't be deceived by all these miracles, falling down, breakthroughs, and deliverances. Healings, deliverances, signs, wonders, miracles, breakthroughs, and prosperity are small things to God. The One Who made the whole universe, what can He not do? His Concern is your soul, because He has determined, by an everlasting decision, that no sin, unrighteousness, or iniquity will cross the gate of Heaven.

The Business of God is drawing people to Jesus Christ, and getting them prepared for the Rapture and Heaven. Every other thing is extra and secondary. Think of it! God loved man so much that He sent His Son to die for men. Why didn't He wipe out all sins, since His Son has died? Why does He still require that you MUST believe in His Son?

If you have not understood the horror and penalty of Hell Fire, consider the terrible nature of Hell Fire by considering that Jesus Christ allowed Himself to be insulted and crucified by ordinary men, so that men will not enter Hell Fire. Just as God values a soul more than all the gold and silver of this world, He did not consider His Life dear to Him; but He gave His Life up for you, so that you will not end in Hell Fire.

But if you chose to spend everlasting torment and punishment in Hell Fire, God will execute it for you. Of all the multitude of people in the world in Noah's time, only Noah and his family were saved from the Flood that destroyed the whole world. It was only Lot and his family that escaped the fire from Heaven, of all the multitude of people in Sodom and Gomorrah.

Though God delivered all the Israelites with a Mighty Hand, and they experienced Divine and supernatural manifestations, yet, God destroyed all of them (who had come to age) that sinned against Him, except Joshua and Caleb. And even in this dispensation, He has told us that it is only few people that will be saved. Why? Is it because He does not love them? No!

Rather, it is because men (even when they call themselves Believers and preachers) are stubborn and obstinate; they choose what they want to obey, and despise God's Word and Spirit. But the Word of God has this for the Believers: "You believe that there is One God. You do well. Even the demons believe – and tremble!" (Jas 2:19). God will wait for everybody at His Judgment.

And those of you women that design your blouses to show us your breasts and armpits, get ready to face the Judgment Seat of God. Those of you that cut and divide your skirts to show us your laps, to help and encourage the devil to spread his lust-wave, prepare for your eternity.

Those who paint their faces and wear artificial nails, encouraging the activities of satan, who invented those lipsticks and cortexes, what will you do if when you appear before God's Judgment, He tells you, "You said these things didn't matter, but they matter to Me; depart to Hell Fire, which is prepared for satan and those that obey him"? And any design of dressing (male or female) that glorifies the devil and encourages his desires and works are from him.

The spirit of the antichrist tells people to combine Christianity with worldliness; they decide what they want, and use Bible quotations to deaden their consciences (as satan quoted the Scriptures to Jesus Christ). And, inasmuch as many people dress and appear like Godly ladies and women, while keeping hatred, bitterness, unforgiveness, etc in their hearts (which will still send you to Hell Fire if you don't repent), how much more will the inside of many of those who don't care about their outward appearance be worse!

When you hear some preachers say that they preach and teach the Word of God, you need to pity them; because they have been blinded by the devil to put materials things before the souls of men. In the last chapter of the Bible, the Word says, "He who is unjust, let him be unjust still;

he who is filthy, let him be filthy still; he who is righteous, let him be righteous still; he who is holy, let him be holy still.

"'And behold, I am coming quickly, and My Reward is with Me, to give to every one according to his work'" (Rev. 22:11-12). THE WISE WILL LISTEN TO THE SPIRIT OF GOD, BUT THE STUBBORN WILL LAUGH OVER THESE THINGS AND RIDICULE THE LORD; BUT WAIT TILL THE COMING OF JESUS CHRIST!

To be sincere with you, if you have all the blessing, anointing and falling down, deliverance, healing, breakthrough, and miracles that God can give to any person, if you lose Heaven, you lost everything and gained nothing. Let no one deceive you: Many agents of the kingdom of darkness pretend to be ministers of Jesus Christ; and the devil uses them to keep people's focus out of Heaven, but on earthly and material things.

Even, many ministers who were called by God have been led astray by the devil, so that they are used to deceive other Believers by making them to set their minds on the things of the earth. Study the Bible by yourself to find out what God wants from you: what you should do and avoid. Be open to the Spirit of God, and don't harden your heart to what you want, so that He can lead and direct you to please God. Jesus Christ died for us; what have we done for Him?

The highest achievement you can have in life is that you are in Christ, and when Jesus Christ looks at you, He doesn't see any impediment which can withhold you from being raptured if He were to come now! Therefore, let us cleanse ourselves from all filthiness (sin) of the flesh and spirit, perfecting holiness in the Fear of God (2 Cor. 7:1).

The highest thing that separates God from satan is holiness; and this is why the angels sing, "Holy, Holy, Holy, Lord God Almighty…" and not, "Power, Power, Power, Holy Lord God…." God will allow you into His Heaven if you are poor, sick, and suffering without sin; but if you have all the miracles, deliverance, breakthrough, success, prosperity, healing, health, and prophecies with sin or disobedience, He will tell you: "Without holiness, no eye shall see the Lord."

If you love the Lord, then keep His Commandments (Jn 14:15). And why will you, after you have spoken in tongues, prophesied, cast out demons, and done mighty works in His Name, hear, "I never knew you; depart from Me, you who practice lawlessness"? A word is enough for the wise!

Satan, the devil, has blinded and gripped the Roman Catholics with idolatry, and taken captive many Pentecostals and charismatics with worldliness and it-doesn't-matter. Some people are concerned with, "Do not judge." But if you knew the millions of people who are going to Hell Fire, because of false, fake, half-bred, unbiblical, selfish, hardened, satanic, and demonic apostles, prophets, evangelists, pastors, teachers, and ministers, you would have long gone to seek God's Face in Bible study and prayer with fasting.

Others are of, "Let the wheat and the tares grow together till the Last Day," without knowing that the wheat and the tares will always grow together till the Last Day. But God Himself has sent many people to emphasize strongly that not all the plants are wheat; but there are tares among the wheat and in the church-world, so that people can decide beforehand whether to be a wheat (and plan for Heaven) or a tare (and wait for Hell)!

However, still know that it is not all supernatural revelations that come from God and His Spirit. In these days when God is revealing mysteries and hidden things to many people, to warn us of eternal realities (though the Bible contains eternal realities in it), know that the devil will also be giving his own revelations and visions to people.

The purpose of the devil in doing this is to lead men to sin and stubbornness, to put confusion among Christians, and to make Believers to not believe God-given revelations and visions. Originals are imitated; but we do not have to do away with the original because of the imitation!

Also, if you are listening to a testimony of someone telling you what Jesus Christ told him (or what he believes that Jesus Christ told him), you should be sensitive enough to separate (detect) what the Lord Jesus Christ told him and what he himself might add, in attempt to explain something to clarify issues.

However, many times, visions may be symbolic with the actual interpretation being given to the person in his heart/spirit. This is one danger of dreams' interpretations; some people have even made books of interpretations of different kinds of dreams.

Whereas they may be right (or nearly right) in many cases, yet some things are symbolic; and they can mean different things to different people. But even at that, the person who had the dream, vision, or even heard the audible voice, can add or subtract something(s) in attempt to tell us what he received, consciously or unconsciously.

A Biblical example may be seen in the about three places in the Book of Acts of the Apostles, where the encounter of Saul (Paul) with Jesus Christ is narrated by Paul himself (with Luke or and Luke). If you are very sensitive, you will perceive that the three accounts are not exactly the same, even though it was the same Paul or/and Luke who gave the report/testimony.

The spirit of man works with the mind and brain of man while he is giving a testimony; and there are things which you may not remember in some occasions. Similar examples are seen in the four Gospels Books.

Mathew and John were among the apostles of Jesus Christ; but Mark and Luke were not among the twelve apostles of the Lord. You may realize, if you are careful and sensitive, that there are times when more than one of them reported the same incidents, but the accounts were not exactly the same.

It is not that any of them lied, but whereas Mathew and John might have heard directly from the Mouth of Jesus Christ, Mark and Luke might have heard from a report of what Jesus Christ said.

And even the ones, who heard directly from His Mouth and saw the miracles, healings, and encounters, with their own eyes, had different levels of mental understanding and spiritual development, not to talk of the possibility (as humans) of forgetting some things at some times.

And John himself said, "And Thomas answered and said to Him, 'My Lord and my God!' Jesus said to him, 'Thomas, because you have seen Me, you have believed. Blessed are those who have not seen and yet have believed.'

"And truly Jesus did many other signs in the presence of His Disciples, which are not written in this Book; but these are written that you may believe that Jesus is the Christ, the Son of God, and that believing you may have life in His Name (Jn 20:28-31).

"Then Peter, turning around, saw the Disciple whom Jesus loved following, who also had leaned on His Breast at the supper, and said, 'Lord, who is the one who betrays You?' Peter, seeing him, said to Jesus, 'But Lord, what about this man?'

"Jesus said to him, 'If I will that he remain till I come, what is that to you? You follow Me.' Then this saying went out among the brethren that this Disciple would not die. Yet Jesus did not say to him that he would not die, but, 'If I will that he remain till I come, what is that to you?'

"This is the Disciple who testifies of these things, and wrote these things; and we know that his testimony is true. And there are also many other things that Jesus did, which if they were written one by one, I suppose that even the world itself could not contain the books that would be written. Amen" (Jn 21:20-25).

Notice that in the issue concerning Jesus Christ, Peter, and John (who was writing), the Lord's Statement was misunderstood. And this can also happen in giving of testimonies of revelations, visions, and mysteries.

But unconsciously, unknowing, and unwillingly misinterpreting, misunderstanding, mispresenting, adding to, or subtracting from the vision or revelation given to you is different from when you consciously, carefully, and knowingly misinterpret, mispresent, add to, or subtract from the revelation or vision given to you or to somebody else.

To this end, the Bible says, "For I testify to everyone who hears the Words of the prophecy of this Book: If anyone adds to these things, God will add to him the plagues that are written in this Book;

"And if anyone takes away from the Words of the Book of this prophecy, God shall take away his part from the Book of Life, from the Holy City, and from the things which are written in this Book" (Rev. 22:18-19).

However, this is not an excuse for you to say, interpret, or present what you do not understand, unconsciously or unknowingly, because the Bible also says, "My brethren, let not many of you become teachers, knowing that we shall receive a stricter judgment.

"For we all stumble in many things. If anyone does not stumble in word, he is a perfect man, able also to bridle the whole body" (Jas 3:1-2).

INDECENT DRESSING AND WORLDLY APPEARANCE

Writing to Timothy, Apostle Paul said, "Take heed to yourself and to the Doctrine. Continue in them, for in doing this you will save both yourself and those who hear you" (1 Tim. 4:16). This means that it is possible for both you and those who believe (look up to) you to not be saved, because of wrong doctrine and practice. And you know that he was writing to a preacher and minister of the Gospel who had some (many) Believers (people of God) under him.

A New Testament apostle, writing to New Testament Believers, wrote: "Therefore, having these promises, beloved, let us cleanse ourselves from all filthiness of the flesh and spirit, perfecting holiness in the Fear of God" (2 Cor. 7:1). Notice that Apostle Paul spoke of the filthiness of the flesh and spirit. Surprisingly, he put the filthiness of the flesh before the filthiness of spirit. But many will forget (or wilfully ignore) the filthiness of the flesh, while many will still not make their followers to be conscious of the filthiness of spirit.

And the Word of God, which cannot be broken, but endures forever, says, "…present your bodies a living sacrifice, holy, acceptable to God, which is your reasonable service. And do not be conformed to this world…" (Rom. 12:1-2). God looks at your heart, as well as your body, which is to be presented holy and acceptable to Him as a living sacrifice.

If the devil doesn't get you with lying, he will try to get you with pride; if he doesn't get you with fornication, he will try to get you with bitterness, hatred, unforgiveness, cheating, or stealing. If he doesn't get you with murder, he will try to get you with examination malpractice or falsification of result or age. If you say that you will not do this or that, because God told you not to do it, he will tell you to do it just once, confess, and God will mercifully, lovingly, and faithfully forgive you.

The devil tries as much as possible to take you to Hell Fire, because he knows that God can neither compromise His Standard nor condole sin. The devil, satan, was created as the holy Lucifer; but he became the wicked and evil satan, because of pride and rebellion.

Adam was formed as the pure and holy Adam; but due to disobedience to the Commandment of God, he became the sinful Adam. Do you know that the Father even removed His Face from Jesus Christ, as He carried the sins of the world on the Cross of Calvary, so that Jesus Christ cried out, saying, "My God, My God, why have You forsaken Me?"

The same blindness that holds many Roman Catholics, so that no matter how you tell them that worshipping images and praying to (or through) Mary (or, do they call it honouring her?) is unbiblical and anti-God, they do not seem to understand, is also holding many Pentecostals, orthodoxes, evangelicals, and charismatics, so that no matter how you tell them that indecent dressing and worldly appearance is unbiblical and anti-Christ, they hope and say that it doesn't matter.

But the devil will try as much as he can to hold you blind, captive, and disobedient until you find yourself in Hell Fire with no second chance. And many people don't even know that many people who carry Bible and call Jesus are actually agents of satan in disguise.

To this end, the Bible says, "For such are false apostles, deceitful workers, transforming themselves into apostles of Christ. And no wonder! For satan himself transforms himself into an angel of light. Therefore it is no great thing if his ministers also transform themselves into ministers of righteousness, whose end will be according to their works" (2 Cor. 11:13-15).

Apostle Peter, writing in the New Testament, to those who were born again, said, "Now if the righteous one is scarcely saved, where will the ungodly and the sinner appear?" (1 Pet. 4:18). When our Lord Jesus Christ says that He will tell many people on the Day of Judgment that He never knew them because they were workers of iniquity, He was speaking of those who had been born again, filled with the Holy Spirit, spoken in tongues, prophesied, cast out demons, and done mighty signs and wonders in His Name (Matt. 7:21-23).

I was passing a church when I saw somebody who was leading a prayer session speaking in tongues. She was seriously speaking in tongues, walking to and fro; but, behold, though I was inside a bus along the road (there was a kind of traffic slowdown, or rather, the bus was moving slowly), I saw part of her breasts all the way from the road due to the 'open-breast' blouse she was wearing; how much more the people with her there inside the church! Hell Fire has enlarged itself to accommodate very many people (Isa. 5:14).

The devil will tell you that there is no God; if you overcome him, he will say, "Okay, there is God, but there is no Jesus Christ." If you say that there is Jesus Christ Who died for you, he will say, "Okay, there is Jesus Christ, but wait till tomorrow before you give your life to Him." If you win him by giving your life to Jesus Christ, he will tell you: "You have the Righteousness of Jesus Christ; it is not by your righteousness that you were saved; therefore, don't worry how you live your life because you are the Righteousness of God; and as for outward appearance, what God looks at is the heart."

If you can't sacrifice small things like your dressing and appearance for Jesus Christ, can you lay down your life for His Sake? And He tells us that anyone who loves his life more than Him is not worthy of Him. Jesus Christ is coming very soon; get ready to receive Him.

If it is contrary to the Word of God, then it is from satan – the devil and God's archenemy – who deceived Eve (from the beginning) with: "Did God really say…." That which is against God and His Word cannot be from God, the Maker of all things Who holds the whole world in His Hands, because God's Word and His Spirit agree. Whatever glorifies the devil, and does not glorify God, is not of God.

The Lord Jesus Christ, Who defeated satan on the Cross of Calvary about two thousand years ago, is the Same – yesterday, today, and forever. He is coming very soon; get ready to meet Him: Heaven and Hell are real; let no one deceive you!

Many of those girls, ladies, and women, that expose their breasts (or breast cleavages), laps, and armpits in churches, in streets, at schools, in your compounds, in buses and cars, in markets, on Facebook, etc, are not just people who dressed seductively; make no mistakes about it! Many of them are agents of the kingdom of darkness, who have sold their souls to the queen of the coast and satan, the devil (who is their chief coordinator), to destroy the souls of men through lust, fornication, and adultery, because they want to entice, persuade, force, and drag people to Hell at any cost.

They may pretend to be Christians, harmless, good people, and ignorant of what they are doing; but they are out to serve the intent, plan, and purpose of the devil. This is one reason why many of them will not adhere to any preaching, teaching, instruction, or advice to get them dress like girls, ladies, and women who appreciate God's Work in them and value their bodies.

Many of them are blind agents of satan (because they do not know that satan is directly using them), while many of them are conscious agents of the kingdom of darkness and witches (who are doing and carrying out what they were told to do in the kingdom of satan, the fallen Lucifer). For many of them, only deliverance can change their mentality and mindset.

The Bible says, "For you were bought at a price; therefore glorify God in your body and in your spirit, which are God's" (1 Cor. 6:20). The Bible says that you should glorify God with both your body and your spirit, the two of which belong to God. When you are washing your plate, do you wash only the inside? No; but you wash both the inside and the outside, to be happy and satisfied. Why will you think otherwise with God?

The Bible says that if your eye causes you to sin, you should pluck it out (Matt. 5:29). If you can't leave lipstick, cortex, earrings, and weavon, can you pluck out your eye for the salvation of your soul if necessary? Your eye and lipstick, cortex, earring, or weavon, which one do you esteem above the other?

The Bible says, "Do not love the world or anything in the world. If any man loves the world, the Love of the Father is not in him; for all that is in the world: the lust of the eyes, the lust of the flesh, and the pride of life come not from the Father, but from the world. And the world passes away with its lusts, but he who does the Will of God abides forever" (1 Jn 2:15-17).

Adulteries, fornications, murders, and thefts are outward acts; yet the Lord says that they come from the heart and defile a man (Matt. 15:17-20). Eating with unwashed hand will not defile you, because you did not have evil thoughts to eat the food. But you can also eat with evil thoughts, like: gluttony and drunkenness.

Therefore using of lipsticks, weavons (wigs), artificial nails, etc defiles you, because it comes from evil thoughts of accusing God of imperfect creation and loving worldliness. And wearing seductive dresses and attire of the harlot come from the evil thoughts of wanting to expose your sensitive parts to command ungodly attention.

God calls hatred murder, calls lust fornication, calls changing your nature worldliness, calls dressing seductively causing your brother to fall, and calls painting yourself works of the flesh and of the devil. Lust is desire to fornicate; and God calls both the desire and the act the same thing – fornication. Using weavons and applying lipsticks and cortexes is to change God's Image which He made.

The Bible says, "A good tree cannot bear bad fruit, nor can a bad tree bear good fruit. Every tree that does not bear good fruit is cut down and thrown into the Fire. Therefore by their fruits you will know them. Not everyone who says to Me, 'Lord, Lord,' shall enter the Kingdom of Heaven, but he who does the Will of My Father in Heaven.

"Many will say to Me in that Day, 'Lord, Lord, have we not prophesied in Your Name, cast out demons in Your Name, and done many wonders in Your Name?' And then I will declare to them, 'I never knew you; depart from Me, you who practice lawlessness!'" (Matt. 7:18-23).

In some churches, people collect up to two, three, or more different kinds of offerings on Sundays; but they fail to tell their members to dress well. Is this hypocrisy or compromise? People put time, energy, and other kinds of efforts to convince (or will I say, pressurize?) people to give tithes/offerings and sow seed-faith; but when it comes to dressing, they will hypocritically say that the Holy Spirit will teach the Believers in Christ how to dress well.

Being born again is of the spirit (heart) of man by the acceptance of the Lord Jesus Christ (Jn 3:6). So someone can receive Jesus Christ while she is indecently dressed. Jn 3:3 says that unless one is born again, he cannot see the Kingdom of God. Jn 3:5 says that unless one is born of water and the Spirit, he cannot enter the Kingdom of God. The water there refers to the Word of God, according to Eph. 5:26. Being born again gives you the ability to become a child of God (Jn 1:12), so that you can live the way that God wants.

So whoever wants to enter (and not just to see) the Kingdom of God must be born again (led and directed) of the water (the Word of God) and the Spirit of God (Jn 3:5). To this end, Paul wrote to born again Believers to present their bodies a living sacrifice, holy and acceptable to God, and to renew their minds (Rom. 12:1-2). They themselves were to do the presenting and the renewing (God was not going to do it for them). This is why Paul himself said that he beat his body and brought it under subjection to his spirit, so that after he had preached to others, he himself will not be a castaway (1 Cor. 9:27).

So the one who knows the good he or she is to do, and does not do it, is sinning (Jas 4:17). And sinners spend eternity in Hell Fire. He who refuses to present his body a living sacrifice, holy and acceptable to God, is disobedient; and disobedient people go to Hell Fire. Remember that Adam was pure before God until he disobeyed God; and Lucifer was holy before God until iniquity was found in him.

Yes, if you receive Jesus Christ now with all your heart, while you are indecently dressed, God will wash away your sins and make you His child, and can even fill you with the Holy Spirit. But when you go to your house, the Spirit of God will speak to your heart to dress decently; if you refuse to obey, you will become a disobedient person (a fallen Adam). If you don't repent before you die or Jesus Christ comes, disobedient people go to.... Paul did not only preach faith towards Jesus Christ; rather, he preached faith towards Jesus Christ and repentance from dead works (Acts 20:21).

And the Word says, "Beware of false prophets, who come to you in sheep's clothing, but inwardly they are ravenous wolves. You will know them by their fruits. Do men gather grapes from thornbushes or figs from thistles? Even so, every good tree bears good fruit, but a bad tree bears bad fruit. A good tree cannot bear bad fruit, nor can a bad tree bear good fruit. Every tree that does not bear good fruit is cut down and thrown into the Fire. Therefore by their fruits you will know them.

"Not everyone who says to Me, 'Lord, Lord,' shall enter the Kingdom of Heaven, but he who does the Will of My Father in Heaven. Many will say to Me in that Day, 'Lord, Lord, have we not prophesied in Your Name, cast out demons in Your Name, and done many wonders in Your Name?' And then I will declare to them, 'I never knew you; depart from Me, you who practice lawlessness!'" (Matt. 7:15-23).

Apostle Paul, writing under the Unction, Anointing, and Inspiration of the Holy Spirit, said, "In like manner also, that the women adorn themselves in modest apparel (New International Version says, "Dress modestly, with decency and propriety"), with propriety and moderation, not with braided hair or gold or pearls or costly clothing, but which is proper for women professing Godliness, with good works" (1 Tim. 2:9-10, the New King James Version).

And Apostle Peter, being another witness, said, "Whose adorning, let it not be that outward adorning of plaiting the hair, and wearing of gold, or of putting on of apparel; but let it be the hidden man of the heart, in that which is not corruptible, even the ornament of a meek and quiet spirit, which is in the Sight of God of great price" (1 Pet. 3:3-4, the King James Version).

May you be changed by the Word of God! And may you learn to listen to the inner voice and witness in your spirit by the Holy Spirit, instead of following the multitude. May the Almighty Lord God give you wisdom and understanding in all things! Amen!

And instead of putting these things aside, criticizing them, or even getting annoyed over them, open your heart to the Holy Spirit and let Him speak to you further in your inner man: don't follow the multitude of disobedient and hardened people!

For the benefit of doubt, the things I have written down, as inspired by the Holy Spirit, are applicable to any tribe, people, nation, or country of the world, whether they are civilized or uncivilized, advanced or not advanced, developed or underdeveloped. To clarify you further, these things are applicable to Americans, Europeans, Asians, Africans, and others.

Let me state, categorically and without mincing words, that any preacher (no matter how anointed you may be, no matter your Knowledge of God, and no matter the years of service in the Kingdom of God), who encourages the use of cortex, lipstick, wigs or weavons, jewellery (jewelry), artificial nails, etc is encouraging the activities of the mermaid.

Much of the current wave of sexual immorality came from these things, even as they also use their demonic ladies and women to pull men into lust, fornication, and adultery. The only woman in the Bible who painted herself was Jezebel; and do you like the Jezebelic lifestyle and spirit? Beware of the attire of the harlot and prostitute! (Prov. 7).

If you do, you are encouraging, knowingly or unknowingly, the purposes and plans of the marine (water) kingdom of darkness, and the activities of the devil (satan), who is their chief-coordinator. You can fight against God without your knowledge; and you can encourage the devil without your knowledge.

And I will add that we preachers are responsible for most of the things happening in the world today, both on the positive side and on the negative side. All these people who misbehave and live their lives however they want, don't they go to churches?

When someone comes to church with his sin-partner (what many people call girl-friend), and leaves the church with the same sin-partner, without fear or shame, is it not enough to prove to you that the preachers are responsible for much of the evil in the society?

There is a way that seems right to a man, but its end is the way of death (Prov. 14:12; Prov. 16:25). God is warning us, because He loves us and does not want anyone to perish. But just as they never listened to Noah, many will not listen to the Truth; and just as Sodom and Gomorrah perished without Lot, those that will listen to God and do His Word and Will, will be saved!

Concerning the Bible passages we read before, I want you to see that there is the ornament or beauty of the spirit (heart). The word – fine – is not in the original text; and that is why it is italicized in the New King James Version. Apparel (according to the King James Version) or fine apparel (according to the New King James Version) refers to fashion and worldly ways of designing clothing. God wants you to look 'good'; but He detests worldly fashions.

Putting your mind on costly clothing makes clothing your idol. But how costly is the costly? Costly and expensive clothes encourage pride and idolization. For instance, if they make this clothing material as a material for the 'reigning' or 'current' people, then you have to remove yourself from it, because you are a different person – God's son or daughter.

People dress indecently and seductively these days, especially girls, ladies, and women. Of course, some men dress indecently also. But whereas even unbelieving men dress decently, many ladies who claim they are Christians, who go to different churches and call on the Name of the Lord, dress indecently to work, school, shopping, and even church.

The dressing and outward appearance of Christians must be different from those of unbelievers. If a Muslim will value covering herself well, how much more should you value it? The problem is that many people will find it easier to manage bondage than liberty. But do not use your liberty as an opportunity for sin and disobedience (Gal. 5:13).

Concerning jewellery (jewellery is British English, while jewelry is American English), Apostle Paul stated, "…that the women adorn themselves…not with…gold or pearls…" (1 Tim. 2:9, the New King James Version). The King James Version also says, "…women adorn themselves…not with…gold, or pearls…." Apostle Peter stated: "Do not let your adornment be merely outward…wearing gold…" (1 Pet. 3:3, the New King James Version). Now, take up your own New King James Version of the Bible, and read this portion of the Scripture. There you will see that the word 'merely' is italicized, which is to say that it is not in the original Greek text of the Bible.

Italicized words in the King James Version (which is the authorized version) or the New King James Version of the Bible are added for clearer understanding, and are not in the original Greek text; but I believe that this 'merely' added in the New King James Version, which, I thank

God, is not added in the only authorized version of the Bible – the King James Version – was added because of human acceptance over time based on demonic deception.

This is why you may see some versions of the Bible which will add 'merely' or 'only' without even italicizing it, which will make someone who doesn't have a certain level of understanding of versions and editions of the Bible to think that the words 'merely' or 'only' are in the original Greek text (and it is not there). Versions of the Bible (like KJV, NKJV, NIV, ASV, etc) are 'straight' translations of the Bible from the original Greek text, while editions of the Bible (like the Living Bible, Good News, etc) are 'interpreted' translations/descriptions of the Bible, either from the original Greek text or from a version of the Bible.

For your confirmation, the King James Version says, "Whose adorning let it not be that outward…wearing of gold…." There is no 'only' or 'merely' there. Apostle Peter said, "Let it not be outward wearing of gold (which is jewellery)." And Apostle Paul said, "Women are not to adorn themselves with gold or pearls (which, also, is jewellery). For the benefit of doubt, first, Apostle Peter didn't say anything about modesty. Secondly, hear Apostle Paul himself: "…women adorn themselves in modest apparel…" (1 Tim. 2:9).

Read it again from your own Bible, and you will see that he spoke of modest apparel, and not modest braiding of the hair or of wearing of gold or pearls (There is no such thing as modest braiding of the hair or modest wearing of jewels for Christians and Believers who want to make Heaven). We will see apparel and modest apparel, in dressing or clothing, later.

Some translations used 'modest appearance' instead of 'modest apparel', saying that the women should adorn themselves in modest appearance; but any translation, edition, or version of the Bible that uses 'appearance' either made mistake or purposely put it there to deceive people. Don't you know that some translations, editions, or versions of the Bible were done by some people to represent what they believe and accept? And you have got to know that the devil has agents (conscious or no conscious) in this regard. The Greek word used there is katastole, which means: apparel, dress, or clothing; it does not mean appearance.

Concerning plaiting or braiding of the hair (plaiting is British English, while braiding is American English), Apostle Paul clearly stated: "…that the women adorn themselves…not with braided hair…" (1 Tim. 2:9). Apostle Peter stated: "Whose adorning let it not be that outward adorning of plaiting the hair…" (1 Pet. 3:3, the King James Version). Apostle Peter said, "Don't adorn yourself by plaiting your hair." Apostle Paul said, "Don't adorn yourself with braided hair."

Neither Peter nor Paul spoke of modest plaiting or braiding of the hair, though Paul spoke of modest apparel. There is no modest braided or plaited hair. Your hair is to be natural as God made it. If it grows to the extent you find it difficult to comb it, then you can reduce it, but not as low as men's hair. Braiding or plaiting of the hair didn't come from God, but from the devil.

American, European, African, Asian, and Australian demons can give (or has given) American, European, African, Asian, and Australian methods and systems of braiding or plaiting of the hair. No matter how long the custom or culture has existed, the Bible says, "No braiding or plaiting of your hair, as a Christian woman." To dress the hair is to arrange someone's hair into a special style; and the devil has given braiding, plaiting, and weaving of the hair as ways in which many women and ladies dress or arrange their hair.

Concerning apparel or clothing, Apostle Paul clearly stated: "…that the women adorn themselves…not with…costly clothing" (1 Tim. 2:9, the New King James Version). The King James Version says, "…not with…costly array." Apostle Peter stated: "Whose adorning let it not be that outward adorning of…putting on apparel" (1 Pet. 3:3, the King James Version). The New

King James Version says, "Do not let your adornment be…putting on fine apparel." If you read the New King James Version, you will see that the word 'fine' is italicized, which means that it is not in the original Greek text. Therefore, Apostle Peter says, "Don't adorn yourself with apparel."

Apostle Paul said, "Don't adorn yourself with costly clothing or array." He said, "Adorn yourself in modest apparel." According to the Longman Dictionary of Contemporary English, 1995 edition, apparel is a formal word used for clothes, especially those worn for special occasions. So, apparel refers to special clothes. This not talking of normal clothes, but special clothes: this is talking of fashion and/or costly clothing. They are to use inexpensive or moderately priced clothes or clothing.

The Bible commands women to use modest apparel (1 Tim. 2:9). This particular, "In like manner also, that the women adorn themselves in modest apparel…" is not even talking of its price, but its style. According to the Longman Dictionary of Contemporary English, 1995 edition, modest clothing covers the body in a way that does not attract sexual interest. How many of our women, ladies, and girls dress modestly – in ways that do not attract sexual interest?

God hates dressing like the people of the world. He said: "And it shall be, in the day of the Lord's Sacrifice, that I will punish…all such as are clothed with foreign apparel" (Zeph. 1:8). Foreign apparel speaks of the kind of dressing that is not for God's people.

The Bible says, "Now when Jehu had come to Jezreel, Jezebel heard of it, and she put paint on her eyes…and looked through the window" (2 Kgs 9:30, the New King James Version). The King James Version says, "…she painted her face…." Painting your eyes, lips, and face is demonic and Jezebelic.

The Word says, "Now when Jehu had come to Jezreel, Jezebel heard of it, and she…adorned her head, and looked through the window" (2 Kgs 9:30, the New King James Version). The King James Version says, "…she…tired her head…." The New International Version says, "…she…arranged her hair…." Arranging, adorning, plaiting, braiding, or weaving the hair is demonic and Jezebelic.

Why didn't the Bible say, "Now when Jehu had come to Jezreel, Jezebel heard of it, and she looked through the window," but, "Now when Jehu had come to Jezreel, Jezebel heard of it, and she painted her face and adorned her head, and looked through the window." It was because she painted her face and adorned her head (or, arranged her hair) to look seductive and unnaturally attractive to seduce Jehu.

The Bible tells us that man looks at outward appearance (1 Sam. 16:7). Even in the secular world, appearance can decide your acceptability in many areas of life. Escape for your dear life; run before it is too late. The five foolish virgins lost their target. Remember that they were virgins, but they lacked something they didn't remember or deem necessary.

Please, open your eyes well, well; the devil has intruded into the Church: his ministers now parade themselves as ministers of Jesus Christ, to deceive and destroy the souls of the children of men.

Be careful of any church where people are allowed to dress anyhow to, no matter how anointed you may think the preacher is or how knowledgeable he is concerning the Bible. It is a different case when unbelievers dress anyhow to crusades, maybe, for the first time.

The Bible says that out of the abundance of the heart, the mouth speaks. Your actions and your words show what is on the inside of you. Your physical appearance reveals your inner man. If you don't care about what people think about your indecent dressing, then your spirit has a serious problem, and your mind has been corrupted. I don't care what you may think about it.

Even unbelievers will find it difficult to believe you are a Christian when you dress indecently as they do. There must be a difference between the dressing of a Christian and a non-Christian.

Many ladies think that they attract marriage partners by dressing seductively. Well, you can only attract a carnal man when you dress that way. How can a reasonable spiritual man decide to marry someone that is worldly in appearance? Will you paint your face with lipstick, eye-pencil, and decorative powder as the wicked and ungodly women, Jezebel, painted hers (2 Kgs 9:30)?

Concerning the dressing or arranging of the hair, using of weavons (or wigs) and attachments is devilish and worldly. Many of those weavons are actual human hairs that were cut and sold. Many of the weavons and attachments are manufactured with demonic materials to enslave the children of men.

I don't care whether you call it wool or what; it is still an attachment. You can't confuse God; He knows more than you do! Even, the using of thread to wind your hair (as many Believers do) is still attachment and unnatural hair. If you don't know, it is not a Christian style of hair-style but traditional style.

If you doubt this, check it out and see that traditional unbelievers use thread for their hair too. As a woman, wash your hair and comb it; there are suitable combs made for long hairs. Allow your hair to be natural; and you can pack it or allow it fly. And I am not telling you to cut your hair low like the general size of that of men of the same race as you, except you are going to cover it or wear cap on it, even outside the church.

Also, when you use weavons and attachments, when you perm and jerry curl your hair, you are saying that God is stupid (or, is an imperfect Creator) to have made your hair the way He made it. Relaxing your hair artificially (whether you call it science or technology) is of the devil. When people refuse to cover their hairs, they resort to worldly means of weavons for a covering. Of course, your must have a sign of authority on your head in church meetings or gatherings, as a woman. What do you lose by veiling your hair?

Much of those things women use for beauty and for their hair, in perming and jerry-curling, is manufactured from alantoin extracted from aborted babies. The worst is that some men even fry their hair.

I read a story of a woman who when she was still a young sister was warned by God to desist from using attachments on her hair. And anytime she disobeyed that Instruction, God will chastise her. She told God that there were other good Christians that were using attachments, and referred to one particular woman who was a spiritual mother to them, whom she saw as a model.

The story had it that then (as at the time of the reporting) the sister is married to a pastor for many years then, and she is a strong pillar in the ministry doing exploits for the Lord. On the other hand, she then makes her hair with attachment, weavons, and other materials without any further warning from the Lord. And she said that her relationship with the Lord is still intact.

This story, though 'funny', is painful. Can you see how someone who believes in Jesus Christ can so much love the things of this world to the extent that her conscience will get hardened to do what God told her not to do, and even make God to give her over to a reprobate mind, and also refuse to speak to her again, because she loves doing her own thing instead of God's Thing? And she still 'believes' that God is happy with her!

Start appreciating your hair the natural way God made it. If you find it difficult to comb it, then reduce it to manageable or easily-combable size, but not as low as the general size of that of men from the same race as you (the men who have the kind of hair that you have). This will solve all these problems of perming the hair, relaxing the hair, 'jerry-curling' the hair, wearing of weavons or wigs, braiding or plaiting your hair with natural hair, attachments, wool, and thread.

If your hair is very long, as a woman, it is good; but the Bible says, "If a woman has a long hair," and not, "When a woman has a long hair." If you have the kind of strong hair that will not be long (or very long) in its natural state without relaxing it artificially, then reduce it to manageable or easily-combable size, but not as low as the general size of that of men from the same race as you (the men who have the kind of hair that you have). Also, the use of veil, hair scarf, and caps can help you remove unnecessary worries.

Satan has entered the Church and has deceived many. Many are sincerely deceived. Those cortexes, lipsticks, make-ups, and many other painting materials and cosmetics, apart from being worldly, are manufactured from demonic materials, aborted babies' placentas, and human fat and blood. This is a mystery that many have not realized. When people use those things, they get demonic problems they don't know where they came from.

Blouses that show too much of your back; tight-fitting and revealing dresses; mini-skirts; spaghetti or line-sleeve and transparent dresses; blouses showing your breast; cobweb and body-hug dresses; blouses revealing your belly; and any such dresses are devilish, satanic, demonic, and worldly.

For men, sagging your trousers and dread-locking your hair are satanic also. Women shouldn't put on trousers, because they look more decent in skirts and gowns. In biology, when women mature, their buttocks get enlarged; this is why when they wear trousers, they reveal their body contours and look seductive.

Any attire or dress that glorifies the devil, and does not glorify God, is worldly and devilish. There are no two ways about this matter. If you doubt this, wait till the Day of Reckoning when you will cry and wail in Hell Fire! Then you will repent one thousand times in a short while without any second chance.

We now come to the issue of earrings, necklaces, and bangles. These things are worldly also. God made you look fine; what advantage is it in decorating your body, which is the Temple of the Holy Spirit, with those things?

We wear cloths and dresses to cover our nakedness. Before Adam sinned, we didn't even need dresses, for God's Glory covered us. Earrings were classified among foreign and ungodly things which Jacob purified his household from; and he buried them, after he had collected them from all the members of his household and those that were with him (Gen. 35:1-5). The Knowledge of God advanced from Abraham, to Isaac, and to Jacob.

God hates jewellery (jewelry) and ornamenting your body. Get rid of rings, chains, bangles, necklaces, and such things. Jewellery is designing your body with jewels. To God, it is idolatry; and the devil uses it to make women look worldly and seductive. By this, he seduces our men into lust, fornication, and adultery more easily.

Even though you may argue, can you prove to me why you need them when God made you beautiful? The problem is that many of these things have continued for so long that many don't even know why they do what they do. Personally, I don't see those things as beauty; and God does not like them.

Some argue that God told the Israelites to collect those things from the Egyptians as they departed from Egypt. Well, if you had not known it, God did not tell them to collect them from them because He wanted them to be given to jewellery. Those things were Egyptian and foreign, even though the Israelites might have been influenced by them after having stayed there for four hundred years.

He told them to collect them from them because they were made from gold, silver, and other materials; and they were to plunder Egypt. Those materials were needed for construction and other works by them and for the Work of God. Where do you think that they would have got the gold for the construction of the sanctuary and tabernacle?

See the Bible speak: "And when the people heard this bad news, they mourned, and no one put on his ornaments. For the Lord had said to Moses, 'Say to the children of Israel, "you are a stiff-necked people. I could come into your midst in one moment and consume you. Now therefore, take off your ornaments, that I may know what to do with you."'" So the children of Israel stripped themselves of their ornaments by Mount Horeb" (Exo. 33:4-6).

God spoke to His people, after they had used their ornaments to make a calf and worshipped it as the god that brought them out of Egypt, and said, "…take off your ornaments…." Is it not clear enough? The Israelites removed their jewellery and stripped themselves of their ornaments, because God commanded them to do so; will you yourself obey God's Voice today and save your soul from Hell?

Also, notice that verse 5 didn't say, "The Lord said to Moses…" but, "For the Lord had said to Moses…." In order words, they didn't just remove the ornaments on their own in verse 4. Verse 4 happened because the Lord had instructed it. And verse 6 affirms that they stripped themselves of their ornaments.

Also, notice that because they still needed the materials from which the ornaments were made – gold, silver, etc – for construction purposes, God didn't tell them to throw away those ornaments; they kept them, not for future wearing of them, but for the preservation of the materials of gold, silver, etc, for which purpose He told them to collect them from the Egyptians in the first place – to be used for construction works.

To this end, the Bible says, "'Take from among you an offering to the Lord. Whoever is of a willing heart, let him bring it as an offering to the Lord: gold, silver, and bronze….' They came, both men and women, as many as had a willing heart, and brought earrings and nose rings, rings and necklaces, all jewellery of gold, that is, every man who made an offering of gold to the Lord.

"Everyone who offered an offering of silver or bronze brought the Lord's Offering. And everyone with whom was found acacia wood for any work of the service, brought it" (Exo. 35:5,22,24). I didn't say this for you to keep your jewels, because you must not.

Someone may ask, "But why did God tell the Israelites to put the jewellery on their wives, sons, and daughters?" The answer is not hard, if you are sincere and God opens your eyes. Many times, we don't see the Truth of the Word of God when we read the Bible, because we already have what we want it to say in our minds, and we force it to say the very thing!

Hear God: "And I will give the people favour in the sight of the Egyptians; and it shall be, when you go, that you shall not go empty-handed. But every woman shall ask of her neighbour, namely, of her who dwells near her house, articles of silver, articles gold, and clothing; and you shall put them on your sons and your daughters. So you shall plunder the Egyptians" (Exo. 3:21-22, the New King James Version).

The King James Version (which is the only authorized version of the Bible) says, "But every woman shall borrow of her neighbour, and of her that sojourneth in her house, jewels of silver, and jewels of gold, and raiment: and ye shall put them upon your sons, and upon your daughters; and ye shall spoil the Egyptians" (Exo. 3:22).

Notice that the purpose of the borrowing and the putting on was to plunder the Egyptians. The Hebrew word used there is 'shaal'. It means 'borrow', and in some instances, may be rendered/translated as 'ask' or 'request'. It is true that the NKJV used 'ask' instead of 'borrow'; but what God told them was to borrow them from them. Why?

Hear the Bible: "Afterwards Moses and Aaron went in and told Pharaoh, 'Thus says the Lord God of Israel: "Let My people go, that they may hold a feast to Me in the wilderness."' And Pharaoh said, 'Who is the Lord that I should obey His Voice to let Israel go? I do not know the Lord, nor will I let Israel go.'

"So they said, 'The God of the Hebrews has met with us. Please, let us go three days' journey into the desert and sacrifice to the Lord our God, lest He fall upon us with pestilence or with the sword'" (Exo. 5:1-3). Look at what Pharaoh said, "You are idle! Idle! Therefore you say, 'Let us go and sacrifice to the Lord'" (Exo. 5:17).

After some plagues, Pharaoh said, "Go, sacrifice to your God in the land." And Moses said, "It is not right to do so, for we would be sacrificing the abomination of the Egyptians to the Lord our God. If we sacrifice the abomination of the Egyptians before their eyes, then will they not stone us?

"We will go three days' journey into the wilderness and sacrifice to the Lord our God as He will command us." So Pharaoh said, "I will let you go, that you may sacrifice to the Lord your God in the wilderness; only you shall not go very far away. Intercede for me" (Exo. 8:25-28).

After other plagues, Pharaoh said, "Go, serve the Lord; only let your flocks and your herds be kept back. Let your little ones also go with you." But Moses said, "You must also give us sacrifices and burnt offerings, that we may sacrifice to the Lord our God. Our livestock also shall go with us; not a hoof shall be left behind. For we must take some of them to serve the Lord our God, and even we do not know with what we must serve the Lord until we arrive there" (Exo. 10:24-26).

I put those portions of the Scripture to help you understand why they were to borrow the jewels. In what they told Pharaoh, they were going on a three-day journey into the wilderness to sacrifice to the Lord their God. And it seems that what Pharaoh understood from their statement(s), was that they were going on a three-day journey into the wilderness to sacrifice to the Lord their God, and after the sacrifice, they would come back to Egypt.

Was God deceiving the Egyptians then? No, He is God; and that was His Method of plundering the Egyptians, as He had told Abraham that his descendants, after serving a foreign land, would come out with great possessions (Gen. 15:14). And notice that neither God nor Moses told any of them that they would come back after the sacrifice!

In God's Sight, the Egyptians were paying for having held His people for hundreds of years in their land. He was punishing them for punishing His people. The same kind of thing happened when Jesus Christ was crucified. The devil, in his desperation, killed Jesus Christ; but it was after He was killed that satan realized that Jesus Christ had to shed His Blood in order to redeem mankind.

Then satan, wanting Jesus Christ to come down from the Cross, entered some people, and they said, "If You are the Son of God, come down from the Cross, and we will believe You (Matt. 27:41-43)"; but it was too late! The Bible says, "Which none of the rulers of this age knew; for had they known, they would not have crucified the Lord of Glory" (1 Cor. 2:8).

What I want you to know is that it was after the Israelites had left Egypt that the Egyptians actually realized that Israel was gone! And this added to their punishments, because there were drown in the Red Sea when they pursued Israel. The Bible says, "Now it was told the king of Egypt that the people had fled, and the heart of Pharaoh and his servants were turned against the people; and they said, 'Why have we done this, that we have let Israel go from serving us?'" (Exo. 14:5).

So, you can see, if you want to, why God said, "Borrow those articles and put them on your wives, sons, and daughters." They were not going to ask for it and keep it in their purses; you borrow things for urgent need. And that was why they had to put the articles on them: It was borrowed articles, which their wives and children were in urgent need for use in the special sacrifice they were going to make for their God in the wilderness after a three-day journey.

For those who want to wear wrist watch, it must not be with chains, for it would be the same as wearing chains. If you want to wear wrist watch (not for beauty, but for keeping time), use the one that is made of plastic, rubber, or leather belt; and let it be of simple and inexpensive type, because it is for checking time and not for fashion. For this same reason, your waist belt must not be the chain type; and it is to be the simple type. And don't even wear the rubber or plastic wrist bangles which carry different kinds of advertisement/write-ups, whether of church, ministry, Bible, Christianity, or whatever.

The Bible says that God looks at the heart (I Sam 16:7). The Word of the Lord says that the Almighty does not look as man looks. How does man look? He looks at the outward appearance. This means that outward appearance is very important in our relationship with men, because they would look at our appearance. Could it be that God does not see in the physical? How can He, Who created the physical out of the spiritual, not see the physical, while we that were created see it?

The Bible says that out of the abundance of the heart, the mouth speaks. This means that what we say has something to do with what is in our heart (which we don't see). The appearance of men could be deceitful. An armed robber could dress like a banker or a pastor. Why will he do that? Because he knows that the appearance of the banker or the pastor is appreciated by responsible people.

However, the banker or the pastor will never want to dress like the armed robber (if there is how they dress). Why would he not want to dress like that? Because he knows that armed robbery is one of the ills of the society.

My brethren, how you dress and how you appear matter before people (responsible people) even when they don't confront you. From this day, make up your mind to glorify God in your dressing no matter the cost. Make up your mind not to offend God through your dressing.

I tell you, many of the girls, ladies, women, boys, young men, and grown up men you see in the towns are agents of the kingdom of darkness. Even many children are witches, and they have direct and conscious relationships with the dark kingdom. Of course, there are blind witches, who don't have conscious relationship with demons and fallen angels, but are demonically remote-controlled.

Will it surprise you to be told that there are many agents of the kingdom of darkness in many churches? Many operate as preachers; some operate as deacons, deaconesses, and elders; others operate as group leaders; still, many are in the choir and in other departments.

It is not that God wants it to be so, or that it is so in every church. It is because many churches, fellowships, and ministries are not at the place God wants them to be, that agents of the kingdom of darkness come into their midst and relax. This is not just saying that we are the Pentecostals or the charismatics, and we speak in tongues always.

Brother, have you ever asked yourself where all those people that flood into your church are going to? People will come to church with their girl-friends, and leave the church with their girl-friends, without fear and shame. If they had tried it in the Early Church, they would have seen what would have happened to them!

The increase of evil in these last days is not only because of the desperation of the devil. As a matter of fact, the devil has always been desperate since the time of Adam. Preachers are responsible for much of it. Apart from preachers who are direct agents of satan, many preachers who were called by God have compromised the Word of God and Christian standards, because of ignorance, fame, and love of money.

Many want to be known as the most popular preacher, the richest preacher, or the most influential preacher. Others want to have the largest congregation, the fastest growing church, or the biggest cathedral. Many ministers have lost the vision of the souls of men, and they are interested in money and other material things.

Why do Christians dress and appear like the people of the world? It is because there are many Jezebels and agents of the kingdom of darkness (especially the mermaid water kingdom) in many churches. This is why many preachers and churches have accepted what they used to call sin before, as being good and harmless now.

Many of them get committed in church activities, that the pastors wouldn't even know that they are agents of the kingdom of darkness; and the pastors begin to promote them, thereby helping them in their seductive and destructive works. When they dress that way and speak their demonic tongues, giving their demonic prophecies, the pastor and others will welcome them.

They will say, "Since this sister dresses like this, wears this, and paints this way, and yet is too spiritual, then nothing is really wrong with these things." And the devil will ask the other Believers and Christians, "Did God really say that it is sinful to dress this way, wear weavons, and paint this way?"

Then the other Believers and Christians will become 'sincerely' deceived (if sincerity is applicable at all, because many of them want it; and if you stop or forbid them, they will criticize and hate you). And when the pastor sees that many or majority of his members are like that, it will be as if water was poured on his spiritual energy to speak against those things.

I have observed that girls, ladies, and women like what appeals to the eyes. I am talking of believing girls, ladies, and women. In fact, the Christianity of many of them doesn't reach that side. If you speak against their worldly appearance, you will become their enemy. They will try as much as possible to find what they will use to justify themselves, because they want to look attractive and 'sharp.'

This is the same thing that put the world into the mess it is in today. In the beginning: "The woman saw (and they still see) that the tree was good for food, that it was pleasant to the eyes (Have you seen and confirmed what I am saying?), and a tree desirable to make one wise, she took of its fruit and ate" (Gen. 3:6).

My sister, whether or not you like it, the way to Heaven is a narrow way. And the Bible says, "Enter by the narrow gate; for wide is the gate and broad is the way that leads to destruction, and there are many who go in by it. Because narrow is the gate and difficult is the way which leads to life, and there are few who find it" (Matt. 7:13-14).

Luke added something when he said, "Strive to enter through the narrow gate, for many, I say to you, will seek to enter and will not be able" (Lk. 13:24). How many people are willing and ready to strive to enter through the narrow gate?

Yet, don't be deceived by appearance, because many agents of the kingdom of darkness dress like Christian ladies, to deceive people into thinking that they are Christians. To this end, know that some of them wear long skirts, tie headties, and wouldn't paint their lips. Be careful, so that the devil will not trap you down!

These days are last days, and the devil is fighting tooth and nail to draw as many people as he can to Hell Fire, to suffer eternal torment and punishment with him. The devil hates the human race with great passion; the human agents he uses are deceived into thinking that he loves them.

We are talking of indecent dressing and outward appearance. And what we have said so far concerns other areas of the life of a Christian. There are many things that people (Believers) do today, and say that they do not matter. It may strike your mind to know that even many unbelievers know that Christians should not live or be those ways.

You have to decide what you want. Do you want to please God or yourself? Do you want to obey the Truth or false teaching? Do you want to make it to Heaven or Hell? Do you want to receive abundant reward from the Lord or suffer loss? Make your decision now before it becomes too late!

Worldliness has crept into the lives of many Believers, especially in these last days. But one thing is that God's Word and Standard cannot change for any person or group of persons. God's Word is forever settled in Heaven: God hates worldliness. Worldliness is living like the people of the world. And concerning what we are discussing, it is appearing like the people of the world.

One of the major problems in many churches today is what somebody called 'churchiality without Christianity.' It is going to church, without being born again. It is being born again, without being committed to the Lord Jesus Christ. It is to be led and directed by the flesh, instead of being led and directed by the Word of God and His Holy Spirit.

Because many are in the churches, without being born again and committed to the Lordship of Jesus Christ, they live and appear like the people of the world; and before you know it, many Believers start joining or following them to live and appear like the people of the world, because they assume that those people, since they are members of our churches, are fellow Believers.

James put this matter in a strong form: "Adulterers and adulteresses! Do you not know that friendship with the world is enmity with God? Whoever therefore wants to be a friend of the world makes himself an enemy of God. Or do you think that the Scripture says in vain, 'The Spirit Who dwells in us yearns jealously (or, lusteth to envy, KJV)?'" (Jas 4:4-5).

What are you thinking, as you are reading this material? That you will change tomorrow? Tomorrow may be too late. Furthermore, if you don't make up your mind and take the right decision, accompanied by prayer, the devil can come and remove the Word from you. You may find out that the same Word that is burning in your heart now will not be felt much by you tomorrow.

How did people who rejected worldliness before accept it latter? By carelessness, lust of the flesh and the eyes, and by false teachings. A woman told me that she can never use weavon (or, is it attachment?) again, not just because I said it, but because she has known the truth about it. Brother, before you know what happened, she had started using it again. God told me the woman loved the world.

When preachings go forth, the women and ladies repent, cry, weep, and sob more than the men. Yet they are the ones that are easily deceived and led astray more than the men. Why is this the case? Apostle Paul said that it was not the man that was deceived, but the woman (1 Tim. 2:14).

If you see the kinds and appearances of dresses that parents put on their children, you will weep, if your understanding has been sharpened along this line. And those parents will expect those children to stop wearing those kinds of dresses when they grow up. They have been deceived, and they think they are wiser than God, Who said, "Train up the child in the way he should go, and when he/she is old he/she will not depart from it" (Prov. 22:6).

Any skirt or gown that is at the knee level as you are standing, which when you sit down, people can see your laps (even if it is a small part of your laps) is from the devil. Any skirt or gown that will require your covering yourself with handkerchief when you sit down is of demons (demon-inspired design). Any skirt or gown which when you sit down in a car, either as the driver or as a passenger, somebody can see your laps, originated from the wisdom of satan.

Read Exodus 20:26. Read also Exodus 28:42. If God was so much interested in the nakedness of His priests (which were even men) not being seen by people, how much more in this New Testament does He not want the nakedness of His daughters to be seen by men! And you say that you are a New Testament priest: why then are you not happy with making your gowns and skirts to be long enough to prevent people from seeing your laps (even when you are sitting down)?

Many women and ladies live in hypocrisy: when there is cold, the women cover themselves well to avoid it; but they will not care if their dressing is instigating lust and causing men to go Hell. Do they love Jesus Christ in reality?

In clearer words, the gown or skirt of a Christian and Godly woman, lady, or girl should not be shorter than halfway between her knee and her ankle, as she is standing up. This will guard against people seeing her laps when she sits down. These modern-day short (knee-level) gowns and skirts came from the wisdom and plans of the devil and his devils, whether or not you believe this Truth! The devil is very subtle and crafty.

If God is not interested in your body (or how you appear), why do you ask for (or claim) bodily healing or Divine health on your body? Many Believers allow the devil to deceive and mislead them with foolishness. How can you do try-and-luck (bet) with your eternal destiny in Heaven or Hell, when there wouldn't be any second chance?

What many people bind the devil of, are nothing but the works of the flesh. If you refuse to take up your responsibility, by obeying the Word of God, you will open a way for the devil; because he, who breaks the hedge, will be bitten by the serpent. Obey God, and those devils will leave by themselves! This will make it possible for you to have fewer things to pray and fast about.

The problem of many churches today is the presence of mixed multitude and great multitude. Yes, great multitude is good; but are you directing their hearts to the Lord and His Word? Today, you see unbelieving chorus leaders and musicians in the church. Many of them sing under the influence of drugs and alcohol. Some of them smoke. What a pity!

This is why you see worldly tones of music being played in many churches today. When you hear worldly tones of reggae, disco, awilo, makosa, etc, you should know that the end time is here with us. They will call God, Jesus, and speak Biblical things in the music; but the tone and beat is demonically programmed and attracts demons.

Choreographic dance is of the devil, for at least two reasons. First, it sends lustful impulses and thoughts to male watchers, which is one of the reasons why the devil introduced it into churches. Also, it makes people to put and focus their attention on the dancers and their body movements instead of focusing on worshipping God. Also, traditional dances are not to be used in the church, because they originated from demons who inspired those heathen traditions.

Concerning music and dancing, the Bible says, "Now the works of the flesh are evident, which are...revelries...of which I tell you beforehand, just as I also told you in time past, that those who practice such things will not inherit the Kingdom of God (Gal. 5:19-21).

"For we have spent enough of our past time in doing the will of the Gentiles – when we walked in...revelries..." (1 Pet. 4:3). According to the Longman Dictionary of Contemporary English, revelry means wild noisy dancing. God is against worldly, satanic, and demonic dancing, music, and tones, even in the church!

The Word of God tells us to prove or test all things, and to hold fast what is good (1 Thes. 5:21). Apostle John put it this way: "Beloved, do not believe every spirit, but test the spirits whether they are of God; because many false prophets have gone out into the world (1 Jn 4:1). Apostle Paul gave us another striking Word when he said, "Let two or three prophets speak, and let others judge" (1 Cor. 14:29).

Have you seen that even prophecies are to be judged and tested with the Word of God and the intuition or witness in your spirit by the Holy Spirit? When we talk of false prophets, many people seem to detect or suspect possible false prophets from their states or countries, and they count the foreign preachers as true ministers. My brother, they exist – locally, nationally, and internationally.

If they were preaching and teaching the Truth, without bringing people into satanic and demonic bondages, I wouldn't have been so much concerned. Why? Because Jesus Christ spoke to His Disciples, saying, "The scribes and the Pharisees sit in Moses' seat. Therefore whatever they tell you to observe, that observe and do, but do not do according to their works; for they say, and do not do" (Matt. 23:2-3).

They also use the Bible, quoting it to you, as the devil quoted it to Jesus Christ in the wilderness, to deceive people. They mix the Bible with the doctrines and teachings of demons and seducing spirits, and they deceive many. People hear them and say, "That is a great man of God!" People clap hands for them, and say, "Ride on, pastor!"

How do you know a false minister? By his words and practices. If his teachings and practices are against Sound Doctrine, run away from him. If he is interested in your money and not your soul, run away from him.

I am not just talking about somebody who may be making a minor mistake, because somebody may make a mistake (though God doesn't want it). But many of them know what they are doing. They know that they are working for the devil. They know they are working for money and fame.

I will tell you that many (or most) of all these beauty salons in town are owned by agents of the kingdom of darkness. Even those who are not direct or conscious agents have been demonized, in that their minds have been influenced or obsessed by the devil into doing that business, because the business glorifies the devil a lot.

When your business expands the works of the kingdom of darkness, are you not their agent? Whether or not you attend their night meetings, you are working for them. I know that, just as many Believers use those materials ignorantly, there are people who do the business, though they are not conscious or direct agents of the kingdom of darkness.

Yet, it doesn't change the fact that they are standing or working for the devil. Am I saying that women shouldn't take care of their hair? No, but they should do it in a Godly manner. Every sincere Christian lady or woman, who seeks to know, will be directed by the Holy Spirit on how to take care of her hair.

Therefore, if you take care of people's hair, as a Believer, you have to do it in a Godly manner. Any business that glorifies the devil and expands the kingdom of darkness, cannot be from God.

The beauty salons, the beauty stores, and the fashion centres, what do they stand for? The person that sales bleaching creams, and helps people to call God stupid for giving them the skin complexion they have, is he or she working for God or for satan? I will rather tell you the Truth and you hate me, than thwart the Word of God, and your blood will be on my head; after all, I am not interested in your sinful money!

If you are a tailor or a clothing designer/maker, what type of dresses and wears do you make for your customers/clients? We have demonic fashion designers also. They tell our good Christian ladies and women, "This style will not make you look 'sharp' and attractive." They will not use the word – seductive, because they are bent to deceive.

And before you know what is happening, you will see a Christian girl, lady, or woman wearing what will show us her armpits, her breasts, and her laps. Some demonic ladies will even carry those types of wears, and sit in front of the church congregation, so as to attempt to lead the man of God on the altar into lust and fornication, so that he will be reduced to an ordinary man, like the Philistines, with their Delilah, did to the 'powerful' Samson.

So, when you sell those marine weavons, demonic attachments, satanic nails, devilish cortex, bloody make-ups, and many other things in the group, are you a Christian, a Believer, or a Disciple? If you are a disciple, are you a disciple of satan or a Disciple of the Lord Jesus Christ? Who are you working for? What do you stand for?

Even those of you, who will make a long skirt, and divide (or, will I say, 'tear') that long skirt at the back, side, or front so that it reveals what a miniskirt or a short-skirt reveals, are you saying that you don't know what you are doing? If you say you did it to be able to walk freely, then why did you make a tight-fitting skirt in the first place? Others will cut their blouses or gowns to show us their back.

Get ready, for judgment is coming. I am not a prophet of doom, but a prophet of the Word of God; and I know that the Great Judge is ready to judge all unrighteousness! Therefore, count your soul more precious than your appearance now!

Those worldly and fashionable wedding gowns should be abolished for Believers and churches. Those wedding gowns are made to be glamorous, flamboyant, gorgeous, and for show and fashion. You may say that it is your day; but the Bible says, "Let your moderation be known unto all men. The Lord is at hand" (Phil. 4:5). Many people even go to the extent of making or using wedding gowns that reveal their sensitive parts.

Men wear (or make) normal wears or suits that they still wear even after the wedding ceremony. Therefore, the bride's wear or dress should be made to be normal and in such a way as to be something she can still wear at any other time after the wedding ceremony. It can be a gown or a skirt and blouse. Yes, make it to look good, but not something for fashion, show, or glamour.

Saying things like this may seem somehow, because my wife used wedding gown during our wedding. Even though the one she used covered her, yet, if I were to wed now, I cannot allow my wife to wear the conventional wedding gowns (even though now, weddings are done in many churches with those wedding gowns), because it does not reflect moderation, humility, Christ-likeness, and the Bible: it shows excesses for show.

But just because I didn't know the Truth at that time will not make me not to say the Truth when I know it. For instance, 'naturally', I myself hated (and I still hate) rings; but when I married, I loved (I think it was not just a liking) wearing wedding ring (maybe for the love of a husband for the wife). But I cannot wear a wedding ring again, because it is still a ring. Will I encourage wearing wedding rings because I loved or worn it?

Formerly, when people had good sense and judgment, the blouses of women were made in such a way that they didn't have buttons at the front, from their chest to their waist. But now, satanic fashion designers have designed what they call blouses for women which have spaced buttons from their chests downwards. And when they wear them, their breasts will push the material, so that someone can see their breasts from the spaces between the buttons.

The devil knew what he did in that demonic design. If their blouses are to be made that way, then they must have very well sealed zips, and not spaced buttons. When people listened to their consciences, men's shirts were made with spaced buttons, because men don't have breasts that will push open their chests. And don't wear those hanging blouses, which when you sit down or lift up your hands, your underwear will be exposed. Say "Amen!"

Men must button up their shirts (that is, they are not to leave their chests open). If you, as a woman, must wear a blouse with buttons, make sure it is not the kind that will reveal your breast or brassiere in-between the buttons. Zips are preferable to buttons for women's blouses; complete undivided blouses with neither zips nor buttons are best for women. Those short hanging jackets worldly women wear are satanic.

If many of our ladies and women will devote the energy they use to beautify themselves, to work on their spirit and soul, brother, many husbands will be running to their homes immediately they are through with their work and business. However, even in the homes of many Believers, the husbands prefer to stay away from home as much as possible.

When you talk to your husband as if he doesn't have authority over you, do you think that he will want to stay with you? This is one of the reasons why many unbelieving husbands go after strange women, because when they see the lady that will honour and respect them, the devil tells them, "Have you seen?"

And the Bible says, "Wives, likewise, be submissive to your own husbands, that even if some do not obey the Word, they, without a word, may be won by the conduct of their wives, when they observe your chaste conduct accompanied by fear" (1 Pet. 3:1-2).

On this issue of the dressing of the women, women should make their dresses – blouses, skirts, gowns, and wrappers – in such a way that they will cover their sensitive parts. When you dress, people shouldn't see your laps, breasts, and armpits. Make your skirts in such a way that even when you sit down, people shouldn't see your laps. If you use handkerchief to cover it when you sit down, are you hypocritical?

Your sensitive parts are for your husband; therefore reserve them for him, and not for us. When you keep on straightening your skirts or you use handkerchief to cover your laps as you are sitting down, why didn't you tell them to make it longer than it is, when they were making it? Or, are you deceiving yourself?

Use the blouses that were made with well-sealed zips. Condemn those blouses which, when you put them on, people, other than your husband, see your breasts in-between buttons; you understand? You are a Christian, and not an unbeliever! The neck of your blouse is to be in such a way that even when you bend down, no one will see your breast.

Don't wear body-hug dresses, because they reveal your body contours. Don't wear see-through dresses. What do I mean by see-through dresses? In physics, the scientists talk of transparent, translucent, and opaque materials. The translucent materials are semi-opaque and semi-transparent. The see-through dresses are the semi-covering and semi-uncovering dresses.

Many Believers wear short-skirts, and they 'think' that because the skirts are not miniskirts, then nothing is wrong with the skirts. A sincere, serious, and dedicated Christian whose mind is in Heaven (and whose eye has not been blinded by the devil) will not be comfortable wearing a short-skirt. A short skirt or gown is the one which when you sit down, somebody can see any part of your laps; while a miniskirt or mini-gown is the one which even when you are standing up, somebody can see your laps.

If, as a man, I open the back or front of my shirt the way some women open the back or front of their blouses and gowns, will you be happy? And if a man will not open his front or back, how much more the women!

Your armpits are not to be seen when you lift up your hands; therefore, the sleeves of your blouses and gowns must be made, both in length and in design, in such a way as to guard against this.

In your church, ministry, or fellowship, be mindful of the dressing and appearance of those who minister, speak, or appear before the crowd, especially those that appear before them often; because they, consciously or unconsciously, tell the rest of the people how they should dress and appear.

To this end, the pastor and minister should be mindful of how his wife dresses and appears, because many women, ladies, and girls in the church, ministry, or fellowship will likely learn from her. Many churches, ministries, and fellowships that dress and appear like the people of the world became that way because of the ministers' wives and other women leaders and ministers.

And don't even wear shorts or trousers inside your skirt or gown; use your appropriate underwears. Somebody may say that she will wear shorts to avoid being raped; but it is God Who keeps and protects you. By the way, even trousers will not stop being raped; but God will stop it. The person who can forcefully rape you can also pull the trousers; and at gunpoint, if you fear weapons instead of believing and trusting God, you yourself will pull the trousers out. But if you do the right thing, angels of God are there to intervene on your behalf. Also, don't use trousers for night-wears: don't allow the devil to deceive you.

Be careful of the pictures and signs that are drawn or imposed on your blouses, shirts, wears, and dresses. The devil puts satanic, demonic, devilish, and occult pictures and signs on some wears and dresses to entangle and enslave people. Those pictures and signs can attract and permit the presence of demons and their works.

Do not use Lycra material to make your dresses and clothes. Lycra material is a material that stretches, which is used for making tight-fitting clothes. This is because it tights your body and shows your body contours, thereby sending lustful messages and impulses to the opposite sex. God hates the use of it for dresses and clothes.

Do not send your children to any school where they are forced to wear sleeveless dresses and clothes as their school uniform: they will end up corrupting them. And the schools which use such school uniforms either have demonic targets from the leadership, have been deceived by the devil and his demons, or they have satanic workers/teachers (conscious or unconscious). Of course, this is not to say that all schools where they wear sleeved dresses and clothes are free from demonic works.

Men dress up to cover their chest and back; who then designed (or planned the design of) the open chest blouses or gowns that show women's breasts' cleavage and breasts, or the open back blouses or gowns that show their back? It could be no other beings/people than satan and his associates; they are the beings/people that stand against the Will of God and promote lust among men.

For those who say that they use pairs of trousers to guard against cold, the human race has been in existence for about six thousand years on the surface of this earth: Did people not keep themselves safe from cold from the beginning of the human race till about some decades ago when women started wearing trousers, which many of them hypocritically call slacks?

You, as a Christian lady, should appear natural. What do we men lose by appearing natural? You may say you want to attract people, but you are attracting men (whether or not they are Believers) who have not known the Truth, because those things get me annoyed, when I see them on the bodies of believing ladies and women. Therefore, all those lipsticks, cortexes, demonic/artificial nails, and paint or pencil will not be required.

Somebody asked me, saying, "Can I use brown powder since I use white powder?" One needs to wonder why some women want to look horrible the way they look. Why do people really want to paint themselves as if they are buildings that need to be painted and repainted? Many of those women seem not to know that their minds have been obsessed by demons, and they 'do not even know' what they are doing to themselves. I wonder why many husbands allow their wives to dress and appear the way they appear! Some men even tell their wives to look that horrible.

Well, as for the question of, "Can I use brown powder since I use white powder?" Why do you want to use the brown powder? The Bible says, "Moreover, when you fast, do not be like the hypocrites, with a sad countenance. For they disfigure their faces that they may appear to men to be fasting. Assuredly, I say to you, they have their reward. But you, when you fast, anoint your head and wash your face, so that you do not appear to men to be fasting, but to your Father Who is in the Secret Place; and your Father Who sees in secret will reward you openly" (Matt. 6:16-18).

Here Jesus Christ tells you to use ointment on your head and wash your face instead of disorganizing your head (hair), wearing sackcloth, and sitting on ashes, to appear to men to be fasting. But notice that the purpose for anointing your head (rubbing oil/ointment on your hair) and washing your face is for you to look normal, so that people will not know that you are fasting.

Of course, it is not compulsory that you anoint your head and wash your face whenever you fasting, because if you were to be in the desert, on the mountain, or in the room alone, where people will not see you, you may decide to neither anoint your head nor wash your face, at least for some time. However, the purpose of the anointing (rubbing) and washing is to appear normal.

So, whereas somebody may use white powder to remove or neutralize oil on his or her face, another person may just wipe his or her face with a handkerchief to remove the oil that might have been accumulated on his or her face, maybe due to heat. But why will you even paint/parch your face with white powder or brown powder? Do you want white or brown colour for your face and 'building'?

Therefore, apart from the brown powder issue, there is certainly a difference between using white powder to neutralize oil on your face and using white powder to paint your face. So, apart from using white powder to neutralize oil on your face, using white powder (maybe the medicated one) to stop or treat heat rashes on your body, or for any other good special case(s), do not even paint your face with white powder for beauty. Of course, this concerns both males and females.

Don't put your mind on costly or expensive things. Never be obsessed by them. Moderately priced and inexpensive clothing is good for the women. It helps to prevent pride. Don't pressurize your husband to buy expensive things for you; for it will not be to your advantage. If the man starts misbehaving and disobeying the Word of God in order to satisfy you, you will suffer it more.

Why? Because when someone starts stealing, lying, or cheating, the fellow can also start following strange women, since they are all from the same heart. Any person, who can be committing evil and hiding it from men, without fearing God Who sees all things, can do what you may not believe.

God said to Jacob, "Arise go up to Bethel and dwell there; and make an altar there to God, Who appeared to you when you fled from the face of Esau your brother." And Jacob said to his household and all who were with him, "Put away the foreign gods that are among you, purify yourselves, and change your garments. Then let us go up to Bethel...."

So they gave Jacob all the foreign gods which were in their hands, and the earrings which were in their ears; and Jacob hid (buried) them under the terebinth tree which was by Shechem. And they journeyed, and the Terror of God was upon the cities that were all around them, and they did not pursue the sons of Jacob (Gen. 35:1-5).

Earrings were among the things they purified themselves from to be clean before God. The Egyptians, Babylonians, Assyrians, Mesopotamians, and the other foreign and heathen nations were given to these things, just as the people of the world today. When you leave the world, you will also leave these things.

And piercing your ear to wear earrings is of the devil. Why do you pierce your ear? Are you a slave? If your ears were pierced by your parents, having repented from it, how can you wear earrings in it again? Where then is your repentance?

When God told Moses to tell the children of Israel to collect those things from the Egyptians, God wanted to plunder the Egyptians, because they made those things from gold and silver. And the Israelites, instead of keeping those things for the construction of the Ark of the Testimony and other things, they started with using them to construct a calf which they worshipped, and said that it was the calf that brought them out of Egypt (Exo. 32). God was very angry with them for that act; and had it not been that Moses interceded for them, He would have wiped them out!

People wear and use things that bring them into the bondage of the devil, even unknowingly. And God says that His people are destroyed for lack of knowledge (Hos. 4:6); and His people have gone into captivity, because they have no knowledge (Isa. 5:13). When you use the things that God has condemned, you are selling yourself to the devil, and he will oppress you. The devil, satan, is a master-strategist: he wants to have your spirit, soul, and body; and if he doesn't get this one, he will go for the other.

Earrings, bangles, rings, necklaces, and such things are not needed on your body by God. They promote the desire of the devil, which is ornamenting your body. Even wedding rings won't be necessary. Of course, you would have seen some who would even put an extra ring on top of the wedding ring to make it look more beautiful. Who even invented the wedding ring as a means of distinguishing the married from the unmarried? Get rid of wedding rings and engagement rings from your fingers, brothers and sisters! Your soul is much more precious than wedding rings and engagement rings.

Some people try to use Abraham (or his servant) to defend themselves in this issue; but they fail to know that Abraham didn't know everything at the same time. Before Jacob grew up and matured, having come from Isaac of Abraham (many years after Abraham), they would have known how God reacts to those things.

Remember that Abraham was a heathen and idol worshipper (from Ur of the Chaldeans – Babylonians) before he was called by God; and he had learned their ways. It still took some time to refine him. Abraham lied on two different occasions, because of fear (and Isaac also lied over his wife, because of fear). Does that make lying good, because Abraham lied?

If your dresses are worldly in appearance, condemn them, because of Jesus Christ and your soul. Don't be afraid, for God is able to provide you with new good dresses. Don't put your trust in man, no matter what he owns: put your trust in God, and His angels will bring all you need to you in due time.

The same things that were happening when God destroyed the whole earth with the Flood are happening now. The same things that the Israelites (God's people) did, for which God destroyed them in the wilderness, are happening today in many churches.

When God destroyed the world, they didn't carry arms for Him; they didn't shoot at Him with guns: they were disobedient to His Commands, and they lived to gratify the lusts of their eyes and the desires of their flesh.

And the same things that happened to the people of old, will happen to many (even Believers) in the Last Day, but in a different dimension – Hell Fire. The Church is giving the Lord Jesus Christ more 'headache' and trouble than the world! But just as the Jews didn't believe Prophet Jeremiah until they were engulfed in the disaster that God brought upon them, many will not believe this Message and Word until they will end in Hell Fire.

God is not from any nation, and He owns all nations. Though we know, from the Bible, that God has a special link with the nation of Israel, yet, He is not from Israel. Israel cannot dictate for Him; and He will not change His Standard because of Israel. God cannot change His Standard for anyone and for any church. No matter how anointed you are, no matter what you may have, all came from God.

Many people do the things they do, because they think that since people from this or that nation do the same things, they must be right; but this is not true in the ultimate sense. The thing that many people seem to fail to understand is that the devil is working in every nation of the earth.

No matter the nation you may come from, the devil had been working in your nation before you were born, and he will continue to work there. The devil has succeeded to work in many nations without being recognized.

There are many things that are being done in some nations of the world, which people don't see as having come from the devil. For instance, when a country legalizes abortion, whether or not they know it, the work of the devil is being fulfilled in their midst.

God hates abortion; for no one has right to take any other person's life. No matter the theory or proposition medical science may make to make abortion look good, they are just dancing to the tone of the devil's deception. Once the zygote has been formed, a human being has come.

Let us consider the issue of women liberation movements. Have you noticed the rate of divorce and juvenile delinquencies these days? These are the long-term effects of women liberation movements.

When women decide to abandon their basic responsibilities in pursuit of secondary issues, the devil is at work, whether they recognize it or not. Women have the responsibility to be helpers suitable to their husbands.

We will now consider the issue of whether it is good for women to put on trousers. One thing about dresses is that they are meant to cover the person putting them on, whether they are men or women.

Gowns, wrappers, skirts, blouses, trousers, shirts, etc, are to cover the person wearing them. I want you to know that over the years, in every continent (America, Europe, Africa, Asia, etc), there have been changes in the modes of their dressing.

However, any dressing or change in dressing that does not glorify God is satanic and demonic, no matter what any person may think or say, even though you may not have it in mind as you put them on. That is the Truth. The devil prefers to work under cover and without being noticed.

When women put on sleeveless blouses, mini-skirts, tight-fitting and partly transparent (revealing) dresses, they are glorifying satan, and helping him to fulfil his purpose, whether or not they know it.

As I said before, considering the biological features of women, women should not use pairs of trousers. Why? When a woman is matured sexually, one of the features that biologists tell us will be noticed in her is enlarged buttocks. Have you never noticed that trousers show their body contours for everybody to see? Trousers reveal their buttocks and laps seductively.

Now, don't say that you are going to allow your children wear pairs of trousers, and when they mature they will stop using them. If you train them up that way, when they are old, they will not depart from it (Prov. 22:6).

But seductive dresses or dressing seductively helps the devil spread his lust wave, and people get into the sins of lust, fornication, adultery, etc. Some will say that whoever wants to fall will fall; but you and I know that some things can make someone fall, when he wouldn't have fallen without them.

Let the Spirit of God lead you, and do not be led by your mind and thought. Trousers are neither an American culture nor a British culture. It started at a time, and got so much opposition there then; but over so many years later, the opposition has waned so much that some think it is their culture.

After all, was there anything like America until Amerigo sailed past the Atlantic Ocean and found the land which was later developed to be America? And it is Britain that developed and colonized America before they got their independence. And all countries and continents of the world will appear before God for judgment.

Know this once again: any dressing that helps the devil fulfil his will, plan, and purpose is from him. If you can't stop dressing this or that way because of Jesus Christ, can you lay down your life for Him? (Matt. 10:39). Don't you want to be worthy of Him?

Christians (both males and females) should avoid wearing jeans materials for some reasons. Jeans tight your body to show your body-contours. Jeans seem to have been made/designed by the devil to provoke rough, wild, and worldly feeling and lifestyle, as evident in the fact that you may see some of them as stone-wash jeans, jeans which look like they have been decolourized (or partly decolourized), perforated jeans with different kinds of openings, patched jeans with pieces of the material sewn on it, torn jeans proudly worn as style (whereas other clothing materials that are torn would make the same person feel ashamed), jeans trousers or shorts with rough cutting or design at the edges, etc.

If the physical appearance of many Believers are worldly, how much more the sins of spirit and soul (inward sins) that are hidden from us! If many Believers don't care about their worldly appearance, how much more do they care less concerning the hidden sins (inward sins) which we do not see!

God hates tribal marks and tattooing your body, as He said, "You shall not make any cuttings in your flesh for the dead, nor tattoo any marks on you: I am the Lord" (Lev. 19:28). No matter the kind of design or picture you tattoo yourself with, it is evil.

Funky (modern and fashionable) style of hair cut like what is called 'punk', 'afro-cut', etc must not find its place in you. Also, leave your hair the natural shape it has in haircut; and avoid carving it, for it gives it an unnatural or/and fashionable shape.

There are many reasons why Christians should not use weavons. Using weavons is like telling God that He is stupid and imperfect for giving you the kind of hair you have. It is like bleaching, which many do; they feel that God should have made them fair in complexion instead of dark. But on the Day of Judgment, you will find out that you tried to degrade God. Using relaxer and hair extensions for your hair or another person's hair is demonic and satanic in origin, and leads to Hell Fire.

The Word says, "For this reason God gave them up to vile passions. For even their women exchanged the natural use for what is against nature. Likewise also the men, leaving the natural use of the woman, burned in their lust for one another, men with men committing what is shameful, and receiving in themselves the penalty of their error which was due" (Rom. 1:26-27).

This place implies turning the nature to artificial/perversion in women/men. Turning the nature to artificial/perversion in women/men does not only apply to lesbianism and homosexualism. Of course, the Bible emphasized on homosexualism here; but on the side of the women, it says, "…women exchanged the natural use for what is against nature."

And you see the exchanging of the natural for what is against nature and God's Plan, Wisdom, and Ability in bleaching the skin, perfuming the body, painting the nails with cortex, fixing of artificial nails, frying and perming the hair, artificially relaxing and extending the hair, painting the face with lipstick and eye-pencil, dyeing the hair, fixing of eyelashes, using and wearing of weavons and attachments, tattooing the body, etc.

And, "The Wrath of God is revealed from Heaven against all ungodliness and unrighteousness of men, who suppress the Truth in unrighteousness, because what may be known of God is manifest in them, for God has shown it to them" (Rom. 1:18). You can see that God has given and shown you the reason why you shouldn't change His Handiwork; therefore, if you do, then you decided to corrupt yourself, turn yourself against God, suffer unnecessary things in this earth, and finally deprive yourself of Heaven!

God asked whether a leopard can change its spot, because He has made it that way (Jer. 13:23); and many human beings say, "God, we are wiser than You and leopards, and we know how to change our skin." The Ethiopians would have refused to change their skin in the old times; now many of them may do it because of science and technology.

It is like those who use high-heel shoes to increase their height, because they feel that they should be taller than they are. When Jesus Christ tells you not to worry about your height, because you can't add a cubit to it (Matt. 6:27), you say, "God, I know how to increase my not-good size in height."

Some use perfume to say, "Why must people not identify my scent? This natural neutral 'scent' is too boring!" Why do people try to bring themselves into different bondages? Others use breast-pads to make their breasts look big and seductive. When you see some others paint themselves with powder, you wonder why they want to look that way in the first place!

Never Say That God Said What He Did Not Say!

Many others say, "God, it is not now that I should have grey (gray) hair; I am still young." (Grey is British English, while gray is American English). And they end up dyeing their hair. Many spend hours designing themselves – time they should have used for Godly and spiritual things. The silver-haired head is a crown of glory, if it is found in the way of righteousness (Prov. 16:31). The glory of young men is their strength, and the splendour of old men is their grey head (Prov. 20:29). Silver-haired or grey head is the Handiwork of God!

Also, many of those weavons are real human hair which were cut and sold. How can you be wearing another person's hair as a Christian lady or woman? This is worldliness; this is satanic and demonic; sister, the ground you are treading on is dangerous.

Then, even though some of those weavons may be synthetic or artificial (which the first point still condemns), many of those weavons ladies use are manufactured in the water-kingdom of darkness and brought to this earth for sales to contaminate the people of the world.

The thing that some people don't know is that some companies which exist physically on this earth came from the dark kingdom of satan, especially the water-world of the devil. In fact, many things we see physically came from the dark kingdom. Even many legal and morally good things (like pre-fabricated food) we see are manufactured in the dark kingdom, some of which I wouldn't mention here.

This is why you need to pray over and sanctify the things that you use, especially edible things. But how will you want to sanctify the things that the Lord has rejected and condemned (like weavons, artificial nails, wet-lips, lipsticks, eyelashes, etc)? You are already offending God!

Everything is not demonic, don't misunderstand me; don't live in fear either, because greater is He that is in us than he that is in the world. The anointing breaks every yoke of the enemy. But many Christians create loopholes for the devil through sin, disobedience, and worldliness.

You need to be watchful and sober, because if you are not, the devil can lead you into sin and worldliness; and if the Lord Jesus Christ meets you in that state at His Coming, or you die in that state, you will miss Heaven and go to Hell.

But that is not God's Plan for you; and He did not bring you out of the world to condemn you later. Therefore, don't condemn yourself. You condemn yourself by despising His Word and the Promptings of His Spirit.

Many are busy 'binding and loosing' the devil while they are the ones that are inviting the devil. Preachers and ministers, many of you are busy saying you are destroying the works of the devil, while the devil is binding people comfortably through worldliness among Believers. May their blood not be on your hands because you refused to tell them the Truth!

Some say that it is not written in the Bible that you must not smoke. Okay, continue to destroy your body, which is the Temple of God (1 Cor. 3:16), until you hear, "Get behind Me, you who practice iniquity!" Cigarette is a destructive tool of satan, the devil. It is suicide in disguise.

Others say that it is alright to drink alcohol as far as you don't get drunk (or in small quantity). Firstly, assuming that the wine which Apostle Paul told Timothy to drink was not a totally non-alcoholic wine, little sense should have told you that if the Believers of the New Testament were drinking it in small quantity, Apostle Paul wouldn't have needed to tell Timothy to take small of it as medicine.

Even if you have stomach problem, do you now envy that archaic and unrefined medical practice when you have always wanted development and civilization, just because you want to satisfy your flesh? Will you have the boldness to defend yourself before God on the Judgment Day? Can you forsake alcohol for God and for your soul?

Secondly, according to the Dake's Annotated Reference Bible's explanation of 1 Tim. 5:23, "With two kinds of wine mentioned in the Scripture – one, unfermented new wine found in the cluster (Isa. 65:8), we can be assured that Timothy was not urged to take the intoxicating kind to strengthen him." Someone may ask, "If this is true, then why did he tell him to drink little of it?" First, you don't even have to drink non-alcoholic drink to excess.

Second, who knows whether they (Timothy was his disciple and associate) had altogether stopped drinking even non-alcoholic wine as a kind of self-denial, continuous partial fasting, or living the fasted life, even as John the Baptist did not eat and drink all kinds of even morally good food and drinks? Even now, many Believers and ministers decide to (or, are commanded by God) to stop or minimize the intake of certain kinds of food or/and drinks as a way of self-denial and living the fasted life.

The Bible says, "Who has woe? Who has sorrow? Who has contentions? Who has complaints? Who has wounds without cause? Who has redness of eyes? Those who linger long at the wine; those who go in search of mixed wine. Do not look on the wine when it is red, when it sparkles in the cup, when it swirls around smoothly; at the last it bites like a serpent, and stings like a viper. Your eyes will see strange things, and your heart will utter perverse things" (Prov. 23:29-33).

Here, the Bible says, "Do not look on the wine…." Can you take a small amount of what you are not supposed to look on to? That is to say, "Don't even desire any amount of wine or alcohol." Whether the wine contains 1% or 5% of alcohol, it is still alcohol and sinful. Can you allow small amount of alcohol to take you to Hell?

When a company that manufactures wine puts '5% alcohol' on the label of the wine, it shows that they know the difference between wine that is free from alcohol and the one with alcohol. And there was no alcoholic content in the wine that Jesus Christ made. No wonder the master of the feast said, "…You have kept the good wine until now!" (Jn 2:10). Jesus Christ made a good quality wine with a difference!

People used to abort unborn human beings in secret before; now satanic and demonic laws have empowered them. And subtly and craftily, the enemy (satan, the devil) has 'moralized' abortion in certain birth-control measures.

People used to smoke secretly before; now they are bold to smoke anyhow outside. Homosexuals and lesbians used to practice their wickedness in secret and darkness, being ashamed of it; now they even boast that they are homosexuals and lesbians. Boasting and waiting for damnation in Hell Fire!

The devil has penetrated and destroyed many people through films. Most of those films from Hollywood, Nollywood, and others promote the works of the devil. Even, many (or most) of the so-called Christian films still advertize and promote the works of the devil.

When films are promoting immorality, indecent dressing, vices, violence, hatred, and other demonic activities, do they promote God? Be careful with the type of film that you and your family watch! Many of those films are dedicated to the devil to serve his interest and increase sales; and so, playing them attracts the presence of demons into your house (and to the watchers). Watching of wrestling, karate, horror films, and many others are inspired by the devil.

So, you film director, producer, actor, or actress, whose interest are you serving? Who is inspiring you, and who are you working for? Sometimes, the devil will wittingly package some of the films in such a way that they look harmless; but ultimately, his interest is being promoted.

Just as many Believers and ministers preach and teach heresies and anti-Christ, anti-God, and unbiblical doctrines and practices, when half-baked and non-Biblically sound Believers direct and produce their so-called Christian films, they end up expanding false teachings and doctrines.

The Internet is a major way that the devil uses to enslave the children of men. Through the Internet, the devil has made many people to go into indecent dressing, lust, and sexual immorality. In Twitter, Facebook, Google, etc, you will see things that can lead you away from the Word of God, if you are not careful, disciplined, and determined.

There are many satanic, demonic, and occult websites in the Internet. Even many of those sites, blogs, and websites which were not opened by conscious agents of satan have things that can still make you to be corrupted and polluted if you are not careful. Many times, even when you are doing something else in the Internet, they will start flashing you with seductive pictures and worldly things.

You might have observed that many of the programmes, movies (films), music, and activities that are spread by televisions, digital satellite stations, cables networks, and radio stations are satanic and demonic in origin. Therefore, be careful of what you watch and ponder on, and what you allow your children and family to watch, listen to, and be exposed to.

Beware of the cartoons that you allow your children to watch, because many of those cartoons are demonic, and they are capturing souls for the devil. Evil spirits possess people when they watch some cartoons. Also, many of the video games that people play are demonic and satanic; and they get people who play them demonized. Horror films are from the devil, and they promote his plans and works.

These are apart from the time that people spend on these things and more, and the passion with which they pursue and get attached to them, thereby making them their gods. When you use the time you should use for God and His Things for activities that do not glory His Name, the Jealous God gets jealous and angry!

Change your name if it is satanic and demonic. Dissociate yourself from any satanic, demonic, and ungodly name. Don't you say that what you confess is what you possess? Why then do you want satanic, demonic, or negative confession on what you are called by? Do you think that God will like to call you by satanic or demonic names?

Concerning the covering of the hair, the Bible says, "Every man praying or prophesying, having his head covered dishonours his head. But every woman who prays or prophesies with her head uncovered dishonours her head, for that is one and the same as if her head were shaved. For if a woman is not covered, let her also be shorn. But if it is shameful for a woman to be shorn or shaved, let her be covered.

"For a man indeed ought not to cover his head, since he is the Image and Glory of God; but woman is the glory of man. For man is not from woman, but woman from man. Nor was man created for the woman, but woman for the man. For this reason the woman ought to have a symbol of authority on her head, because of the angels.

"…Judge among yourselves. Is it proper for a woman to pray to God with her head uncovered? Does not even nature itself teach you that if a man has long hair, it is a dishonour to him? But if a woman has long hair, it is a glory to her; for her hair is given to her for a covering. But if anyone seems to be contentious, we have no such custom, nor do the churches of God" (1 Cor. 11:4-16, New King James Version).

I want you to notice that it did not say that her 'long hair' is given to her for a covering, but her hair. I also want you to notice that this place is talking about covering the hair, and not about long or short hair. To convince you that it is speaking of covering or veiling your hair, the Bible says, "Every man praying or prophesying, having his head covered dishonours his head" (verse 4).

Covering the hair indicates using something (not your hair) to veil your hair. Forget about the distortion of the Bible: according to the Longman Dictionary of Contemporary English, 'veil' is a thin piece of material worn by women to cover their faces at formal occasions such as weddings or for religious reasons.

You can see that this portion of the Scripture is dealing with veiling yourself, as a woman, and not about long or short hair. Speaking of long or short hair, it says, "Does not even nature itself teach you that if a man has long hair, it is dishonour to him?" (verse 14). This is to say that, naturally, long hair doesn't befit a man.

Speaking on the being good if a woman has a natural long hair, it says, "But if a woman has long hair, it is a glory to her; for her hair is given to her for a covering" (verse 15). This is why I ponder on it when I see Christian women cut their hair as low as a man's hair (and I am talking of even outside the church building).

If a woman has to cut her hair as low as men's hair in any given society or nature of hair (because the nature or natural texture of the hair will affect the length), then she should also be ready to wear cap on it, because, naturally, it doesn't befit a woman, except that 'human civilization' and disregard for God-ordained procedures has gripped many. This is what these women liberation movements, which are inspired by satan, have caused over time: disregard for God-ordained authority and natural tendencies.

And know that it didn't say that the long attachment or weavon of the woman is given to her for a covering, because God didn't give any woman any attachment or weavon. Therefore the attachment or weavon on the head of the woman is no glory, but satanic and demonic bondage, whether or not she knows of it.

It says, "But if a woman has long hair…" and not, "When a woman has long hair…." So your hair may not be 'long' or very long, but should not be as short as men's hair in the race/nation you are from (I am not talking of mixed society: where the society is mixed, consisting of people from different nations and races, then use the shortness of men's hair from the same nation or race as you to ascertain the minimum length of your hair); but it is best long, as far as the being 'long' or very long is not achieved by perming or artificially relaxing your hair or with the use of attachments or weavon!

If you find it difficult to comb it or keep it neat, then shorten, reduce, or cut it, to the length that you can comb it well and keep it neat; but do not let it be as low as the general length of the hair of the men from the same race or nation as you, except you are going to wear cap or hair scarf on it as you go around.

Look at what verses 4 and 7 say: "Every man praying or prophesying, having his head covered dishonours his head. For a man indeed ought not to cover his head, since he is the Image and Glory of God; but woman is the glory of man." This is telling a man, who already has a short hair (or may decide to be shorn) to not cover his hair in the church. To be shorn is to shave someone's hair clean, as you would shear the skin of the sheep. Is this not clear enough that what the Bible is talking about here is covering the hair and not short or long hair?

And verses 5 and 6 say: "But every woman who prays or prophesies with her head uncovered dishonours her head, for that is one and the same as if her head were shaved. For if a woman is not covered, let her also be shorn. But if it is shameful for a woman to be shorn or shaved, let her be covered." And this place is saying that the woman whose hair is not covered (veiled) in the church is the same as being shorn (shaving her hair clean).

And verse 10 says that a woman should have a symbol of authority on her head because of the angels. That is either to teach the angels submission to God, or in order not to grieve the angels of God, who, normally, are present in any Believers' meeting; because angels don't like disorder and unrighteousness. Lucifer and his cohorts rebelled against God; they were angels, just like the present obedient angels. Genesis 24:65 says: "...So she took a veil and covered herself." Rebekah, whose hair was already long, took a veil to cover herself to show respect for Isaac.

The Greek word used in verses 6 and 7 of First Corinthians, chapter eleven, for covered and cover is 'katakalupto'. Katakalupto means veiled. It had been a custom for ages for women to be veiled. Only public prostitutes in the East went without veils. But those who want all they can do to avoid covering their hair use: "But if a woman has long hair, it is a glory to her; for her hair is given to her for a covering" (verse 15). They misapply this verse to do what they want to do.

For whoever may be contentious about these things, Apostle Paul wrote: "We have no such custom, nor do the churches of God" (verse 16). Could he be saying that there is no custom of covering hair when he took many verses to persuade the women to cover their hair? I don't believe so; rather, I believe that he is talking of the custom of the contentious person saying that it makes no difference if women cover their hair {or even try to convince people that covering of hair is not for Believers (those in the church, or their church)}.

Many people do not take time to consider some things about the design of many women dresses – gowns, blouses, and skirts. Consider how the design and making of even average unbelieving men are – how they do not expose their armpits, laps, and chests. Just take time to consider the length of the sleeves of their shirts (even their short-sleeved shirts) and that of their trousers; and I know that the men also want fresh air.

Compare it with how many women move around with gowns, blouses, and skirts that show people their armpits, laps, breasts, and shapes. Can you not detect that satan and mermaid spirits are at work in the lives of many women (even Believers) whether or not they are aware of it, as far as dressing is concerned? The devil wants to corrupt men and the human race; and one great weapon he uses is women and their dressing.

Please, if you are a Believer, when you go to buy an already-made dress, check the design and method of their making before buying them. And when you meet a dress designer and maker for your dresses, tell them how they should make your dresses. No wonder the world (which is ruled by satan) has decided to call them fashion designers, because many of them design what satan and demons inspire and tell them to design!

Just take time to consider how those satan-inspired fashion designers design and make women dresses! Some of them will make a long gown, but they will make its sleeves to be so short (and even sleeveless) so that the armpits will be the point of attraction and seduction.

Some other demons-prompted designers will make the blouse that has a good length of sleeve, but they will 'cut' the back or the front in such a way as to show their back, breasts, and breast cleavages; because what satan wants to seduce men through the blouse is her breasts and exposed body.

Others will make long skirts, but they will cut and divide the skirt at the back, by the side, or at the front, because the point of seduction is their laps. Then others will design and make short skirts and gowns which when the women wearing them sit down people will see their laps and even underwears, because that is the heart and desire of the devil.

And others will not care and make mini-skirts, so that even if they are standing, people will be seeing their laps and what they call long legs. Do you know that many women (even Believers) are serving the devil, even without their knowledge? And surely, serving the devil has rewards (or do I say punishments?).

I wonder why many women spend hours in making and dressing their hair with attachments, wool, and thread! This is the love of the world and idolatry in operation. Notice that the modern frying of hair and the use of attachment were not even in existence among the unbelieving Israelites and Jews of the days of the Early Church, and also among the Gentiles of the places where Paul ministered! Therefore they had no business writing about frying of hair and the use of attachments (they did not even know the possibility or the reality of people trying such abominations).

You can use map to check the places where Apostle Paul ministered in his first, second, and third missionary journeys to see whether the inhabitants of those places (except possible immigrants) have the kind of hair which those that fry their hair and use attachments to make their hair long use nowadays.

Yes, they wrote about braiding or plaiting, and also of jewellery, which existed in their days among the unbelievers and possibly among some Believers who had carried their worldly lifestyle of hair dressing into their Christian faith. And you can see what they wrote about braiding/plaiting the hair, use of jewels, and wearing of fashions and costly clothing and apparel (and women relationship with their husbands) in First Timothy 2:9-10 and First Peter 3:1-6.

When God created everything, He saw that all the things He created were good, that the Bible says, "Then God saw everything that He had made, and indeed it was very good" (Gen. 1:31). Who are you to challenge the Handiwork of God? Bleaching your skin, painting your face, perming your hair, wearing weavons, dyeing your hair, painting your nails, etc are ways of challenging God's Creative Ability.

Someone may say, "But Jesus Christ said that it is not what enters a man that defiles the man, but what comes out of the man" (Matt. 15:11). You have to understand well what He was saying. But if what goes into a man doesn't defile a man, why did Jesus Christ rebuke the church in Thyatira for allowing Jezebel to teach His Servants to eat things sacrificed to idols? (Rev. 2:20). And when there was a debate/argument on what the Gentile Christians should keep, why did the counsel at Jerusalem tell them to abstain from things polluted by idols, from strangled meat/animals, and from blood? (Acts 15:20).

Somebody may say that Apostle Paul said that idol is nothing, but fail to see that he said that if your brother will be offended, because you ate the meat sacrificed to idol, you are to avoid it (1 Cor. 8; Rom. 14). When somebody says that Jesus Christ said that not what enters a man defiles a man, but what comes out of the man, he doesn't even know that they were discussing about washing of the hands before eating.

By the way, does vomiting defile you before God, since it came out of you? And those who want to destroy themselves have used that excuse to drink alcohol and smoke cigarettes, destroying their bodies, which is for God and should be kept holy for our God. Think of it! If the Believers were already drinking alcohol by little measure, why will Apostle Paul tell Timothy to use little wine for his stomach's sake (as a kind of soothing medicine, in that their ancient and unrefined medical practice)?

A WORD IS ENOUGH FOR THE WISE! Shall we continue to sin that grace may increase? (Rom. 6:1) Is faith without works not dead? (Jas 2:17). What will make Jesus Christ to tell those that had prophesied, cast out demons, and done mighty works in His Name, that He never knew them? (Matt. 7:21-23). Surely, they had known Christ before. I am not reducing righteousness and holiness to physical things, physical appearance, and dress code alone? Why did the Word of God put the sin of the flesh first before sin of spirit in Second Corinthians 7:1?

Some people say that we are laying unnecessary burdens on people. Which burden (if it were even to be a burden, as you think) is greater than sacrificing small things for Jesus Christ and Heaven? If you can't deny yourself of small things, because of Heaven, can you lay down your life for Jesus Christ? He who loves his life more than Christ Jesus is not worthy of Him.

By the way, have you ever seen it in the Bible that Apostle Paul gave ordinances to New Testament Believers? He wrote, saying, "Now I praise you, brethren, that you remember me in all things and keep the traditions (ordinances, the King James Version) just as I delivered them to you" (1 Cor. 11:2). Was he putting burdens on them? Certainly the Corinthian church was a 'Gentile' church.

Apostle Paul wrote: "But beware lest somehow this liberty of yours become a stumbling block to those who are weak. And because of your knowledge shall the weak brother perish, for whom Christ died? But when you thus sin against the brethren, and wound their weak conscience, you sin against Christ. Therefore, if food makes my brother stumble, I will never again eat meat, lest I make my brother stumble" (1 Cor. 8:9-13).

Writing to the Galatians, he said, "For you, brethren, have been called to liberty; only do not use liberty as an opportunity for the flesh, but through love serve one another. And those that are Christ's have crucified the flesh with its passions and desires. If we live in the Spirit, let us also walk in the Spirit" (Gal. 5:13,24,25).

Jesus Christ rebuked the scribes and the Pharisees, not because they paid tithes (because God commanded them to pay tithes), but because they neglected justice, mercy, and faith, while paying tithes (Matt. 23:23). Will you cancel tithe (for example), because they neglected justice, mercy, and faith? Certainly, no! Or you will still be disobeying God.

In other words, because somebody can dress virtuously and Godly like a Christian and still be evil, immoral, and wicked on the inside, will not cancel the fact and Truth that a Christian is to dress and appear like a Christian. By that, I mean that Christians and Believers are to dress decently, Godly, and Biblically. Inside and outside, you are to be like Christ – Christian.

As a woman, it is either you decide to worship and serve God in Spirit and Truth, or you join the rest of the women and ladies who follow their minds instead of the Mind of God. Writing to the Corinthians, Apostle Paul said, "But I fear, lest somehow, as the serpent deceived Eve by his craftiness, so your minds may be corrupted…" (2 Cor. 11:3).

The devil deceived Eve at the Garden of Eden by craftiness, just as he has been deceiving many women and ladies today, especially in the areas of indecent dressing and worldliness. When God told Adam and Eve to avoid the fruit of the tree of knowledge of good and bad, telling them that they will die any day they eat from the fruit, satan came afterwards to tell Eve: "You will not surely die…" (Gen. 3:4).

But what happened when they ate the fruit? They died spiritually, being separated from the Life of God. Apart from the spiritual death, God had intended that they live forever; however, when they disobeyed God, they could now die physically after some years. Though you may not see the punishment for your disobedience now, if you don't repent and change, know that you can't enter into the Kingdom of Heaven. Do you want to end in Hell after speaking in tongues and carrying Bible?

The Bible says, "For you were bought at a price; therefore glorify God in your body and in your spirit, which are God's (1 Cor. 6:20). But if you are led by the Spirit, you are not under the

Law (Gal. 5:18). Both your body and your spirit are God's – belong to God – and you have to glorify God in both of them.

Furthermore, it is those who are led by the Spirit of God who are not under the Law. The essence of God making us to not be under the Law is because He expects us to be led by His Spirit. But if your flesh and desires still lead you, then you are not led by the Holy Spirit; and there is danger.

The Book of Romans says that those who are led by the Spirit of God are those who are the sons of God. You wash both the outside and the inside of your plates. Why do you think of the opposite concerning God and His people? Certainly, God wants both the inside and the outside of His people to be clean, purified, and holy.

Many people talk against many things in the name of Old Testament; but they will readily teach about blessings from the twenty-eighth chapter of the Book of Deuteronomy, and expound tithes and offerings from the third chapter of the Book of Malachi – both in the New Testament.

Let us know that we have not arrived in Heaven yet; therefore, we are to be careful of how we live our lives and of the utterances we make, including how we think and reason. Let us always be open to the Holy Spirit to direct and lead us all the days of our lives till we see the Face of Jesus Christ in Heaven.

(For an in-depth Scriptural study on this subject, refer to the book: Indecent Dressing and Outward Appearance by GODSWORD GODSWILL ONU)

ABOUT THE BOOK

The Power and Authority of the Believer reveals the great power, ability, and authority that the Lord has given to the Church (His Body). The Believer has been empowered by the Lord Jesus Christ to overcome the devil and the world. We have the power and authority to trample on satan, his fallen angels and demons, witches and wizards, and all the power and works of the devil, and nothing shall by any means hurt us! Have you started using that power and authority?

ABOUT THE AUTHOR

Apostle Godsword is the President and Overseer of WHOLE LIFE SPIRIT-WORD MINISTRIES (a.k.a. HOLY GHOST AND GODSWORD CHRISTIAN NETWORK). Godsword, a Teaching Prophet and Evangelist, is a Minister of the Lord Jesus Christ who believes in the Demonstration of the Spirit and Power and takes delight in the Declaration and Teaching of the Word and Will of God.

Godsword Godswill Onu studied Building Construction in his First Degree, and later had Master of Urban and Regional Planning (MURP) from Abia State University, Uturu.

BOOKS BY APOSTLE GODSWORD

1. *75 Great Biblical and Spiritual Truths (As Inspired by the Holy Ghost)*
2. *Preparing for Our Maker (The Cry of the Spirit and the Lord's Witness)*
3. *Lessons from the Seven Churches*
4. *Vessels and Instruments of Honour and Dishonour*
5. *Divine Protection*
6. *The Power-filled Life*
7. *From Glory to Glory*
8. *Always and Without Ceasing*
9. *The Whole Life from God to Men*
10. *Right and Wrong Thinking, Belief, and Confession*
11. *He Came to Set You Free*
12. *A Better Covenant Based on Better Promises*
13. *Apostles, Prophets, Evangelists, Pastors, and Teachers*
14. *Being Strong in the Lord*
15. *Real Freedom and Gain*
16. *Faithfulness and Diligence in Stewardship*
17. *Heirs of God and Joint-heirs with Christ*
18. *Open and Closed Heavens and Doors*
19. *A Heaven to Gain, and a Hell to Avoid*
20. *The Anointing and Power of the Holy Spirit*
21. *The Glory, Presence, and Power of God*
22. *The Fulness of the Blessing of the Gospel*
23. *Prosperity and Success*
24. *Seducing Spirits and Doctrines of Demons*
25. *My God and Father*
26. *The Works of the Flesh and Youthful Lusts*
27. *The Spiritual Christian*
28. *The Commandments of the Lord and Master*
29. *The Total Man*
30. *The Virtuous Woman*
31. *Contending with the Forces of Darkness*
32. *Developing a Strong Relationship with God*
33. *Secrets to God's Miracle-working Power*
34. *Concerning the Roman Catholics*
35. *Ministers-Workers Training Manual*
36. *The Christian Virtues*
37. *The God-approved Minister*
38. *Taking It by Force*
39. *God's Generals*
40. *Blessings, Curses, and Spiritual Attacks*
41. *Pressing Towards the Mark*
42. *My Father's Business*
43. *Walking in the Anointing*
44. *The Weapons and Armour of Our Warfare*
45. *Tithes and Offerings*
46. *Greater Levels and Glory (An Annual Reading)*
47. *God is Not from Any Nation*
48. *The Power and Authority of the Believer*

49. Sin, Disobedience, and Rebellion
50. Wisdom, Knowledge, and Understanding
51. The Christian Marriage and Home
52. Patience, Endurance, and Longsuffering
53. Indecent Dressing and Outward Appearance
54. Keys to Financial Prosperity
55. Witnesses and Ministers of the Word
56. False Prophets, Teachers, and Ministers
57. I Give You Dominion
58. Making Your Calling and Election Sure
59. Prayer and Fasting
60. Christians, Disciples, and Followers
61. Understanding the Strategies of Your Enemy
62. The Fruit of the Spirit
63. Obedience, Holiness, and Righteousness
64. Excellence in Life and Godliness
65. Being Led by the Holy Spirit
66. Knowing and Following God's Will
67. Manifesting God's Glory
68. Confronting Your Confrontations
69. The Church of Jesus Christ
70. Power Over All Devils and Evil
71. The Power of Faith
72. Filled with the Fulness of God
73. The Man of God
74. Signs and Wonders
75. Pursue, Overtake, and Recover
76. More Than Conquerors
77. Redefining Christianity
78. Prosperity in Every Area
79. Godliness
80. Being an Example to the Believers
81. Diligently Obeying the Voice of God
82. A Crown of Righteousness
83. Evangelism by Power
84. The Fellowship of Other Believers
85. The Kingdom of Light and of God
86. Casting Out Devils
87. A Friend of God
88. Watchfulness, Vigilance, and Sobriety
89. Perfecting the Saints
90. Called, Chosen, Faithful, and Glorified
91. Acts and Signs of Believers
92. Secrets to Successful Ministry
93. Preaching and Teaching the Word
94. The Work and Ministry of the Holy Spirit
95. Demonstration of the Spirit and Power
96. The Ministry of Angels
97. Walking Worthy of God
98. The Qualities of a Christian

99. Running the Race
100. The End-time Realities
101. The Ministry Gifts
102. Soldiers of Christ
103. Government by the People of God
104. Jesus Christ Comes Very Soon
105. Being Fruitful and Productive
106. The Unstoppable Christian and Minister
107. The Gifts of the Holy Spirit
108. Perfect and Blameless
109. The Kingdom of Darkness and of Satan
110. Divine Health and Healing
111. Tests, Temptations, Trials, and Wilderness Experiences
112. The Power of Prayer
113. The Manifestation of the Sons of God
114. The Lord Jesus Christ
115. The Word of the Living God
116. Love
117. Earnestly Contending for the Faith
118. Becoming a Prayer-warrior
119. Revival
120. Partakers of the Divine Nature
121. Fasting, Discipline, and Self-control
122. The Gifts and the Calling of God
123. Testing and Proving All Things
124. Pulling Down Strongholds
125. Giving to God and to Men
126. The Unsearchable Riches of Christ
127. From Faith to Faith
128. The More Abundant Life
129. Being on Fire for God
130. Agents of the Kingdom of Darkness
131. The Power of Spoken Words
132. Arise and Shine
133. There is Power in Praise
134. The Promises of the Lord
135. Spiritual Hunger and Thirst
136. The Untouchable Christian
137. The Overcomer
138. Commissioned with Power
139. Our Lord and Master
140. God Cares for You
141. Worshipping in Spirit and in Truth
142. Operating in the Supernatural
143. Repentance and Restitution
144. Warnings from the Lord
145. Divine Direction and Strategy
146. Power Encounter
147. Pleasing God
148. The God that Answers by Fire

149. Serving God, Your Maker
150. Speaking in Tongues and the Gift of Prophecy
151. The Life and Ministry of Jesus Christ
152. Apostle Paul's Life and Ministry
153. Lessons from the Life of Moses
154. Abraham, the Father of Faith
155. David, the Man After God's Own Heart
156. Peter, the Leader of the Apostles
157. Joseph, the Dreamer
158. Joshua, the Finisher of Moses' Assignment
159. Samuel, the Prophet and Judge of Israel
160. Job, God's Man
161. Prophets Elijah and Elisha
162. Adam, the First Man, and Noah, God's Favourite
163. Isaac and Jacob, the Patriarchs of Israel
164. Aaron and Barnabas, the Helpers of the Men of God
165. Daniel, Shadrach, Meshach, and Abed-Nego
166. Sarah, Deborah, Esther, Ruth, and Mary Magdalene
167. Miriam, Martha, and Sapphira
168. Isaiah, Jeremiah, and Ezekiel, the Prophets
169. Saul, Solomon, and Asa, the Kings Who Disappointed God
170. Jehoshaphat, Hezekiah, and Josiah, the Kings Who Pleased God
171. Stephen, the Martyr, and Philip, the Evangelist
172. Ahab, Nebuchadnezzar, and Herod, the Wicked Rulers
173. Gideon, Jephthah, and Samson
174. Ezra and Nehemiah, the Men Who Feared God
175. The Apostolic Ministry
176. The Prophetic Ministry
177. The Evangelistic Ministry
178. The Pastoral Ministry
179. The Teaching Ministry
180. Knowing and Understanding God
181. The Extraordinary Life
182. The Pathway to Good Leadership
183. The Christian Youth
184. False Religions, Beliefs, and Teachings
185. Witches and Wizards
186. Foundations
187. The Anointed
188. Spiritual Authority
189. None of Those Diseases and Sicknesses
190. The Power of Temperaments and Emotions
191. The Christian Rituals of Water Baptism, the Lord's Supper, Laying on of Hands, Etc
192. Dignity and Integrity
193. Tempted and Tried by the Devil
194. The Deliverance Ministry
195. The Healing Ministry
196. The Prayer Ministry
197. The Events of the End of Ages and Eternity

198. The Music Ministry
199. The Laws of God's Kingdom
200. You Can Pay the Price!
201. Missions and Missionaries
202. Exceedingly Abundant Grace
203. Keep on Doing Good
204. Islam and Muslims
205. Fear Not!
206. Laying Up Treasures in Heaven
207. You Are a Watchman
208. Fulfilment
209. You Are God's Battleaxe
210. The Name of the Lord
211. God Has the Final Say!
212. The Blood of Jesus Christ
213. Sunday School and Bible Study Manual
214. Altars, Spiritual Gates, and Covenants
215. Enduring to the End to Be Saved
216. Destroying the Works of the Destroyer
217. Visions and Dreams
218. The Pathway to Greatness
219. Should We Send Back to Sender?
220. Vows, Oaths, and Swearing
221. Comforting and Encouraging One Another
222. Do You Really Love God?
223. Backsliding and Falling Away
224. Why Bad Things Happen to Good People
225. Mastering and Defeating Weak Points
226. Conditions for Answered Prayers
227. Rejoice in the Lord Always!
228. Watch and Pray!
229. Waiting Upon the Lord
230. Looking Up Unto God!
231. The Spirit of Love, Mercy, and Grace
232. Orderliness

Any of the titles (ebooks) can be bought/downloaded immediately. And the printed books, if it is not available at your local bookstore, can be ordered.

NEVER PIRATE ANY OF THE EBOOKS/BOOKS!

For enquiry, you may contact Apostle Godsword Godswill Onu, by calling or texting him on +2348030917546.

Made in United States
Orlando, FL
10 May 2023